DOCTOR · WHO

The Shooting Scripts

DOCTOR · WHO

The
Shooting Scripts

Foreword by Russell T Davies

BBC
BOOKS

CONTENTS

FOREWORD BY RUSSELL T DAVIES

SC.1 EXT. BBC PRISON NIGHT

A flash of lightning illuminates a tall, forbidding building. The INTERVIEWER approaches, fearful, knocks on the door. It opens. A hideous, cowled WRAITH beckons her into the darkness.

SC.2 INT. PRISON CORRIDOR NIGHT

The WRAITH leads the INTERVIEWER down a long, dark corridor lined with padlocked doors. The first door is labelled LESLEY JOSEPH. The second, CELEBRITY SLEEPOVER. The third, WHY DON'T YOU, and from within, children can be heard crying bitterly down a tin-can-and-string telephone.

The Wraith unlocks the last door, labelled DOCTOR WHO 2005–2037. Deep breath, then the Interviewer steps inside, as the Wraith flees . . .

SC.3 INT. PRISON CELL NIGHT

The INTERVIEWER enters. In a pool of moonlight, RUSSELL T DAVIES sits on a milk crate. He is ageing, tired, and yet somehow beautiful.

RUSSELL We meet again. Come in, my child. Do sit. No doubt you've come to ask about my remarkable career, how I came to be enthroned here, in TV Towers, as King of the Airwaves, in my robes of ermine and silk.

INTERVIEWER But you're naked.

RUSSELL And you're crying.

INTERVIEWER These two facts are connected. But I came to ask about *Doctor Who*, way back in 2005. How did you set about bringing back such an old show?

RUSSELL With love. As simple as that. The programme's history and reputation had gathered dust. All those jokes about wobbly sets and rubber monsters and Daleks not getting up stairs, that was just another layer of dust. But I remembered when I was a kid. When it was new. All of us would gather round the telly for *Doctor Who*, all the kids in class, boys and girls, and the teachers and your mum and dad and your nan and people on the bus. Everyone watched it. Everyone loved it. But then they grew up and moved on, and maybe they got a little bit embarrassed about it all. And they forgot. They just forgot. All we had to do to the concept was wake it up, to imagine it again, with all the wit and bravery they'd first had, all the way back in 1963.

INTERVIEWER And you had to find new viewers, of course.

RUSSELL Oh yes. To hell with nostalgia! The most important viewers of all were the ones who'd never seen it, never even heard of it. They had DVDs stuffed full of Slayers and Captains and Knights and Wizards, but there was something missing. Something sweet and daft and terrifying and very, very British. They needed the Doctor, but they just didn't know it.

INTERVIEWER And the scripts were part of that?

RUSSELL Oh yes. Scripts are everything.

INTERVIEWER Well, it could be argued that scripts are just a starting point, that the look, the feel, the style, the pace of the show were just as important. That back then, in Old Cardiff Town, you had to gather the best production team that you could possibly get. That you found a Doctor and Rose in Christopher Eccleston and Billie Piper who elevated the production to a whole new level, alongside wonderful and imaginative directors. That your design teams – sets, costumes, CGI, make-up – set new standards and created a new, vibrant *Doctor Who*. That the whole thing was a magnificent team effort.

RUSSELL No. It was just the scripts.

INTERVIEWER But not even –

RUSSELL The scripts.

INTERVIEWER But wha–

RUSSELL Scripts.

INTERVIEWER Bu–

RUSSELL Scriz.

A long silence.

INTERVIEWER So what went wrong?

RUSSELL I don't know what you mean! That 2029 season was a triumph! 'Doctor Who and the Space Frog', that was one of mine! Starring Ornella Muti as the Frog, and Michelle McManus as the Space. Oh, glorious days! And then casting myself as the Rani, genius! And frankly, the comedy musical black-and-white cartoon naked episode was *not* a gimmick! Oh, they stopped me too soon! I had such plans! Such revivals in store! *Howard's Way*, with puppet mice! *Shine On Harvey Moon*, actually on the moon! *Celebrity Wrestling* –

INTERVIEWER I'm sorry, that's ridiculous, I've heard enough, I think I should be going –

She hurries to the door, but as she's about to go, Russell calls out – quieter now, calmer, sadder, and yet still beautiful –

RUSSELL But tell me. *Doctor Who*. Is it still running?

INTERVIEWER Yes, yes it is.

RUSSELL And who's playing the Doctor now?

INTERVIEWER Romeo Beckham.

Pause. Then Russell smiles, gently.

RUSSELL Actually … I bet that works.

INTERVIEWER It does. People love it. They really, really love it.

She smiles at him, then goes. Silence falls over the cell. The distant call of owls, from outside. Russell sits in the weak moonlight, lost in memory. In one eye, the glint of a solitary tear.

Then the WRAITH runs in, throws off his cloak, does a funny little dance and makes noises with his armpit, and they hoot with laughter!

Fade to black.

INTRODUCTION BY HELEN RAYNOR, SCRIPT EDITOR

The title of this book is *Doctor Who – The Shooting Scripts*. And I bet, without even thinking about it, you're assuming that these are – well, the 'definitive' scripts of the new series, season one, *'as seen on TV'*.

They aren't. Because you can watch all these episodes on DVD, for starters. We wanted this book to offer a real insight into the whole process of getting an episode from script to screen, in all its naked authenticity – not just provide glorified subtitles. So, what are these 'shooting scripts', then? Are they in any way 'definitive'? And where does the nakedness come in? I'll begin at the beginning . . .

A script can go through any number of drafts from the word 'go', and for all sorts of reasons. There are editorial decisions – key issues of story, character, tone, structure – which are endlessly debated between writer, producer, executive producer, script editor and director. 'Shouldn't the servant girl be at the heart of this episode?' 'How do we dramatise Evil?' 'Can we see Captain Jack's bum – please?' Vital elements of the script which all change and evolve across successive drafts.

Then there are the practicalities of production. As we get closer to filming, the questions of *how* it all gets done become more pressing. The aim is always to serve the script and the story, but the conversation has to be two way. Everyone directly involved with the shoot all feeds in – the designer, visual effects team, casting director, location manager – all via the script editor, to keep the writer sane. 'You don't want a *real* pig, do you?' 'Can we fit a Dalek in the lift? A Slitheen in a toilet?' Oh – and the script has to fit the shooting schedule. We're trying to fit sixteen days of filming into twelve days? Better go to another draft.

Round about now – when the schedule is being drawn up, about eight weeks before filming starts – we 'lock' the script (essentially, this means scene numbers are fixed; crucial for all the schedules and lists being drawn up). So – are these locked scripts the 'definitive' scripts?

Oh no. Because all manner of things can happen between locking the script and the start of filming. Lines change, stage directions get tweaked, scenes are added and cut. The script editor practically moves in with the writer – got to hang on to what's great about the script; be practical, but keep the boldness, the magic.

Given that all these changes are now happening to a locked script, when a scene is cut, the scene is simply listed as 'OMITTED'. This means that the scene was never filmed. When a scene is *added*, it appears as an 'A', 'B' or 'C' scene (or as far down the alphabet as you need to go).

And before you know it, it's day one of filming. So surely, by now, the script has reached the 'definitive' stage? I mean, the thing's being filmed now . . .

If only! But now we're at the mercy of the weather. Things that don't go 'bang' when they're supposed to. Things that *do* go 'bang' when you didn't know they could. Peculiarities of the location that only emerge on the day (the oven-like temperature of a basement, for example – not much fun if you're an Auton). That dog that only starts barking when someone shouts 'action!'. Sickness, aeroplanes, traffic jams . . . clambering from its chrysalis, the butterfly script we've nurtured so lovingly for months is now at the most exciting but vulnerable stage of its life cycle. More OMITTED scenes appear, along with more 'A', 'B' and 'C' scenes (Episode 5 is the winner here, boasting an 'E' scene).

Generally the OMITTEDs predominate at this stage; the instinct under pressure being to simplify rather than elaborate. However, often in cutting a scene, we lose something crucial to the story that we need to pick up elsewhere, so we either add to an existing scene, or create a new one. Stage directions in scenes added during filming often read as if they are 'suggesting' solutions for production, referring to material already filmed, or sets we can use easily (Ep.2, sc.8A, for example, or Ep.4, sc.13A). You get the occasional hint of a long dark night of the soul here, when the plaintive phrase: '... or whatever we can afford' crops up.

Before you know it, we get to the last day of the shooting schedule. Everything we wanted to film, that could be filmed, has been filmed. Those crumpled and stained pages (coffee, not tears, hopefully) constitute the Final Shooting Script. Which is, surely ... the *'definitive'* script ...?

Nope. Because now editing and post production begin, and an episode can change radically here. The raw material of filming is edited into one version, then another, and another (like drafts of the script). Scenes get cut, the order of scenes changes, and everything from computer generated imagery (CGI) to sound effects and music are added. Oh, and Automatic/additional Dialogue Replacement (ADR). You need additional dialogue for all sorts of reasons; the odd line is fluffy, you want some out of vision (OOV) dialogue to explain something – you find that Davina McCall is available to be the voice of *Big Brother*, so you add some juicy lines for her.

Finally, post production comes to an end. From the final (MASTER) tape, a TX (transmission) script is typed up. Word for word, an exact copy of what happens on screen. *As seen on TV.*

Is THIS the 'definitive' script? Yes! But wouldn't it be boring if we published that? So, the scripts published here are the Final Shooting Scripts. Scripts as they were when filming had finished, but before the episodes went into the edit.

There will be variations between what you see on screen, and what you read here. You'll find different action, shots, and dialogue, and the odd brand-new scene that otherwise would never have gone further than cast and crew. Any lines *not* in this book are ADR lines, which, of course, were never part of the original shooting script.

You'll also see the thousand and one intriguing things that distinguish one writer's script from another, and the incidental beauties that still make me laugh (in Ep.13, in a tense sequence with Rose's future at stake, Russell pauses to wonder: 'Can a Beetle have a tow-bracket?'). Charlotte, the book editor, has kindly removed typos and spelling mistakes to spare our blushes but otherwise, these scripts read exactly as they did when Elwen Rowlands and I printed them off our PCs in Cardiff. Which means, among other things, punctuation is used to indicate delivery, and give an impressionistic sense of how the script 'comes off the page'; *not* to conform to the rules and consistencies of grammar, before we get any letters.

So here they are. The Final Shooting Scripts of the first series of the new *Doctor Who*. I hope you enjoy them as much as we did.

And the nakedness? Ask Captain Jack.

SCRIPT NOTES

Scenes which are marked 'OMITTED' were cut after the scripts and scene numbers were locked, but before filming started. Episode 2 scenes 20, 38A and 38B, found here in the final shooting script, were never filmed as they were dropped during filming.

A few FX shots (e.g. Ep.2 sc.16) were never achieved as written, and additional FX material was created that wasn't specified in the shooting script. Likewise, some shots of lift shafts, with lifts ascending or descending (Ep.6 sc.74, Ep.12 scs 42 and 60) were dropped. Other (cheaper!) ways were found of illustrating the same moment, e.g. filming the lift floor-counter.

Ep.3 sc.23 was never filmed as per the script, but some of the dialogue was lifted and added to the end of sc.21.

Ep.13 contains a sequence and lines in sc.97 which weren't in the shooting script, or issued as amendments (the Female Programmer manages to blind a Dalek before she gets killed). This was an 'on the spot' innovation suggested by director Joe Ahearne, looking to get maximum drama out of the moment. For speed's sake, the formal machinery of script amendments was bypassed, and he just rang Russell to discuss it ('I was in a train station, I remember . . . ').

INT. – interior

EXT. – exterior

OOV – out of vision

V/O – voiceover

FX SHOT – 'FX' (effects) are added in post production (Daleks pouring out of their spaceship in Ep.13 is a 'pure' FX shot, whereas the Dalek 'laser bolt', or the Nanogenes' golden cloud are FX added to filmed material)

CGI – computer generated images/imagery

LONG LENS SHOT – creates 'depth' in a picture

WIDE MATTE SHOT – FX house adds 'matte paintings' to add to, and enhance, the actual set (like the 'Bad Wolf' sign in Ep.13)

WS – wide shot (a more 'panoramic' view – opposite of close up)

CU – close up

BCU – BIG close up!

PRACTICAL/PRAC LIGHT – anything 'practical' needs to take place on set, on the day the scene is actually being filmed

f/g – foreground

b/g – background

beat – a dramatic pause, of sorts – added to highlight a key moment in the script

clears frame – an actor or object moves out of the picture you're looking at

greenscreen – a 'green screen' provides a blank canvas for the FX house to work with. In Ep.9, when Rose flies across London during an air raid, Billie was filmed suspended in a harness against a greenscreen floor and walls, and virtually everything else was created in post production.

NB Not all writers use these terms; in fact, most don't. Technical knowledge and vocab can help, but would-be writers shouldn't be intimidated by it.

Full cast lists for each episode, along with lots of behind-the-scenes pictures and videos about the making of this *Doctor Who* series, can be found at bbc.co.uk/doctorwho.

Episode 1

Rose
By Russell T Davies

This had to be more than a script. This had to be a pitch, a budget, a template, a mission statement, an ideal. Because we were in an unusual position with the 2005 series of *Doctor Who* — it was greenlit before a single word had been written. Talk about lucky!

But that put more than the usual pressures on this first adventure. It had to convince everyone – and I mean everyone within the BBC, long before the viewing public got involved – that their faith hadn't been misplaced; that an old, tired, niche, cult sci-fi show could work in the mainstream once again. No pressure, then.

Every scene, every beat, every character had to operate as a signal, telling everyone – accountants, designers, writers, management – what we wanted. Defining what *Doctor Who* is to be. Monsters? There's the Nestene. The everyday world? Hello, Jackie. Mystery? That's the Doctor. The ordinary-turned-sinister? Dummies! A very British bleakness? Clive dies in front of his wife and son. Jokes? The London Eye. A lack of sci-fi technobabble? Anti-plastic. Heartbreak? Hmm, I never quite achieved that – it doesn't kick in until Episode 2, damn it. And so on, each moment carrying a much bigger agenda.

The script was even bigger in scale, at first. Two key sequences proved to be too ambitious for the schedule and had to be rewritten.

When the Doctor and Rose first escape in the department store's lift, the lift was to stop in the shaft and then get attacked by Autons bursting through the roof and the floor. We saved thousands by cutting that, but I was glad to see it go; it was more important to end the chase and get Rose home. Then, there was an extended sequence with the plastic arm in the Tylers' flat. It was a much more vicious fight, resulting in the Doctor and Rose barricading themselves in the kitchen, leaving Jackie in danger in the bedroom. Cut! But I still miss it. We get an 'armless joke instead, which isn't as good. Oh well.

Thanks must go to Executive Producer Julie Gardner's husband, Jeremy. At one point, worrying about the tone of the show, I thought that maybe the inclusion of the London Eye was a bit ... well, daft. Julie described it to Jeremy. He laughed. The scene stayed in. I love a laugh.

Of course, the most important thing to say about 'Rose' is that it was written entirely from Rose Tyler's point of view. The Autons provide the plot, but the story is all about her. (There's an old Hollywood saw, describing the vital difference between plot and story. Plot is: the King died and then the Queen died. Story is: the King died and then the Queen died of a broken heart.) I'd love to tell you that months of analysis went into the decision to focus on Rose, but the fact is, it didn't take a second. Some things are just instinct, and all the rest is hindsight. Hidden amongst a million options, there is one way to write something. And finding that one way is my job.

Russell T Davies

1 EXT. FX SHOT

The planet Earth drifting in space, silent, serene. Suddenly – the beep-beep-beep of an alarm clock.

CAMERA races towards the Earth, plunging down, down, down through clouds, revealing the UK, down towards London, a grid of buildings, zooming down to a block of flats –

2 INT. ROSE'S BEDROOM DAY 1 0730

CU a black, square alarm clock. A hand slams it off. ROSE TYLER sits up in bed, gathers herself for a second. She's 19, her bedroom's a mess, she's got another bloody day at work, and she's so much better than this. Ho hum. Deep breath, and Rose throws the quilt off.

MUSIC, fast, loud, over sc.3 to 9: good chart track.

3 INT. TYLERS' KITCHEN DAY 1 0750

ROSE gives her MUM a quick kiss, runs out of the door.

4 EXT. TYLERS' FLAT DAY 1 0751

ROSE runs for the stairwell. The flat's on the third floor – a sprawling complex of grey walkways and concrete balconies.

5 EXT. CITY SHOPPING STREET DAY 1 0835

ROSE hops off the bus, hurries along. She clears shot, CAMERA drifts for a second, over to the shop windows: elegant DUMMIES, frozen in their finery.

6 INT. DEPARTMENT STORE DAY 1 1000

A huge John-Lewis-type store. The windowless expanse of the women's clothing dept. ROSE carries a stack of jumpers.

7 EXT. CITY SHOPPING STREET DAY 1 1300

ROSE and her boyfriend MICKEY SMITH having a sandwich, on a bench. Mickey's 22, cheeky, laddish, a good catch.

JUMP CUT: both laughing like mad.

JUMP CUT: kiss goodbye, they head off, separate directions.

8 INT. DEPARTMENT STORE NIGHT 1 1800

Shutters rattling down over the doors, the shop closing. ROSE heads towards the last open door, with MATES. But a SECURITY GUARD holds up an A5 padded envelope, smiles. Mates laugh; Rose groans, grabs the envelope, runs back –

CUT TO Rose running into the lift, slams the button.

9 INT. LIFT SHAFT NIGHT 1 1802

Top shot of the lift. As it descends, MUSIC fades away, echoes, gone, Rose heading for a different world . . .

10 INT. BASEMENT CORRIDOR NIGHT 1 1803

Lift opens, ROSE steps out. Empty. Just the dull roar of boilers, the feeling of pressure. It's a long, grim, service corridor, lined with pipes and forgotten boxes. She goes to an office door, it's locked. She calls through:

ROSE Wilson? I've got the lottery money, Wilson? You there?

Silence. She calls down the corridor:

ROSE I can't hang about, they're closing the shop, Wilson?
(pause)
Ohh come on.

A flicker of shadow at the end of the corridor, gone –

ROSE Hello?

She's more alert now. The pressure getting to her. She walks towards the far end, voice less certain:

ROSE Hello? Wilson, it's Rose.

Silence. Rose opens a door, goes through.

 1 ROSE

11 INT. BASEMENT ROOM NIGHT 1 CONTINUOUS

Darkness. ROSE reaches for the light switch. Pools of light snap on; the rest of the room stays pitch black. It's a big storage space, lined with pipes and cables. And full of shop-window DUMMIES. Sixty, male and female – not neatly arranged, but crowded in, all caught in different lifeless poses. Stark illumination from the lights, steep shadows on smooth, expressionless faces. (No wigs, the hair's part of the sculpture, like a statue.)

ROSE ... Wilson?

She crosses the room to the far door, tries it, it's locked. Behind her, the first door she came through swings. Slam! Rose runs back, pushes, but it won't open.

ROSE Oh you're kidding me.

A noise behind her, a clatter – she turns, fast. Nothing. Absolute stillness. Rose unnerved:

ROSE Is that someone mucking about?

Another noise. Rose walks to the centre of the room, scared but defiant, looking at the dummies. Quiet:

ROSE Who is it?

She looks round. The dummies' faces – the empty stares. And then – not suddenly, no shock – at the back of the room, one DUMMY's head slowly turns to look at her. Rose is holding her breath. Scared. Fascinated. The dummy – a good distance away, behind so many others – tilts its head slowly from side to side, studying her. Then its entire body shifts, as though to get a better look at her, curious. Rose keeps quiet, controlled:

ROSE Okay. You got me, very funny –

Suddenly six more dummies – spaced across the room – jerk their heads round simultaneously. Rose startled, angry:

ROSE Right, I've got the joke. Whose idea was this, is it Derek? Is it? Derek, is this you?

The seven dummies flex and stretch, uncoiling, as though waking, with careful, slow actions. Another twenty jerk alive. (Some stay frozen throughout.) The FIRST DUMMY (male, in a beautiful suit) seems the most intent on her. It steps round the others, elegant, precise. All the dummies are turning to face her, but Rose is aware of the original's approach. Still brave, still defiant, she nevertheless backs up against the wall ... the dummy's tall.

Dead eyes stare down. Rose stares up. Slowly, the dummy lifts its arm above its head.

On Rose, rising terror. The dummy's arm is right above its head, a karate chop –

From behind Rose, someone's hand grabs her hand, tight – she turns to look – a MAN is right behind her and he just says:

THE DOCTOR Run!

The dummy's arm swings down – and shatters into the wall. Rose and the man are running. She'd backed up against a third door and this leads to –

12 INT. BASEMENT CORRIDOR #2 NIGHT 1 CONTINUOUS

A long, dark corridor, barely lit, a nightmare tunnel. ROSE and the MAN run, hand in hand. Rose looks back: the DUMMIES are following. And they can *run*. Filling the corridor with an awful plastic clatter, closer and closer.

The man pulls Rose into a lift –

13 INT. LIFT NIGHT 1 CONTINUOUS

The MAN and ROSE run in – he slams the button – the doors go to close. A DUMMY'S ARM reaches through – the doors close on the arm, trap it. The arm flexes, reaching out. The man grabs hold of the arm, grapples with it – teeth clenched, the arm's strong. Through the gap in the door: the impassive plastic face, surrounded by more DUMMIES, reaching out –

Rose stands at the back of the lift, staring, lost. Madmen!

The man heaves – and the arm comes off! Rose horrified!

The lift doors close. It starts to go up. A strange calm.

ROSE ... You pulled his arm off.

THE DOCTOR Yup.

And he chucks it to Rose. She catches it, stares. It's not flesh, it's solid.

THE DOCTOR Plastic.

ROSE Oh very clever, nice trick, who are they then, students? Is this a student thing or what?

THE DOCTOR Why would they be students?

ROSE I don't know!

THE DOCTOR Well you said it, why students?

ROSE Cos ... to get that many people, all dressed up and being stupid, they've got to be students.

He smiles; he likes her.

THE DOCTOR That makes sense. Well done.

ROSE Thank you.

THE DOCTOR They're not students.

ROSE Whoever they are, when Wilson finds them, he's gonna call the police.

THE DOCTOR Who's Wilson?

ROSE Chief electrician.

THE DOCTOR Wilson's dead.

Ping, lift arrives, door opens, the man strides out. Rose follows –

14 EXT. LIFT NIGHT 1 CONTINUOUS

The MAN comes out, ROSE following, still holding the plastic arm. (The doors close behind them.)

ROSE That's not funny, that's sick, I've had enough of this now, who are you then, who's that lot down there?

He whips out a thin metal tube, which glows at the end.

THE DOCTOR Hold on, mind your eyes –

He holds it against the lift button-panel, the tube whirrs. *Bang!* – the panel explodes in a shower of sparks. Big smile off the man, he strides away – Rose having to run after him.

ROSE I said, who are they?

14A INT. DEPARTMENT STORE CORRIDOR NIGHT 1 CONTINUOUS

The MAN walks along, ROSE following in his wake, still holding the plastic arm.

THE DOCTOR They're made of plastic, living plastic creatures, and they're being controlled by a relay device in the roof, which would be a great big problem *if!* I didn't have this –

From his jacket, he brandishes a '*24*'-style bomb, with slabs of explosive strapped to a metal LED display –

THE DOCTOR – so I'm gonna go upstairs and blow it up and I might well die in the process but don't you worry about me, no! You go home, go on, go and have your beans on toast.

He jolts open a fire door, pushes her –

15 EXT. STREET OUTSIDE STORE NIGHT 1 CONTINUOUS

A quiet side-street, where the service doors and trade entrances of big shops are located. ROSE is shoved out.

THE DOCTOR Don't tell anyone about this, cos if you do, you'll get them killed.

Slam, he's gone. Rose is left alone. Shaken.

Pause. Door opens again –

THE DOCTOR I'm the Doctor, by the way, what's your name?

ROSE Rose.

THE DOCTOR Nice to meet you, Rose –
(draws attention to the bomb he's carrying)
Run for your life!

Slam, he's gone again.

16 EXT. CITY SHOPPING STREET NIGHT 1 1808

ROSE, still holding the plastic arm, runs onto the main street, but slows to a halt. Running feels daft, faced with the sheer normality of it all. Her POV: A few late SHOPPERS, PEOPLE waiting for a bus. A taxi scorches past, blaring its horn. The real world.

She's lost: did any of that really happen? She lifts up the plastic arm, looks at it. And, behind her, the roof of the store explodes – a ball of flame.

WIDE SHOT: burning debris falling to the ground, people running, cars screeching to a halt. Alarms go off, screams (no one hurt, just panic). And in the middle of the chaos, Rose just stands there, numb. Holding the arm.

17 OMITTED

18 INT. TYLERS' FLAT NIGHT 1 2045

(The Tylers' flat: a hallway – two bedrooms and a bathroom leading off – leading to the living area at the back of the flat, a living room and kitchen, separated by a door.) JACKIE's in the kitchen on a chunky white cordless phone, taking a cuppa through to the living room, for ROSE, who's more herself now, with the plastic arm on the table.

JACKIE I know, it's on the telly, it's everywhere, she's lucky to be alive. Honestly, it's aged her, skin like an old Bible. Walk in here now, you'd think I was her daughter.
(looks up)
Oh, and here's himself –

Because MICKEY SMITH's just coming in – alarmed, to Rose:

MICKEY I've been phoning your mobile, you could've been dead! It's on the news and everything, I can't believe it, your shop went up!

He gives Rose a hug.

ROSE I'm all right, look, I'm fine, don't make a fuss.

MICKEY But what happened?

ROSE I don't know.

MICKEY What was it though, what did it?

ROSE I wasn't in the shop, I was outside, I didn't see anything.

Interrupted by Jackie, holding out the phone –

JACKIE It's Debbie-on-the-end, she says she knows a man on the *Mirror*, five hundred quid for an interview.

ROSE Oh that's brilliant, give it here.

She takes the phone, clicks it off, slams it down.

JACKIE Well you've got to find some way of making money, your job's kaput and I'm not bailing you out –
(phone rings, she grabs it)
Bev, she's alive! I've told her, sue for compensation . . .

Jackie wanders off to the kitchen b/g, chatting.

MICKEY What you drinking, tea? That's no good, you're in shock, you should have something stronger.

ROSE I'm all right.

MICKEY Come on, you deserve a proper drink, let's go down the pub, you and me, my treat, how about it?

ROSE Is there a match on?

MICKEY I'm thinking of you.

ROSE There's a match on, isn't there?

MICKEY That's not the point. But I could just catch the last five minutes.

She's not annoyed, just smiles:

ROSE Go on then. I'm fine, really, go on. And get rid of that.

He gives her a quick kiss, she gives him the plastic arm.

MICKEY (waves with the arm)
Bye bye.
(pretends it's strangling him)
Akkkk . . .
(stops)
See ya!

And he goes.

19 EXT. TYLERS' FLAT NIGHT 1 2050

Ground floor. MICKEY runs down the steps, saunters along, passing tall, steel, cylindrical bins.

He tosses the plastic arm up, into the bin, gone. As he hurries on and clears shot, a slight track in on the bin . . .

20 INT. ROSE'S BEDROOM DAY 2 0730

CU alarm clock, beep-beep-beep – ROSE slams it off, sits up. Remembers. Sinks back down.

21 INT. TYLERS' FLAT DAY 2 0900

ROSE sitting with a coffee, glum, as JACKIE, in a dressing gown, walks through from the kitchen.

JACKIE There's Finch's, you could try them, they've always got jobs.

ROSE Oh great, the butcher's.

JACKIE Might do you good. That shop was giving you airs and graces.

Jackie goes through to her bedroom, becomes an OOV voice. Rose just sitting there, a bit lost, empty.

JACKIE OOV And I'm not joking about compensation, you've had genuine shock and trauma. Arianna got two thousand quid off the council, just cos the man at the desk said she looked Greek. I know she *is* Greek, but that's not the point, it was a valid claim.

Rose hears a clatter, a swinging noise. She looks down the hall – the cat-flap in the front door is swinging to and fro. Something sinister in its gentle motion.

Rose stands, walks down the hall, stops at Jackie's bedroom.

ROSE Mum, you're such a liar. I told you to nail down that cat-flap, we're gonna get strays.

JACKIE I did it weeks back.

ROSE You thought about it.

Rose continues down the hall. She reaches the door, crouches down, looking at the carpet, seeing three twisted nails. Rose picks one up, puzzled.

And then, right in front of her, the cat-flap swings, as though bumped from outside – just a sway, to and fro . . .

Rose edges down, takes hold of the cat-flap . . . She lifts it up . . . peers through . . .

A face, filling the gap. THE DOCTOR!

Rose jumps to her feet, opens the door –

22 EXT. TYLERS' FLAT DAY 2 0902

Door opens, to reveal THE DOCTOR, just standing up.

THE DOCTOR What are you doing here?

ROSE I live here.

THE DOCTOR Well what do you do that for?

ROSE Because I do. And I'm only at home cos someone blew up my job!

THE DOCTOR (whirrs his device)
I must've got the wrong signal. You're not plastic, are you?
(taps her head)
Nope, bonehead. Bye then.

He walks off. ROSE follows, grabs his arm, pulls him back.

ROSE You, inside, right now.

She shoves him in, slams the door.

23 INT. JACKIE'S BEDROOM DAY 2 0903

ROSE in the doorway (THE DOCTOR behind her), to JACKIE:

ROSE It's about last night, he's part of the inquiry, give's ten minutes.

Rose goes, the Doctor lingers, just looking around.

JACKIE She deserves compensation.

THE DOCTOR Oh, we're talking millions.

Beat; Jackie looks at him properly, turns coy.

JACKIE I'm in my dressing gown.

THE DOCTOR Yes you are.

JACKIE There's a strange man in my bedroom.

THE DOCTOR Yes there is.

JACKIE Anything could happen.

THE DOCTOR No.

And he goes. Jackie nonplussed.

24 INT. TYLERS' FLAT DAY 2 0904

THE DOCTOR walks into the living room.

ROSE Don't mind the mess, coffee?

THE DOCTOR Might as well, thanks, just milk.

She goes to the kitchen.

INTERCUT: ROSE brewing up, barely glancing round; the Doctor looking around, bored and fascinated at the same time. [Speeches run simultaneously.]

ROSE We should go to the police. Seriously. Both of us. And I'm not blaming you, even if it's some sort of joke that just went wrong ... Cos it said on the news, they found a body. I suppose that's Wilson. I didn't really know him, but all the same ... He was nice though, he was a nice bloke. We owe it to him. If we are gonna tell the police though, I want to know what I'm saying. I want you to explain everything.

THE DOCTOR (picks up *Heat*)
Huh! That won't last. He's gay and she's an alien.
(riffs through a paperback, reads it in a second)
Aaah, sad ending.
(reads an envelope)
'Rose Tyler'.
(looks in mirror)
Could've been worse. Look at the ears!
(picks up a deck of cards, a masterful curved shuffle)
Luck be a lady ...
(they fly everywhere)
Or maybe not.
(hears a scrabbling)
Who's that then ...?
(looks behind settee, calls to Rose)
Have you got a cat?

The plastic arm – alive! – leaps up, grabs his throat.

CUT TO Rose, in the kitchen, making coffee, her back to the living room. In b/g, maybe even out of focus, the Doctor staggers past, silent, being strangled.

ROSE No, we did have, but that was years back. Now we just get strays, they come in off the estate.

She turns, carries two coffees into the living room. Her POV: the Doctor is now on the settee, being strangled, gripping the plastic arm with both hands.

Rose is calm, puts down the coffee.

ROSE I told Mickey to chuck that out. You're all the same, give a man a plastic hand and off he goes. Anyway, I don't even know your name, Doctor what-is-it?

The Doctor pulls off the arm, it goes flying. Fast zoom into CU Rose, shocked.

The arm slaps on to her, palm open across her whole face, sticking, gripping tight – the Doctor leaps over –

He grapples with the arm, Rose struggling, mute, the Doctor digging out his metal device. Fighting all the time, he tries to get the device to whirr at the right pitch.

The device hits a clear, high note – the Doctor jams it right up against the plastic arm, and it stops. He pulls it off Rose's face, Rose heaving for breath. The arm's now inflexible, dead plastic. The Doctor just smiling:

THE DOCTOR S'all right, I've stopped it.
(slaps it against his palm)
There you go, see?
(chucks it to Rose)
Harmless.

ROSE D'you think?

And she hits him with it.

24A EXT. STAIRWELL DAY 2 0914

Concrete stairwell. THE DOCTOR's sauntering off, down the stairs – happy, holding the arm. ROSE is running after him.

ROSE Hold on a minute, you can't just go swanning off –

THE DOCTOR Yes I can, here I am, this is me, swanning off, see ya.

ROSE But that arm was moving, it tried to kill me!

THE DOCTOR Ten out of ten for observation.

ROSE You can't just walk away! That's not fair, you've got to tell me what's going on –

THE DOCTOR No I don't.

24B EXT. TYLERS' ESTATE DAY 2 0915

THE DOCTOR strides on, ROSE chasing after him. But then she stops, strong:

ROSE All right then. I'll go to the police! I'll tell everyone! And you said, if I do that, I'll get people killed, so! Your choice. Tell me, or I start talking.

And he's stopped too, looking at her, smiling.

THE DOCTOR Is that supposed to sound tough?

ROSE . . . Sort of.

THE DOCTOR Doesn't work.

Said with a big smile, which makes her smile too, even though she's puzzled.

ROSE Who *are* you?

THE DOCTOR Told you, I'm the Doctor.

ROSE Yeah, but Doctor what?

THE DOCTOR Just the Doctor.

ROSE 'The Doctor'?

THE DOCTOR Hello!

ROSE Is that supposed to sound impressive?

THE DOCTOR . . . Sort of.

Another smile between them. She walks up to him, more relaxed, all confidential.

ROSE Come on then, you can tell me, I've seen enough. Are you the police?

THE DOCTOR No, I was just . . . passing through. I'm a long way from home.

ROSE But what have I done wrong? How come those plastic things keep coming after me?

THE DOCTOR Oh, like the entire world revolves around you! You're just an accident, you got in the way, that's all.

ROSE It tried to kill me!

THE DOCTOR It was after me, not you. Last night, in the shop, I was there first. You blundered in, almost ruined the whole thing! This morning –
(of the arm)
I was tracking it down, it was tracking *me* down, it only fixed on you, cos you'd met me.

ROSE So what you're saying is . . . the entire world revolves around *you*?

THE DOCTOR Sometimes, yeah.

ROSE You're full of it.

THE DOCTOR Sometimes, yeah.

ROSE But all this plastic stuff … Who else knows about it?

THE DOCTOR No one.

ROSE What, you're on your own?

THE DOCTOR Who else is there? You lot, you just watch telly and eat chips and go to bed, and all the time, right underneath you … there's a war going on.

She takes the arm off him.

ROSE Okay. Start from the beginning.

25 EXT. TYLERS' ESTATE DAY 2 0920

THE DOCTOR and ROSE (holding the plastic arm) walking along, more like friends, now.

ROSE … I mean, if we go with living plastic – and I don't even believe that, but if we do – how did you kill it?

THE DOCTOR The thing controlling it projects life into the arm, I just cut off the signal, dead.

ROSE So that's … radio control?

THE DOCTOR Thought control.

He's gentle with her:

THE DOCTOR You all right?

ROSE Yeah.
(pause)
So … who's controlling it, then?

THE DOCTOR Long story.

ROSE But what's it all for? I mean, shop window dummies, what's that about? Is someone trying to take over Britain's shops?

Both laughing.

THE DOCTOR No!

ROSE Well, no!

THE DOCTOR It's not a price war.

ROSE No.

Laughter stops, with:

THE DOCTOR They want to overthrow the human race. And destroy you. D'you believe me?

ROSE No.

THE DOCTOR But you're still listening.

ROSE Really though, Doctor. Tell me. Who are you?

Both at a halt, now. The Doctor smiling, muses:

THE DOCTOR D'you know like we were saying? About the Earth revolving.
(pause)
It's like when you're a kid, the first time they tell you that the world is turning. And you just can't believe it, cos everything looks like it's standing still.
(right at her)
I can feel it.

He holds her hand. The two of them, joined together; a gradual tilt to the image, the feeling of suppressed power.

THE DOCTOR The turn of the Earth. The ground beneath our feet is spinning at a thousand miles an hour, the entire planet is hurtling round the sun at sixty-seven thousand miles an hour, and I can feel it, we're falling through space, you and me, clinging to the skin of this tiny little world, and if we let go –

He lets go. Back to normal. Rose shaken, steps back.

THE DOCTOR That's who I am. Now forget me, Rose Tyler. Go home.

He takes the plastic arm off her, turns and walks away. Rose's POV: a wide, beautifully bleak urban landscape, the Doctor walking away, in the general direction of a free-standing 8-ft blue wooden box.

Rose sighs, turns, goes. She turns a corner, heading for the flats, walking but slowly becoming aware of ... a distant noise. Getting louder, a heavy, groaning, grinding noise, like ancient engines rising and falling.

A wind springs up around Rose. Newspapers whipped up into a sudden vortex, spinning. The noise rising.

Suddenly Rose is running, back the way she came. The noise fades away as Rose rounds the corner – the urban landscape's empty: the Doctor, the box, vanished.

26 INT. MICKEY'S FLAT DAY 2 1000

MICKEY opens the door, ROSE standing there.

MICKEY Wa-hey, kit off, here's my woman!

ROSE Oh shut up.

Quick kiss, she steps in, smiling. The flat is a lads-together mess. Bikes and crates and old clothes. Mickey saunters down to the kitchen

MICKEY Coffee?

ROSE Only if you wash the mug, and I don't mean rinse, I mean wash, can I use your computer?

MICKEY Any excuse to get into the bedroom.

And Rose goes in. Pause, he makes coffee, then remembers:

MICKEY Don't read my e-mails!

27 INT. MICKEY'S BEDROOM DAY 2 1010

A comfy mess of a room, with an old PC on a littered desk. ROSE with a coffee, looking at the screen.

She's in Google. CU screen: she types *Doctor*, presses *search*; it blinks to – *17,700,000 results*.

She laughs. Tries again. Types *Doctor living plastic*, presses *search*; *55,300 results*.

Closer on Rose, fed up. But she thinks, sits up, types. Extreme CU on the letters, as they blink into existence: *Doctor blue box*. She presses *search*, and gets *493 results*.

Rose clicks on the first result – a home-made web page opens. Bold letters: *DOCTOR WHO?* Then a blurred photo of the Doctor. Underneath: *Have you seen this man?* Underneath that: *Contact Clive!*

28 EXT. SUBURBAN STREET DAY 2 1600

The essence of suburbia – not too posh, just normal. Semi-detached houses, small front lawns. A battered Beetle just pulling up, MICKEY driving, ROSE in mid-argument:

ROSE ... You're not coming in, he's safe, he's got a wife and kids –

MICKEY And who told you that? He did! That's exactly what an internet lunatic murderer would say –

Rose slams the door, heads off, with a polite smile at a NEIGHBOUR, who's just putting out his wheely bin.

29 INT./EXT. CLIVE'S HOUSE DAY 2 1602

Front door opens, a 7-year-old BOY looks up at ROSE.

ROSE Um, hello, I've come to see Clive, we've been e-mailing.

BOY Dad! It's one of your nutters.

Boy wanders off, CLIVE appears – 40, flustered, smiling.

CLIVE Sorry, hello! You must be Rose. I'm Clive. Obviously.

ROSE I'd better tell you now, my boyfriend's waiting in the car, in case you're going to kill me.

She indicates MICKEY, in the car, glaring. Clive waves.

CLIVE No, good point, yes! No murders!

Clive's wife CAROLINE calls out OOV:

CAROLINE Who is it?

CLIVE It's something to do with the Doctor, she's read the website.
(to Rose)
Come on through, I'm in the shed.

Rose goes through, Caroline appears, top of the stairs.

CAROLINE She? She's read a website about the Doctor and she's a she?

30 EXT. CLIVE'S SHED DAY 2 1610

A wooden shed in a small back garden – dark, lit by a desklight. It's CLIVE's den, a cocoon of clippings and magazines. Clive sits at his PC, ROSE beside him.

CLIVE ... A lot of this stuff's quite sensitive, I couldn't just send it to you. People might intercept. If you know what I mean.
(digs through papers)
You see, if you dig deep enough, and keep a lively mind, then this 'Doctor' keeps cropping up, all over the place. He's in political diaries, conspiracy theories, even ghost stories. No first name, no last name, just 'the Doctor', always 'the Doctor'. And the title seems to be passed down, from father to son, it appears to be an inheritance. This one's your Doctor, isn't it?

He indicates the website *DOCTOR WHO?* photo, on screen.

ROSE Yeah.

He opens a file thick with old papers, felt-penned *FILE 9*.

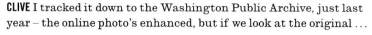

CLIVE I tracked it down to the Washington Public Archive, just last year – the online photo's enhanced, but if we look at the original . . .

He flicks through photos, each one widening, the Doctor becoming part of a crowd – wider: a crowd in shock; wider: lining a road; wider: a familiar, terrible car . . .

CLIVE The 22nd of November, 1963, the assassination of President Kennedy. And there he is.

ROSE Must be his father.

CLIVE Going further back . . . April 1912, a photograph of the Daniels family of Southampton, and friend . . .

B&w photo, a 1912 family, formal pose, with the Doctor.

CLIVE The day after this was taken, they were due to sail for the New World. On the *Titanic*. But for some unknown reason, they cancelled the trip, and survived. And here we are – 1883, another Doctor –

A line drawing of the Doctor.

CLIVE – Look, the same lineage, he's identical – this one was washed up on the coast of Sumatra, on the very night that Krakatoa exploded.

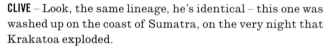

Clive drawing Rose in; both loving the myth.

CLIVE The Doctor is a legend, woven throughout history. When disaster comes, he is there. He brings the storm in his wake, and has one constant companion.

ROSE Who's that?

CLIVE Death.

31 EXT. SUBURBAN STREET DAY 2 1612

MICKEY's bored. Drumming his hands on the steering wheel. His POV: suburban stillness. No one around. Perfect calm, almost sinister in itself.

Then – Mickey glances across, did he see . . . ?

He's looking at a wheely bin, about twenty feet away. It's just settling back into its position, Mickey missing the actual move. Mickey stares. Nothing.

And then it moves. It turns towards him, six inches, stops.

32 INT. CLIVE'S SHED DAY 2 1612

CLIVE intense, ROSE believing.

CLIVE If the Doctor's come back, if you've seen him, Rose, then one thing's for certain. We're all in danger.

33 EXT. SUBURBAN STREET DAY 2 1612

Mickey's bemused, sits up to see if there's anything at the base of the bin. Nothing. No slope.

Then the wheely bin rolls forward, just six inches, stops. Mickey gets out of the car, saunters over to the bin. Still smiling. He looks round the bin, either side. No string. He flips open the lid, confident –

MICKEY Come on then –

Nothing, it's empty.

34 INT. CLIVE'S SHED DAY 2 1612

CLIVE And if he singled you out, if the Doctor's making housecalls … then God help you.

35 EXT. SUBURBAN STREET DAY 2 1612

MICKEY goes to walk off, takes his hands off the bin – and the plastic stretches, like melted cheese. He's stuck to the bin. He's horrified, wails, lifts his hands up further – the elastic strands of grey-wheely-bin plastic stretching out, pulling taut.

And it snaps back! He's jerked towards the bin.

Scared now, Mickey pulls back again, really hard, struggling, sweating, the plastic stretching out …

And this time, it snaps back hard. Mickey's pulled head-first into the bin. He cries out – a muffled scream – then there's another heave. Mickey's legs are swallowed inside, and the lid swings up, slams shut, whap!

And all is calm. Pull back, gently; suburbia restored.

36 INT. CLIVE'S SHED DAY 2 1612

ROSE and CLIVE, still intense.

ROSE But who is he? Who d'you think he really is?

CLIVE I think all these pictures are the same man. I think he's immortal. I think he's an alien from another world.

Hold on Rose. She just blinks.

37 EXT. SUBURBAN STREET DAY 2 1616

ROSE walks to the car, gets in, breezy –

ROSE All right, he's a nutter. Off his head. Complete online conspiracy freak, you win! So what are we doing tonight? I fancy a pizza.

And only now, CAMERA swings over to MICKEY. Smiling. Bright. Like it's a new word:

MICKEY Pizza! Puh-puh-puh-puh-pizza!

ROSE Or Chinese.

MICKEY Pizzaaaaaaaa!

CU Mickey, the engine roars, as he twists the wheel. The wild grin. White teeth. The shine of his skin.

38 OMITTED

39 INT. RESTAURANT NIGHT 2 1850

Nice, but not too posh, a step above Café Rouge (with ROSE *not* out of her depth). Rose musing, MICKEY studying her.

ROSE D'you think I should try the hospital? Suki said they had jobs going, in the canteen.
(sighs)
Is that it then, dishing out chips? I could do A-Levels. It's all Jimmy Stone's fault, I only left school cos of him and look where he ended up. What d'you think?

MICKEY So where did you meet this Doctor?

ROSE Oh sorry, was I talking about me for a second?

MICKEY Cos I reckon, it all started back at the shop, am I right? Was he something to do with that?

ROSE No.

MICKEY Come on.

Rose awkward, guilty.

ROSE Sort of.

MICKEY What was he doing there?

ROSE I'm not going on about it, Mickey. I know it sounds daft, but I don't think it's safe. He's dangerous.

MICKEY But you can trust me, sweetheart –
(blinks, robotic)
Babe –
(blinks)
Darling –
(blinks)
Sugar –
(blinks)
Non-specific term of affection –
(normal again)

You can tell me anything. Tell me about the Doctor, and what he's planning, then I can help you, Rose, that's all I want to do, sweetheart/babe/darling/sugar/non-specific term of affection.

ROSE (unnerved)
What are you doing that for . . . ?

A WAITER appears, proferring champage – but stay on Rose and Mickey, the waiter just a blur, black jacket, head OOV.

WAITER Excuse me, your champagne.

MICKEY We didn't order champagne.
(to Rose, cold)
Where's the Doctor?

The Waiter whisks the champagne round to Rose.

WAITER Madam, your champagne.

Rose doesn't even look up, unnerved by Mickey's intensity.

ROSE That's not ours –
(to Mickey)
Mickey, what is it, what's wrong?

MICKEY I need to find out how much he knows, so where is he?

WAITER Doesn't anybody want this champagne?

MICKEY Look, we did not order –
(looks up)
Ah, gotcha.

Rose looks up – the waiter is THE DOCTOR. And he's shaking the champagne bottle like mad.

THE DOCTOR Don't mind me, I'm just toasting the happy couple. On the house!

And the Doctor aims the bottle, pops the cork. It hits Mickey. But his whole face bends in, like sponge, absorbing the blow – and then *boings!* back to normal shape. Mickey chews, then spits out the cork. Big smile.

MICKEY Anyway!

Rose stands, steps back, horrified, joining the Doctor.

Mickey lifts up his arms – both hands are now big, flat, hard chisels. He stands, swipes down – slicing the table in half. Everyone in the restaurant now looking, gobsmacked, as the Doctor dives forward, grabs Mickey in a headlock. They struggle, Mickey flailing, the Doctor yanking until Mickey's head comes off.

CUT TO MIDDLE-AGED COUPLE, the WOMAN screams. The Doctor holds up Mickey's head. Which is still alive.

MICKEY'S HEAD Don't think that's gonna stop me.

CUT TO Middle-aged Couple, the MAN screams.

Rose smashes the fire alarm.

ROSE Get out! Everyone, out, now!

Panic, DINERS run, scream. Headless-Mickey-chisel-hands is blind but still lashing out wildly, sends tables flying. The Doctor and Rose run through swing-doors, to the kitchens –

40 INT. RESTAURANT KITCHEN NIGHT 2 CONTINUOUS

THE DOCTOR (carrying MICKEY's head) and ROSE run through. The KITCHEN STAFF are already panicked by the alarm.

ROSE All of you, get out!

Rose and the Doctor run through – out. Next second, headless-Mickey-chisel-hands blunders through, sends a WAITER and a stack of plates flying, charges on, wild, terrifying in his clumsiness and strength –

41 EXT. RESTAURANT YARD NIGHT 2 1853

A plain concrete yard, very high walls. THE DOCTOR (carrying MICKEY's head) and ROSE run out, top speed. The Doctor slams the door shut – it's an old riveted metal door. The Doctor whirrs his device against the lock, the door stays fast. *Whump!* The creature inside hammers against the door. Rose runs for the gate. Locked. Pulls on it. Trapped! The hammering on the door is strong, she's panicking.

The Doctor's calmly digging out keys, wandering over to the tall blue box, standing in the middle of the yard. It's got a sign across the top: *POLICE PUBLIC CALL BOX.*

ROSE Open the gate, use that – tube thing, come on!

THE DOCTOR (holds up device)
Sonic screwdriver.

ROSE Use it!

THE DOCTOR Naah, tell you what, let's go in here.

And he just steps into the box, gone.

ROSE You can't just hide in a wooden box – !

Whump! The banging gets harder, louder. Rose is frantic, runs to the gate again, heaves – *whump!* She pulls with all her might – *whump!* –

ROSE He's gonna get us!

Whump! A huge buckle in the middle of the door –

ROSE Doctor – !

In a blind panic, Rose runs into the box –

42 INT. TARDIS NIGHT 2 CONTINUOUS

– into a big, wide, wonderful room. ROSE stops dead. THE DOCTOR's far away, busy at a central six-sided console, which is a jam of all sorts of technology, big old 60s' buttons and futuristic devices. And around that, high above, the shine of epic, alien design, the whole place humming with suppressed energy.

Rose stares. Then she steps back out –

43 EXT. RESTAURANT YARD NIGHT 2 CONTINUOUS

– into the yard. *Whump!* A chisel hand slices through the metal door. ROSE runs back inside –

44 INT. TARDIS NIGHT 2 CONTINUOUS

– back into the mysterious room, slams the wooden door shut behind her.

ROSE It's gonna follow us!

THE DOCTOR The assembled hordes of Genghis Khan couldn't get through that door, and believe me, they have tried, now shut up for a minute –

During this, THE DOCTOR keeps working, happy. He's whirring away at MICKEY'S HEAD, balanced on the console, with the face now reduced to just dead plastic. The Doctor pulls wires out of the console and down from the roof, like a switchboard operator, shoving them into the skull. For ROSE's benefit:

THE DOCTOR Y'see, the arm was too simple, but the head's perfect, I can use it to trace the signal back to its source.

He jams in a final wire, then turns to Rose; studying her, fascinated. Rose keeps level, holding back the terror:

THE DOCTOR Right. Where d'you want to start?

ROSE Um. The inside's bigger than the outside.

THE DOCTOR Yes.

ROSE It's ... alien.

THE DOCTOR Yes.

ROSE Are you alien?

THE DOCTOR Yes.
(pause)
Is that all right?

ROSE Yeah.

THE DOCTOR It's called the TARDIS, this thing. T-A-R-D-I-S, that's Time And Relative Dimensions In Space –

Rose goes to cry, holds in a sob, right on the edge.

THE DOCTOR That's okay. Culture shock. Happens to the best of us.

But *this* is what she's upset about:

ROSE Did they kill him? Mickey? Did they kill Mickey? Is he dead?

THE DOCTOR Oh. I didn't think of that.

ROSE He's my boyfriend, and you pulled off his head, and they copied him, and you didn't even *think*? And now you're just gonna let him melt.

THE DOCTOR Melt – ?!

He spins round – the head is melting. It oozes away over the console. The Doctor runs over, furious:

THE DOCTOR No no no no no –

He pulls chunky, stiff levers; keeps operating as the wheezing engine-noise starts up. A glass column at the centre of the console starts to rise, fall and rotate.

The whole room lurches. Deep, ominous creaks from high up, the dangerous grinding of old metal. Rose looks down: the panels of the floor are shifting slightly, uneasy.

ROSE ... What are you doing?

THE DOCTOR Following the signal ... it's failing, wait a minute – I've got it ...
(rips panels off)
Ohhh no you don't, no no no no NO!
(pulls huge lever)
Almost there, almost there –

And he runs for the door, the engine noise falling away.

ROSE You can't go out there, it's not safe –

Rose agonised, but then she runs after him, to help –

45 EXT. EMBANKMENT NIGHT 2 1856

ROSE stops dead in the doorway.

The police box is now in a completely different place. A quiet stretch of the Embankment; the lights of London. THE DOCTOR is looking out over the Thames, pissed off, as Rose steps out, carefully.

THE DOCTOR Lost the signal. I got so close.

ROSE We've moved. Does it ... fly?

THE DOCTOR It disappears there and reappears here, you wouldn't understand.

ROSE But if we're ... somewhere else, what about the headless thing? It's still on the loose.

THE DOCTOR It melted with the head, are you just gonna witter on all night?

Pause. Then, quietly:

ROSE I'll have to tell his mother.

The Doctor looks at her, blank.

ROSE Mickey. I'll have to tell his mother he's dead, and you just went and forgot him *again*! You were right. You are alien.

THE DOCTOR Listen, if I did forget some kid called Mickey –

ROSE He's not a kid!

THE DOCTOR – it's because I'm busy, trying to save the life of every stupid ape blundering about on top of this planet, all right?

ROSE All right!

THE DOCTOR Yes it is!

Silence. Then, sulky, both like kids:

ROSE If you're an alien, how come you sound like you're from the north?

THE DOCTOR Lots of planets have a north.

Pause. Still sullen, but both gradually warming up:

ROSE What's a 'police public call box'?

THE DOCTOR It's like a telephone box, from the 1950s, it's a disguise.

ROSE Okay. And, this living plastic ... What's it got against us?

THE DOCTOR Nothing. It loves you. You've got such a good planet, lots of smoke and oil, plenty of toxins and dioxins in the air – just what the Nestene Consciousness needs. Its foodstock was destroyed in the War, all its protein planets rotted. So. Earth. Dinner.

ROSE Any way of stopping it?

The Doctor takes out a glass tube, blue liquid inside.

THE DOCTOR Antiplastic.

ROSE Antiplastic?

THE DOCTOR Antiplastic! But first of all, I've got to find it.
(all energy again)
How can you hide something that big in a city this small?

ROSE Hold on, hide what?

THE DOCTOR The transmitter. The Consciousness is controlling every single piece of plastic, so it needs a transmitter to boost its signal.

ROSE And what does it look like?

THE DOCTOR Like a transmitter! Round. And massive. Somewhere slap-bang in the middle of London.

He's facing Rose, his back to the river, being framed by . . . the London Eye.

THE DOCTOR A huge, metal, circular structure, like a dish, like a wheel, radial, close to where we're standing, it must be completely invisible . . .
(notices Rose)
What?

She just indicates with a nod, like he's stupid.

The Doctor looks round at the Eye, looks back at Rose.

THE DOCTOR What?
(looks round, looks back)
What is it, what?
(looks round, pause, looks back)
Oh.
(looks round, looks back, big smile)
Fantastic!

46 EXT. A BRIDGE ACROSS THE THAMES NIGHT 2 1900

THE DOCTOR and ROSE run across the bridge, the city shining behind them. Running to save the world. They take each other's hand, exhilarated.

47 EXT. THE LONDON EYE NIGHT 2 1920

The London Eye looms above, turning against the night sky. THE DOCTOR and ROSE run to a halt on the concourse, a good distance back from the official entrance.

The Doctor looks across the river: London at night.

THE DOCTOR Think of it. Plastic. All over the world, Every artificial thing, waiting to come alive. The shop window dummies, the phones, the wires, the cables.

ROSE The breast implants.

Beat.

THE DOCTOR Still, we've found the transmitter. The Consciousness must be somewhere underneath.

ROSE looks over the Embankment wall.

ROSE What about down there?

The Doctor looks; a grille, down by the river's edge, with light and smoke rising up . . .

THE DOCTOR Looks good to me.

48 INT. UNDERGROUND LAIR NIGHT 2 1935

Darkness. THE DOCTOR and ROSE walk down a metal staircase. It's dark, cramped. The Doctor eases open a rusting door.

They walk into a nightmare factory.

Nothing hi-tech. It's a dark, greasy metal chamber, all riveted dirty steel, like the guts of a battleship. Old ladders and signs on the wall, like this was once a human workspace. Now, metal walkways and gantries, rickety and unsafe, are suspended above [greenscreen the floor] a huge vat of thick, churning liquid, like molten steel, glowing yellow, with streaks of violent red and orange.

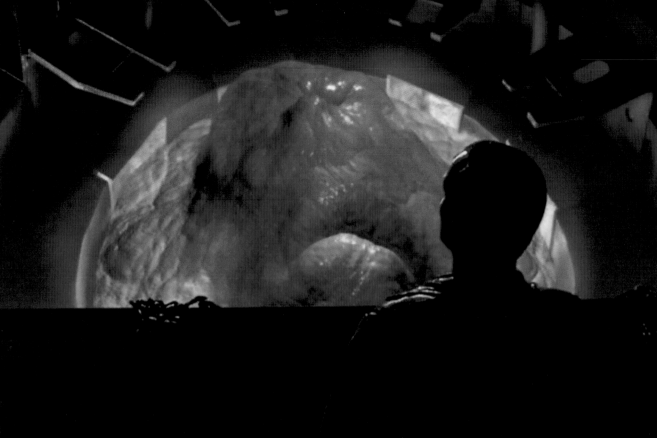

The Doctor and Rose lit from below. All around them, a series of pulleys, made of chains, crank up and down; a primitive mechanical system which lifts and then tips troughs of glowing liquid into the vat below, feeding it.

The Doctor and Rose looking down, quiet:

THE DOCTOR The Nestene Consciousness. That's it, inside the vat, a living plastic creature.

ROSE Well then, tip in your antiplastic and let's go.

THE DOCTOR I'm not here to kill it. I've got to give it a chance.

The Doctor steps forward, proclaims, formal:

THE DOCTOR I seek audience with the Nestene Consciousness under peaceful contract, according to Convention Fifteen of the Shadow Proclamation.

A rumbling fills the air, a deep, strange alien voice. The vat bubbles, churns.

THE DOCTOR Thank you. If I might have permission to approach.

But Rose sees –

ROSE Oh my God –

She runs across the gantry to a ragged, grimy figure, curled up in a ball. It's MICKEY, terrified, like an animal.

ROSE Mickey! Oh my God, Mickey, it's me, it's okay, it's all right –

MICKEY That thing, down there, the liquid, Rose, it can *talk* ...

ROSE Oh you're stinking!
(calls down)
Doctor, they kept him alive!

The Doctor is walking down to the next level, to a platform above the centre of the vat.

THE DOCTOR Yeah, that was always a possibility, keep him alive to maintain the copy.

ROSE What, and you *knew* that? And you never said?!

THE DOCTOR Can we keep the domestics for outside, thank you.
(formal again:)
Am I addressing the Consciousness?

Rose stares, boggles, as a huge blister forms on the surface of the vat. And the blister stays inflated, settles into the shape of a face – huge, many metres across – flat on the horizontal, staring up. It's a rudimentary, blank face, blind eyes, like a basic dummy's features. But the mouth can move, talk. A voice fills the air. Rose chilled: harsh alien vowels, reverberating all around.

CONSCIOUSNESS [*A rumble of acceptance, greeting.*]

The Doctor reaches the lower level, stands forward.

THE DOCTOR Thank you. If I might observe. You infiltrated this civilisation by means of warp-shunt technology. So may I suggest, with the greatest respect, that you ... shunt off.

CONSCIOUSNESS [*Anger!*]

THE DOCTOR Oh don't give me that! This is an invasion, plain and simple, don't talk about constitutional rights –

CONSCIOUSNESS [*Fury!*]

THE DOCTOR I – am – *talking*!

The vat simmers, resentful. The Doctor strong, heartfelt:

THE DOCTOR This planet is just starting. These stupid little people have only just learnt how to walk, but they can achieve so much more. / On their behalf, I'm asking you, please. Just go.

But at /, behind the Doctor, two DUMMIES step out of the shadows, both in sharp black suits. Unseen, they walk forward in silence.

ROSE Doctor!

Too late – FIRST DUMMY grabs the Doctor, pins his arms back, the SECOND DUMMY slides its hand into the Doctor's pocket. It holds up the tube of blue liquid.

THE DOCTOR I wasn't gonna use it, that was just ... insurance –

First Dummy keeps holding the Doctor as Second Dummy takes a good few steps away with its prize, stands to the side.

CONSCIOUSNESS [*Roars, furious!*]

THE DOCTOR I was not attacking you, I was trying to help ... I swear, I'm not your enemy, I'm *not* –

CONSCIOUSNESS [*Talks fast, accusing.*]

THE DOCTOR ... What d'you mean? No. Ohhh no. Honestly, no ...

It's suddenly a lot more serious, he looks round, in dread. Rose follows his line of vision, sees above them, on the topmost level, a pool of light slam on, revealing: the TARDIS. The Doctor is genuinely disturbed, now.

THE DOCTOR Yes, that's my ship, it's mine.

CONSCIOUSNESS [*Accuses him.*]

THE DOCTOR That's not true! I should know, I was there, I fought in the War, it wasn't my fault.
(agonised)
I couldn't save your world. I couldn't save any of them.

CONSCIOUSNESS [*Roars – a command!*]

It's charging up, the vat flickering, churning. Pools of light slam on; the whine of dynamos, systems activating.

ROSE What's it doing?

THE DOCTOR It's the TARDIS. The Nestene's identified it as superior technology, it's terrified, it's going to the final stage. The invasion is starting, right now – get out, Rose, just leg it!

In the middle of the noise and rage and fear, Rose gets out her mobile. Clicks a name. As the chamber activates around her, she's very small and frightened, as she phones:

ROSE ... Mum?

49 EXT. CITY SHOPPING STREET NIGHT 2 1940

INTERCUT with ROSE in the UNDERGROUND LAIR.

JACKIE's on her mobile. She's just leaving a city-centre police station. She's clutching a sheet of paper, triumphant.

JACKIE There you are, I was just gonna phone – you *can* get compensation, I said so, I've got this document-thing off the police. Don't thank me!

ROSE Where are you?

JACKIE I said, I'm in town.

ROSE Go home. Mum, go home, right now, just go home – (static on phone)

JACKIE You're breaking up, I'm just gonna do a bit of late-night shopping, I'll see you later, ta-ra!

Jackie hangs up, walks on. Her path away from Rose's shop takes her down a main shopping street.

Jackie clears frame, stay on the windows. The DUMMIES.

50 INT. UNDERGROUND LAIR NIGHT 2 1941

ROSE on her mobile, clicking the number again and again.

ROSE Mum? Mum?

THE DOCTOR's still being held fast by FIRST DUMMY:

THE DOCTOR It's the activation signal! It's transmitting –

He looks up.

51 EXT. THE LONDON EYE NIGHT 2 1941

Arcs of blue electricity begin to streak along the spokes of the giant wheel.

CUT TO TOURISTS, staring up, awestruck.

CUT TO the electricity bolts, going wild.

52 INT. UNDERGROUND LAIR NIGHT 2 1941

CU ROSE, looking up. Horrified. A whisper:

ROSE . . . The end of the world.

The huge plastic face smiles:

CONSCIOUSNESS [*Begin!*]

53 EXT. THE LONDON EYE NIGHT 2 1942

And the London Eye transmits. The entire circle pulses, like the RKO transmitter, with a massive, reverberating hum.

54 EXT. CITY SHOPPING STREET NIGHT 2 1942

A windowful of DUMMIES. They jerk. Just a fraction. Awake. They turn slowly, flexing, in their elegant clothes.

CUT TO CLIVE and CAROLINE and their SON, walking along.

CLIVE A budget is a budget, Caroline, there's no point in me creating a spreadsheet if you're going to spend summer money in winter months.

CAROLINE Oh my God – !

DUMMIES in the window behind her jerk awake.

CAROLINE I thought they were dummies! I could've had a heart attack. Oh, don't tell me it's rag week.

But Clive's looking around. Suspecting . . .

CUT TO JACKIE. She's stopped, looks round the street, seeing dummies moving in all the windows. SHOPPERS are stopping. Staring. Some laughing.

CUT TO the first windowful. The dummies step forward. The front one raises its hands, karate chop – the glass shatters.

55 INT. UNDERGROUND LAIR NIGHT 2 1943

The chamber is now full-pitch, the pulse of the signal, the entire room steaming, groaning.

CONSCIOUSNESS [*Victory!*]

THE DOCTOR Rose, get out! Just run! RUN!

ROSE is despairing, but turns to MICKEY, pulls him up.

FIRST DUMMY is still holding THE DOCTOR from behind, and now starts pushing him towards the platform's edge. The vat boiling below, wild and hot.

56 EXT. CITY SHOPPING STREET NIGHT 2 1943

JACKIE looks round. DUMMIES are stepping down from every window. All sorts of different shapes and sizes. And it's all strangely calm; SHOPPERS just looking, bemused. Jackie turns to see THREE CHILD DUMMIES walk out of the doors of Daisy-&-Tom-type shop. Faces just ovals, no features at all.

CUT TO the far end of the street. CAROLINE's scared, CLIVE steps forward. A DUMMY turns to face him. Enraptured:

CLIVE It's true. Everything I've read. All those stories, it's all true.

The dummy lifts up its arm to point at him. The wrist is hinged, its hand swings down. Revealing a metal tube.

And Clive's so sad, because he knows what happens next: the dummy fires.

57 INT. UNDERGROUND LAIR NIGHT 2 1943

FIRST DUMMY pushes THE DOCTOR towards the edge ... HIGH SHOT: the Doctor framed against the Nestene face below, as it stares up, joyous.

CONSCIOUSNESS [*Join me!*]

CUT TO ROSE, helping MICKEY along, the gantry swaying. They reach the TARDIS. Rose pushes the door, but it won't give. She hammers at it, but it's no use. A whisper:

ROSE I haven't got a key ...

She sinks to the floor. The terrible noise muffled. Mickey's just shivering. Rose is desolate.

58 EXT. CITY SHOPPING STREET NIGHT 2 1944

JACKIE stands frozen. The world has gone insane: DUMMIES firing. SHOPPERS running, screaming. (NB, see the shots fired, but not the actual impact, cut around that.)

A MAN has a CHILD DUMMY clinging to his back. CAROLINE and SON run past, screaming.

At the far end, a car is burning. Sirens wail.

A phalanx of dummies walks down the street. Calm, elegant. Jackie's crying. Heaving for breath. She's tucked away to one side, backing away from the madness. Behind her: a bridal shop. Jackie's staring out, not seeing THREE BRIDE DUMMIES in different white dresses step forward, raise arms, swipe – glass shatters. CU Jackie, turning round, screaming –

59 INT. UNDERGROUND LAIR NIGHT 2 1944

TRACK IN TO ROSE, huddled by the TARDIS, tiny, wretched . . .

Except she's not. Never will be.

She looks up. Fire in her eyes.

Hero shot, she stands, rising into frame.

60 EXT. CITY SHOPPING STREET NIGHT 2 1944

JACKIE backs away. The THREE BRIDE DUMMIES have fixed on her. Walk towards her with terrifying elegance.

As Jackie backs away, SHOPPERS run left to right, panic all around, no one to help her. She's backed against the wall opposite. She slides to the floor, helpless.

The brides approach.

61 INT. UNDERGROUND LAIR NIGHT 2 1944

ROSE steps forward, determined. MICKEY stays by the TARDIS, scared to death.

MICKEY Rose, don't, leave him – !

THE DOCTOR's struggling, held by FIRST DUMMY, right on the edge, but he looks up. He sees Rose. Eye contact. He's desperate; he *needs* her.

62 EXT. CITY SHOPPING STREET NIGHT 2 1944

JACKIE cowers on the floor, looking up. THREE BRIDE DUMMIES lift arms, point at her. Their hands swing down. Aim . . .

63 INT. UNDERGROUND LAIR NIGHT 2 1945

ROSE pulls a big red fire-axe off the wall.

MICKEY There's nothing you can do!

Rose pulls at one of the vertical chains hanging down in the cavern. It pulls free, but not completely, still attached above her head to a big, crude ceiling bolt. As she swings the chain to wrap around her arm:

ROSE I've got no job. No A-Levels. No future. But I'll tell you what I have got. Jericho Street Junior School, under-7's gymnastic team –

She swings the axe, *schunk!*; severs the bolt.

ROSE I got the bronze!

And she leaps off the platform and swings – right across the chamber. The chain rattles through its pulley so she's going *down*. Rose's POV: swinging down towards THE DOCTOR –

The Doctor grins, flips forward and down, sends FIRST DUMMY flying over his head, into the vat, which at the same time leaves the Doctor crouching so that Rose swings over him, right into the SECOND DUMMY. Second Dummy falls off the platform. CU the tube of blue liquid, falling out of its hand, down into the vat, on to the huge Nestene face –

CONSCIOUSNESS [*Screams!*]

64 EXT. CITY SHOPPING STREET NIGHT 2 1945

The THREE BRIDE DUMMIES jerk. Twitch.

65 INT. UNDERGROUND LAIR NIGHT 2 1945

The Nestene face roars in pain, the vat boiling madly. THE DOCTOR grabs hold of ROSE. Grinning.

THE DOCTOR Now we're in trouble.

66 EXT. CITY SHOPPING STREET NIGHT 2 1945

JACKIE looks round. All the DUMMIES along the street are spasming, confused.

67 INT. UNDERGROUND LAIR NIGHT 2 1945

THE DOCTOR and ROSE race up the stairs towards the TARDIS. The whole room is shaking, girders falling from the roof. The Doctor unlocks the TARDIS door, shoves MICKEY inside, follows. But Rose stops in the doorway. Looks down.

The face-bubble dissolves, the vat boiling and bursting. Dying. Screaming, as it turns a pure, dazzling white. Rose smiles. Gotcha! She goes inside – rubble cascading down as the vat ruptures in its death throes. The groaning engines of the TARDIS start up, as the molten plastic glows, filling the screen with white ...

68 EXT. CITY SHOPPING STREET NIGHT 2 1945

All the DUMMIES clatter to the floor. Lifeless. They tumble into component pieces, arms and legs separating.

A BRIDE's head rolls at JACKIE's feet.

She looks round. Everything's stopped. The devastation. The awful silence. The SURVIVORS.

69 EXT. ALLEYWAY NIGHT 2 1947

MICKEY runs out of the TARDIS like a mad thing.

It's an alley in the city centre: at the end, a normal city-centre street. The wail of sirens in the distance. Mickey stumbles, falls to the floor, looks back in terror: ROSE just saunters out, with her mobile, speed-dials –

ROSE Mum?

70 EXT. CITY SHOPPING STREET NIGHT 2 1947

JACKIE in the wreckage, on her mobile.

JACKIE Rose, don't go out of the house! It's not safe, there are these things, they were shooting, they –

71 EXT. ALLEYWAY NIGHT 2 1947

ROSE hangs up, smiling, reaches MICKEY, kneels by him.

ROSE Well. Fat lot of good you were.

But Mickey suddenly points, scared, at THE DOCTOR, standing in the TARDIS doorway, casual.

THE DOCTOR Nestene Consciousness?
(clicks fingers)
Easy!

ROSE Oh yeah! You were useless in there, you'd be dead if it wasn't for me.

THE DOCTOR Yes I would. Thank you.

A smile between them.

THE DOCTOR Right! I'll be off then. Unless ... I dunno. You could come with me. This box isn't just a London hopper, it can travel anywhere in the universe. Free of charge.

MICKEY Don't, he's an alien, he's a *thing* –

THE DOCTOR He's not invited. What d'you think?

Pause; she's so tempted.

THE DOCTOR You can stay here. Fill your life with work and food and sleep, or you could go ... everywhere.

ROSE Is it always this dangerous?

THE DOCTOR Yes.

She stares. But Mickey grips her.

ROSE ... I can't. I've got to go and find my mum. And someone's got to look after this stupid lump.

THE DOCTOR Okay. See you around.

He steps into the TARDIS.

Rose and Mickey stand as the ancient engines start up. And they finally see it happen, how this machine works: the light on the roof blazes, a wind springs up, litter circling in the air, as the Police Public Call Box simply ... fades away.

Silence. Hold on Rose. Bereft.

They turn away. Mickey clings to her.

ROSE Let's go home.

They walk towards the plain, normal world ... but then the noise comes back. Rose turns, the TARDIS reappears. The Doctor leans out, pats the doorframe.

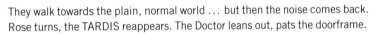

THE DOCTOR By the way, did I mention? It also travels in time.

And he goes back inside. Leaves the door open.

On Rose. She turns to Mickey.

ROSE Thanks.

MICKEY Thanks for what?

ROSE Exactly.

She gives him a quick kiss. Turns to face the TARDIS.

And she runs. Rose's POV: rushing top speed towards the blue box. And she's never been so happy – CU Rose running as the almighty shriek of the cliffhanger music scorches in and accelerates her through the door ...

Into adventure.

Episode 2

The End of the World
By Russell T Davies

Everyone expects an Episode 1 to be big, and for an Episode 2 to calm down. So I did the opposite. Bear in mind that budget meetings were still happening while this was being written, so I deliberately made this script impossible! And d'you know what? We made it. That still staggers me. What a production team!

I could feel this spiralling beyond a sensible cost even as I wrote (my Executive Producer's hat weighs heavily, sometimes). Platform One, the shuttles, the aliens, the fans, the Earth exploding. And then, bored of grandiloquent villains in capes, I dreamt up Cassandra, inspired by the 2004 Oscars' ceremony; those once-beautiful women reduced to nodding china lollipops. But I knew Cassandra would cost a penny. And having made her immobile, I then had to invent the Spiders. And they couldn't be daft little wind-up toys, so they'd have to be added to the CGI list ... Oh God!

But we only cut one thing, in the end. Which is a miracle! Originally, as Platform One went into meltdown, the section containing the Manchester Suite and the Viewing Gallery broke free of its moorings and tilted 90 degrees, so that Rose and all the aliens slid down the floor, as it became the wall, and on to the

windows, which became the floor. And then the windows start
cracking underneath them (like that bit in the caravan, in
Jurassic Park 2). We got quite far in the production process before
that was abandoned. I can't believe we even considered it, now!

Of course, the whole thing's practically a tribute to Douglas
Adams, that late, great genius. It's funny, cos when *Doctor Who*
fans list their favourite story from the original series, they rarely
mention *The Pirate Planet*. Not because it isn't good, but maybe
because it's good on a whole new scale; it seems to exist in its own
little world. I remember watching it when I was fifteen, and the
sheer ferocity of the ideas lifted my little head off. And some
things you love so much, you don't even realise you're using them;
they just become part of you. I swear, even with Douglas Adams in
mind, *The Restaurant at the End of the Universe* didn't consciously
occur to me while writing this. When it was eventually pointed
out to me, it's bleedin' obvious! But I was aware of using the word
'meme', lifted from the writing of Adams' great friend, Richard
Dawkins. I'd like to think that at some point, off-stage, the Doctor
explained the concept of a meme to Rose, so that by the end of the
series, she's practically creating her own meme, of sorts, with
the Bad Wolf. Or maybe I think about this stuff too much.

My sister complained about this episode, cos it doesn't work as
a whodunnit: 'I like to work it out!' But it's *not* a whodunnit! I mean,
if the murderer had turned out to be, say, Mr and Mrs Pakoo –
well, who cares? There's only one person you want the murderer to
be, and yes, it's her! That's not a whodunnit, more of an ihopeitsher.

Russell T Davies

OA INT. TARDIS DAY 3

The TARDIS in flight. The groan of the engines; underneath, the hum of power, but it's calm; THE DOCTOR's flying well, the captain of his ship, grinning as he uses the controls; showing off a bit. ROSE smiling, loving it. (This is just a few minutes after their final scene of ep.1.)

THE DOCTOR Right then, Rose Tyler. You tell me, where d'you want to go? Backwards or forwards in time, your choice, what's it gonna be?

ROSE Forwards.

THE DOCTOR How far?

ROSE One hundred years.

He operates controls. Loving it. Engines lurch.

THE DOCTOR There you go. Walk out of those doors, it's the twenty-second century.

ROSE Kidding.

THE DOCTOR That's a bit boring though, d'you wanna go further? Five hundred years.

ROSE Go on then.

He operates controls. Engines lurch.

THE DOCTOR The year twenty-five hundred.
(smiles)
Further?

ROSE Fine by me.

He operates controls. Engines lurch.

THE DOCTOR Ten thousand years in the future. Step outside, it's twelve thousand and five. The New Roman Empire.

ROSE (laughs)
You think you're so impressive.

THE DOCTOR I am so impressive!

ROSE You wish.

THE DOCTOR Right then. You asked for it. I know exactly where to go. Hold on!

And he slams every control going, wham, wham, wham! The TARDIS does a good spin, Rose has to hold on; like they're really flying. The Doctor operating the controls like a maestro. Rose still entranced by it all, even as she holds on tight to the console; the rise and fall of the rotor; the creaks from the roof; the lights from the floor.

And then *slam!* The Doctor brings everything to an absolute halt. Engines dead, no movement.

Rose straightens up:

ROSE Where are we ...?

He's just confident, gestures to the doors.

ROSE What's out there?

He just indicates again, out you go. Rose smiling, a bit scared, goes to the door ...

1 INT. VIEWING GALLERY DAY 3 1500

The TARDIS door opens, ROSE looks out, then steps out.

A simple, elegant room; cool, dark walls in deep colours. The room rakes downwards in a series of wide steps, like a private cinema without seats; but instead, each step has a handrail in front. Evidently, this is meant to look out on to something. But the steps face only another dark-metal wall, which is gradually curved both vertically and horizontally. In b/g, the deep, constant hum of engines.

THE DOCTOR follows Rose out. She looks at him, like she's unimpressed, challenging him to prove something. He just smiles, confident, crosses to a computer panel on the wall, whirrs the sonic screwdriver against it.

The curved wall starts to slide down. Rose stands forward at a handrail, as she sees: the Earth. They're right above the planet; it fills the lower half of the wide window. Clouds, oceans and continents in beautiful, vivid colours. And all around, the black void of space. Far off, the white light of the Sun.

Rose looks at her world, stunned. The absolute beauty of it. The Doctor joins her, quiet:

THE DOCTOR You lot, you spend all your time thinking about dying. Like you're gonna get killed by eggs, or beef, or global warming, or asteroids. But you never take time to imagine the impossible. That maybe you survive.

(pause)

This is the year five-point-five-slash-apple-slash-twenty-six. Five billion years in your future. And this is the day …

(looks at wristwatch)

Hold on …

He looks up. And the Sun explodes. The star bursts into a fierce red, and with a *wooomph!* a wave of yellow expands from it – in all directions, expands. The Earth stands proud, occasional waves of thick orange gas rippling in front of it, but leaving it unharmed.

THE DOCTOR This is the day the Sun expands. Welcome to the end of the world.

2 EXT. FX SHOT: PLATFORM ONE

Platform One, suspended against space. With no need to be aerodynamic, it's a sprawling three-mile-wide grid of scaffolding structures (not too far from current notions of a space station). The grid supports a central rod, dotted with windows; the Luxury Area.

Tiny against the Platform, two shuttles head towards docking. As they do so, CAMERA sails round, to reveal Platform One suspended above the Earth. Over this:

COMPUTER VOICE *Shuttles five and six now docking. Guests are reminded that Platform One forbids the use of weapons, teleportation and religion. Earthdeath is scheduled for 15:39, followed by drinks in the Manchester Suite.*

3 INT. PLATFORM ONE CORRIDOR DAY 3 1505

A simple corridor. THE DOCTOR leads ROSE along, both having heard the computer voice:

ROSE So, when it says guests, does that mean ... people?

THE DOCTOR Depends what *you* mean by people.

ROSE I mean people, what do *you* mean?

THE DOCTOR (big smile)
Aliens!

ROSE There's aliens on board?

THE DOCTOR Should be, yup. Is that okay?

ROSE ... Yeah, fine. What sort of aliens, what do they look like?

THE DOCTOR No idea, let's find out.

ROSE But what are they doing on board this spaceship, what's it all for?

THE DOCTOR It's not a spaceship, it's more like an observation deck. The great and the good are gathering to watch the planet burn.

ROSE What for?

THE DOCTOR Fun.

Another door, he whirrs the screwdriver, the door opens.

4 INT. THE MANCHESTER SUITE DAY 3 CONTINUOUS

A huge, deep room – massive floor space. It's got all the cool and calm of a modern art gallery, or a Philippe Starck hotel; largely empty, with shiny floors. Muted colours. Tall, thin display cases are dotted about, but sparsely, it's very minimalist. THE DOCTOR continuing, heading for the window:

THE DOCTOR Mind you, when I say the great and the good, what I mean is, the rich.

ROSE But hold on, they did this once on *Newsround Extra*. The Sun expanding, that takes hundreds of years.

THE DOCTOR Millions. But the planet's now the property of the National Trust, they've been keeping it preserved – see down there?

Orbiting the Earth, a tiny glint of light.

THE DOCTOR Gravity satellites, holding back the Sun.

ROSE The whole planet looks the same as ever, I thought the continents shifted and things.

THE DOCTOR They did, and the Trust shifted them back. That's a Classic Earth. But now the money's run out, and nature takes over.

ROSE How long's it got?

THE DOCTOR About half an hour. Then the planet gets roasted.

ROSE Is that why we're here – I mean, is that what you do? Jump in at the last minute and save the Earth.

THE DOCTOR I'm not saving it. Time's up.

ROSE But what about the people?

THE DOCTOR It's empty. No one left. They've all gone.

She looks at the planet; feels tiny.

ROSE Just me, then.

STEWARD Who the hell are you?

The STEWARD's hurrying towards them, across the wide floor. He's 30, professional, blue-skinned, wearing a simple variation on a suit, carrying an electronic clipboard.

THE DOCTOR Oh that's nice, thanks.

STEWARD But how did you get in? This is a maximum hospitality zone, the guests have disembarked, they're on their way, any second now –

THE DOCTOR No, that's me, I'm a guest, I've got an invitation –

The Doctor gets out a small leather wallet – the kind that would hold a policeman's ID badge – shows it to the Steward.

THE DOCTOR Look, it's fine, look, there, you see? 'The Doctor plus one', I'm the Doctor, this is Rose Tyler, she's my plus one, s'that all right?

STEWARD Well, obviously. Apologies, etcetera. Right, if you're on board, we'd better start – enjoy!

The Steward hurries off. The Doctor shows ROSE the wallet. It just contains blank paper.

THE DOCTOR The paper is slightly psychic, it shows them whatever I want them to see. Saves a lot of time.

ROSE He's … blue.

THE DOCTOR Yep.

Pause.

ROSE Okay.

A whine of feedback – the Steward's at a glass lectern to one side, on a microphone.

STEWARD Thank you, broadcasting to all quarters, here we go then, right –
(deep breath)
We have in attendance the Doctor and Rose Tyler, thank you, all staff to their positions!

He claps his hands, STAFF come scurrying out from all over the place. They are CHILDREN with blue skin, in simple, black, stagecrew-type clothes, wearing black helmets with a visor covering their eyes, just the blue chin visible. They make a shrill, chittering noise.

Rose stares. (Also, throughout, play off the Doctor – glancing at Rose, monitoring her reactions.)

STEWARD Thank you, quick as we can, and now, might I introduce the next honoured guest. Representing the Forest of Cheem, we have Trees, namely Jabe, Lute and Coffa –

Rose looks, as a door opens – the FOREST walks in. Three humanoid figures in white robes, but with bark for skin. Their 'hair' is a series of thin branches, with the occasional leaf, twined back like wicker.

STEWARD Thank you, there will be an exchange of gifts to represent peace, if you could keep the room circulating, thank you – next, from the solicitors Jolco and Jolco, we have the Moxx of Balhoon –

Rose looks, another door opens – the MOXX is a little creature on a big cushion.

STEWARD Might I remind you, the Moxx of Balhoon carries the standard health warning. Next, from Financial Family Seven, the Adherents of the Repeated Meme –

Rose looks, another door – five cowled, monk-like figures, faces hooded in darkness, like the Ghost of Christmas Future crossed with a Dementor. A sinister hum follows them round.

STEWARD Guests should take note that the Adherents will be reciting the meme at thirty-minute intervals. And next, of course, the sponsor of the main event, our friend from the Silver Devastation, please welcome, the Face of Boe.

Rose looks. Staff-children wheel in a big glass tank, containing a 5-ft-high scaly alien FACE, wreathed in smoke. As this goes on, in b/g, the Steward continues with his introductions, more guests arriving.

STEWARD Next, I bid welcome the ambassadors from the City State of Binding Light, please note that oxygen levels must be strictly monitored in the ambassadors' presence.
(enter extra aliens)
Next, straight from the exalted clifftops of Rex Vox Jax, the inventors and copyright holders of hyposlip travel systems, the Brothers Hop Pyleen, thank you.
(enter extra aliens)
And next, ladies and gentlemen. A little treat. Dodging the papparazzi to make his way here, travelling incognito, it's none other than cybernetic hyperstar, Cal 'Spark Plug' MacNannovich and his entourage, thank you very much.
(enter extra aliens)
Next, of course: Mr and Mrs Pakoo.
(enter extra aliens)
And now, pray bid welcome to the chosen scholars of Class Fifty-five from the University of Rago Rago Five Six Rago.
(enter extra aliens)

Foreground, over all the above, the exchange of gifts begins. The Doctor and Rose stay where they are, and JABE, the Tree, approaches. She's female, elegant, 30. She carries a tray of little tubs of earth, each sprouting a plant.

Rose just staring at the alien.

JABE The gift of peace, I bring you a cutting of my grandfather.

The Doctor takes the plant, hands it to Rose.

THE DOCTOR Thank you, yes, gifts, um, I bring you in return . . . air from my lungs.

He breathes on her. She's delighted.

JABE How intimate.

THE DOCTOR (flirting)
There's more where that came from.

JABE I bet there is.

JABE moves on, smiling, as the Moxx wobbles up.

THE DOCTOR The Moxx of Balhoon, I bring you the gift of air from my lungs.

Breathes on him. The Moxx has got a big, deep voice:

MOXX OF BALHOON My felicitations upon this historical happenstance, I bring you the gift of my bodily saliva.

Like Spit the Dog, the Moxx spits, *hoik – tuh!* Rose gets an eyeful, flinches.

THE DOCTOR Thank you very much.

One cowled ADHERENT approaches.

THE DOCTOR Ah, the Adherents of the Repeated Meme, I bring you air from my lungs.

The Adherent's voice is like a whisper from the grave:

ADHERENT A gift of peace. In all good faith.

From the Adherent's sleeve, a metal/organic claw gives the Doctor a stainless-steel orb. Then it looks at Rose. Rose's POV: the blackness of the cowl. Its terrible breath. This is really getting to her now, the freak-show.

STEWARD And last but not least, our very special guest. Ladies and gentlemen and trees and multiforms: consider the Earth, below. Its countless empires have risen and fallen and risen again. In memory of this dying world, we call forth . . . the Last Human. The only remaining member of her species. I bring you the final representative of humanity itself, the Lady Cassandra O'Brien Dot Delta Seventeen.

Rose looks at the last door – CASSANDRA glides in. A metal frame, six foot tall, three feet wide. Only an inch deep. And stretched across that frame, a piece of canvas – bolted into the frame, pulled tight. Except this isn't canvas. It's skin. Right in the middle, there are two eyes and a mouth. No nose, no chin, nothing but eyes and mouth. The eyes are bulging, but the mouth has no depth; it's just lips and teeth, no actual mouth behind it. When the lips are open, you can see right through. The whole frame is supported on a sleek metal truck. At the base, in a glass jar, a brain bubbles and glows from within, wires connecting it to the frame.

Cassandra is flanked, a few steps behind, by two SURGEONS – hospital robes, faces covered by medical masks and hats, eyes covered by heavy, complicated glasses – like the sort an optician uses mid-test, to slot in different lenses. Cassandra is posh, fluttery and coy.

CASSANDRA Oh now don't stare! I know, I know, it's shocking, isn't it? I've had my chin completely taken away, and look at the difference, look how thin I am! Thin and dainty! I don't look a day over two thousand – moisturise me! Moisturise me!

The Surgeons hand-pump a fine mist over her.

CASSANDRA You're too kind. And all of you. Gathered here. For me.

During this, Rose quietly walks round. Follow her POV, tracking round Cassandra, establishing that she's literally flat; nothing behind her at all, except the bulge of the back of her eyes. Rose fascinated, horrified.

CASSANDRA Truly, I am the Last Human. My father was a Texan, my mother was from the Arctic Desert.
(emotional)
They were born on the Earth, and they were the last to be buried in its soil. I have come to honour them, and say goodbye. No tears, no tears . . .

Surgeon #1 dabs her eye with a hanky.

CASSANDRA I'm sorry. Excuse me.
(bright smile)
But I bring gifts! Behold! From Earth itself, the last remaining ostrich egg.

Surgeon #2 carries the ostrich egg forward, puts it in a central work-of-art display case.

CASSANDRA The ostrich was made extinct in the Great Bird Flu of 2051. Legend says it had a wing-span of fifty feet, and blew fire from its nostrils. Or was that my third husband? Oh, no, don't laugh, I'll get laughter-lines, stop! Oh! Mercy! And here! Another rarity, some Old Earth entertainment –

Staff-children wheel in a 1950s' jukebox.

CASSANDRA According to the archives, this was called an i-Pod, it stores classical music from humanity's greatest composers. Play on!

MUSIC: 'Tainted Love', Soft Cell.

STEWARD Refreshments will now be served, Earthdeath in thirty minutes' time.

The guests mingle, Jabe approaching the Moxx, another Tree talking to the Face, the third Tree congratulating Cassandra, the Adherents standing alone, brooding, while Staff-children carry in simple, unadorned food on trays. Rose looks round. Her POV: the bark-skin. The Face. Cassandra.

On Rose. Genuinely freaked out, only just holding on. Quietly – still carrying the gifts – she steps out, gone.

The Doctor's watching, follows. As he reaches the door:

JABE Doctor.

He turns. Jabe the Tree is holding up a small, thin screen, portable DVD-size. It flashes, taking his photograph.

JABE Thank you.

For some reason, this unsettles him. But he follows Rose.

CUT TO the Steward, just crossing the room, as the Adherent steps forward. It offers him a stainless-steel orb.

ADHERENT A gift of peace. In all good faith.

STEWARD Um, no, you're very kind, but, I'm just the Steward.

ADHERENT A gift of peace. In all good faith.

STEWARD Well, thank you, of course, yes. If you'll excuse me.

The Steward hurries on, passing Jabe the Tree. He clears – stay on her, as she talks to her portable screen.

JABE Identify species.

The screen gives complicated bleeps, like it's not happy.

JABE Please identify species.

On screen: her 'photo' of the Doctor, bleached white, lines of computer code scrolling across him. Again, unhappy bleeps. Jabe thumps the device.

JABE Now stop it, identify his race, where's he from?

The screen pings, success. Slow track in to CU Jabe. Staring at the result. Awestruck. She locks at the door through which the Doctor left, almost frightened, then back to her scanner.

JABE Impossible . . .

But continue the track past Jabe, on to her Adherent stainless-steel orb, behind Jabe, forgotten on a shelf. Unseen, the orb jolts. Rolls a little. A tiny crack appears round its diameter. A spindly metal leg pushes out . . .

5 INT. STEWARD'S OFFICE DAY 3 1512

A small official space, though still with a view of the Earth. The STEWARD enters, puts down his clipboard, and the Adherent's Orb, sits at his desk – it's cluttered with plastic pages. The Steward swigs from an old coffee mug, winces. The computer bleeps.

STEWARD Yes, all right, hold on . . .
(angry bleep)
What's that?
(long, angry bleep)
Well how should I know?
(presses switch)
Would the owner of the blue box in Private Gallery Fifteen please report to the Steward's office. Guests are reminded that the use of teleportation devices is strictly forbidden under the peace treaty of five-point-four-slash-cup-slash-sixteen, thank you . . .

But during this, unnoticed: the Adherent's Orb jerks. Cracks open. A leg pushes out. Then more legs. And a sly, thin METAL SPIDER scuttles out – only about eight inches in diameter. It hurries up the wall, its legs making a tiny *tic-tic-tic* noise.

6 THRU 8 OMITTED

8A INT. PLATFORM ONE ROOM/SHAFT DAY 1512

An open room, leading off from a main corridor. A wide window (if this can be achieved with a translight – just the glow of space, the sun, from outside?). ROSE stands there, lost in thought, looking down. CUT TO her POV: FX SHOT, the Earth (stock, from the shots we've already ordered?).

She hears foosteps, turns, looks round – one of the STAFF has walked in, with a toolbox. This is RAFFALO – an adult, of restricted height. Blue, like the Steward. No helmet, but in regulation black. Humble, she just gets to work. One wall has a number of discreet service panels; she starts to examine the readings on the lower panel. Pause, then:

ROSE Sorry, I'm not in the way, am I?

No reply.

ROSE It's just – I was just wondering, am I allowed in here?

RAFFALO You have to give us permission to talk.

ROSE Um. You have my permission.

RAFFALO (nice smile)
Thank you. And you're not in the way, guests are allowed anywhere.

ROSE Okay. And, what's your name?

RAFFALO Raffalo.

ROSE Raffalo?

RAFFALO Yes miss. I won't be long, I've just got to do some maintenance . . .

Raffalo inspects the wall panel. Part of it is a grille. CUT TO INT. SHAFT, the other side of the grille. Raffalo peering through, but not seeing, beneath her line of vision. A SPIDER scurries past, in the dark, with a quiet, sinister *tic-tic-tic* . . .

Over this:

RAFFALO There's a tiny little glitch in the Face of Boe's suite. Something must be blocking the system, he's not getting any hot water.

CUT OUT OF SHAFT, Raffalo now digging a device out of her toolbox, unscrewing the panel, during the following:

ROSE So . . . you're a plumber?

RAFFALO That's right, miss.

ROSE They still have plumbers.

RAFFALO Hope so, or I'm out of a job.

ROSE Where are you from?

RAFFALO Crespallion.

ROSE Right. And, is that a planet . . . ?

RAFFALO No, Crespallion is part of the Jaggit Brocade affiliated to the Scarlet Junction Convex Fifty-six. And where are you from, miss? If you don't mind my asking.

ROSE No, not at all, I'm . . .

She looks out of the window again. REPEAT FX SHOT: the Earth, the Sun, the strangeness of it all.

ROSE I dunno. It's a long way away. I just sort of hitched a lift, with this man. Didn't even think about it. And I don't even know who he is. He's a complete stranger.
(pause, then snaps out of it)
Anyway. Don't let me keep you. Good luck with it.

Rose heads off.

RAFFALO Thank you, miss. And . . . thank you for the permission. Not many people are that considerate.

ROSE (smiles)
That's okay. See you later.

And Rose goes.

As soon as she's gone, Raffalo lifts off the panel.

RAFFALO Now then ...

She presses a metal button on her tunic.

RAFFALO Control, I'm at Junction Nineteen, I think the problem's coming from here, I'll go inside and have a look.

Raffalo squats down, looks into the maintenance shaft. Her POV: the shaft, darkness. Ominous music, danger ... then, the sound of the *tic-tic-tic*.

RAFFALO What's that? Is there something in there?

And from the darkness, a spider calmly walks forward. Looks at her. Studying her. Its red light shining. The tiny red light plays across her face.

RAFFALO Who are you, then, are you part of the cleaning system? Are you that upgrade they were talking about?

The spider scuttles away, back into darkness.

RAFFALO No, don't ...

Raffalo shuffles further in. From outside: just her legs now sticking out of the shaft.

RAFFALO Hold on! If you're an upgrade, I just need to register you, that's all. Come back!
(silence)
I didn't mean to scare you. I'm sorry, I'm just a Grade H, they don't tell me anything. Hello?

In the darkness: the pinpoint of red light comes on. The light shines on Raffalo's face.

RAFFALO There you are. Now, all I need to do is register your ident ...

In the dark: a second pinpoint of red light.

RAFFALO Oh, there's two of you. Got yourself a little mate?

Then a third pinpoint. Raffalo a little worried; three pinpoints on her face.

RAFFALO I think I'd better report this to Control, how many of you are there ...?

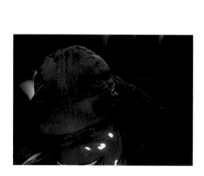

A fourth pinpoint. Fifth, sixth, seventh, eighth, ninth, tenth, more and more, blinking on, in the darkness. Each pinpoint shining onto Raffalo's face. Scared now. The darkness is dotted with dozens of red lights. Raffalo's face is covered in pinpoints of light. A whisper:

RAFFALO ... What are you ...?

And suddenly the CAMERA rushes in to her face, an attack –

CUT TO ROOM, Raffalo's feet start to kick – thrash –

RAFFALO No! Noooo – !

And *whoosh!* Legs disappear, she's pulled into the shaft. CAMERA starts to calmly pull back, with only her voice:

RAFFALO Help me – oh someone *help me!*

And then a terrible cry. And then silence.

9 INT. VIEWING GALLERY DAY 3 1514

ROSE sits on the top step. Looking at the view; the Earth, the red Sun, the yellow void. And all the while, she's passing the Adherent's Orb from hand to hand.

COMPUTER VOICE *Earthdeath in twenty-five minutes.*

ROSE Oh, thanks.

She puts the orb down at her side, picks up Jabe's plant.

ROSE Hello? Can you speak?

CU orb. It cracks open, the legs flex out . . .

ROSE My name's Rose. That's a sort of plant. We might be related.
(beat)
I'm talking to a twig.

The SPIDER is beetling round behind Rose . . .

10 INT. PLATFORM ONE CORRIDOR DAY 3 1514

THE DOCTOR walks along. Ahead of him, STAFF-CHILDREN have got the TARDIS on a simple trolley. Tilted at an angle, it's being wheeled off, Staff-children fussing away.

THE DOCTOR Oy now, careful with that, park it properly. No scratches.

A Staff-child thrusts something into his hand, and they wheel the TARDIS off. The Doctor looks bemused. It's a cloakroom ticket. Behind him, out of focus, a SPIDER scurries up the wall . . .

11 INT. VIEWING GALLERY DAY 3 1514

The METAL SPIDER is behind ROSE. Interested in her. It extends a spindly leg towards her . . .

The door slides open, THE DOCTOR enters.

THE DOCTOR Aye aye.

Unseen, the spider quickly *tic-tic-tics* away. It vanishes into a grille, gone.

12 INT. DUCTS DAY 3 CONTINUOUS

The METAL SPIDER crawls into the duct-space, hurries along. It passes a SECOND SPIDER, busy on its own mission, digging its legs into a computerised junction box. A THIRD SPIDER scuttles past, then a fourth,

all on different paths, like this is a spiders' crossroads, *tic-tic-tic-tic-tic-tic* . . .
It's crawling with them. Platform One is infested.

13 INT. VIEWING GALLERY DAY 3 1515

The DOCTOR's now sitting next to ROSE.

THE DOCTOR What d'you think, then?

ROSE Great, yeah. Fine. Once you get past the slightly psychic paper.
(beat; blurts out:)
They're just so . . . alien! The aliens are so alien, you look at them,
and they're . . . alien.

THE DOCTOR Good thing I didn't take you to the Deep South.

Pause, as she registers that. Calm, more neutral:

ROSE Where are you from?

THE DOCTOR All over the place.

Pause.

ROSE They all speak English.

THE DOCTOR You just hear English. It's a gift of the TARDIS.
Telepathic field, gets into your brain, translates.

ROSE . . . It's inside my brain?

THE DOCTOR Well. In a good way.

ROSE (colder)
Your machine gets inside my head? It gets inside and changes my
mind and you didn't even ask?

THE DOCTOR (thrown)
I never thought of it like that –

ROSE No, you were too busy thinking up cheap shots about the Deep
South –
(livid)
Who are you, then, Doctor, what are you called, what sort of alien
are you?

He tries to stay flippant:

THE DOCTOR I'm just the Doctor.

ROSE From what planet?

THE DOCTOR Well it's not as if you'd know it –

ROSE Where are you from?

THE DOCTOR Why does it matter?

ROSE Tell me who you are!

THE DOCTOR (sudden anger)
This is who I am, right here, right now, all right? All that counts is
here and now, and this is me!

ROSE (matches him)
Yes, and I'm here too, cos you brought me here, so tell me!

He stands, angry – walks down the steps, right up to the window. Hold the pause, a stand-off.

Rose takes a breath; recovers.

ROSE Okay.
(pause)
As my mate Shareen says, don't argue with the designated driver.

He half smiles, still moody. She walks down to him.

ROSE I can't exactly phone for a taxi.
(gets out her mobile)
No signal. We're out of range. Just a bit.

And he smiles properly, friends again, and takes the phone off her; something to interest him.

THE DOCTOR Tell you what – with a little bit of jiggery-pokery ...

He takes the phone, slips the battery out, digs in his pocket, slots in a new, jet-black battery. And during this, they revert to their natural banter:

ROSE Is that a technical term, jiggery-pokery?

THE DOCTOR Yes, I came first in jiggery-pokery, what about you?

ROSE No, I failed hullabaloo.

He hands the mobile back. The screen's active, normal.

ROSE You're kidding.

He just smiles, daring her. Rose clicks onto names, finds MUM. She dials. Rose holding her breath. Then:

JACKIE OOV Hello?

ROSE ... Mum?

14 INT. TYLERS' KITCHEN DAY 1 1100

INTERCUT with ROSE, sc.13, VIEWING GALLERY: Rose standing against the glass, in which the Earth and Sun are reflected.

A bright, ordinary day in 2005, UK, Earth. JACKIE's on the phone, getting clothes out of the washing machine.

JACKIE Oh what is it, what's wrong, what have I done now? This red top is falling to bits, you should get your money back – go on, you never phone in the middle of the day, it must be something, what?

Rose laughs, more out of shock.

JACKIE What's so funny?

ROSE Nothing. You all right though?

JACKIE Why wouldn't I be?

ROSE What day is it?

JACKIE Wednesday all day, have you got a hangover? Hey, tell you what, put a quid in that lottery syndicate, I'll pay you back later.

ROSE Yeah, look, um. I was just phoning cos ... I might be late home.

JACKIE (more serious)
Is there something wrong?

ROSE No, I'm fine. Top of the world. See ya.

15 INT. VIEWING GALLERY DAY 3 CONTINUOUS

ROSE hangs up. Gobsmacked.

THE DOCTOR Think that's amazing, wait till you see the bill.

ROSE That was five billion years ago. So ... She's dead now. Five billion years later, my mother's dead.

THE DOCTOR Bundle of laughs, you are.

A small lurch in the background engine noise, the gallery shudders slightly. THE DOCTOR instantly alert. Delighted!

THE DOCTOR That's not supposed to happen.

16 INT. DUCTS DAY 3 1517

The junction box is burning, fizzing with sparks. The METAL SPIDER *tic-tic-tics* away, work to do ...

17 INT. STEWARD'S OFFICE DAY 3 1517

The STEWARD's a bit panicked, talking to Control.

STEWARD Well what was it? I'm just getting green lights at this end –
(intercom, polite)
Honoured guests are reassured that gravity pockets may cause slight turbulence, thanking you.
(back to Control)
The whole place shook! I felt it! I've hosted all sorts of events on Platforms One, Three, Six and Fifteen, and I've never felt the slightest tremor. I warn you, if this lot decide to sue – ! I'm going to scan the infrastructure, wait a minute –
(presses buttons)
What's that ...?
(computer burbles. Worried, serious:)
Control. I don't want to worry you, but I'm picking up readings. Something's crept under the security codewalls. I'm picking up ... traces, I don't know, lots of them, right inside Platform One. I think perhaps we should evacuate –
(computer burbles)
How should I know? They're small, the scan says they're metal ...
(computer burbles)
I don't know what they look like!

He stops dead as one of the METAL SPIDERs skitters out of a grille in the computer-panel on his desk, *tic-tic-tic*.

STEWARD Although I'd imagine they look rather like that . . .

He crouches down. The faceless spider seems to study him.

STEWARD You're not on the guest list. How did you get on board . . .?

The spider turns, scuttles over to the computer panel, lifts up a spindly leg. Pushes a button. He realises:

STEWARD No — !

A humming starts up, and the Steward turns to the window, horrified. The calm COMPUTER VOICE announces:

COMPUTER VOICE *Sunfilter descending. Sunfilter descending.*

A previously invisible layer of glass in the window is sliding down. Now, it becomes clear how much the sun is being polarised; as the filter descends, the naked glass above it glows with a shocking bright white light.

COMPUTER VOICE *External temperature four thousand degrees. Sunfilter descending . . .*

The Steward slams the button —

STEWARD No no no no no — sunfilter *up*! Control! Respond! Sunfilter UP!

The screen keeps lowering. The Steward raises up his arms, blinded by the light, and he glows a terrible white . . .

18 INT. CORRIDOR OUTSIDE STEWARD'S OFFICE DAY 3 1518

The METAL SPIDER struggles through a tiny gap in the doorframe, then hurries off down the corridor, *tic-tic-tic* . . . CUT TO the door, which has a glass panel in the centre, and a sign, 'STEWARD'S OFFICE'. Bright white light flares in the glass and around the edges of the door.

A scream. Which abruptly stops.

19 INT. THE MANCHESTER SUITE DAY 3 1519

Dotted around the room: JABE; STAFF-CHILDREN with a TREE; CASSANDRA entertaining the other TREE, the two SURGEONS at her side; far away, the ADHERENTS, still and solemn.

On Jabe, as she sees THE DOCTOR hurry in, with ROSE. They go straight to a computer panel on the wall. The Doctor stabs buttons, getting readings. Jabe takes a deep breath. Calms herself. Assumes a smile, approaches them as though everything's normal.

THE DOCTOR . . . That wasn't a gravity pocket, I know gravity pockets and they don't feel like that . . .
(becomes aware of:)
What d'you think, Jabe? Listen to the engines, they've pitched up about thirty hertz, is that dodgy?

JABE It's the sound of metal, it doesn't make any sense to me.

THE DOCTOR Where's the engine room?

JABE I don't know.
(closer, intimate)
But the maintenance duct is just behind our guest suite, I could show you. And ... your wife.

THE DOCTOR (flirting)
She's not my wife.

JABE Partner?

THE DOCTOR No.

JABE Concubine?

THE DOCTOR Nope.

JABE Prostitute?

ROSE Whatever I am, it must be invisible, d'you mind? Tell you what, you two go and ... pollinate, I'm going to catch up with the family. Quick word with Michael Jackson.

She indicates Cassandra.

THE DOCTOR Don't start a fight.
(offers arm to Jabe)
I'm all yours.

Jabe takes his arm, they head off.

ROSE And I want you home by midnight.

And she heads off towards Cassandra.

CUT TO the Adherents, far off, watching. Their ominous hum. They turn, in unison, glide out of the room.

20 INT. PLATFORM ONE CORRIDOR DAY 3 1521

The sonic screwdriver whirrs against a panel, as:

COMPUTER VOICE *Earthdeath in fifteen minutes.*

The door slides open. THE DOCTOR and JABE look into a maintenance corridor. He's all smiles, loves investigating.

THE DOCTOR This is more like it –

He steps forward. Jabe's still flirtatious, and fascinated by him.

JABE Now then, Doctor, that's far enough, you know full well that we're not allowed inside.

THE DOCTOR You're the one who brought me here!

JABE Only to look. It specifically says in the guidelines, guests are supposed to stay inside the Luxury Quarter.

THE DOCTOR Oh come on, break a few rules.

JABE I'm a royal branch of the Forest, I have a reputation to maintain.

THE DOCTOR And I bet that gets boring – all the more reason to come with me!

JABE Are you trying to make me a law-breaker?

THE DOCTOR You must've been a sapling once. Blowing in the breeze, sneaking outside the orchard, hanging out with the bad flowers, remember what it was like? Let's have a bit of fun. Or, you can stay here and vegetate. What d'you think?

Pause. Then Jabe smiles, cheeky, inspired by him, and they head inside together –

21 INT. MAINTENANCE CORRIDOR DAY 3 CONTINUOUS

THE DOCTOR and JABE step through. A clear divide between Maintenance and Luxury – this is a short, dark, cramped corridor, lined with gun-metal pipes and machinery. As the Doctor and Jabe edge their way along, on the move:

THE DOCTOR Who's in charge of Platform One, has it got a captain or what . . .?

JABE There's just the Steward and the staff. All the rest is controlled by the metalmind.

THE DOCTOR What d'you mean, the computer? And who controls that?

JABE The Corporation. They move Platform One from one artistic event to another.

THE DOCTOR But there's no one from the Corporation on board?

JABE They're not needed. This facility is purely automatic, it's the height of the Alpha Class, nothing can go wrong.

THE DOCTOR Unsinkable?

JABE If you like. The nautical metaphor is appropriate.

THE DOCTOR Oh, you're telling me. I was on this other ship once, they said it was unsinkable. I ended up clinging to an iceberg, wasn't half cold – so what you're saying is, if we're in trouble, there's no one to help us?

JABE I'm afraid not.

THE DOCTOR (big, sudden grin)
Fantastic!

JABE I don't understand, in what way is that . . . 'fantastic'?

THE DOCTOR Oh, I'm not one for swanning round with delegates and cocktails. Bit of trouble, just my thing.

JABE That's a strange attitude.

THE DOCTOR I'm a strange man.
(reaches out)
Careful –

He takes her hand, helps her step over a pipe. A smile between them, and they keep moving on.

THE DOCTOR Tell me, Jabe, what's a tree like you doing in a place like this?

JABE Respect for the Earth.

THE DOCTOR Oh come on, everyone gathered on this Platform is worth zillions.

JABE Well. Perhaps it's a case of having to be seen at the right occasions.

THE DOCTOR In case your share prices drop – I know your lot, you've got massive forests, roots all over the place. And there's always money in land.

JABE All the same, we respect the Earth, as family. So many species evolved from that place, mankind is just one. I'm another. My ancestors were transplanted from the planet down below, I'm a direct descendant of the tropical rainforest.

THE DOCTOR Hold on . . .

Because they've reached another door.

The Doctor whirrs the sonic screwdriver at the panel – this one's tougher: resists. He has to keep beeping to different frequencies.

Jabe leans against the wall beside him. Studying him. More cautious. Her real agenda:

JABE And what about your ancestry, Doctor? Perhaps you could tell a story or two. Perhaps a man only enjoys trouble, when . . . there's nothing else left.

Silence. He doesn't look at her, keeps working, grim.

JABE I scanned you earlier.
(no reply)
The metalmachine had trouble identifying your species. It refused to admit your existence. And even when it named you, I wouldn't believe it. But it was right.
(moves closer)
I know where you're from.

He keeps working, grim, ignoring her.

JABE Forgive me for intruding. But it's remarkable that you even exist. I just wanted to say . . .
(beat)
How sorry I am.

Only now, he looks at her. And he's wild, hollow, wretched. She reaches out, simply touches his arm, in sympathy. Which he accepts.

Ping!, the computer panel finally responds. The Doctor breathes in – resuming his old self again, in a single second, as the door opens –

22 INT. VENTILATION CHAMBER DAY 3 CONTINUOUS

A fan. A standard fan, four identical blades radiating out from a central pivot, the blades turning. And lined up behind the first fan, a second fan. Behind that, a third fan. These fans are 50 ft in diameter; each blade roughly 25 ft, swooshing round on a massive scale. The three fans are connected through the central pivot, all three strung along a thick metal rod. The pole spans across a metal-walled, Death-Star-type chasm; the fans are suspended above a drop which sheers away into darkness far below.

Underneath all fans is a thin white bridge, stretching across the chasm. The lowest point of the blades slices above the bridge by about an inch.

THE DOCTOR and JABE stand in the doorway, which opens out on to the bridge. Below them, the sheer drop. Ahead of them and above them, the three massive fans, constantly turning. The 25-ft blades are steady but slow, calmly revolving. They circle down, at their lowest point, right in front of the Doctor and Jabe.

The Doctor and Jabe look up, around, taking in the view, the noise, the majesty of it all. And then:

THE DOCTOR Is it me or is it nippy?

High shot, looking down from above the fans. Out of the Doctor and Jabe's eyeline, on top of the connecting rod, a METAL SPIDER *tic-tic-tics* between the fans ...

23 INT. THE MANCHESTER SUITE DAY 3 1524

The record-arm of the jukebox flips over, more classical music: Alison Moyet, 'Love Letters'. In b/g, not part of this: STAFF-CHILDREN, the FACE OF BOE and the other two TREES, general party milling about.

Foreground, CASSANDRA glides along, with ROSE, Cassandra's two SURGEONS following at a respectful distance. She's leading Rose past the tall, thin display cabinets. And Rose is getting good at taking all this in; registering things, bemused, but not freaking out.

CASSANDRA It's so rare for someone to take an interest in history, bless you. So much of my sweet planet has been looted, or lost.

All on the move, as Rose looks at the first cabinet: an old parchment, labelled *Magna Carta*.

CASSANDRA There are people who think it's just a story, to scare the children. 'If you don't behave, we'll send you to Earth.'

They pass the second cabinet, Rose sees: *Harry Potter and the Philosopher's Stone* (first edition).

CASSANDRA And that's what it becomes today. A story. The final chapter.

Cassandra wheels towards the window, the view – the perfect Earth, the boiling Sun.

CASSANDRA Soon, the Sun will blossom into a red giant, and my home will die.
(sigh)
I've encountered a red giant before. My fourth husband had one. Oh no no no! Too funny! Oh no, Cassandra, behave!
(instant panic)
Oh my God, wrinkle! I've wrinkled! Ow ow ow, I can feel it, ouch, oh damn these laughter lines, I'm too witty for my own good, can you see it, can you see it?

ROSE Where?

CASSANDRA Left eye, left eye, help me!

There's a tiny crease, left eye. The Surgeons run forward.

ROSE It's just a tiny little line –

CASSANDRA Cut it out, cut it *out*!

Surgeon #1 whips out a scalpel, cuts the stretched skin at the edge of the frame, parallel with the eye. No blood, it's like thin leather. Rose winces, can't stop looking.

CASSANDRA Moisturise me, moisturise me! I told you it was getting hotter!

Surgeon #2 sprays, Surgeon #1 has cut a flap of skin loose.

CASSANDRA Stop wasting time, pull it! Pull!

And he tugs on the skin. Pulls it like tough elastic. An awful, creaking, stretching noise.

CASSANDRA Ohhhhh that's lovely. Ohhh you big strong man. And a bit more. Pull it! Ohh!

Surgeon #1 keeps it taut, and whips out a little staple-gun, which bolts the skin to the frame with a *chunk!* Cassandra recovers, like she rather enjoyed it.

CASSANDRA Oh thank you. Oh that's better. Ohhh yes. Moisturise me!

The Surgeons spray her, then retreat to their positions.

CASSANDRA Now where were we?

ROSE I've completely forgotten.

CASSANDRA Oh look, you see, that's where I used to live, when I was a little boy. Down there.

Their POV: North America facing up from the Earth.

CASSANDRA Mummy and daddy had a house built into the side of the Los Angeles Crevasse. Oh, I'd have such fun.

ROSE But what happened to everyone else? The Human Race, where did it go?

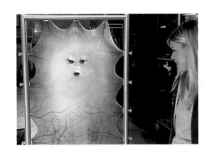

CASSANDRA Everywhere. The colonists, then the imperialists, then the great Space Arks. They say mankind has touched every star in the sky.

ROSE So you're not the Last Human.

CASSANDRA (haughty)
I'm the Last *Pure* Human. The others ... mingled.

ROSE ... What does that mean?

CASSANDRA With other species. Apparently, they're even allowed to marry.
(sharing a secret)
Oh, they call themselves New Humans and Protohumans and Digihumans, even Humanish, but d'you know what I call them? Mongrels.

And Rose is cool; she's got the measure of her now.

ROSE Right. And you stayed behind.

CASSANDRA I kept myself pure.

ROSE How many operations have you had?

Cassandra wheels in closer, like it's girly chat.

CASSANDRA Seven hundred and eight. Next week, it's seven hundred and nine, I'm having my blood bleached. Is that why you wanted a word? You could be flatter, Rose, you've got a little bit of a chin poking out. And my surgeons are the best.

ROSE I'd rather die.

CASSANDRA Honestly, it doesn't hurt.

ROSE (controlled, direct)
No, I mean it. I would rather die. It's better to die than to live like you. A bitchy trampoline.

Cassandra wheels back, huffed.

CASSANDRA Ohh, well what do you know?

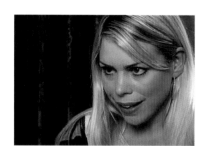

ROSE I was born on that planet. And so was my mum, and so was my dad, and that makes me, officially, the last human being in this room. Cos you're not human. You've had it all nipped and tucked and flattened till there's nothing left, anything human got chucked in the bin. You're just skin, Cassandra. Lipstick and skin.
(beat)
Nice talking.

Rose strides off. Shaken, not triumphant, walks fast –

24 INT. PLATFORM ONE CORRIDOR DAY 3 CONTINUOUS

ROSE walks out, into the corridor, head down, keeps going – she's lost in thought, doesn't notice, till the last second, something blocking the way. She looks up ...

The ADHERENTS. The lead Adherent lashes out, vicious –

25 INT. VENTILATION CHAMBER DAY 3 1528

THE DOCTOR is using the sonic screwdriver to undo a panel of metal on the wall, JABE watching. Behind them, the slow circle of the enormous fans.

THE DOCTOR Fair do's though, that's a great bit of air-conditioning. Sort of nice and old-fashioned. I bet they call it retro. Gotcha!

The panel comes loose, the Doctor heaves it off the wall, exposing wires and circuitry – and a SPIDER. It scampers out, up the wall, fast, *tic-tic-tic* –

THE DOCTOR What the hell is that ...?

JABE Is it part of the 'retro'?

THE DOCTOR Don't think so, hold on ...

The spider's a good 20 ft above their heads. The Doctor holds up the sonic screwdriver, whirrs it up at the spider, as though trying to 'hit' it. But the spider scuttles about, fast, clever. The Doctor aims, but can't pin it down at this distance. The spider *tic-tic-tics* to and fro, escaping –

Jabe steps back. She pulls her arm back behind her head, then whips it out, fast, pointing up. A leafy creeper shoots out of her wrist, with a whip-crack – shoots 20 ft up, knocks the spider off the wall – instantly retracts back into Jabe's wrist, gone. The spider falls, right into the Doctor's hands.

THE DOCTOR Hey. Nice liana.

JABE (blushing)
Thank you. We're not supposed to show them in public.

THE DOCTOR I won't tell anyone.
(studies the spider)
Now then, who's brought pets on board ...?

JABE What does it do?

THE DOCTOR Sabotage.

Interrupted by:

COMPUTER VOICE *Earthdeath in ten minutes, Earthdeath in ten minutes.*

THE DOCTOR And the temperature's about to rocket ... come on –

He races off –

26 INT. THE MANCHESTER SUITE DAY 3 1529

CASSANDRA circles round, in her element, flanked by SURGEONS.
The MOXX OF BALHOON, the FACE OF BOE, the ADHERENTS (and extra
GUESTS?) sweep in through their respective doors. STAFF-CHILDREN
scurry about, offering food and drinks.

CASSANDRA The planet's end, come gather, come gather! Bid farewell to
the cradle of civilisation, let us mourn her with a traditional ballad.

The jukebox pipes up: 'Toxic', Britney Spears. The music's piped through
Platform One. At varying volumes, this song backs the entire sc.27–33
sequence.

The tiny Moxx of Balhoon trundles into foreground, vexed:

MOXX OF BALHOON Has anybody witnessed the personage of the
Steward? Where is he?

27 AND 28 OMITTED

29 INT. CORRIDOR OUTSIDE STEWARD'S OFFICE DAY 3 1530

COMPUTER VOICE *Earthdeath in nine minutes, Earthdeath in
nine minutes.*

Bright white light is pouring horizontally out of the glass panel in the office
door. THREE STAFF-CHILDREN are hopping about, wailing, lamenting –
genuine grief – as THE DOCTOR and JABE run up, horrified. The Doctor
runs forward, ducks under the burning light, to get to the computer panel
on the far side of the door.

THE DOCTOR All right, look out, get back!

He whirrs at the panel with the sonic screwdriver. A Staff-child grabs him
by the waist and clings to him, crying.

COMPUTER VOICE *Sunfilter rising, sunfilter rising.*

The stream of light lifts up, being cut off from inside.

JABE Was the Steward in there?

THE DOCTOR You can smell him.

The Staff-child wails. The computer panel burbles, the Doctor looks at it.

THE DOCTOR Hold on. There's another sunfilter. Programmed to descend . . .

30 INT. VIEWING GALLERY DAY 3 1531

ROSE lies on the floor. Just waking from unconsciousness. She groans. Looks round, blinks, dazed. Britney Spears still being piped through, faintly. And it takes a second for this to register:

COMPUTER VOICE *Sunfilter descending. Sunfilter descending.*

She hears a mechanical hum, turns to look at the window. And it's easy to work out what the computer means. A thin slice of burning white light appears along the length of the top of the wide window. And begins to descend . . .

31 INT. PLATFORM ONE CORRIDOR DAY 3 1531

THE DOCTOR belts along, top speed.

32 INT. VIEWING GALLERY DAY 3 1531

ROSE hammering on the door. Yelling, furious:

ROSE Let me out! *Let me out!*

She looks round. The glaring white light lowers, burning the wall as it slowly sinks down, down, down . . .

33 INT. VIEWING GALLERY/CORRIDOR OUTSIDE DAY 3 1531

Smoke rising from the door as THE DOCTOR runs up, immediately starts whirring at the computer panel. (The b/g Britney song rising in volume, driving this.)

THE DOCTOR Anyone in there?

ROSE Get me out!

She appears at the glass panel. Casual:

THE DOCTOR Oh, well it would be you.

ROSE Open the door!

THE DOCTOR Hold on, give's two ticks . . .

COMPUTER VOICE *Sunfilter rising. Sunfilter rising.*

ROSE looks: the light begins to lift. The computer panel sparks.

COMPUTER VOICE *Sunfilter descending. Sunfilter descending.*

The light begins to lower. The Doctor whirrs away frantically:

THE DOCTOR Just what we need. The computer's getting clever –

ROSE Stop mucking about!

THE DOCTOR I'm not mucking about! It's fighting back –

The light's at head height, Rose has to sink down.

ROSE Open the door!

THE DOCTOR I know!

CU Doctor, whirring the sonic screwdriver.

The door's on the uppermost step. To escape the light, Rose slithers across the floor, down to the next step. The light keeps lowering – light's burning through the glass panel now. The Doctor has to flinch away to the side, keeps working – Rose is down to the lowest step, terrified.

The Doctor's furious, grits his teeth, and desperately rams the sonic screwdriver right into the controls, so it's stuck halfway in, the panel sparking.

COMPUTER VOICE *Sunfilter rising. Sunfilter rising.*

The light begins to rise – keeps rising. Doctor tries the door, it won't open.

THE DOCTOR The whole thing's jammed, I can't open the door – stay there, don't move.

He runs off, leaving the sonic screwdriver jammed in.

ROSE Where'm I gonna go? Ipswich?

COMPUTER VOICE *Earthdeath in five minutes, Earthdeath in five minutes.*

34 INT. THE MANCHESTER SUITE DAY 3 1532

Britney out. Serious atmosphere. JABE has got the attention of CASSANDRA and SURGEONS, the MOXX OF BALHOON, the FACE OF BOE, ADHERENTS and STAFF-CHILDREN (and extra GUESTS?), all spaced across the suite. Jabe holds the METAL SPIDER in one hand, her scanner in another.

JABE The metalmachine confirms. The spider devices have infiltrated the whole of Platform One.

THE DOCTOR enters, in a world of his own, just takes the spider off Jabe, fiddles with it, letting them carry on:

CASSANDRA How's that possible? Our private rooms are protected by a codewall – moisturise me, moisturise me!

MOXX OF BALHOON Summon the Steward!

JABE I'm afraid the Steward is dead.

The Staff-children wail.

CASSANDRA Oh, shut them up, someone!

MOXX OF BALHOON Who killed him?

CASSANDRA This whole event was sponsored by the Face of Boe, he invited us. Talk to the Face, talk to the Face!

Quiet authority, no need to lord it over them:

THE DOCTOR Easy way of finding out. Someone brought their little pet on board. Let's send it back to master.

He puts the spider on the floor. Stands back. All eyes on the spider. It scuttles forward. Pause. All staring. The spider makes a half-turn right, then left – then it *tic-tic-tics* across to the Adherents. They stand still, but the hum becomes a dangerous growl.

CASSANDRA The Adherents of the Repeated Meme! J'accuse!

The Doctor's still casual, strolls across to the Adherents.

THE DOCTOR That's all very well, and really kind of obvious, but if you stop and think about it –

The lead Adherent shoots out its metal/organic claw, but the Doctor grabs it, stops it dead, mid-swing; surprisingly strong. Hold, as he stares into the Adherent's cowl. Then he rips the arm off. The whole arm comes loose – claw, forearm, then some bulbous ganglia. The Adherent just stands stock still.

THE DOCTOR A repeated meme is just an idea, and that's all they are, an idea –

He snaps one of the ganglia. The Adherents collapse into nothing. Their robes just sink to the ground, empty.

THE DOCTOR Remote control droids, nice little cover for the real troublemaker.
(kicks the spider)
Go on, Jimbo. Go home.

And the spider *tic-tic-tics* away. Follow it across the floor . . . it scuttles up to a metal base. Pan up . . . to Cassandra. She looks at the Doctor, sneers.

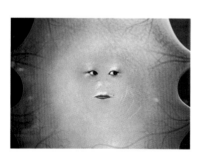

CASSANDRA I bet you were the school swot and never got kissed. At arms!

The Surgeons step forward, armed with their sprays.

THE DOCTOR What you gonna do, moisturise me?

CASSANDRA With acid. You're too late anyway, my spiders have control of the mainframe. Ohh, you all carried them as gifts, tax-free, past every codewall, I'm not just a pretty face.

THE DOCTOR Sabotaging a ship while you're inside it, how stupid is that?

CASSANDRA I'd hoped to manufacture a hostage situation. With myself as one of the victims, the compensation would have been enormous.

THE DOCTOR Five billion years, and it still comes down to money.

CASSANDRA D'you think it's cheap, looking like this? I'm the Last Human, Doctor . . . me, not that freaky little kid of yours. Flatness costs a fortune, I need a complete skin transplant. I'm growing clones in my cellar, they're just waiting to be peeled.

MOXX OF BALHOON Arrest her! The infidel!

CASSANDRA Oh shut it, pixie, I've still got my final option –

COMPUTER VOICE *Earthdeath in three minutes, Earthdeath in three minutes.*

CASSANDRA And here it comes. You're just as useful dead, all of you. I've got shares in your rival companies, they'll triple in price as soon as you're gone. My spiders are primed and ready to destroy the safety systems. How does that Old Earth song go? Burn baby, burn.

JABE Then you'll burn with us.

CASSANDRA Well, yes, except ... Ohh, I'm sorry, I know the use of teleportation is strictly forbidden, but ...

Cassandra and the Surgeons begin to shimmer, blue light.

CASSANDRA I'm such a naughty thing.
(sharp, command)
Spiders, activate!

35 INT. DUCTS DAY 3 1535

A SPIDER explodes (not huge, just enough to rupture it).

CUT TO a SECOND SPIDER exploding.

CUT TO a THIRD SPIDER exploding.

36 INT. THE MANCHESTER SUITE DAY 1535

A spider-sized explosion from a grille. The room shudders, and the lighting switches to an alarming red. CASSANDRA and SURGEONS are shimmering, fading from sight.

CASSANDRA Force-fields gone, with the planet about to explode. At least it'll be quick. Just like my fifth husband. Oh shame on me!
(disappearing)
Bye-bye, my darlings. Bye-bye.

And she's gone.

COMPUTER VOICE *Heat levels rising. Heat levels rising.*

MOXX OF BALHOON Reset the computer!

JABE Only the Steward would know how –

THE DOCTOR No, we could do it by hand, there's got to be a system-restore switch –
(running out)
Jabe, come on, you lot, just ... chill.

He runs out, Jabe following.

37 EXT. FX SHOT DAY 3 1536

The sun glares hotter, redder. CAMERA soars around Platform One, glaring with reflected light, above the still-perfect Earth. Over this:

COMPUTER VOICE *Earthdeath in two minutes.*

38 INT. MAINTENANCE CORRIDOR DAY 3 1536

THE DOCTOR and JABE run into the maintenance corridor, top speed, Platform One groaning all around them.

38A INT. VIEWING GALLERY DAY 3 1536

ROSE pressed up against the blackened wall (though no expanse needed – this scene can be shot tight).

COMPUTER VOICE *Warning! Platform One unsafe. Warning! Platform One unsafe.*

And over that – her mobile rings! Rose gets it out, sees the ident, answers, overjoyed –

ROSE Mum?

38B INT. TYLERS' KITCHEN DAY 1 1134

INTERCUT with ROSE in the VIEWING GALLERY. JACKIE with some damp food cartons, the fridge and freezer wide open. She's fast, bristling, keeps on the move.

JACKIE No, listen, I won't keep you, but I switched the freezer off by mistake, it's all defrosted, so we're having a mixed bag tonight, I've got paella and beefburgers and that tex-mex thing –

ROSE Never mind that, it doesn't matter –

JACKIE Don't have a go at me! If you labelled those plugs like I said, then I wouldn't be in this mess! All I'm saying is, don't have a big sandwich cos there's plenty for your tea. Now off you go, I won't keep you –

ROSE No don't hang up! Mum? You still there?

JACKIE You get back to work, go on.

ROSE No, but I'm not ... I mean, I don't have to ...
(helpless)
Thing is, you don't have to rush off, you could just ... stay on the line. Talk to me.

JACKIE Oh I like that! Every time I phone up, you haven't got time, now all of a sudden you're begging. Well excuse me, I'm not hanging on your every word, I'm a very busy woman – I'll see you tonight –

And she hangs up.

ROSE Mum – ?!

But no one's there. Just the ominous:

COMPUTER VOICE *Warning, abandon ship. Warning, abandon ship ...*

39 THRU 47 OMITTED

48 INT. VENTILATION CHAMBER DAY 3 1537

The door slides open, THE DOCTOR and JABE stare, frozen. The three massive fans are now whizzing round twice as fast, spinning like mad, with an almighty *whuk-whuk-whuk* –

THE DOCTOR Oh, and guess where the switch is.

49 INT. VIEWING GALLERY DAY 3 1537

COMPUTER VOICE *Exterior breach. Exterior breach …*

ROSE sits against the back wall, hot, trapped. But then she looks up. A noise. A terrible noise. A crack begins to trace a path across the window, with the awful sound of icebergs breaking …

50 INT. THE MANCHESTER SUITE DAY 3 1537

The STAFF-CHILDREN begin to scream, wail, point. The TREES, the MOXX OF BALHOON and the FACE OF BOE all turn to face the window … and cracks begin to streak across the glass.

MOXX OF BALHOON We're going to die!

51 INT. VENTILATION CHAMBER DAY 3 1537

THE DOCTOR has ripped a panel off the doorframe, revealing a big, stiff metal lever. He heaves it down – the fans slow, just a little. He steps forward, lets go of the lever – it shoots upright – the fans speed up. JABE steps forward, struggles to hold the lever down.

THE DOCTOR You can't, the heat's gonna vent through this place.

JABE I know.

THE DOCTOR Jabe. You're made of wood.

JABE Then stop wasting time. Time Lord.

A smile between them. Absolute trust. The Doctor turns to face the first fan, as:

COMPUTER VOICE *Safety systems failing. Safety systems failing.*

52 OMITTED

53 INT. VIEWING GALLERY DAY 3 1538

ROSE pinned against the wall, terrified. More and more cracks scatter across the glass –

54 INT. VENTILATION CHAMBER DAY 3 1538

THE DOCTOR's taken his jacket off, stands right up against the first fan. So close; the blades whooshing round, impossibly fast, with a terrifying *whuk-whuk-whuk*. If he can just time it right, in the second's gap between blades . . .

The Doctor – the blades . . . He goes forward, a single fast step – through to the other side!

55 INT. VIEWING GALLERY DAY 3 1538

ROSE staring, horrified – the cracks are beginning to glow, as the heat and light from outside force their way through –

56 INT. VENTILATION CHAMBER DAY 3 1538

THE DOCTOR faces fan two, with fan one whizzing behind him. The noise, the pressure. But the *whuk-whuk-whuk* rises in pitch, the fan increasing speed. He looks back – JABE clings to the lever, keeping it down, willing him on. The Doctor looks at fan two. Braces himself –

57 INT. VIEWING GALLERY DAY 3 1538

A terrible *crack!* Solid light streams through the glass, following the shape of the crack. It lances to the back of the room. ROSE has to scrabble to one side to escape it –

58 INT. VENTILATION CHAMBER DAY 3 1539

THE DOCTOR takes a breath, one step forward – through the second fan!
No time to waste, he faces the third …

59 OMITTED

60 INT. THE MANCHESTER SUITE DAY 3 1539

Solid white light forces its way through the cracks in the glass – STAFF-
CHILDREN and TREES run to avoid it, scream, panic. Light slams into the
MOXX OF BALHOON, he screams, flares white –

61 INT. VENTILATION CHAMBER DAY 3 1539

JABE holds down the lever with all her strength, shaking. Smoke is starting
to rise from her body. THE DOCTOR faces the third fan. Braces himself …

A dying cry – he turns. Only just visible through the first two fans: Jabe,
burning. Still looking at the Doctor, but helpless. Then her body falls –
CU Jabe's arm leaving the lever as she dies. The lever slams back upright.

The Doctor despairs, but has to turn back round, as the third fan speeds up,
whuk-whuk-whuk –

62 INT. VIEWING GALLERY DAY 3 1539

ROSE is pressed right up against the wall/steps, terrified. The naked white
light is shafting through to her left, to her right, she's trapped in a small space
in the middle –

COMPUTER VOICE *Earthdeath imminent.*

63 INT. VENTILATION CHAMBER DAY 3 1539

CU THE DOCTOR. The fan is impossibly fast, *whuk-whuk-whuk*. He tries
to step forward, but the blade almost skims him; he jolts back, scared –

COMPUTER VOICE *Planet explodes in ten, nine, eight* –

64 INT. VIEWING GALLERY DAY 3 1539

CU ROSE, about to die, the light closer on each side –

COMPUTER VOICE *– seven, six, five* –

65 INT. VENTILATION CHAMBER DAY 3 1539

COMPUTER VOICE *– four …*

But then the word just echoes away, all b/g noise sliding into nothing as THE DOCTOR simply lifts his head, closes his eyes, summoning an absolute calm. He is completely in control of this single second.

He steps forward. Through the blades, out to the other side. And he snaps back to reality – the noise, the countdown. There's a massive lever on the wall, he grabs it with both hands, slams it down –

THE DOCTOR Raise shields!   **COMPUTER VOICE** – *three, two, one –*

66 EXT. FX SHOT DAY 3 1539

Platform One shimmers. A transparent, rippling force-field blossoms around it, a protective bubble.

The Earth explodes. The planet scatters violently into chunks of rock and clouds of gas, spiralling in all directions. Debris flies around Platform One. But it remains untouched, safe behind its shields. Sailing through the apocalypse.

67 INT. VIEWING GALLERY DAY 3 1540

All the noise and fury stop.

COMPUTER VOICE *Exoglass repair. Exoglass repair.*

The light pulls away, as though sucked back outside. The crack-lines in the glass seal up, disappear.

On ROSE. Recovering. Alive.

68 OMITTED

69 INT. VENTILATION CHAMBER DAY 3 1542

The fans are back to normal speed, a slow, lazy spin. THE DOCTOR is just returning to the doorway. He looks down (though CAMERA does not), smoke rising from JABE. He stands there, gathering himself. Furious.

70 INT. THE MANCHESTER SUITE DAY 3 1550

The door slides open and ROSE – bedraggled, exhausted – steps in, looks around, still stunned. Given its minimalism, the mess isn't too bad – the cabinets broken and tilted, maybe the odd patch of fire (if possible), being doused by STAFF-CHILDREN. The two TREES are recovering, helping each other to walk. Staff-children help the FACE OF BOE, mopping the outside of its tank with cold water. But other Staff-children have gathered around the MOXX OF BALHOON's cushion. It's charred. They tip out the Moxx; just dust. The Staff-children wail and lament.

Then, on the far side, THE DOCTOR walks in. Rose stays back, unnerved; a controlled anger blazing out of him. She watches as he approaches the Trees, says something, holds their hands. And Rose can guess what's happened,

as the Trees begin to cry, comfort each other. Then the Doctor walks across the room, looking through the debris. Still looking, he sees Rose. A grim smile.

ROSE . . . All right?

THE DOCTOR Oh, I'm full of ideas. Bristling with 'em! Idea number one: teleportation through five thousand degrees needs some sort of Feed.

He finds the ostrich egg, still intact, picks it up.

THE DOCTOR Idea number two: this Feed must be hidden nearby.

He smashes the egg in his hands. Inside, a chunky black-metal device.

THE DOCTOR Idea number three: if you're as clever as me, then a teleportation Feed can be *reversed*.

He twists a dial on the Feed, looks up. And CASSANDRA shimmers back into view. She's mid-sentence, as though laughing with friends, just turning round.

CASSANDRA – Ohhh, you should've seen their little alien faces, all helpless and bleating and . . .
(realises)
Oh.

THE DOCTOR The Last Human.

CASSANDRA So. You passed my little test. Bravo! This makes you eligible to join, um, the Human Club –

THE DOCTOR People have died, Cassandra. You murdered them.

CASSANDRA It depends on your definition of people.
(vicious)
And that's enough of a technicality to keep your lawyers dizzy for centuries. Take me to court then, Doctor, and witness the effect of beauty upon the legal system. Oh, I will dazzle them! Charm the sternest jury. Seduce the stiffest judge. You stand in court, and watch me smile and cry and flutter –

THE DOCTOR And creak?

CASSANDRA And what?

THE DOCTOR Creak. You're creaking.

CASSANDRA What . . .?

And she is. An awful, dry, pulling noise. Cassandra's skin is stretching on its frame. She panics:

CASSANDRA I'm drying out! Oh sweet heavens, moisturise me, moisturise me! Where are my surgeons, my lovely boys? It's too hot!

THE DOCTOR You raised the temperature.

CASSANDRA Oh dear God, have pity! Moisturise me! I'm too dry, oh Doctor – I'll do anything, please, I'm sorry –

Rose steps forward, joins the Doctor, quiet:

ROSE Help her.

THE DOCTOR Everything has its time. And everything dies.

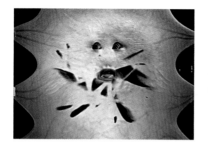

CASSANDRA I'm too young! I'm too young!

Cassandra wails as her skin stretches, pulling tight – and she snaps. An eyeball goes flying over Rose's shoulder.

CUT TO Cassandra, now just strips of flat skin flapping on the edge of an empty frame, like pieces of burst balloon.

Rose is horrified. The Doctor just walks away.

71 INT. FX SHOT DAY 3 1600

Platform One stands against a new, calm sky, clouds of solid gas, curls of dust and rock; the remains of the Earth lit in red and orange, from the still-burning Sun. Shuttles rise from the scaffolding, departing.

COMPUTER VOICE *Shuttles four and six departing. This unit now closing down for maintenance. Closing down ...*

72 INT. THE MANCHESTER SUITE DAY 3 1600

ROSE, alone, stands at the window, the room only half-lit. Her POV: the slow shift of gas, dust and rubble, drifting through space. All that's left of her home. She becomes aware of someone behind her, turns. THE DOCTOR stands a good distance away. A gentle smile, almost apologetic. More his old self again. Quiet:

ROSE The end of the Earth. It's gone. And we were too busy saving ourselves. No one saw it go. All these years, all that history, and no one was looking. It just ...

Pause. Then he holds out his hand.

THE DOCTOR Come with me.

73 EXT. ALLEYWAY DAY 3 1600

The TARDIS door opens, ROSE looks out, then steps out. It's a small alleyway, bricks and bins, but she walks down, knowing what she'll find the far end. Sounds of the real world only filter in as she steps out –

74 EXT. PICCADILLY CIRCUS DAY 3 CONTINUOUS

ROSE steps out into Piccadilly Circus. She looks around, filled with the sights and the noise, like she's never seen them before. It's the most ordinary day in 2005, UK, Earth. Shops, traffic, pavements. Life going on. PEOPLE hurrying past, in worlds of their own. WORKERS and TOURISTS and KIDS and *BIG ISSUE* SELLERS. No one looking at her.

THE DOCTOR appears at her side, gentle.

THE DOCTOR You think it's going to last forever, people and cars and concrete. But it won't. One day, it's gone. Even the sky.

Silence. Not sad, Rose only taking in the size of this, understanding it. Hold the pause, and then, maybe saying this for the first time:

THE DOCTOR My planet's gone. It's dead. It burnt like the Earth, it's just rocks and dust. Before its time.

ROSE What happened?

THE DOCTOR There was a War. And we lost.

ROSE A war with who …?

But he's just staring ahead, no reply.

ROSE What about your people?

THE DOCTOR I'm a Time Lord. I'm the last of the Time Lords. They're all gone. I'm the only survivor, I'm left travelling on my own, cos there's no one else.

Pause.

ROSE There's me.

Now, he looks at her, serious.

THE DOCTOR You've seen how dangerous it is. D'you want to go home?

ROSE I don't know. I want …
(pause)
Can you smell chips?

THE DOCTOR (smiles)
Yeah.

ROSE I want chips.

THE DOCTOR Me too.

ROSE Right! Before you get me back in that box, chips it is, and you can pay.

THE DOCTOR Um. No money.

ROSE What sort of date are you? Come on, tightwad. Chips are on me.
(holds out her hand)
We've only got five billion years till the shops close.

He takes her hand, and they saunter off together. Wide shot, gradually losing the Doctor and Rose as they walk through the crowds, chatting and laughing, on the most ordinary day in the world.

The Unquiet Dead
By Mark Gatiss

Doctor Who was dead: to begin with. This must be distinctly understood or nothing wonderful can come of the story I am going to relate…

This script – at various points called 'The Crippingwell Horror', and 'The Angels of Crippingwell' – began as a short paragraph in the new series 'bible', and would be the first trip back in time for the new TARDIS crew. It was to feature Charles Dickens, aliens made of gas and be set in Victorian Cardiff. Those few provisos got me immediately excited. I've an Auton-like affinity for historical stories and have been in love with the morbid, ebony-black grotesqueness of the nineteenth century since I was knee-high to a funeral mute.

At the very first script meeting, I was keen to express something intimately bound up in the magical, satsumas-at-Christmas feel of the show as I remembered it. That is: the very notion of travelling in time. What would it really be like, I pondered, to creak open that police-box door and glimpse a world long gone, a world, as Rose observes 'a hundred thousand sunsets ago'? I wanted a moment, amidst the madness, for this to be properly explored. 'That's wonderful,' said Russell. 'But it's not a moment. It's what the whole story is about.'

The first few drafts were set in a house run by the imposing Mrs Plumchute whose servant, Gwyneth, has lost her little brother to diphtheria. Gwyneth goes to see a reading by Dickens and asks him whether he thinks there is life beyond the grave. The great man thinks not. How is it, then, that she saw her dead brother at her window only the night before? Heading for Italy in 1860 to witness Garibaldi's famous taking of Naples, the Doctor and Rose become embroiled, instead, in the machinations of the only true medium in the place, one Noah Sneed. Thinking he has made contact with the spirits of the dead, he is in fact in tune with the alien Gelth who have sinister plans for the corpses in the nearby cemetery . . .

Although several plot strands remained constant, the big change came in the tone of the episode. It was all far too grim, with the dead boy wandering about, and also terribly convenient that Crippingwell cemetery was just next door! Relocating to an undertaker's suddenly allowed a lot more of the black humour which is my stock-in-trade, and I can remember the opening scene and Sneed's 'We've got another one!' coming in one joyous rush.

The other major change was the concentration on Gwyneth. Everyone fell in love with her in the first draft, and so it was eventually she who inherited the original Sneed's psychic powers and tragic end.

When I was little, scribbling stories in my jotter featuring Jon Pertwee's battle with the Yeti, or the thirties-set Auton story in which they develop an affinity for bakelite (hey, that's good!), I would never have believed I'd write for the real *Doctor Who*. But that Christmas-Yet-to-Come, well, came, and I'm thrilled and honoured to be part of this wonderful new beginning.

Mark Gatiss

1 TARDIS NIGHT

Chaos! A wild flight, engines groaning, floor lurching, lights dipping. THE DOCTOR and ROSE are clinging to the console. He pulls himself from one panel to another, slamming down stiff levers. Loud, enjoying it:

THE DOCTOR Hold that one down!

ROSE I'm holding this one down!

THE DOCTOR Hold them both!

ROSE It's not gonna work –

THE DOCTOR Oi! I promised you a time machine, and that's what you're getting. You've seen the future, now let's have a look at the past – (stares at panel)
1860! How does 1860 sound?

ROSE What happened in 1860?

THE DOCTOR Let's find out! Hold on – here we go!

He slams down a big, important lever –

2 FX SHOT: TIME VORTEX

The TARDIS spins through the whirlwind of the space/time vortex, disappearing away, into history . . .

3 INT. CHAPEL OF REST NIGHT

Calm, quiet, solemn. CU on a shaded gas-mantle. The tap's turned, gas hisses out and is lit by GABRIEL SNEED. The panelled room groans with lilies and mourning crepe. Centre: an open coffin. Sneed, a disreputable undertaker, turns to a young male mourner, MR REDPATH.

SNEED Sneed and Company offers its sincerest condolences, sir, in this most trying hour.

REDPATH moves to the coffin, stifles a sob. Inside, a gentle-looking old lady, MRS PEACE.

REDPATH Grandmama had a good innings, Mr Sneed. But she was so full of life, I can't believe she's gone.

SNEED Not gone, Mr Redpath. Merely sleeping.

REDPATH May I have a moment . . .?

SNEED Of course. I shall be next door should you require anything.

Sneed goes out. Redpath bows his head in prayer. Suddenly MRS PEACE's hand shoots up, grabs Redpath by the throat. The dead woman's pale, dead eyes snap open.

Choking, Redpath struggles with his reanimated grandparent. Smash! A vase of lilies goes over – the door's thrown open. Sneed stands there. And he just rolls his eyes and *tuts*. Then he runs forward, prises Mrs Peace's hand off

Redpath's throat. But Redpath collapses, dead. Sneed picks up the coffin lid and pushes it down onto Mrs Peace's body, yelling off:

SNEED Gwyneth! Gwyneth! Get down by here! We've got another one!

The coffin lid is suddenly thrust upwards, clobbering Sneed, who drops, unconscious, to the floor. Then one side of the coffin is smashed out, with one blow, so Mrs Peace can sit up, stand, and walk – a slow, dead walk, but not too zombified – to the door to the street.

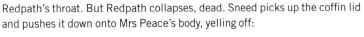

4 EXT. SNEED AND COMPANY, STREET NIGHT 4 CONTINUOUS

A quiet off-town-centre street, light snow drifting down. MRS PEACE throws open the door. She walks towards CAMERA, and a ghostly WRAITH, a mournful face, hovers over her own, like cigarette smoke – an echoing cry, wailing into – OPENING CREDITS.

4A INT. SNEED'S KITCHEN NIGHT

[Start scene with spare footage of EXT. SNEED's, if possible, from sc.4 – without Mrs Peace, just the snow falling, and SNEED OOV:]

SNEED Gwyneth! Where are you girl, Gwyneth!

CUT TO INT. KITCHEN: GWYNETH, the maid, hurries in, to find Sneed in a state.

SNEED Where've you been, I was shouting!

GWYNETH I was in the stable, sir, breaking the ice for old Samson –

SNEED Well get back in there and harness him up, we're going out!

GWYNETH Whatever for, sir?

SNEED The corpses are getting lively again! Mr Redpath's grandmother, she's up and on her feet, she's out there somewhere, on the streets, we've got to find her.

GWYNETH Oh Mr Sneed, for shame, how many more times? It's ungodly!

SNEED Don't look at me like it's my fault, I'm just as much a victim in all this! No one pities me, do they? Come on, hurry up, she was eighty-six, she can't have got far!

GWYNETH What about Mr Redpath? Did you deal with him?

SNEED No, she did.
(mimes throttling)

GWYNETH Oh but that's awful, sir! What have you done with him?

SNEED Gwyneth, I'm an undertaker, what d'you think I did with him? He's all laid out and past caring.

GWYNETH But that's murder!

SNEED Ahh, but if the murderer is already dead, I'm not sure it counts.

GWYNETH Mr Sneed, I know it's not my place, and forgive me for speaking out of turn, sir, but this is getting beyond now. Something terrible is happening inside this house, we've got to get help –

SNEED And we will, as soon as I've got that dead old woman locked up safe and sound. Now stop prevaricating girl – get the hearse ready! We're going bodysnatching!

5 EXT. STREET AND ALLEYWAY NIGHT

Down a dark alleyway, a light begins to flare, ancient engines groan, snowflakes rise and scatter. And the TARDIS fades into view.

6 INT. TARDIS NIGHT

Smoke rising from the floor and the console. THE DOCTOR and ROSE thrown onto the floor, both recovering, but smiling (no matter what, they have such a good laugh together):

ROSE Blimey.

THE DOCTOR Telling me! You all right?

ROSE Think so, yeah. Nothing broken. Did we make it, where are we?

THE DOCTOR (studies a panel)
I did it! Give the man a medal. Earth, Naples, December 24th, 1860.

ROSE That's so weird. It's Christmas.

THE DOCTOR All yours.

ROSE But it's like . . .
(quiet, smiling)
Think about it, though. Christmas 1860 happens once, just once, and then it's finished, it's gone, it'll never happen again. Except for you. You can go back and see days that are dead and gone. A hundred thousand sunsets ago. No wonder you never stay still.

THE DOCTOR Not a bad life.

ROSE Better with two.

Hold the moment between them, the smile. Then, energy –

ROSE Come on then – !

She runs to the doors, but –

THE DOCTOR Oi, oi oi! Hold it, where d'you think you're going?

ROSE 1860.

THE DOCTOR Go out there dressed like that, you'll start a riot, Barbarella. There's a wardrobe down there, first left, second right, third on the left, go straight ahead, under the stairs, past the bins, fifth door on your left. Hurry up!

7 EXT. STREET AND ALLEYWAY NIGHT

TARDIS b/g, then throw focus foreground, as a HEARSE creeps along, complete with black-plumed horses, a dark harbinger stealthily padding through the night. Sitting in the cab, eyes darting left and right – SNEED, and GWYNETH. Hushed:

SNEED Not a sign. Where is she? Wandering corpses! It's a disgrace! Lord, if word of this ever gets out ...

GWYNETH There's something awful queer going on, Mr Sneed. What are we to do?

SNEED Get her back and under wraps, that's what. Ooh, I can remember when undertaking was a respectable business. Laying out. Embalming. Stitching up the jawbone, those were the days.

GWYNETH She's vanished into the ether, sir. Where can she be?

Sneed brings the horses to halt, turns to Gwyneth, grim.

SNEED You tell me, girl.

GWYNETH What d'you mean ...?

SNEED Gwyneth, you know full well.

GWYNETH (scared)
Oh no, sir, I can't.

SNEED Use the sight.

GWYNETH It's not right, sir, it's forbidden –

SNEED (leans in close)
You're my servant, you'll do as I instruct. Find the old woman, or you're dismissed. Now look inside, girl. Look deep. Where is she ...?

CU Gwyneth, looking to the distance, eyes wide, voice faint; a psychic vision, underscored by eerie music.

GWYNETH ... She's ... Ohh, she's lost, sir. She's so alone. Oh my Lord. So many strange things in her head.

SNEED But where?

GWYNETH She was excited. About tonight. Before she passed on, she was going to see ... *him*.

SNEED And who's him?

GWYNETH The great man. All the way from London, the Great, Great Man ...

MIX TO:

8 INT. DRESSING ROOM NIGHT

CHARLES DICKENS sits alone. He's 57, dapper, his beard well trimmed; but he's weary, grey-skinned. Lost in contemplation. It takes a second or two for him to hear:

STAGE MANAGER Mr Dickens? Mr Dickens? Excuse me, sir, Mr Dickens, this is your call. Are you quite well, sir?

DICKENS Yes. Splendid. So sorry!

STAGE MANAGER Time you were on, sir.

DICKENS Absolutely. I was merely, uh ... brooding a little, that's all. Christmas Eve. Not the best of times to be alone.

STAGE MANAGER Did no one travel with you, sir? No lady wife waiting out front?

DICKENS I'm afraid not.

STAGE MANAGER You can have mine if you want.

DICKENS (small laugh)
I wouldn't dare. I've been rather ... well, let us say, clumsy, with family matters. I've left an ugly path of broken hearts behind me, and I've not been forgiven. The sins of the past, eh? Thank God I'm too old to cause any more trouble.

STAGE MANAGER You speak as if it's all over, sir.

Dickens looks up. On the wall, a poster: December 24, 1869, The Taliesin Lodge, Cardiff. MR CHARLES DICKENS will be reading from his many and sundry works, a free performance to honour the Children's Hospital ...

DICKENS Oh, it's never over! On and on I go. The same old show.
(grim smile)
I'm like a ghost, condemned to repeat myself for all eternity . . .

STAGE MANAGER Never too late, sir, you could think up some new turns.

DICKENS No, no. Even the imagination grows stale. I'm an old man, perhaps I've thought of everything I will ever think.
(deep breath, stands)
Still. The lure of the lime-light is as potent as a pipe, eh? On with the motley!

And Dickens follows the stage manager out.

9 INT. BACKSTAGE NIGHT

CU DICKENS as he follows the STAGE MANAGER through darkness.
As he walks, he loses the weariness, straightens up, breathes in, assumes a smile, summons the twinkle in his eye, with every step –

10. INT. THEATRE NIGHT

– so that as DICKENS steps out on to the stage, he's very much the Great Man. Wry, sparkling, in his element as the audience applauds. He bows, smiles, shines.

CUT TO THE AUDIENCE. And in the middle of a centre row, just staring, not clapping: the awful face of MRS PEACE.

11 INT. TARDIS NIGHT

ROSE steps forward, in her 1860 dress, hair pinned up appropriately.
And she looks stunning.

THE DOCTOR Blimey.

ROSE Now don't laugh.

THE DOCTOR You look . . . beautiful. Considering.

ROSE Considering what?

THE DOCTOR That you're human.

ROSE I think that's a compliment. Aren't you gonna change?

THE DOCTOR I've changed my jumper! Come on –

He holds out his hand, but she pushes past.

ROSE You stay there, you've done this before. This is mine –

She hurries to the TARDIS door, excited, opens it. Snowflakes flutter in . . .

12 EXT. ALLEYWAY NIGHT

ROSE stands in the police-box doorway and gazes out. A few snowflakes drift in through the open TARDIS door. A beat as she looks up at the snow-filled night sky.

She looks down. A drift is already forming on the threshold of the TARDIS. She puts one foot forward, plants it in the virginal snow, then lifts her foot back inside. The imprint of her shoe is left in the snow. Rose smiles, delighted, then steps out properly. THE DOCTOR appears behind her, follows her out.

THE DOCTOR Ready for this?

She's excited, lets him take her hand. She's holding her breath, as they hurry down the alley, and he's grinning –

THE DOCTOR Here we go. History.

The Doctor and Rose disappear round the corner.

13 EXT. CARDIFF SQUARE NIGHT

ROSE and THE DOCTOR arrive at a crossroads. Pull out from Rose, astonished, and the Doctor, beaming (he never tires of this), to a WIDE SHOT: a wide, busy, snowy town square. LADIES and GENTLEMEN in their finery, the POOR in plainer clothing, CAROLLERS, KIDS running, horse-drawn carriages rattling to and fro, braziers burning. The full majesty of history.

Hold, then CUT TO the hearse pulling up outside the theatre. SNEED jumps off, GWYNETH following.

GWYNETH In there, sir, I'm certain of it –

CUT TO the Doctor and Rose, walking along. The Doctor just giving a coin to a newsvendor, taking a paper; Rose just beaming, overjoyed, taking it all in.

THE DOCTOR I got the flight a bit wrong.

ROSE I don't care.

THE DOCTOR It's not 1860, it's 1869.

ROSE I don't care.

THE DOCTOR And it's not Naples.

ROSE I don't care.

THE DOCTOR It's Cardiff.

Pause, keep walking.

ROSE ... Right.

14 INT. THEATRE NIGHT

DICKENS stands at a lectern, in full flow. A fine orator; the best! The AUDIENCE is enraptured.

DICKENS 'Now, it is a fact, that there was nothing at all particular about the knocker on the door of this house and yet, let any man explain to me, if he can, how it happened that Scrooge, having his key in the lock of the door, saw in the knocker, without its undergoing any intermediate process of change: not a knocker, but Marley's face!'

A gasp from the audience, genuine shocks and thrills.

DICKENS 'Marley's face. With a dismal light about it like a bad lobster in a dark cellar.'
(more fearful)
'It looked at Scrooge as Marley used to look ...'
(disturbed)
It looked like ...
(horrified)
Oh my Lord, it looked like *that!*

And with a trembling finger, Dickens points. MRS PEACE is staring at him, but her eyes are blazing blue, and a ghost-like blue wraith is slowly rising out of her.

DICKENS What phantasmagoria is this?

Then Mrs Peace stands, lets out an unearthly cry – and the ectoplasmic WRAITH streams from her mouth and nostrils! It has a vague child's face, but it's blurry, unformed. It rises up, wailing, still attached to Mrs Peace's mouth by a blue smoky strand. The gas-light dips.

Screams! The CROWD panic, and start to run –

15 EXT. CARDIFF SQUARE night

THE DOCTOR and ROSE hear screams –

THE DOCTOR That's more like it!

And they're both running –

16 INT. THEATRE FRONT–OF–HOUSE night

As the AUDIENCE run out – screams, terror! – SNEED and GWYNETH are trying to push their way in.

SNEED Let me through! Let me through!

17 INT. THEATRE night

MRS PEACE is now standing, the WRAITH still attached to her mouth by a thin, smoky strand. The creature itself, though anchored, circles in the air, wailing, desperate. MEN and WOMEN still yelling, panicking, running out.

CUT TO DICKENS, on the stage, genuinely affronted.

DICKENS Stay in your seats, I beg of you! It is a lantern show, it's trickery!

He looks round. The STAGE MANAGER is in the wings, scared, quaking. And Dickens is actually upset, tearful:

DICKENS Is this what I am become? The target of feeble jokes? Am I reduced to this?

CUT TO SNEED and GWYNETH arriving at the back.

GWYNETH There she is, sir!

SNEED I can see that! Whole bloomin' world can see it!

18 INT. THEATRE FRONT-OF-HOUSE NIGHT

MEN and WOMEN still running out, yelling, sobbing, as THE DOCTOR and ROSE push through –

19 INT. THEATRE NIGHT 4 CONTINUOUS

THE DOCTOR and ROSE run in. See MRS PEACE. Look up – see the WRAITH, spiralling.

THE DOCTOR Fantastic!

Then Mrs Peace clamps her jaw shut, and the ghostly strand is broken. The old woman collapses, dead again. The wraith rises up, free, spiralling faster, frantic. The auditorium is rapidly clearing, but the Doctor sees a man on the stage, runs down to him –

THE DOCTOR Did you see where it came from?

DICKENS Ah! The wag reveals himself, does he? Well, I trust you're satisfied!

CUT TO Rose. She's stayed at the back of the auditorium. With everyone else's eyes on the wraith, only she sees . . .

During all the above, SNEED and GWYNETH, just looking like part of the CROWD, have been hurrying along the rows of seats to get to Mrs Peace; now, they've reached her. Sneed hoists the body over his shoulder –

ROSE Oi! Leave her alone –

Gwyneth looks back, scared, but Sneed, carrying Mrs Peace, is heading to the far side of the auditorium, to a side-door (the equivalent of a fire-door).

Gwyneth follows. Rose hoists up her skirts, charges after them, calls out –

ROSE Doctor! I'll get them –

CUT TO the Doctor, clambering up on stage.

THE DOCTOR Be careful!
(to Dickens)
Did it say anything? Can it speak? I'm the Doctor, by the way.

DICKENS Doctor indeed! You look more like a navvy.

THE DOCTOR What's wrong with this jumper?

A wail: the Doctor turns, to see the wraith slither away, into one of the gas-mantles, gone. The gas-lighting rises back up.

THE DOCTOR (more to himself)
Gas. It's made of gas . . .

20 EXT. CARDIFF SQUARE NIGHT

PEOPLE still running, some standing, crying, others drawn towards the commotion. On ROSE, hurrying out of the theatre. Her POV: SNEED and GWYNETH, shoving MRS PEACE into the hearse. Rose runs towards them, muttering:

ROSE How d'you run in these things . . . ?
(calls out)
Oi! You two! What are you doing?

Sneed darts away behind the hearse, Gwyneth faces Rose.

GWYNETH Oh it's a tragedy, miss, don't you worry yourself, me and the master'll deal with things. Fact is, this poor lady's been taken with a brain-fever and we have to get her to the infirmary –

Rose grabs hold of Mrs Peace's hand.

ROSE She's cold. She's dead. Oh my God, what did you do to her?

But Sneed's hand comes in, fast, pressing a cloth pad over her face. ROSE struggles, but loses consciousness.

GWYNETH What d'you do that for?

SNEED She's seen too much! Get her in the hearse!

Gwyneth's miserable, but helps to lift ROSE up –

CUT TO THE DOCTOR, running out of the theatre – looks round. His POV: Rose being shoved into the hearse.

THE DOCTOR Rose!

He runs, but the hearse rattles off into the night. Before it disappears we clearly see the lettering on the side of the hearse; 'Sneed and Company'. And an address – '7 Temperance Court, Llandaff'.

DICKENS has followed the Doctor, limping, agitated.

DICKENS You're not escaping me, sir! What do you know about that hobgoblin? A projection on glass, I suppose, who put you up to it?

THE DOCTOR Yeah, thanks, not now, mate –

The Doctor spots a splendid-looking coach parked across the street, runs over. Shouts up to the DRIVER:

THE DOCTOR Oi! You! Follow that hearse!

DRIVER Can't do that, sir.

THE DOCTOR Why not?

And Dickens is still following!

DICKENS I'll tell you why not, I'll give you a very good reason why not. Because this is my coach!

THE DOCTOR Well get in then!
(to Driver:)
Move!

He shoves Dickens inside. CUT TO CU wheels, hooves; CUT TO the carriage, giving chase –

21 INT. COACH NIGHT

Rattling along, THE DOCTOR bangs on the ceiling.

THE DOCTOR Come on! You're losing them!

The DRIVER looks down through the trap in the ceiling.

DRIVER Everything in order, Mr Dickens?

DICKENS No, it is not!

The Doctor turns and looks at DICKENS.

THE DOCTOR What did he say?

DICKENS Now let me say first, I'm not without a sense of humour but –

THE DOCTOR Mr Dickens?

DICKENS Yes.

THE DOCTOR Charles Dickens?

DICKENS Yes!

THE DOCTOR *The* Charles Dickens?

DRIVER Should I remove the gentleman, sir?

THE DOCTOR Charles Dickens! You're brilliant, you are! Completely, one hundred per cent brilliant! I've read 'em all! *Great Expectations,* I love that book! *Oliver Twist* – and what's that one with the ghost?

DICKENS Ah, you mean the old bear Scrooge –

THE DOCTOR No, no, no, the one about the trains. *The Signalman,* that's it! Terrifying! Best short story, ever! You're a genius.

DRIVER D'you want me to get rid of him, sir?

DICKENS Um. No, I think he can stay.

THE DOCTOR Honestly Charles – can I call you Charles? – I'm such a big fan.

DICKENS A big what?

THE DOCTOR Fan. Number one fan, that's me!

DICKENS How are you a 'fan' exactly? In what way do you resemble a means of cooling oneself?

THE DOCTOR No, it means fanatic. Devoted to you! Mind you, I've got to say, that American bit in *Martin Chuzzlewit*, what's all that about? Was that just padding or what, I mean, it's rubbish, that bit.

DICKENS I thought you were my ... *fan?*

THE DOCTOR Oh well, if you can't take criticism. Go on, do the death of Little Nell. It cracks me up –
(suddenly)
No! Sorry! Never mind that –
(bangs roof)
Faster! Come on!

DICKENS Who's inside that hearse?

THE DOCTOR My friend. She's only nineteen and it's my fault. She's in my care and now she's in danger.

DICKENS Then why waste my time with dry old books? This is far more important – driver! Be swift! The chase is on!

22 INT. CHAPEL OF REST NIGHT

SNEED lays ROSE out on a table. (MRS PEACE is back in her coffin, next to REDPATH, now in his own unadorned coffin.)

GWYNETH The poor girl's still alive, what are we going to do with her?

SNEED I don't know! I didn't plan any of this, did I? Is it my fault if the dead won't stay dead?

GWYNETH Then whose fault is it, sir? Why is this happening to us?

GWYNETH clears frame. Reveal the gas-mantle, behind her. It flares with unnatural light. And a distant whispering, chattering sound, like many voices, far away ...

23 EXT. SNEED AND COMPANY, STREET NIGHT

DICKENS's coach pulls up outside SNEED AND COMPANY, a tall, plain town-house. They see: the hearse, horses tethered to a lamppost. THE DOCTOR gets down from the coach, followed by Dickens.

THE DOCTOR Not exactly hidden. Which makes it more dangerous, they're amateurs.

DICKENS Doctor, let me lead. Dressed like that, they'll show you to the tradesman's entrance.

THE DOCTOR Lead on then, Charlie.

DICKENS No one calls me Charlie.

THE DOCTOR The ladies do.

DICKENS (embarrassed)
... How d'you know that?

THE DOCTOR (grinning)
Told you. I'm your –

DICKENS 'Number one fan', yes.

And he marches forward.

24 INT. SNEED AND COMPANY, HALLWAY NIGHT

SNEED and GWYNETH hurrying along –

SNEED I did the Bishop a favour once. Made his nephew look like a cherub even though he'd been a fortnight in the weir. P'raps he'll do us an exorcism on the cheap!

From off, a heavy knock at the front door.

SNEED Say I'm not in! Tell 'em we're closed! Just get rid of 'em!

25 INT. CHAPEL OF REST NIGHT

On her table, ROSE groans and stirs. She opens her eyes and immediately regrets it. Still woozy, she sits up. Blinking, dazed, she gathers her senses. And while Rose faces forward, behind her, MR REDPATH sits bolt upright in his coffin.

26 EXT. SNEED AND COMPANY, STREET NIGHT

GWYNETH opens the front door. DICKENS stands there, indignant, THE DOCTOR a step back.

GWYNETH I'm sorry sir, we're closed.

DICKENS Nonsense, since when did an undertaker's keep office hours? The dead don't die on schedule, now I demand to see your master –

GWYNETH He's not in, sir.

DICKENS Don't lie to me, child, summon him at once!

GWYNETH I'm awfully sorry, Mr Dickens, but the master is indisposed.

THE DOCTOR (quietly)
Having trouble with your gas?

He indicates. Dickens and Gwyneth look round – the gas-mantle in the hall is blazing with unnatural light, accompanied by a terrible whispering . . .

DICKENS What the Shakespeare is going on . . . ?

27 INT. CHAPEL OF REST NIGHT

REDPATH arches his head back, breathes in. A blue ectoplasmic form rushes out of the gas-mantle, into his mouth and nostrils, settling over his face. He breathes it in, with a low, awful moan, which makes ROSE jump, turn. She watches wide-eyed, as the weird vapour settles into Redpath, disappears. And Redpath gets out of his coffin.

ROSE . . . Are you all right?

He keeps walking towards her.

ROSE You're kidding me, yeah? You're just kidding. You are, you're kidding, aren't you?
(beat)

Okay, not kidding.

Scared, she hops down, runs to the door, it's locked. Redpath advances towards her.

Then MRS PEACE sits up –

28 INT. SNEED AND COMPANY, HALLWAY NIGHT

THE DOCTOR stands beneath the flaring gas-light, pressing his ear to the wall. DICKENS and GWYNETH looking on.

GWYNETH You're not allowed inside, sir –

CU the Doctor; the distant whispering . . .

THE DOCTOR There's something in the walls. The gas-pipes. Something's living inside the gas . . .

29 INT. CHAPEL OF REST NIGHT

ROSE throws a big vase at REDPATH, it smashes against him. MRS PEACE is now on her feet, advancing.

Rose hammers on the door.

ROSE Let me out!

30 INT. SNEED AND COMPANY, HALLWAY NIGHT

THE DOCTOR, DICKENS, GWYNETH hear:

THE DOCTOR That's her!

And he's running –

31 INT. CHAPEL OF REST NIGHT

ROSE shoves the table on which she was lying at REDPATH and MRS PEACE – turns back to the door, hammers –

ROSE Oi! Let me out! Open the door!

32 INT. SNEED AND COMPANY, CORRIDOR 1 NIGHT

SNEED standing in the way as THE DOCTOR and DICKENS race along, followed by a helpless GWYNETH –

SNEED How dare you, sir! This is my house –

But the Doctor just barges past.

33 INT. CHAPEL OF REST NIGHT

CU ROSE hammering on the door – REDPATH's dead hand comes in, covers her mouth, pulls her back out of shot. Next second, the door is kicked, slams open – THE DOCTOR stands there for a second, DICKENS, SNEED and GWYNETH behind him, horrified – then the Doctor just steps forward:

THE DOCTOR I think this is my dance, thank you –

And he just takes Rose's hand, elegantly pulls her out of Redpath's grip, and into his arms.

A stand-off, as the living look at the dead. Quiet, awed:

DICKENS It's a prank. Must be. We're under some mesmeric influence.

THE DOCTOR No we're not. The dead are walking.
(to Rose)
Hi.

ROSE Hi. Who's your friend?

THE DOCTOR Charles Dickens.

ROSE ... Okay.

THE DOCTOR (to the dead)
My name's the Doctor. Who are you, then? What do you want?

Redpath speaks, a thin, unearthly wail:

REDPATH/GELTH *Failing! Open the rift. We are dying. Trapped in this form. Cannot sustain. Help us ...*

Then Redpath and MRS PEACE suddenly arch their heads back. The transparent blue wraiths pour out of them. The bodies collapse, dead, as the wraiths spiral in the air, swirl away, into the gas-lights, gone.

And all is calm.

34 INT. SNEED'S PARLOUR NIGHT

A comfortable, wood-panelled parlour. ROSE in a fine temper, walking-stick in hand, right at SNEED, while THE DOCTOR sits, happy to watch. DICKENS stands back, unwilling to join in, uneasy. GWYNETH meekly handing out tea.

ROSE First of all you drug me, then you kidnap me – and don't think I didn't feel your hands having a quick wander, you dirty old man –

SNEED (quailing)
I won't be spoken to like this –

ROSE And then you stack me in a room full of zombies! And if that isn't enough, you swan off and leave me to die! So come on! Talk!

SNEED It's not my fault, it's this house! Always had a reputation. Haunted. But I never had much bother, till about three months back. Then the stiffs – er, the dear departed – started getting restless.

DICKENS Tommyrot!

Simultaneously (Sneed b/g; on the Doctor):

SNEED But you witnessed it! Can't keep the beggars down, sir, they walk. And it's the queerest thing, they hang onto scraps of their old selves. One old fella – used to be a sexton – almost walked into his own memorial service. Like the old lady, going to your performance, just as she'd planned.

Gwyneth gives the Doctor his tea.

GWYNETH Two sugars, sir, just how you like it.

She goes on her way. Hold on the Doctor, watching her for a second, puzzled . . .

DICKENS Morbid fancy.

THE DOCTOR Charles, you were there.

DICKENS I saw nothing but an illusion.

THE DOCTOR If you're gonna deny it, don't waste my time, just shut up.

Dickens cut to the quick, genuinely hurt, stays silent.

THE DOCTOR (to Sneed)
What about the gas?

SNEED That's new, sir. Never seen anything like that.

THE DOCTOR Means it's getting stronger. The rift's getting wider, and something's sneaking through.

ROSE What's the rift?

THE DOCTOR A weak point, in time and space. A connection between this place and another. That's the cause of ghost stories, most of the time.

SNEED That's how I got the house so cheap, stories go back generations. Echoes in the dark. Queer songs in the air. And this feeling, like a shadow passing over your soul. Truth be told, it's been good for business, just what people expect from a gloomy trade like mine.

From above, on Dickens, quietly opening the door. Forgotten, not needed – he slips away.

35 INT. SNEED AND COMPANY, CORRIDOR NIGHT

Quietly, DICKENS sneaks away down the corridor. On a mission of his own. He observes one of the flickering gas-mantles, and, remembering what the Doctor said, he puts his ear against the wall. Listening . . . very faint: the awful whispering sound. Dickens pulls his head away, affronted, mutters:

DICKENS Impossible!

And he moves on.

36 INT. CHAPEL OF REST NIGHT

The coffin lid is lifted up. REDPATH lies there, eyes closed, utterly, and ordinarily, dead. DICKENS heaves the lid down to the side, studies the body. Waves a hand in front of Redpath's eyes. Prods him. Then he waves his hands over the body, moves up and down, all along the coffin, waving –

THE DOCTOR Looking for strings?

THE DOCTOR's in the doorway. Dickens defiant.

DICKENS Wires perhaps. There must be some mechanism behind this fraud.

THE DOCTOR (walks in)
Oh come on, Charles. All right, I shouldn't have told you to shut up. Sorry. But you've got one of the best minds in the world – you saw the creature, made of gas –

DICKENS I cannot accept that –

THE DOCTOR And what does the human body do, when it decomposes? It breaks down. Produces gas. Perfect home for these gas-things, they can slip inside, use the body as a vehicle. Like your driver and his coach.

DICKENS Stop it!

Silence: the Doctor only now realising that Dickens is upset. Pause, as the older man holds back tears.

DICKENS Can it be? That I have the world entirely wrong?

THE DOCTOR (gentle)
Not wrong. There's just more to learn.

DICKENS But all my life, I've railed against fantasists! Dedicated myself to the *real* world. The injustices. The great social causes. I thought I was a force for good. Now you tell me that the real world is a realm of spectres and jack o'lanterns. In which case ... have I wasted my brief span, Doctor? Has it all been for nothing?

37 INT. SNEED'S KITCHEN NIGHT

CU match striking. GWYNETH holds the match to the gas-mantle, lights it. She steps down, putting the matches in her apron. It's a dank, plain kitchen. ROSE is helping, drying plates.

GWYNETH Please, miss, you shouldn't be helping, it's not right.

ROSE Don't be daft, I bet Sneed works you to death. How much do you get paid?

GWYNETH Eight pound a year, miss.

ROSE How much?!

GWYNETH I know! I'd've been happy with six!

ROSE So did you even go to school, or what …?

GWYNETH Course I did, what d'you think I am, an urchin? I went every Sunday, nice and proper.

ROSE What, once a week?!

GWYNETH We had to do sums and everything. To be honest, I hated every second.

ROSE Me too!

Both smiling now, friends.

GWYNETH Don't tell anyone, but one week, I didn't go, I ran away down the Heath, all on my own.

ROSE I did plenty of that, I used to go round the shops with my mate Shareen. We'd go looking at boys.

GWYNETH Well I don't know much about that, miss.

ROSE Oh come on, times don't change that much. I bet you've done the same.

GWYNETH I don't think so, miss.

ROSE Gwyneth, you can tell me. I bet you've got your eye on someone.

GWYNETH I suppose …
(shy)
There is one lad. The butcher's boy, comes by every Tuesday afternoon. Such a nice smile on him.

ROSE Oh, I like a nice smile. Good smile and nice bum.

GWYNETH (laughing, shocked)
I've never heard the like!

ROSE Ask him out. Give him a cup of tea or something, that's a start.

GWYNETH (studying her)
I swear, miss, it's the strangest thing. You've got all the clothes and breeding. But you talk like some sort of wild thing.

ROSE Maybe I am. And maybe that's good. You need a bit more in life than Mr Sneed.

GWYNETH Now that's not fair, he's not so bad, old Sneed. He was very kind, taking me in, cos I lost mam and dad to the flu when I was twelve.

ROSE Oh, I'm sorry.

GWYNETH Thank you, miss. But I'll be with them again, one day. Sitting with them in Paradise. I shall be so blessed. They're waiting for me. Maybe your dad's waiting up there too, miss.

ROSE Maybe. Um … who told you he was dead?

GWYNETH Dunno, must've been the Doctor.

ROSE My father died years back.

GWYNETH But you've been thinking about him lately. More than ever.

ROSE Suppose ...

Rose studying her, now; beginning to wonder.

ROSE How d'you know all this?

GWYNETH Mr Sneed says I think too much, I'm all alone down here. Bet you've got a dozen servants, haven't you?

ROSE (laughs)
No servants where I come from.

GWYNETH And you've come such a long way.

Rose moves closer, fascinated:

ROSE What makes you think so?

Gwyneth stares. Right into Rose's eyes. Looking deep. Rose holds the stare. The eerie underscore ...

GWYNETH I just do. You're from ... London.
(frowns)
I've seen London in drawings, but never like that, all those people rushing about ... half-naked, for shame. So much noise! Those metal boxes, racing past ... and those birds in the sky! No!
(awe-struck)
They're metal as well. Iron birds with people inside. People are flying.
(suddenly scared)
And you. You've flown so far. Further than anyone. The things you've seen. The darkness. The big bad wolf –

Gwyneth breaks away, terrified, staggers back.

GWYNETH Oh I'm sorry, miss. I'm so sorry.

ROSE It's all right –

GWYNETH Can't help it. Ever since I was a little girl, mam said I'd got the sight. She told me to hide it.

THE DOCTOR But it's getting stronger. More powerful. Is that right?

THE DOCTOR's in the doorway; dark, dangerous. All hushed, Gwyneth – and Rose, to some extent – scared of him.

GWYNETH All the time, sir. Every night, now, voices in my head.

THE DOCTOR You've grown up on top of the rift. You're part of it. You're the key.

GWYNETH I tried to make sense of it, sir. Consulted with spiritualists and table-rappers and all sorts.

THE DOCTOR Well that should help. You can show us what to do.

GWYNETH What to do where, sir?

CU the Doctor, grim, but loving it:

THE DOCTOR We're gonna have a seance.

38 INT. SNEED'S PARLOUR NIGHT

THE DOCTOR, ROSE, DICKENS, GWYNETH and SNEED are seated at a round table. Gwyneth in front of the bay window, curtains closed. She's nervous, but excited.

GWYNETH I've seen it done, sir, this is how Madame Mortlock summons those from the land of mists, down in Butetown. Come. We must all join hands . . .

DICKENS I can't partake in this.

THE DOCTOR Humbug? Come on. Open mind.

DICKENS But this is precisely the sort of cheap mummery I strive to unmask. Seances! Nothing but luminous tambourines and a squeeze-box concealed between the knees. The girl knows nothing!

THE DOCTOR Now don't antagonise her. I love a happy medium.

ROSE I can't believe you said that.

THE DOCTOR Come on. We might need you.

Reluctantly, Dickens joins hands with the others.

THE DOCTOR Good man. Gwyneth. Reach out.

Gwyneth begins to breathe heavily.

GWYNETH Speak to us. Are you there? Spirits, come. Speak to us that we may relieve your burden . . .

ROSE Can you hear that . . . ?

DICKENS Nothing can happen, it's sheer folly . . .

The whispering, chattering sound is rising.

ROSE Look at her.

Gwyneth tilts her head back.

GWYNETH I see them! I feel them!

The bluey ectoplasm begins to pour from the gas-mantle. It swirls around the room, takes on the form of the WRAITH. It swirls about above Gwyneth's head. The Doctor and Rose in awe; it's beautiful. Dickens and Sneed fearful. The wraith speaks – but the words rise, fall away, lost.

ROSE What's it saying?

THE DOCTOR It can't get through the rift –
(gentle, but urgent)
Gwyneth. It's not controlling you, you're controlling it. Now look deep. Allow them through.

GWYNETH I can't –

THE DOCTOR Yes you can. Just believe it. I have faith in you, Gwyneth. Make the link.

GWYNETH Yes – !

And Gwyneth takes control; energy fills her; she looks ahead, smiling, ecstatic, transported – and the wraith *blossoms*. An unearthly wind sweeps through the room. The bay windows crash open, glass smashes, curtains blow. All those round the table hold on tight, buffeted, illuminated by a fierce white-blue light.

And above Gwyneth, the full glory of the wraiths. Three of them, a trinity, one above her head and one each side. Ghostly, beautiful female faces, with hair and rags streaming from them as though they're under water.

SNEED Great God! Spirits! From the other side!

THE DOCTOR The other side of the universe.

And the central wraith can speak; a high, wailing voice:

GWYNETH/WRAITH *Pity us! Pity the Gelth! There is so little time. Help us!*

THE DOCTOR What d'you want us to do?

GELTH *The rift. Take the girl to the rift. Make the bridge.*

THE DOCTOR What for?

GELTH *We are so very few. The last of our kind. We face extinction!*

THE DOCTOR Why, what happened?

GELTH *Once we had a physical form. Like you. But then the War came.*

DICKENS What war?

GELTH *The Time War.*

A glance between the Doctor and Rose.

GELTH *The whole universe convulsed. The Time War raged, invisible to smaller species. But devastating to higher forms. Our bodies wasted away. We're trapped in this gaseous state.*

THE DOCTOR So that's why you need the corpses.

GELTH *We want to stand tall. To feel the sunlight. To live again. We need a physical form and your dead are abandoned, they go to waste. Give them to us.*

ROSE But we can't.

THE DOCTOR Why not?

ROSE It's not ... I mean, it's not ...

THE DOCTOR Not decent? Not polite? It could save their lives.

Gwyneth groans, in pain. The voice starts failing –

GELTH *Open the rift. Let the Gelth through. We're dying. Help us ... Pity the Gelth!*

Gwyneth slumps across the table. The Gelth wail, spiral round and vanish into the gas-pipes. Everything is still.

Rose runs to Gwyneth. And then, a sob – Dickens is tearful, shaking.

DICKENS All true. It's all true.

39 INT. SNEED'S PARLOUR NIGHT

GWYNETH lies on a chaise-longue, white as chalk. ROSE dabs a wet cloth against her lips, Gwyneth's eyes flicker open.

ROSE S'all right. You just sleep.

GWYNETH (panics)
But my angels, miss! They came, didn't they? They need me –

She looks round: THE DOCTOR, DICKENS and SNEED are gathered across the room, watching her.

THE DOCTOR They do need you, Gwyneth. You're their only chance of survival –

ROSE I told you, leave her alone. She's exhausted, and she's not fighting your battles.

Like she's said that for the fifteenth time, tension simmering away between the Doctor and Rose.

ROSE (to Gwyneth)
Have a drink of this ...

Allowing the Doctor, Dickens and Sneed to huddle, sotto:

SNEED But what did you say, Doctor? Explain it again, what are they?

THE DOCTOR Aliens.

SNEED Like, foreigners, you mean?

THE DOCTOR Pretty foreign, yeah. From up there.

He points upwards.

SNEED Brecon?

THE DOCTOR Close. And they've been trying to get through from ... Brecon to Cardiff, but the road is blocked, only one or two can slip through. Even then, they're weak, they can only test-drive the bodies for so long. They have to revert to gas, and hide in the pipes.

DICKENS And that's why they need the girl?

ROSE They're not having her.

Opening up the conversation to Rose and Gwyneth again:

THE DOCTOR But she can help. Living on the rift has made her part of it. Gwyneth can open up the rift, make a bridge, and let them through.

Dickens sighs, sits, feeling ancient.

DICKENS Incredible. Ghosts that are not ghosts but beings from another world. Only able to exist in our realm by inhabiting cadavers ...

THE DOCTOR It could work. Good system.

ROSE You can't let them run around inside dead people!

THE DOCTOR Why not? It's just like recycling.

Right at each other:

ROSE Seriously though, you can't.

THE DOCTOR Seriously though, I can.

ROSE But it's just ... wrong. Those bodies were living people. We should respect them, even in death.

THE DOCTOR D'you carry a donor card?

ROSE But that's different, that's ...
(exasperated)
Oh I don't know.

THE DOCTOR It is different, yeah. It's a different morality. Get used to it. Or go home.

They stare at each other; he's at his most alien. The moment broken by Dickens, weary:

DICKENS Not easy, is it, my dear? This new world. Oh, I was so sure of myself. The great Dickens! Every day, checking the papers for my name. Such vanity. When I'm nothing but an old fool.

THE DOCTOR At least you're learning.

DICKENS Learning what? That I'm a spent force? That this addle-headed scribbler is no longer use nor ornament? I didn't need you to tell me that, Doctor.

Pause; he stares into his glass.

The Doctor moves forward, more reasonable with Rose:

THE DOCTOR You heard what they said. Time is short. I can't worry about a few corpses when the last few Gelth could be dying.

ROSE I don't care, you're not using her –

GWYNETH Don't I get a say, miss?

ROSE Well, yes, but, you don't understand what's going on –

GWYNETH You would say that, miss, cos that's very clear inside your head. That you think I'm stupid.

ROSE That's not fair –

GWYNETH S'true though. A simple child, that's what I am to you. Things might be very different where you're from, but here and now, I know my own mind. And the angels need me. Doctor? What do I have to do?

THE DOCTOR You don't have to do anything.

GWYNETH They've been singing to me since I was a child. Sent by my mam on a holy mission, so tell me.

THE DOCTOR We need to find the rift.
(paces around)
This house is a weak spot, so there must be one spot that's weaker than any other. Mr Sneed, what's the worst part of this house? The place where the most ghosts have been seen?

SNEED That would be . . .
(darkly)
The morgue.

A solemn pause.

ROSE No chance you were gonna say gazebo, is there?

40 INT. SNEED AND COMPANY, MORGUE NIGHT

A dank, cement-walled cellar, arched at one end. BODIES on wooden trolleys, covered in white sheets. At one end, a small, iron-gated alcove – the sluice, where bodies are washed down and prepared. The metal door creaks open: THE DOCTOR comes in, ROSE, DICKENS, GWYNETH and SNEED follow.

THE DOCTOR Talk about bleak house.

They all walk in, cautious, spread out. Sotto:

ROSE Thing is, Doctor, the Gelth don't succeed, cos I know they don't. I know for a fact that corpses weren't walking round in 1869.

THE DOCTOR Time is in flux, changing, every second. Your comfy little world could be rewritten like that –
(clicks fingers)
Nothing is safe. Remember that. Nothing.

DICKENS Doctor . . . I think the room is getting colder.

The whispering, chattering sound begins to rise.

ROSE Here they come . . .

The gas-light dims, and ectoplasm billows from a gas-mantle, forming a hazy blue GELTH, which bobs in front of them.

GELTH *You have come to help! Praise the Doctor! Praise him . . .*

ROSE Promise you won't hurt her.

GELTH *Hurry! Please! So little time. Pity the Gelth!*

THE DOCTOR I'll take you somewhere else after the transfer. Somewhere you can build proper bodies. This isn't a permanent solution, all right?

Gwyneth steps forward. She's pale, strangely calm.

GWYNETH My angels! I can help them live.

THE DOCTOR Okay, where's the weak point?

GELTH *Here! Beneath the arch!*

GWYNETH Beneath the arch . . .

She walks forward – the Doctor, Rose, Dickens, Sneed, all staring as Gwyneth stands in the arch, faces them, breathes in, stiffens –

ROSE You don't have to do this –

GWYNETH My angels!

BANG! Eye-searing brightness as the connection is made. Light shining behind Gwyneth. The others stagger back. The Gelth swirls around Gwyneth's head, agitated.

GELTH *Establish the bridge! Reach out to the void. Let us through!*

Gwyneth is wide-eyed, staring ahead. The whispering rises.

GWYNETH Yes! I can see you. I can see you! Come!

GELTH *Bridgehead establishing . . .*

GWYNETH Come to me. Come to this world. Poor lost souls . . .

The whispering sound reaches an ecstatic crescendo.

GELTH *It has begun! The bridge is made. She has given herself to the Gelth!*

Ectoplasmic Gelth begin to stream from Gwyneth's mouth. They swim around the room like fish in a tank . . . *hundreds* of them. Never stopping. Pouring out. Gelth after Gelth after Gelth . . .

DICKENS Rather a lot of them, eh?

And suddenly, the central Gelth transforms. The mournful ghost-face morphs into a vicious smile – mocking laughter.

GELTH *The bridge is open. We descend! The Gelth will come through in force.*

DICKENS You said you were few in number!

GELTH *A few billion! And all of us in need of corpses!*

SNEED steps forward, brave, trying to get through to Gwyneth.

SNEED Now Gwyneth, stop this, there's a good girl. Listen to your master! This has gone far enough, now stop dabbling, child, and leave these things alone, I beg of you.

One of the circling Gelth plunges down, under the sheets of a BODY, which immediately sits up!

ROSE Mr Sneed, get back!

Too late – the body grabs Sneed, begins to throttle him.

CUT TO Rose – the Doctor grabs her, pulls her –

THE DOCTOR Don't go near –

CUT TO Sneed, falling down dead. An orbiting Gelth plunges down and into SNEED's mouth.

THE DOCTOR I think it's going a little bit wrong.

SNEED gets to his feet. Dead, but transformed – his mouth moves, but the Gelth speaks:

SNEED/GELTH *I have joined the legions of the Gelth. Come, march with us.*

DICKENS Oh, Glory!

SNEED/GELTH *We need bodies. All of you, dead. The human race, dead, fit only to become our vessels. The Gelth shall march in victory!*

Gelth stream under the sheets, into all the dead BODIES. Sheets are flung back. The DEAD are on the move, BODIES sitting up, standing . . .

THE DOCTOR Gwyneth! Stop them! Send them back!

But Gwyneth's face is wreathed in a vicious Gelth-face. Again, her mouth moves, but it's the Gelth voice:

GWYNETH/WRAITH *Three more bodies! Convert them! Make them vessels for the Gelth!*

Dickens is at the door, desperate.

DICKENS I'm sorry, Doctor! But I can't! I'm too old, your new world is too much for me – I'm so sorry –

Dickens runs away, gone. Gelth stream out after him, in pursuit. The DEAD advance on the Doctor and Rose –

THE DOCTOR Into the sluice!

They run back, slam the iron gates shut, clang! Trapped!

41 INT. SNEED AND COMPANY, HALLWAY NIGHT

DICKENS runs up to the front door, flings it open, dashes out and slams it behind him –

42 EXT. SNEED AND COMPANY, STREET NIGHT

DICKENS stops, heaving for breath, pressing his back against the door. But then he turns his head, horrified –

A GELTH is squeezing through the door. Its mournful alien face hovers over the lion's head knocker, wailing.

Dickens yells and runs off.

43 INT. SNEED AND COMPANY, MORGUE NIGHT

GWYNETH stands with arms wide, utterly possessed. GELTH continue to pour from her mouth. THE DOCTOR and ROSE are trapped in the sluice, the DEAD massing at the gates, rattling them, reaching their arms through the bars, hands outstretched. SNEED leads them:

SNEED/GELTH *Give yourself to glory! Sacrifice your lives to the Gelth.*

THE DOCTOR I trusted you. I pitied you!

SNEED/GELTH *We don't want your pity! We want this world and all its flesh.*

THE DOCTOR Not while I'm alive.

SNEED/GELTH *Then live no more!*

And the dead attack with renewed vigour. The gate is beginning to give, the bolts in the wall flaking . . .

44. EXT. STREET NIGHT

DICKENS is still running. The GELTH rockets overhead –

GELTH *Failing ...! Atmosphere unsuitable ...!*

And it streaks into the gas-lamp, whoosh, gone. Dickens goes to hobble off, guilty, ashamed ... but then he stops. Looks back. At the gas-lamp.

DICKENS Gas ...
(an idea)
The gas!

Inspired! He runs back towards the house.

45 INT. SNEED AND COMPANY, MORGUE NIGHT

The DEAD clamour at the sluice-gates. THE DOCTOR and ROSE shrink back against the far wall. Quiet, scared, close:

ROSE But I can't die. Doctor, I can't, tell me I can't. I haven't been born yet, it's impossible for me to die. Isn't it?

THE DOCTOR I'm sorry.

ROSE But it's 1869, how can I die now?

THE DOCTOR Time's not a straight line, it can twist into any shape it likes. You can be born in the twentieth century and die in the nineteenth. All because of me. I brought you here.

ROSE Not your fault. I wanted to come.

THE DOCTOR And what about me? I saw the fall of Troy. World War Five. I was pushing boxes at the Boston Tea Party. Now I'm gonna die in a cellar, in Cardiff!

ROSE And it's not just dying. We become one of them.

They shrink back further, as one of the dead leers forward.

ROSE We'll go down fighting, yeah?

THE DOCTOR You bet.

ROSE Together.

THE DOCTOR Yeah.

He takes her hand.

THE DOCTOR I'm glad I met you.

ROSE Me too.

And in the middle of this nightmare, they've still got a brave smile for each other.

46 INT. SNEED AND COMPANY, HALLWAY NIGHT

DICKENS races into the house and turns on the nearest gas-tap – but doesn't light it. He rushes to the next – turns it on, rushes to the next , turns it on, rushes on –

47 INT. SNEED AND COMPANY, MORGUE NIGHT

DICKENS bursts in, pressing a handkerchief to his face –

DICKENS Doctor! The gas! Turn on the gas! All of it, now!

He races to a gas-mantle and twists the tap. Gas hisses out. All the DEAD are massed by the sluice-gate, but two of them turn, to see Dickens –

THE DOCTOR What are you doing?

Dickens runs to a second tap, then a third. More hissing.

DICKENS I might be an old fool but I understand basic science, sir! Turn on quickly, turn on the gas! Flood the place!

THE DOCTOR Brilliant! Gas!

THE DOCTOR turns on one sluice gas-tap, ROSE another.

ROSE What, so we choke to death instead?

Dickens runs to a fourth tap, a fifth –

DICKENS Am I correct, Doctor? They're gaseous creatures –

THE DOCTOR Fill the air with gas – it'll draw them out of the host, suck them into the air, like poison from a wound –

DICKENS I hope – Oh lor – !

Because REDPATH and MRS PEACE walk in, heading for him. At the same time, three bodies from the sluice-gate lumber in his direction. Dickens is trapped against the wall.

DICKENS I rather hope this theory will be validated soon. If not immediately.

CUT TO the Doctor, ripping the gas-pipe off the wall –

THE DOCTOR Plenty more –

Redpath and Mrs Peace lurching up to Dickens, reaching out, when Redpath falters. Stumbles. Tips his head back: the ectoplasmic GELTH is pulled out of him.

GELTH *Noooo* …

Then the Gelth is pulled from Mrs Peace and the three advancing dead – the human bodies collapse.

DICKENS It's working!

The dead at the sluice-gate – including SNEED – turn, as though lost, and arch their heads back. Gelth stream up to the roof, out of their mouths, gone.

CUT TO the Doctor and Rose – Rose coughing – pulling open the sluice-gate, stepping out. They look up. LOW ANGLE, the Doctor and Rose: the entire ceiling is a writhing sea of thousands of Gelth. All of this, with the banshee wail and the hiss of the gas, louder and louder …

THE DOCTOR Gwyneth! Send them back! They lied, they're not angels!

And the smoky blue Gelth-mask lifts from Gwyneth's face, though she remains in position. Her own voice comes through:

GWYNETH ... Liars ...?

THE DOCTOR Look at them! If your mother and father could look down and see this, they'd tell you the same. They'd give you strength. Now send them back!

ROSE Can't breathe –

THE DOCTOR Charles, get her out.

ROSE Not leaving her –

GWYNETH They're too strong ...

THE DOCTOR Remember that world you saw? Rose's world? All those people. None of it will exist, if you don't send them back through the rift!

GWYNETH Can't ... send them back.
(stronger)
But I can hold them. Hold them in place. Hold them here ...

Still staring ahead, she reaches into her apron and takes out the box of matches.

GWYNETH Get out.

ROSE You can't!

GWYNETH Leave this place.

Rose goes to run forward, but the Doctor grabs her. Fierce, intense, right at her:

THE DOCTOR Rose, get out, go now. I won't leave her while she's still in danger, okay? Now go!

And terrified, coughing, Rose runs, with Dickens, out. The Doctor looks up – the Gelth swarm around the roof, screaming. The Doctor runs forward, to Gwyneth.

THE DOCTOR Come on. Leave that to me –

But Gwyneth just stares ahead. The Doctor's puzzled. He feels Gwyneth's neck. She doesn't react, keeps staring. The Doctor's lost, disturbed. Then, very quiet:

THE DOCTOR I'm sorry.
(kisses her forehead)
Thank you.

Then he runs –

48 INT. SNEED AND COMPANY, HALLWAY NIGHT

ROSE and DICKENS, coughing, run out – gas hissing –

49 INT. SNEED AND COMPANY, MORGUE NIGHT

GWYNETH stares ahead: eyes shining. GELTH swoop down, to swarm all around her, screaming their rage, but she smiles – holds the match against the box ...

50 INT. SNEED AND COMPANY, HALLWAY NIGHT

THE DOCTOR runs – gas hissing –

51 INT. SNEED AND COMPANY, MORGUE NIGHT

And GWYNETH is blissful as the match sparks –

52 EXT. SNEED AND COMPANY NIGHT

THE DOCTOR hurtles through the front door – the house ignites –

53 FX SHOT, SNEED'S HOUSE NIGHT 4

Sneed and Company *whoomphs* with flame, and explodes!

54 EXT. SNEED AND COMPANY, STREET NIGHT

And then silence. The ash fluttering down. A haze of rubble and flame foreground.

On THE DOCTOR, getting up from the snow, as DICKENS and ROSE run up.

ROSE She didn't make it . . .

THE DOCTOR I'm sorry. She closed the rift.

DICKENS At such a cost. The poor child.

THE DOCTOR I did try, Rose, but ... she was already dead. I examined her. Gwyneth had been dead for at least five minutes.

ROSE (spooked)
What d'you mean?

THE DOCTOR I think she was dead from the moment she stood in the arch.

ROSE But ... she can't have been, she spoke to us, she helped us, she saved us. How could she have done that ...?

Beat.

DICKENS 'There are more things in Heaven and Earth than are dreamt of in your philosophy.' Even for you, Doctor.

ROSE She saved the world. A servant girl. And no one will ever know.

And the three of them stand there, solemn, lit by the fire, in the snow, in the night.

55 EXT. ALLEYWAY NIGHT

THE DOCTOR and ROSE stand outside the TARDIS, with DICKENS.

THE DOCTOR If you don't mind, Charlie boy, I've just got to pop into my, um ... shed. Won't be long.

ROSE (to Dickens)
What are you going to do now?

DICKENS I shall take the mail-coach back to London, quite literally post-haste; it's the wrong time of year to be on my own. I shall spend Christmas with my family, and try to make amends. After all I've seen tonight, there's nothing more vital.

THE DOCTOR You've cheered up.

DICKENS Exceedingly! This morning, I thought I knew everything in the world. Now I know I've barely started. And what an appetite I have, Doctor! All these huge, wonderful notions! I am inspired, I must write about them!

ROSE D'you think that's wise?

DICKENS Oh, I shall be subtle, at first. *The Mystery of Edwin Drood* still lacks an ending. Perhaps the killer was not the boy's uncle, perhaps he was not of this earth! *The Mystery of Edwin Drood and the Blue Elementals*! I can spread the word, and tell the truth!

THE DOCTOR Good luck with it.
(shakes hands)
Nice to meet you, fantastic!

ROSE Bye then. And thanks.

To Dickens's surprise, she gives him a kiss on the cheek.

DICKENS Oh my dear! How modern. Thank you. But I don't understand, in what way is this goodbye, where are you going?

THE DOCTOR Into the shed. You'll see.

DICKENS 'Pon my soul, it's one riddle after another with you. But Doctor – in amongst all the revelations, there's one mystery you haven't explained. Answer me this. Who are you?

THE DOCTOR Just a friend. Passing through.

DICKENS You seem to know so much of future times. And I won't intrude, but I have to wonder . . .
(quiet, a bit scared of the answer:)
My books, Doctor. Do they last?

THE DOCTOR Oh yes.

DICKENS For how long?

THE DOCTOR Forever.

And he means it. Dickens smiles.

THE DOCTOR Right then. Shed. Come on, Rose.

DICKENS Both of you, inside that box?

THE DOCTOR Down boy. See ya.

And they head inside.

56 INT. TARDIS NIGHT

THE DOCTOR and ROSE walk across to the console. On the scanner: DICKENS, watching the blue box, puzzled.

ROSE But doesn't that change history, if he writes about blue ghosts?

THE DOCTOR In a week's time, it's 1870. And that's the year he dies. Sorry. He'll never get to tell his story.

ROSE Ohh no. And he was nice.

THE DOCTOR But in your time, he was already dead. We've brought him to life, and he's more alive now than he's ever been. Old Charlie Boy. Let's give him one last surprise . . .

And he eases down a lever . . .

57 EXT. ALLEYWAY NIGHT

DICKENS steps back as the mighty engines ache and wheeze . . . and the TARDIS simply melts away. Dickens stares, amazed, and then delighted. There's a spring in his step, a smile on his face as he turns, walks down the alleyway, out into the world. And in the distance, the Town Hall clock is chiming midnight.

58 EXT. CARDIFF SQUARE NIGHT

DICKENS approaches the square. Appreciating the world around him, and every person in it. As he walks, a PASSER-BY calls out:

PASSER-BY Merry Christmas, sir.

DICKENS God bless us. Every one.

Aliens of London and World War Three

By Russell T Davies

Again, this two-parter was designed to be big. Bear in mind, we had no idea that anyone would be watching this series; we feared a small, niche audience; I certainly felt the shadow of a disaster ahead of us. I've been there before!

So this, four weeks into the run, was written to kick up the dust, to get people talking, to cause a bit of fuss. And if Big Ben and 10 Downing Street get destroyed in the process, well, there we go. That's telly.

I've seen reviews that call this a satire, but it's hardly that. I don't think a few broad pot-shots at the British (and American) governments constitute true satire. It's more like *Spitting Image*.

I was having trouble with Downing Street, at first. It seemed dull. Men in suits, sweating in a crisis. All briefcases and shiny shoes. Then our producer, Phil Collinson, came to the rescue. We were driving through Manchester, talking about Penelope Wilton. I'd worked with her on *Bob & Rose* for ITV1, had loved her and worshipped her, and had always stayed in touch. Phil had been listening to an audio version of her performance in Alan Bennett's *Talking Heads*, and then said, in a heartfelt voice, 'Can't you put her in *Doctor Who?*' And suddenly, there in the car, Downing Street fell into place. An MP you could *like*. A character who would give that environment heart and passion and integrity, and a good few laughs too. It is, I think, the only guest role in this series created for a specific actor.

Episode 4 saw the words Bad Wolf appear for the first time. I just made it up on a whim, cos I liked the idea of the TARDIS being graffiti'd. But then I spent the rest of the episode idly wondering who that kid was, why he wrote those odd words. And, having dismissed notions of Evil Super Villain Kid, a plan began to form, in mid-production. Knowing that Rose would become the Time Goddess at the end of the series, I wondered if a Goddess would imprint herself on the universe, creating things in her image, like the face of Jesus in a bagel. Better still, these signs would actually summon her into existence. That's the sort of stuff you think about in this job, late at night. And then I worked backwards, inserting Bad Wolf references into almost every script. Funnily enough, I never told anyone what I was doing, in case it didn't work, but the design department picked up on it – they didn't even ask what it meant, they just offered to stencil it on Captain Jack's bomb, in German. The idea spread without anyone knowing what it meant. Which is very Bad Wolf in itself.

From wolves to pigs. The poor little Space Pig wasn't in the first draft. Instead, the Doctor argued with Rose and worried about the timelines, or something. Dull, said my script edit session. So I proposed the pig. On the spot. Described it to the room. Julie looked pale and grim: 'I don't like the pig.' It's nasty, having an idea die in your mouth. I said, 'Let me write it.' So I did, and on the page, it came to life and earnt its existence. Which just goes to show, writers aren't there to talk, but to write. Greatest Writing Lesson Ever: stop bloody yapping and get on with it.

Russell T Davies

1 EXT. TYLERS' ESTATE DAY 5 0900

A quiet corner of the estate. The grind of ancient engines; dust stirs, papers scatter, and the TARDIS fades into view. ROSE comes out, walks round, so she can see the whole estate. The same as ever.

Rose takes it all in, as THE DOCTOR joins her.

ROSE How long have I been gone?

THE DOCTOR 'Bout twelve hours.

She laughs, gobsmacked. Then, deep breath, things to do:

ROSE I won't be long. I just want to see my mum.

THE DOCTOR What you gonna tell her?

ROSE I dunno. That I've been to the year five billion, I've met Charles Dickens, and I've only been gone twelve hours.
(pause)
No, I'll tell her I spent the night at Shareen's. See you later.

She walks off, but then turns back.

ROSE And don't you disappear.

A smile between them, and Rose heads off.

2 EXT. STAIRWELL DAY 5 0902

ROSE heads up steps, excited.

3 EXT. ROSE'S ESTATE DAY 5 0902

THE DOCTOR mooches about. Out of place. Kicks a stone. Then he sees something, squints.

CUT TO foreground, a lamppost. A sheet of tatty A4 cardboard is wired to the post, its back to camera, the front – a poster – OOV, facing the Doctor. He walks closer, puzzled.

4 INT. STAIRWELL #2 DAY 5 0903

ROSE hurries up, thinking of her mum, smiling . . .

5 INT. ROSE'S ESTATE DAY 5 0903

THE DOCTOR studies the poster. Realises. Oh my God –

And he runs – !

6 INT. TYLERS' FLAT DAY 5 0904

ROSE, key in hand, saunters in, calls out:

ROSE I'm back! I was with Shareen, she got all upset again, are you in?

Rose walks through, into the living room. JACKIE is standing in the kitchen doorway, in her dressing gown. Staring at her, like she's something strange and terrible.

ROSE So what did I miss? How've you been?

Jackie's still just staring.

ROSE What's that face for? It's not the first time I've stayed out all night.

Jackie's cup of coffee just slides from her hand. Smashes on the floor. Which Jackie doesn't even acknowledge, still staring. Very quiet:

JACKIE . . . It's you.

ROSE 'Course it's me.

JACKIE (starts to cry)
Oh my God, it's you. Oh my God.

Jackie runs to Rose, clings to her, crying, and Rose looks around. On the table, stacks of 5000 leaflets – photocopied white A4 – with Rose's face. And the word MISSING. On top of every stack, her face, MISSING, MISSING, MISSING.

The front door clatters, THE DOCTOR bursts into the living room doorway, slams to a halt.

THE DOCTOR It's not twelve hours, it's twelve *months*. You've been gone a whole year.
(big smile)
Sorry!

7 EXT. ROSE'S ESTATE DAY 5 0930

CU white spray paint, streaking across blue wood. CUT TO WIDER: TARDIS foreground, flats b/g, a 10-year-old SKINHEAD KID spraying graffiti on the TARDIS, big letters, *BAD WOLF*. Over this, a distant voice:

JACKIE OOV The hours I sat here, days and weeks and months, all on my own – I thought you were dead, and where were you? Travelling!

8 INT. TYLERS' FLAT DAY 5 0931

ROSE sits there, grim; JACKIE walks around, never stopping, blazing temper. A young POLICEMAN sits taking notes, and THE DOCTOR stands in the doorway to the hall. Glances between the Doctor and Rose, both ashamed.

JACKIE What the hell does that mean, travelling, that's no sort of answer –
(to the PC)
– you ask her, she won't tell me, that's all she says, travelling –

ROSE That's what I was doing –

JACKIE With your passport still in the drawer? It's one lie after another!

ROSE I meant to phone, I really did, just ... forgot.

JACKIE For a year? You forgot, for a year, and I'm left sitting here? I just don't believe you, why won't you tell me where you've been?

THE DOCTOR Look, it's my fault, I sort of, employed Rose as my ... companion ...

POLICEMAN When you say companion, is this a sexual relationship?

THE DOCTOR/ROSE No!

Jackie goes right up to the Doctor, every bit his equal:

JACKIE Then what is it? Cos you! You waltz in here, all charm and smiles, next thing I know, she vanishes off the face of the Earth! How old are you then, forty, forty-five? What, did you find her on the internet? Did you go online and pretend you're a doctor?

THE DOCTOR I am a Doctor –

JACKIE Prove it. Stitch this, mate –

Slap! Right across his face.

8A INT. TYLERS' FLAT, KITCHEN DAY 5 1000

ROSE and JACKIE coming out of a hug, tearful. They stay close, quiet, Jackie calm now, but honest – which makes it all the more difficult for Rose.

JACKIE Did you think about me at all?

ROSE I did, all the time, but ...

JACKIE One phone call. Just to know you were alive.

ROSE I'm sorry, I really am.

JACKIE But d'you know what terrifies me? That you still can't say. What happened to you, Rose? What can be so bad that you can't tell me? Sweetheart. Where were you?

But Rose is trapped into silence.

9 EXT. ROOF DAY 5 1400

Overlooking London, in the distance. THE DOCTOR and ROSE have escaped up here: wide open space all around. Quiet, calm, but a bit edgy between them, recriminations:

ROSE I can't tell her. Can't even begin. She's never going to forgive me. (pause)
And I missed a year. Was it good?

THE DOCTOR Middling.

ROSE You're so useless.

THE DOCTOR If it's this much trouble, are you gonna stay here now?

ROSE I dunno.
(pause)
I can't do that to her again.

THE DOCTOR Well she's not coming with us.

Which breaks the tension. Laughing, more like old friends:

ROSE No chance!

THE DOCTOR I don't do families.

ROSE She slapped you!

THE DOCTOR Nine hundred years of time and space, and I've never been slapped by someone's mother.

ROSE Your face.

THE DOCTOR It hurt!

ROSE You're so gay.
(pause)
When you say nine hundred years ...

THE DOCTOR That's my age.

ROSE You're nine hundred years old.

THE DOCTOR Yeah.

Serious again, another massive concept for Rose to accept.

ROSE . . . Okay. My mother was right, that's a hell of an age gap.

She walks a few feet away, towards the view. Above her, the huge expanse of plain British sky.

ROSE Every conversation with you just goes mental. But there's no one else I can talk to! I've seen all that stuff, up there, the size of it . . . And I can't say a word. Aliens and spaceships and things, I'm the only person on planet Earth who knows they exist.

And a GREAT BIG SPACESHIP roars overhead! It's the size of a channel ferry, flying low, only a few hundred feet off the ground. A circular, chunky ship, with fins, lights and small portholes, a battered bronze.

Massive noise – in its wake, the rooftop shakes; the Doctor and Rose thrown to the ground. As the ship clears – flying along the horizontal, heading for London – dirty smoke is belching from the rear –

10 EXT. LONDON/FX SHOTS DAY 5 1402

The SPACESHIP roars over London – flames now belching out of the rear, the craft tilting ominously, the engine noise stuttering and failing – something's seriously wrong –

CUT TO the shadow of the ship, passing over London streets –

CUT TO the ship, curving round . . .

CUT TO an explosion at the back of the ship, the engines falling to pieces –

CUT TO BLACK CABS screeching to a halt, a LONDON BUS braking –

CUT TO HIGH SHOT, PEOPLE looking up, horrified –

CUT TO the ship, turning and heading down . . . and it clips the top off Big Ben! A cloud of rubble cascades in all directions as the ship plunges down –

CUT TO the ship smashing into the Thames –

CUT TO PEOPLE, running up to the Embankment to see –

CUT TO the ship, half-submerged, with the Houses of Parliament in the background. It rolls, slowly, onto its side, at a 45-degree angle. The engines belch a final gout of flame and smoke from underneath, and the water churns, hissing. Like the death throes of a dying beast. And finally, it's still.

11 EXT. ROOF DAY 5 1403

ROSE stands up.

ROSE . . . Oh that's just not *fair*.

Her POV: smoke rising from the far-off river, alarms beginning to sound. The city transformed. THE DOCTOR's laughing. Like this is so brilliant! Then he grabs her hand, and off they run –

12 OMITTED

12A EXT. STREET DAY 5 1410

Foreground: a blur of cars, irate DRIVERS getting out, banging on roofs, the beeping of horns. Focus on background, THE DOCTOR and ROSE running to a halt. (And b/g behind them, far off, PEOPLE run to and fro, panic in the air.) Both looking forward, facing the traffic throughout:

THE DOCTOR It's blocked off!

ROSE We're miles from the centre, the city must be gridlocked. The whole of London must be closing down –

THE DOCTOR I know! I can't believe I'm here to see it, this is fantastic!

ROSE Did you know it was gonna happen?

THE DOCTOR Nope!

ROSE D'you recognise the ship?

THE DOCTOR Nope!

ROSE D'you know why it crashed?

THE DOCTOR Nope!

ROSE I'm so glad I've got you.

THE DOCTOR I bet you are! This is what I travel for, Rose: to see history, happening right in front of us!

ROSE Let's go and see it then – never mind traffic, we've got the TARDIS.

THE DOCTOR Umm. Better not. There's already one spaceship in the middle of London, I don't want to shove another one on top.

ROSE Yeah, but yours looks like a big blue box, no one's gonna notice.

THE DOCTOR Oh, you'd be surprised. Emergency like this, there'll be all sorts of people watching. Trust me – the TARDIS stays where it is.

ROSE So, history is happening, and we're stuck here.

THE DOCTOR Yes we are.

Pause.

ROSE We could always do what everyone else does. We could watch it on TV.

And the picture blinks, fizzes: full-frame white noise –

13 EXT. EMBANKMENT DAY 5 1530

TV FOOTAGE, horizontal lines visible. Branded with logos and graphics, scrolling headlines bottom of screen, '*Emergency meeting of the United*

Nations', etc. A hand-held FX SHOT of the broken Big Ben in the distance, – whipping down to REPORTER #1 – young, trying to keep calm – to CAMERA, as though he's being jostled by a crowd.

REPORTER #1 Police are urging the public not to panic – there's a helpline number on screen right now, if you're worried about friends or family –

13A INT. STUDIO

There will be approximately one minute of newsreader footage here, INTERCUT with the rest. Preferably more than one newsreader – the more we can intercut, the better. It needs a worldwide feel. We can also punctuate the news itself better – using already-shot stuff, and new material, we can really emphasise the shock news of the discovery of a BODY. It's a newsflash within the newsflash! (But for now, news script runs as was:)

13B INT. STUDIO DAY 5 1030

AMERICAN REPORTER, against *News* b/g, to CAMERA:

AMERICAN REPORTER The military are on the lookout for more spaceships – until then, all flights in North American airspace have been grounded. The President will address the nation live from the White House, but the Secretary General has asked that people watch the skies –

13C EXT. EMBANKMENT DAY 5 1530

REPORTER #1 to CAMERA:

REPORTER #1 The army is sending divers into the wreck of the spaceship, no one knows what they're going to find –

14 INT. TYLERS' FLAT DAY 5 1630

THE DOCTOR trying to watch TV, JACKIE handing ROSE a coffee. In b/g, an OLD WOMAN, 70, Chinese, is having a beer. [Speeches run simultaneously.]

JACKIE I've got no choice! Either I make him welcome –

ROSE Ohh don't go on –

JACKIE – or I run the risk of never seeing you again!

OLD WOMAN You broke your mother's heart. She sobbed in my arms, she did. I cradled her like a child.

Stuck in the middle of this:

THE DOCTOR Oy! I'm trying to listen!

15 EXT. EMBANKMENT DAY 5 1700

TV FOOTAGE: REPORTER #1 and crew are now being manhandled back from the river's edge by POLICE. The camera's trying to grab shots. REPORTER #1 keeps going –

REPORTER #1 They've found a body – it's unconfirmed, but I'm being told that a body has been found in the wreckage, a body of non-terrestrial origins, it's being brought ashore –

CAMERA whips across – on the shore, a good distance away – tarpaulin tents, POLICE and SOLDIERS and DIVERS, and bulky objects wrapped in white cotton being hauled out of sight . . .

16 INT. TYLERS' FLAT DAY 5 1705

With each new scene, the Tylers' is busier, noisier: now with ROSE, JACKIE, OLD WOMAN and her OLD MAN husband (Chinese, 70) hugging Rose, a GOTH and a BEARDED MAN. THE DOCTOR increasingly sidelined.

OLD WOMAN You broke his heart, disappearing, where's my Rose, he used to say.

OLD MAN You beautiful girl!

JACKIE And I've lost weight, I told her, go missing more often, it does me good. Guess who asked me out? Billy Croot!

The Doctor's being driven mad, leaning forward, trying to listen to the telly.

17 EXT. ALBION HOSPITAL DAY 5 1706

A sign saying ALBION HOSPITAL – police cars, barriers being erected, POLICE and SOLDIERS, etc. REPORTER #1 to CAMERA:

REPORTER #1 We don't know if it's alive or dead, Whitehall is denying everything – but the body has been brought here, Albion Hospital – with the roads closed off, it's the closest to the river –

18 INT. BLUE PETER STUDIO DAY 5 1710

MATT BAKER, to CAMERA, making little cakes.

MATT BAKER . . . and if you stick on the fins with buttercream, that's your very own spaceship, ready to eat. And look, I've put some jelly babies on top, as little aliens.

19 INT. TYLERS' FLAT DAY 5 1710

(B/G: ROSE, JACKIE, OLD WOMAN, OLD MAN, GOTH, BEARDED MAN, a MIDDLE-AGED COUPLE and THREE KIDS now piled in, all talking at once – bedlam – passing pizza and beer to and fro.) THE DOCTOR's trying to watch TV with a TODDLER on his knee. The toddler's got the remote (hence the *Blue Peter*), the Doctor wrestles it off him, peeved; clicks at the TV:

20 EXT. ALBION HOSPITAL DAY 5 1715

REPORTER #1 to CAMERA, then CAM whips across to glimpse GENERAL ASQUITH – a large man, 55, in uniform – keeping his head down, SOLDIERS hurrying him into the hospital.

REPORTER #1 – I'm being told, that's General Asquith, now entering the hospital. The building's been evacuated, patients have been moved out on the streets, the police still won't confirm the presence of an alien body, contained inside those walls –

21 INT. HOSPITAL CORRIDOR DAY 5 1720

Not a ward area, more like the research labs. A long, echoing corridor – shiny floor. Dark, windowless, creepy. SOLDIERS stationed at doorways, on the alert. GENERAL ASQUITH, flanked by SOLDIERS, marches along.

22 INT. MORTUARY DAY 5 1722

GENERAL ASQUITH and SOLDIERS enter. The mortuary's huge, deep, receding away into alcoves and shadows. DR SATO is waiting – she's the pathologist, Japanese, white coat.

GENERAL ASQUITH Let's have a look, then.

Soldiers stay back, Dr Sato leads the General across. CUT TO LOW ANGLE: Dr Sato and the General looking down, on a shape in extreme foreground. Sato pulls the white sheet back. The General disturbed, quiet:

GENERAL ASQUITH ... Good God. And that's ... real, it's not a dummy, or a hoax, or ...?

DR SATO I've x-rayed the skull. It's wired up inside, like nothing I've ever seen. No one could make this up.

GENERAL ASQUITH We've got experts being flown in. Until they arrive ...
(disgusted)
Get that out of sight.

23 INT. HOSPITAL MORTUARY/CORRIDOR DAY 5 1725

Wham! – the steel drawer of a mortuary shelf slides shut, sealing the alien body inside.

GENERAL ASQUITH Thank you.

He turns, goes, walks down the corridor with his SOLDIERS. But DR SATO hurries after him, nervous, but daring to ask:

DR SATO Excuse me, sir. I know it's a state of emergency, and there's a lot of rumour flying around, but ... is it true what they're saying? About the Prime Minister?

The GENERAL stares at her, alarmed. Almost wanting to tell the truth. But the stiff upper lip wins out; he just turns, walks away – the echo of footsteps down the corridor.

24 EXT. DOWNING STREET DAY 5 1730

TV FOOTAGE: a crush of JOURNALISTS, yelling at BLACK CARS pulling up at 10 Downing Street. REPORTER #2 to CAMERA:

REPORTER #2 Mystery surrounds the whereabouts of the Prime Minister, he's not been seen since the emergency began, the opposition is criticising his lack of leadership – oh – hold on –

CAMERA swings round, to grab shots of: JOSEPH 'JOE' GREEN. He steps out of a black car, PRESS yelling, cameras flashing. He's 50, a big bloke in a too-small suit, sweating profusely. He looks out of his depth.

REPORTER #2 OOV No, sorry, that's Joseph Green, MP for Hartley Dale, Chairman of the Parliamentary Commission for Monitoring of Sugar Levels in Exported Confectionery – with respect, hardly the most important man right now –

Joe Green looks back, a scared smile, and as he goes inside –

25 INT. 10 DOWNING STREET RECEPTION DAY 5 1731

Slam! Cutting out of TV footage, back to the real world, as the door shuts out the clamour outside. JOE GREEN pauses, mops his forehead, then launches forward. He hurries through MEN and WOMEN IN SUITS, all running to and fro. INDRA GANESH – late 20s, smart, carrying a red parliamentary briefcase – joins Joe, hurries with him, towards the stairs, fast, muttering:

INDRA Indra Ganesh, sir, Junior Secretary with the MOD, I'll be your liaison –

JOE Where the hell is he?

INDRA If we could talk in private, sir –

A woman tries to follow Joe and Indra – HARRIET JONES, mid-50s, elegant, prim, polite, a lifelong backbencher.

HARRIET Excuse me, um – Harriet Jones, MP for Flydale North –

INDRA I'm sorry, can't it wait?

HARRIET I did have an appointment, at three fifteen –

INDRA Yes, and then a spaceship crashed in the middle of London . . . I think the schedule might have changed!

And Indra hurries Joe upstairs. Harriet's left below, dismayed.

26 INT. DOWNING STREET UPSTAIRS CORRIDOR DAY 5 1735

JOE and INDRA pause for a secret, frantic conversation:

JOE But where is he? Where's the Prime Minister?

INDRA No one knows, sir, he's disappeared. And I have to inform you, that with the city gridlocked and the Cabinet stranded outside London . . . this makes you Acting Prime Minister. With immediate effect.

JOE Oh my Lord! Oh, hold on –

He huffs, holds his stomach and ... burps. A good belch.

JOE Sorry. Nervous stomach. Anyway!

Joe and Indra hurry on, Joe in a sweat.

27 INT. CABINET ROOM CORRIDOR DAY 5 1737

JOE and INDRA hurry down the corridor (an L-shaped corridor – the length now being taken by Joe and Indra – leads to the double doors of the Cabinet Room; the second length then right-angling back into the depths of the building). MARGARET BLAINE and OLIVER CHARLES are waiting, anxious. Margaret's 50, plump, posh, awkward in a badly fitting suit; Oliver's 35, a hulking brute of a man with a distinctive shock of blonde hair.

INDRA Margaret Blaine, she's with MI5.

MARGARET There's no more information, sir, I personally escorted the Prime Minister from the Cabinet Room to his car – this is Oliver Charles, Transport Liaison –

OLIVER The car's disappeared, no record of it, sir, it literally vanished.

JOE Right, inside, tell me everything.

As Margaret and Oliver head into the Cabinet Room, Indra holds out the red briefcase, to Joe, with great solemnity:

INDRA Sir. The Emergency Protocols. Detailing the action to be taken by the government of Great Britain in the event of an alien incursion.

JOE Oh right. Oh good. Oh blimey –

He grimaces. Clenches. And then farts. Indra just blinks politely.

JOE Pardon me. Now get to work!

Joe goes into the office – SLAM!

28 INT. CABINET ROOM DAY 5 CONTINUOUS

Traditional long table and chairs. MARGARET and OLIVER at the far end of the room, waiting, as JOE walks in. He holds up the important red briefcase ... then he just chucks it onto the table, irrelevant. He looks at Margaret and Oliver and smiles. Margaret and Oliver are smiling, dying to laugh. Three big people, three old friends, enjoying their terrible secret.

29 EXT. TYLERS' FLAT NIGHT 5 2230

THE DOCTOR comes out of the flat, heads off, but then:

ROSE And where d'you think you're going?

THE DOCTOR (guilty, caught)
Nowhere. It's just a bit ... human in there. History just happened, and they're talking about buying dodgy top-up cards for half price. I'm off on a wander, that's all.

ROSE Right, there's a spaceship in the Thames, and you're just wandering?

THE DOCTOR Nothing to do with me! It's not an invasion, that was a genuine crash-landing. Angle of descent, colour of the smoke, everything, it was perfect.

ROSE So?

THE DOCTOR So maybe this is it. First contact. The day mankind officially comes into contact with an alien race. I'm not interfering, cos you've got to handle this on your own. That's when the Human Race grows up. Just this morning, you were all tiny and small and made of clay, and now – you can expand!
(pause)
You don't need me, go and celebrate history. Spend some time with your mum.

ROSE Promise you won't disappear.

THE DOCTOR Tell you what. TARDIS key, about time you had one. See you later.

And he chucks her a key, heads off. Rose holds it, delighted – the most precious thing he's ever given her.

30 EXT. TYLERS' ESTATE NIGHT 5 2235

The estate is celebrating: home-made banners on sheets, *HELLO E.T.*
In one flat, a noisy party, kids, a blaze of light, music thumpa-thumping out.
THE DOCTOR walks through it all, heading towards the TARDIS – with a bit more energy, almost sneaky, like he's escaped from Rose.

CUT TO a high walkway, a good distance away. MICKEY SMITH, Rose's ex-boyfriend, is walking along, but stops dead. His POV: the Doctor, reaching the TARDIS, going inside.

MICKEY . . . Oh my God.

And Mickey starts to run –

31 INT. TARDIS NIGHT 5 2236

THE DOCTOR walks in, smiling – home again! – and runs to the console, top speed. He's gleeful, pulls the lever – as big and as stiff as a handbrake – which sends the TARDIS into flight. The room lurches, the engines groan and rise.

32 AND 33 OMITTED

34 EXT. TYLERS' ESTATE NIGHT 5 2236

MICKEY belts along, fast, furious –

MICKEY Oy! Doctor! DocTAAH!

The TARDIS groans and fades out of sight – Mickey runs through the empty space, smack, into the wall.

35 INT. TARDIS NIGHT 5 2236

The whole room shuddering, groaning, sailing the high seas. THE DOCTOR holds on, pulls levers. Steam vents from the console. The Doctor opens a drawer, pulls out a hammer, belts the console, frantic, flying this thing like a madman.

36 INT. MORTUARY NIGHT 5 2245

WIDE SHOT, all quiet and cold. DR SATO at a desk, in a small pool of light, working. There's a small *thunk*. Dr Sato looks up. Listens. Nothing. She gets back to work, filling out papers. *Thunk*. A bit louder, now. Metal. DR SATO stands, scared because she knows which direction the noise came from. The mortuary shelves.

37 INT. HOSPITAL STOREROOM NIGHT 5 2245

The TARDIS door opens, THE DOCTOR looks out. A dark, cramped storeroom. Keeping quiet, the Doctor creeps over to the door, gets out the sonic screwdriver, whirrs – it's loud, he shushes it, clicks to a lower setting, whirrs.

38 INT. MORTUARY NIGHT 5 2245

A regular metallic *thunk ... thunk ... thunk*. DR SATO is slowly crossing the mortuary, towards the source of the noise, heart pounding. TRACK IN TO the steel mortuary shelves. The door of the alien's shelf is clunking, *thunk, thunk, thunk*. Something inside is rocking to and fro. Waking up ...

39 INT. HOSPITAL STOREROOM NIGHT 5 2245

THE DOCTOR whirrs, the lock clicks. He tries the handle. It gives. He swings the door open –

40 INT. HOSPITAL ANTEROOM NIGHT 5 2245

– on to a room full of TWENTY SOLDIERS, feet up, having a coffee, smoking.

Freeze. They look at THE DOCTOR, he looks at them. Then all twenty leap to their feet – the click of twenty safety catches – twenty rifles point at the Doctor.

41 INT. MORTUARY NIGHT 5 2245

DR SATO goes up to the shelf, *thunk, thunk, thunk*, then – *SLAM!* The metal door shoots open –

42 INT. HOSPITAL ANTEROOM NIGHT 5 2245

A scream! All whip round, hearing Dr Sato. THE DOCTOR starts running first, then the SOLDIERS –

43 INT. HOSPITAL CORRIDOR NIGHT 5 2246

Icon shot: THE DOCTOR and SOLDIERS run, fast – a team – down the long, dark, shiny corridor.

44 INT. MORTUARY NIGHT 5 2246

THE DOCTOR and SOLDIERS round the corner, halt. The shelf is open, empty. DR SATO is on the floor, dazed, forehead bleeding, scared:

DR SATO It's alive. Oh my God, it's still alive.

The Doctor runs to her, taking charge; to the soldiers:

THE DOCTOR Spread out, tell the perimeter it's a lockdown.
(beat)
Do it!

With such authority that the soldiers jump to it, run –

45 INT. HOSPITAL CORRIDOR NIGHT 5 2246

The SOLDIERS spread out, on red alert. Moving in silence across the long, dark corridor, silhouettes. They kick open a door, shine in torches. Nothing. Another door, kicked in, torches, nothing. A third door . . .

46 INT. MORTUARY NIGHT 5 2247

THE DOCTOR with DR SATO, helping her up, shaken.

DR SATO I swear, it was dead . . .

THE DOCTOR Coma, shock, hibernation, anything; what does it look like?

Crash! Nearby, something metal knocked over; in the deep shadows of the room, both Doctors alert. A whisper:

THE DOCTOR It's still here.

The Doctor runs to the corridor, silently signals to a SOLDIER. The soldier runs, follows the Doctor back inside. The Doctor signals the soldier, go to Sato – look after her. The soldier runs to her. The Doctor gestures, shush, and he listens . . . They all listen – alert. Dr Sato shaking, terrified.

A noise, movement, in the shadows. The Doctor signals to the soldier, keep back. The soldier stays with Dr Sato, but readies his gun. The Doctor edges along the mortuary slabs, all senses alert.

A scrape nearby – the Doctor ducks down. The soldier's sweating, his gun shaking. The Doctor scampers from one slab to another, keeping low. He can hear breathing. The Doctor's on all fours, keeping his head below the top of the slab. He inches along. The breathing is closer. Crouched down, he edges up to the corner of the slab . . . and the alien peeks round the corner!

It's a PIG. A pink, Earth, farmyard pig – but strangely alive, sentient, standing upright, on two legs, in a spacesuit, gold trim around the collar. It's only 3 ft tall, head level with the Doctor. It blinks at him in surprise.

THE DOCTOR Hello.

And the pig squeals! Runs! – a little 3-ft pig in clothes running across the mortuary, scared, squealing, running for its life. The soldier's unnerved, aims –

THE DOCTOR Don't shoot!

The soldier pulls back. The pig flees into the corridor. The Doctor goes to run, stumbles, keeps going –

47 INT. HOSPITAL CORRIDOR NIGHT 5 2248

SOLDIER #2, halfway down the corridor, turns, horrified – the little PIG, trotters flailing in panic, is running towards him, squealing, scared. The soldier panics – fires. CUT TO THE DOCTOR, running up. Incandescent with rage:

THE DOCTOR What did you do that for?! It was scared! *It was scared!*

WIDE SHOT: more SOLDIERS running up, but staying back, the pig just a shape, unmoving, at the Doctor's feet. The Doctor kneels, upset. Touches it. Grieves for it.

48 INT. TYLERS' FLAT NIGHT 5 2250

ROSE, JACKIE, OLD WOMAN and MAN, GOTH, BEARDED MAN, MIDDLE-AGED COUPLE, THREE KIDS and SKINHEAD raising a glass.

JACKIE Here's to the Martians!

ALL The Martians!

The room stops dead. MICKEY's standing in the doorway, glowering. Rose guilty.

ROSE I was gonna come and see you.

OLD WOMAN Someone owes Mickey an apology.

ROSE I'm sorry.

OLD WOMAN No, not you.

Rose thrown, realises it's Jackie who's shame-faced.

JACKIE Well it's not my fault. Be fair, what was I supposed to think?

On Rose: eh?

49 INT. TYLERS' FLAT, KITCHEN NIGHT 5 2255

JUMP CUT TO MICKEY seething, facing ROSE and JACKIE. All kept sotto, away from the living room. Rose mortified.

MICKEY You disappear, who do they turn to? Your boyfriend. Five times I was taken in for questioning, five times! No evidence, cos there couldn't be, could there? And then I get her. Your mother, whispering all round the estate, pointing the finger. Stuff through my letterbox. All cos of you.

ROSE I didn't think I'd be gone so long.

MICKEY (more upset)
And I *waited* for you. Twelve months, waiting for you and the Doctor to come back.

JACKIE Hold on, you knew about the Doctor? Why didn't you tell me?

MICKEY Yeah, why not, Rose? How could I tell her where you went?

JACKIE Tell me now!

MICKEY Might as well, cos you're stuck with us now, the Doctor's gone. I saw him, just now, that box just faded away.

ROSE What d'you mean . . . ?

MICKEY He's left you. Some boyfriend he turned out to be –

Rose horrified, pushes past him, runs out.

50 INT. MORTUARY NIGHT 5 2255

The PIG is laid out on a slab, its torso respectfully covered with a sheet. THE DOCTOR and DR SATO stand over it, SOLDIERS in b/g. The Doctor dark, grim.

DR SATO I just assumed, that's what aliens look like. But you're saying it's an ordinary pig, from Earth?

THE DOCTOR More like a mermaid. Victorian showmen used to draw the crowds by taking the skull of a cat, glueing it to a fish, and calling it a mermaid. Now someone's taken a pig, opened up its brain, stuck bits on. Then they strapped it inside that ship, made it dive-bomb, it must've been terrified. They even invented a uniform. Gold trim. Space cadet. Everything but dignity. They took this animal and they turned it into a joke.

CU Dr Sato, walking round, consulting her charts.

DR SATO So it's a fake, it's pretend, like a mermaid. But the technology augmenting its brain, that's like nothing on Earth. It's alien. Aliens are faking aliens. Why would they do that . . . ?
(looks round)
Doctor?

But he's gone.

51 INT. HOSPITAL CORRIDOR NIGHT 5 2256

DR SATO runs into the corridor – SOLDIERS looking puzzled, like they saw nothing, no one went past.

DR SATO Doctor!

But in the distance, the groan of ancient engines . . .

52 INT. CABINET ROOM CORRIDOR NIGHT 5 2257

Darker, pools of light, a cool night-time feel. INDRA's got a desk and laptop outside the double doors. He's typing away as HARRIET quietly approaches, with a coffee.

HARRIET I bet no one's brought you a coffee.

INDRA Thanks.

HARRIET My pleasure.

INDRA You still can't get in.

HARRIET Damn. You've seen through my cunning plan.

INDRA (smiling)
Sorry, it's just impossible.

HARRIET Not even for two minutes? I don't get many chances to walk these corridors, I'm hardly one of the babes. Just a faithful backbencher. And I know we've had a brave new world land right on our doorstep, and that's wonderful, I think, that's probably wonderful, but nevertheless, ordinary life keeps ticking away, I just need to enter this paper –

JOE, MARGARET and OLIVER stride out of the Cabinet Room.

HARRIET – Oh, Mr Green sir, I know you're busy, but – could you put this on the next Cabinet agenda ...?
(offers papers)

JOE What is it?

HARRIET Cottage hospitals! I've worked out a system whereby cottage hospitals needn't be excluded from Centres of Excellence. You see, my mother's in the Flydale Infirmary – that's my constituency, you wouldn't know it, tiny little place – but it gave me the chance to draw up –

JOE By all the saints, get some perspective, woman, I'm *busy*!

Joe, Margaret and Oliver march off, Indra having to follow. And Harriet's left alone. But still not defeated. A daring thought pops up ... She looks round, summons the nerve, and sneaks into the Cabinet Room ...

53 INT. CABINET ROOM NIGHT 5 CONTINUOUS

HARRIET stands there for a second, delighted. The famous room; she's never been inside before.

Then she hurries – the red briefcase is still on the table, she opens it, gives her papers a quick kiss, puts them in the briefcase, closes it. She's about to go, but ... she can't help it, she opens the briefcase again, lifts up her papers: underneath, the Emergency Protocols. *TOP SECRET*. She can't resist, starts to read.

54 EXT. TYLERS' ESTATE NIGHT 5 2300

ROSE distraught, standing in the empty space where the TARDIS once was. MICKEY watching, JACKIE just lost.

ROSE But he wouldn't just go. He promised me.

MICKEY He's dumped you, Rose, sailed off into space, how does it feel? You're left behind with the rest of us earthlings. Get used to it!

54A EXT. TYLERS' ESTATE NIGHT 5 2302

Closer to the flats. ROSE walking back, disconsolate, with MICKEY. JACKIE's still bemused.

ROSE ... But he would've said.

JACKIE You two chimps, I don't know what you're on about. What's going on, what's this Doctor done now?

MICKEY He's vamoosed!

ROSE He has not! Cos he gave me this –
(the key)
He's not my boyfriend, Mickey, he's better than that. He's much more important. And he would never –

She stops, stares. The key shines, hums. Joyous:

ROSE I said so!

CU Rose, turning to face the empty space, as the sound of ancient engines begins to build – she's so happy. Then CU Rose, turning the opposite way, realising, horrified:

ROSE Mum! Go inside, now! Don't stand there, just go inside, right now, off you go, go! Mum! Go!

Too late. The TARDIS fades into view.

ROSE Ohh blimey.

Mickey vindicated, Jackie puzzled. Looking for the trick.

JACKIE ... How did you do that then?

55 INT. TARDIS NIGHT 5 2302

THE DOCTOR busy at the console, concentrating hard – testing for signals, radar, etc – as ROSE appears at his side. He just keeps working like they've never been apart.

THE DOCTOR All right, so I lied, I went and had a look, but the whole crash-landing's a fake, I thought so, it was just *too* perfect – I mean, hitting Big Ben, come on! So, I thought, let's go and have a look at the pilot –

ROSE My mother's here.

The Doctor swings round. A good distance back, JACKIE: in shock, looking round, breathing fast, holding her mouth as though she might be sick. MICKEY's next to her, glowering at the Doctor.

THE DOCTOR Ohh, just what I need. Don't you dare make this place domestic!

MICKEY You ruined my life, Doctor. They thought she was dead, I was a murder suspect, all because of you.

THE DOCTOR (to Rose)
You see? Domestic!

MICKEY I bet you can't even remember my name!

THE DOCTOR Ricky.

MICKEY Mickey.

THE DOCTOR No, it's Ricky.

MICKEY I think I know my own name!

THE DOCTOR You *think* you know your own name? How stupid are you?

Then Jackie just whimpers. Runs out.

ROSE (to the Doctor)
Don't go away.
(runs past Mickey)
Don't start a fight.

And Rose runs out.

56 EXT. ROSE'S ESTATE NIGHT 5 CONTINUOUS

ROSE runs out, sees JACKIE running away, and follows.

ROSE Mum! It's not like that, he's not –

Rose stops dead. Struggles – gaaah! – torn between two lives, then yells after her mother:

ROSE Hold on, I'll be up in a minute –

And she runs back into the TARDIS.

57 INT. TARDIS NIGHT 5 CONTINUOUS

ROSE runs back in, past MICKEY, to THE DOCTOR at the console.
Like their conversation never stopped:

ROSE But that was a real spaceship?

THE DOCTOR Yep.

ROSE So it's all a pack of lies. What is it then, are they invading?

MICKEY Funny way to invade, putting the whole world on red alert.

He's quietly come to join them at the console. The Doctor and Rose look at
him. Beat, then:

THE DOCTOR Good point. So what's going on?

58 INT. CABINET ROOM NIGHT 5 2305

HARRIET now sitting in the PM's chair, absorbed in the Emergency Protocols.
But then she hears voices:

GENERAL ASQUITH OOV I've got the White House phoning me direct,
because Downing Street won't return their calls, this is outrageous!
We haven't even started the vaccination programme –

Harriet panics, slams the Protocols inside the briefcase, runs to the door –
too late, they're coming. She runs to a second side door – it's locked, voices
getting louder. Harriet looks round, blind panic, opens another door in the
wood-panelled walls. A fair-sized cupboard, lined with law books. She steps
inside, swings the door to, as GENERAL ASQUITH, JOE, MARGARET and
OLIVER enter.

Harriet's trying to swing the door shut, but doesn't dare risk the click, leaving
a small crack to spy through. Her POV: General Asquith goes to one side of
the table, Joe, Margaret and Oliver to the other, so Asquith is facing Harriet
(unable to see her). The politicians are right in front of Harriet, with their
backs to her. INTERCUT between the office, and Harriet's POV of events.

GENERAL ASQUITH The capital's ground to a halt! Furthermore, we can
only assume that the Prime Minister's disappearance is the direct
result of hostile alien action, and what have you been doing?
Nothing!

JOE I'm sorry, but ... I thought I was Prime Minister now.

GENERAL ASQUITH Only by default!

JOE Ohhh, but that's not fair!
(sly smile)
I've been having so much fun.

He starts to giggle. Margaret and Oliver join in.

GENERAL ASQUITH You think this is fun ...?

JOE It's a hoot, this job.

MARGARET Honestly, it's super!

OLIVER Oh, 'scuse me –

Oliver gurgles and farts, the others laugh. Asquith's no fool, already unnerved, as is Harriet, in hiding.

GENERAL ASQUITH What's going on here? Where's the rest of the Cabinet, why haven't they been airlifted in?

JOE I cancelled it, they'd only get in the way – oops, here I go –

Clutches his stomach, a weird, strangled gurgle.

MARGARET Ohh, and me! I'm shaking my booty –

She jiggles her bum, then lets rip a big fart. Asquith stands, disturbed, like the world's gone insane.

GENERAL ASQUITH Sir. Under Section Five of the Emergency Protocols, it's my duty to relieve you of command. By God, I'll put this country under martial law if I have to –

JOE Ooooh I'm scared! That's hair-raising, I mean literally, look –

Joe reaches up. Grabs his hair. Yanks it back, which pops open a fold running horizontally along the top of his forehead, and inside the fold, embedded in the skin – a zip. And Joe smiles, zips it across. A harsh, flickering blue light activates, like an electrical discharge, all around Joe Green. It's like it draws light away from the rest of the room, the whole office darkening.

On General Asquith. Absolute terror.

The zip goes all the way round, leaving only a hinge, and the top of Joe's head flaps off, like it's made of thin rubber. Joe's face sags, just a mask, and something solid, wet, organic and green begins to struggle out of his open head.

Margaret lifts her hair. Grinning. A zip. She unzips it. Oliver does the same. On Harriet. Terrified. Unable to look away. And now, stay on her restricted POV: the room dark, flickering. The politicians, silhouetted foreground, seem to grow taller. A violent farting noise, compressed air escaping, something huge forcing its way into the world. Harriet can see Asquith. His fear. He's looking up, as a shape rises up, looms over him – all the time, the flickering, the gurgling, and laughter. Terrible, childish laughter. Asquith goes to scream, but is silenced, as something huge and vicious lashes out.

58A INT. TARDIS NIGHT 5 2305

THE DOCTOR is underneath the flooring at the base of the console, clutching big handfuls of wiring, rooting about. MICKEY squats down, to ask:

MICKEY So what are you doing down there?

THE DOCTOR Ricky –

MICKEY Mickey –

THE DOCTOR Ricky, if I told you what I was doing to the controls of my frankly magnificent timeship, would you even begin to understand?

MICKEY Suppose not.

THE DOCTOR Well shut up then.

And the Doctor disappears underneath, busy. Mickey stands, saunters over to ROSE.

MICKEY Nice friend you've got.

ROSE He's winding you up.

Awkward pause. Then quiet, with their old intimacy:

ROSE I am sorry.

MICKEY … Okay.

ROSE I am, though.

MICKEY Every day, I looked. On every street corner, wherever I went. Looking for a blue box. For a whole year.

ROSE It's only been a few days for me. I dunno, it's hard to tell inside this thing, but I swear, it's just a few days since I left you.

MICKEY Not long enough to miss me, then.

ROSE I did miss you.

Pause. Quiet:

MICKEY I missed you.

ROSE Sorry.

MICKEY Yeah.

ROSE So, in twelve months … have you been seeing anyone else?

MICKEY Nope.

ROSE (big smile)
Okay.

MICKEY Mainly cos everyone thinks I murdered you.

ROSE (smile drops)
Right.

Pause.

MICKEY Now you've come back ... are you gonna stay?

THE DOCTOR Got it!

He's clambering back out. The moment broken, Rose heads over, helps to haul him out. Mickey stays on the opposite side of the console, watching them: a good team.

THE DOCTOR Patched in the radar! Looped it back twelve hours, so it's tracked the flight of that spaceship, here we go, hold on –
(bangs scanner)
Come on!

A graphic: the Earth centre, with a line tracing the path of the spaceship, heading from space towards the UK.

THE DOCTOR That's the spaceship, on its way to Earth, see? Except! Hold on –

Presses buttons – the path loops round the Earth in a slingshot.

THE DOCTOR See? The ship did a slingshot, round the Earth, before landing.

ROSE What does that mean?

THE DOCTOR Means it came from Earth in the first place. Went up, came back down. Whoever these aliens are, they haven't just arrived, they've been here for a while. Question is, what have they been doing ...?

59 INT. JACKIE'S BEDROOM NIGHT 5 2308

The noise of all her guests OOV, laughing, singing, arguing. But JACKIE's dazed, lost, sits on her bed. On her portable TV:

60 EXT. ALBION HOSPITAL NIGHT 5 2308

TV FOOTAGE, POLICE, ARMY, barriers b/g. REPORTER #1 to CAMERA, frazzled, tired:

REPORTER #1 ... are there more ships to come? And what's their intention? The authorities are now asking, if anyone knows anything, if any previous sighting has been made, then phone this number. We need your help.

Throughout this: a helpline number, bottom of screen.

61 INT. JACKIE'S BEDROOM NIGHT 5 2308

JACKIE picks up her phone. Urgent, coming to life a bit, she dials the helpline number. Engaged noise.

Rapid sequence, jump cuts: CU REDIAL; CUT TO closer on Jackie, engaged noise; CUT TO CU REDIAL; CUT TO even closer on Jackie, engaged noise; CUT TO CU REDIAL; CUT TO EXTREME CU Jackie, getting more and more frantic.

JUMP CUT TO: Jackie's got through, gabbling –

JACKIE Yes, I've seen one, I really have, an alien, she's not safe – my daughter's with him, oh my God, she's not safe –
(deep breath, calmer)
I've seen an alien. I know his name. He's called the Doctor.

62 THRU 65 OMITTED

66 INT. COMPUTER SCREEN NIGHT 5 2313

CU LETTERING, being typed out on a computer screen: *THE DOCTOR.*

67 INT. JACKIE'S BEDROOM NIGHT 5 2313

CU JACKIE, on the phone, scared:

JACKIE It's a box, a blue box –

68 INT. COMPUTER SCREEN NIGHT 5 2313

CU LETTERING, typing out: *BLUE BOX.*

69 INT. JACKIE'S BEDROOM NIGHT 5 2313

JACKIE She called it a TARDIS –

70 INT. COMPUTER SCREEN NIGHT 5 2313

CU LETTERING, typing out: *TARDIS.* The word is highlighted, flashes red, an alarm sounds –

71 OMITTED

72 INT. DOWNING STREET CONFERENCE ROOM NIGHT 5 2331

A plush reception room, being adapted for a conference. Tables and chairs being laid out, with a video screen at one end, set against a lavish fireplace, velvet curtains.

INDRA and the AIDE run in, top speed. Computers are being installed along one wall, a MINION is on duty at one of them – he steps back for Indra to see – The screen reads: *RED ALERT*.

Indra looks closer: *THE DOCTOR*.

73 INT. CABINET ROOM NIGHT 5 2332

Seen only from HARRIET's restricted POV: GENERAL ASQUITH appears, patting himself down. The original General was a big man, but now he's even bigger, bursting out of his uniform, massively padded.

GENERAL ASQUITH What d'you think, how's the compression? I've got a bit of ballast round the middle –

General Asquith holds his tum, grimaces, farts.

GENERAL ASQUITH That's better!

MARGARET We've really got to fix the gas exchange, it's getting ridiculous.

JOE Oh I don't know, seems very human.

General Asquith grabs hold of what looks like an empty wet-suit, as thin as a kagoule, with a shock of blonde hair.

GENERAL ASQUITH Shame, I quite enjoyed being Oliver. He had a wife, a mistress and a young farmer – God, I was busy.

JOE Better get rid of his skin –

Harriet sees JOE heading for the cupboard. She flattens herself behind the door. The door opens, and effectively hides her. The strange, flimsy wet-suit is slung inside, and the door's closed again.

OOV now, leaving the room:

JOE OOV Back to work.

GENERAL ASQUITH OOV I have an army to command!

MARGARET OOV Careful now, we're not there yet.

During this, Harriet picks up the wet-suit, holds it up, realises what it is. Or was. It was Oliver. The face, the shock of blonde hair. The body-suit skin isn't remotely fleshlike, it's all flimsy, floppy and rubberised now.

The voices from outside have gone. It's safe. Harriet opens the door, steps out. Freezes, as she hears:

INDRA OOV General Asquith –

74 INT. CABINET ROOM CORRIDOR/CABINET ROOM NIGHT 5 2334

JOE, MARGARET and GENERAL ASQUITH halfway down the corridor; INDRA running up, a bit frantic. INTERCUT with HARRIET in the Cabinet Room, listening.

INDRA Sir, we've had a priority alarm, it's Code Nine, confirmed, Code Nine, how d'you want to handle it?

GENERAL ASQUITH Right. Good. Code Nine. And that would mean . . .?

INDRA In the event of the Emergency Protocols being activated, we've got software which automatically searches all communications for key words. And one of those words is Doctor. I think we've found him, sir.

MARGARET What sort of Doctor, who is he?

CU Harriet, as she overhears the vital information:

INDRA OOV Evidently, he's some sort of expert in extraterrestrial affairs. The ultimate expert! We need him, sir, we need him here right now.

75 INT. TARDIS NIGHT 5 2357

THE DOCTOR at the console, surfing the scanner across different channels. ROSE and MICKEY at his side.

MICKEY How many channels can you get?

THE DOCTOR All the basic packages.

MICKEY Sports channels?

THE DOCTOR Yeah, I get the football.
(notices:)
Hold on. I know that lot.

On the scanner:

76 EXT. HEATHROW NIGHT 5 2357

TV FOOTAGE: ACADEMICS and UNITED NATIONS SOLDIERS and COLONELS, being escorted out of the airport, towards black cars, by UK SOLDIERS. Over this, both OOV and in vision:

REPORTER #3 The airport's sealed off, except for this flight, from Geneva, with another due from Washington. Nothing's been confirmed, but it seems the government is flying in alien specialists, those who've devoted their lives to outer space.

77 INT. TARDIS NIGHT 5 2358

THE DOCTOR rewinds the report to footage of the UN representatives, freezes on them, enlarges the shot, during:

THE DOCTOR UNIT, the United Nations Intelligence Taskforce. Good people.

ROSE How d'you know them?

MICKEY He's worked for them. Cos I didn't just sit on my backside for twelve months, Doctor, I read up on you. Look deep enough, on the internet, in the history books, and there's your name. Followed by a list of the dead.

THE DOCTOR That's nice, good boy, Ricky.

ROSE If you know them, why don't you go and help?

THE DOCTOR They wouldn't recognise me, I've changed a bit since the old days. Besides, the world's on a knife edge; there's aliens out there, and fake aliens, I don't want this alien added to the mix. I'm staying undercover, I'd better keep the TARDIS out of sight – Ricky, you've got a car, come on, you can drive –

The Doctor's crossing to the doors, ROSE and MICKEY following.

MICKEY Where to?

THE DOCTOR The roads are clearing, let's go and have a look at that spaceship.

He heads out, fast –

78 EXT. ROSE'S ESTATE NIGHT 5 0000

THE DOCTOR, ROSE and MICKEY step out – and a MASSIVE BEAM OF LIGHT slams down. Huge iconic shot: the Doctor, Rose, Mickey and the TARDIS in a powerful white light, shafting down from the sky. They steady themselves, buffeted as a vicious wind whips up, dust and paper circling up in a vortex. Above them, headlights become visible, alongside the beam. And a ferocious whickering noise. It's a helicopter.

ARMY VANS pull up, all around them; SOLDIERS clambering down, armed with rifles, taking aim. Mickey panics, runs – TWO SOLDIERS run in pursuit – along the balconies; NEIGHBOURS watch, including the OLD MAN and WOMAN, GOTH, BEARDED MAN, MIDDLE-AGED COUPLE, three KIDS and SKINHEAD, standing outside the Tylers' flat.

CUT TO JACKIE, ground floor, running out of a stairwell, a good distance away from the Doctor and Rose. SOLDIERS block the way. They have to physically stop her – Jackie yelling for Rose, inaudible under the roar.

79 EXT. BACK OF THE ESTATE NIGHT 5 0001

The two SOLDIERS race past. MICKEY's hiding by the tall bins. He stays in the shadows, terrified.

80 EXT. ROSE'S ESTATE NIGHT 5 0001

THE DOCTOR and ROSE hold up their hands.

THE DOCTOR Take me to your leader.

80A INT. POSH BLACK CAR

Plush leather, smoked black windows; THE DOCTOR already sitting in the back as ROSE gets in. During dialogue, car starts up, drives off.

ROSE This is a bit posh! If I'd known it was like this, being arrested, I would've done it years ago.

THE DOCTOR We're not being arrested, we're being escorted.

ROSE Where to?

THE DOCTOR Where d'you think? Downing Street.

ROSE (laughing)
You're kidding!

THE DOCTOR (laughing)
No I'm not!

ROSE Ten Downing Street?

THE DOCTOR That's the one!

ROSE I'm going to Downing Street? Oh my God! But how come?

THE DOCTOR I hate to say it, but Ricky was right. I've been visiting this planet, plenty of times, and over the years, I've been ... noticed.

ROSE And now they *need* you.

THE DOCTOR Like it said on the news, they're gathering experts in alien knowledge.
(big smug smile)
And who's the biggest expert of the lot?

ROSE Patrick Moore.

THE DOCTOR Apart from him.

ROSE Oh don't you just love it!

THE DOCTOR Telling you, Lloyd George, he could drink me under the table – who's the Prime Minister these days?

ROSE How should I know? I missed a year!

81 EXT. DOWNING STREET NIGHT 5 0100

BLACK CARS pull up, SOLDIERS and POLICE on duty. The pop and flash of cameras; JOURNALISTS yelling out. THE DOCTOR and ROSE step out. He gives the PHOTOGRAPHERS a big smile, waves – loving it. A POLICEMAN indicates, 'this way'. Rose laughing:

ROSE Oh my God.

Because they're being ushered into Number 10.

82 OMITTED

83 INT. TYLERS' FLAT NIGHT 5 0100

JACKIE with ASSISTANT COMMISSIONER STRICKLAND, a PC and WPC.

JACKIE So she's not in trouble, then? She's all right?

STRICKLAND All I can say is that your daughter and her . . . companion might be in a position to help the country. But I need to know how she made contact with this man. If he is a man.

He sits – and only now, it becomes evident that he's a wide, fat man, his uniform too small. His stomach rumbles ominously. He burps. Smiles.

STRICKLAND (to the PC and WPC)
Off you go. Let me talk to Mrs Tyler on my own, thank you.

84 INT. 10 DOWNING STREET RECEPTION NIGHT 5 0103

HARRIET walks carefully down the stairs, seeing: ARMED POLICE at the edges of the room, ACADEMICS and UN SOLDIERS all around, in heated conversations, hubbub all around. JOE and GENERAL ASQUITH amongst them. HARRIET's pretending everything's fine, trying to glide, though she's terrified. She shows her ID – a photo in her purse – to an ARMED POLICEMAN, voice trembling:

HARRIET Harriet Jones, MP for Flydale North.

MARGARET strides past her, ignoring her, but Harriet shudders. Deep breath. Moves on. Keeping away from Joe and the General. Looking at every guest, searching . . .

INDRA calls out:

INDRA Ladies and gentlemen, can we convene? Quick as we can, it's this way, on the right, and can I remind you, ID cards are to be worn at all times –

THE DOCTOR and ROSE hurry up, keen to get in – Indra stops them, gives the Doctor a laminated pass on a chain, to be worn round the neck.

INDRA That's your ID card – I'm sorry, your companion doesn't have clearance.

THE DOCTOR I don't go anywhere without her –

INDRA No, you're the Code Nine, not her, I'm sorry, uh . . . Doctor, it's the Doctor, isn't it? But she'll have to stay outside.

On that – 'Code Nine . . . Doctor' – CUT TO Harriet. Sharp turn, focus on the Doctor.

THE DOCTOR She's staying with me –

INDRA I'm sorry, but even I haven't got clearance to go in there, I can't let her in and that's a fact –

Harriet's approaching, cautious. [Speeches run simultaneously.]

ROSE I'm all right, you go in.

THE DOCTOR D'you think?

ROSE They're the experts, you should hear what they've got to say.

THE DOCTOR Suppose. Stay out of trouble, then.

HARRIET Excuse me, are you the Doctor ...?

INDRA Oh not now, we're busy, can't you go home?

HARRIET I just need a word, that's all, in private –

INDRA You haven't got clearance, now leave it –

The Doctor walks down the corridor. Indra to Rose:

INDRA I'll have to leave you with security ...

HARRIET That's all right, I'll look after this one. Let me be of some use.

Harriet steers Rose round, takes charge of her. As Indra heads off b/g, TRACK WITH Harriet and Rose as they walk across reception. Harriet sotto, like a spy:

HARRIET Walk with me, just keep walking, don't look round, that's it. (shows her photo)
Harriet Jones, MP for Flydale North.

85 INT. DOWNING STREET CONFERENCE ROOM NIGHT 5 0107

The ACADEMICS and UN SOLDIERS finding seats – all with ID cards round their necks. JOE and GENERAL ASQUITH are at the front of the room. Hubbub, chat, etc. THE DOCTOR sidles in, grabs a seat at the back. Printed agendas are on the table. The Doctor reads one, fast.

86 INT. DOWNING STREET DOWNSTAIRS CORRIDOR NIGHT 5 0108

A quiet alcove, HARRIET with ROSE. And Harriet's losing it now, scared, paranoid.

HARRIET ... This friend of yours, he's an expert, is that right? He knows about aliens ...?

ROSE Why d'you want to know?

But Harriet can't hold on any more, starts to cry.

87 OMITTED

88 INT. DOWNING STREET CONFERENCE ROOM NIGHT 5 0111

GENERAL ASQUITH, with JOE beside him, stands front; all the ACADEMICS and UN SOLDIERS in place.

GENERAL ASQUITH If I can have your attention. Thank you. Now as you'll see from the summaries in front of you, the ship had one porcine pilot –

The Doctor stands up, reading, musing, and he wanders round, like he's talking to himself.

THE DOCTOR Of course the really interesting bit happened three days ago, see? Filed away under Any Other Business. The North Sea, a satellite detected a signal, a little blip of radiation, at five hundred fathoms. Like something's down there. You were just about to investigate, next thing you know –
(looks round)
This happens, spaceship, pigs, massive diversion. From what …?

89 INT. CABINET ROOM NIGHT 5 0110

HARRIET, upset, holding Oliver's body-suit. ROSE scared, though trying to be in control.

HARRIET They turn the body into a suit, a disguise, for the thing inside …

ROSE It's all right, I believe you, it's alien – but they must have serious technology behind this. If we could find it, we could use it –

The wood-panelling is full of cupboards, Rose opens another – a BODY falls out, *slam!*

ROSE Oh my God. Is that …?

HARRIET It looks like …

INDRA Harriet, for God's sake!

They turn, look. INDRA's in the doorway, walks forward.

INDRA This has gone beyond a joke, you can't just wander round –
(sees the body)
Oh my God.
(pause)
That's the Prime Minister.

90 INT. DOWNING STREET CONFERENCE ROOM NIGHT 5 0112

THE DOCTOR's mind racing –

THE DOCTOR If aliens fake an alien crash, and an alien pilot, what do they get …?
(realises, horrified)
Us. They get us. It's not a diversion, it's a trap!

91 INT. CABINET ROOM NIGHT 5 0112

ROSE, HARRIET and INDRA turn away from the BODY, hearing –

MARGARET Ohhh, has someone been naughty?

MARGARET, smiling, walks into the room, her stomach gurgling as she slams the door shut behind her.

92 INT. JACKIE'S BEDROOM NIGHT 5 0112

JACKIE's in the kitchen, making coffee.

JACKIE It was bigger on the inside, I don't know! What do I know about spaceships?

CUT TO ASSISTANT COMMISSIONER STRICKLAND in the living room:

STRICKLAND That's what worries me. You see, this man is classified as trouble, which means anyone associated with him is trouble. And that's my job. Eliminating trouble.

During this, Strickland sighs. Almost regretful. He slides his hand up his forehead. Yanks his hair up.

He starts to open the zip in his head ...

93 INT. CABINET ROOM NIGHT 5 0112

ROSE and HARRIET backing away, as INDRA stands over the BODY; MARGARET strolling closer, smiling.

INDRA – But that's not possible – the Prime Minister left Downing Street, he was driven away –

MARGARET And who told you that? Me.

And as her hands reach up ... CUT TO:

94 INT. DOWNING STREET CONFERENCE ROOM NIGHT 5 0113

THE DOCTOR looking round, realising:

THE DOCTOR This is all about *us*! Alien experts, the only people who might have the knowledge to fight them. All gathered together in one room ...

A massive fart. The Doctor turns to JOE and GENERAL ASQUITH.

THE DOCTOR 'Scuse me, d'you mind not farting when I'm saving the world?

JOE Would you rather silent but deadly?

And Joe starts to laugh, mouth wide and wet. And General Asquith reaches up, unzips – again, the electrical discharge, the flicker of blue light. The top of the General's head flaps open, and a solid green organic mass bulges upwards –

On the Doctor. Fascinated!

95 INT. CABINET ROOM NIGHT 5 0113

The room darkening and flashing with blue light – INDRA standing forward, ROSE and HARRIET behind, all in terror. A thick shape is forcing its way out of MARGARET, much larger than the woman herself. Her whole body sags down, just a flimsy layer, as the creature shucks out of its disguise, wet and green and glistening, with the sound of something being sucked out of hell.

96 INT. TYLERS' FLAT NIGHT 5 0113

JACKIE in the kitchen, stirring the coffee, but looking round as the lights darken, and a blue light flickers.

97 INT. DOWNING STREET CONFERENCE ROOM NIGHT 5 0113

THE DOCTOR, ACADEMICS and UN SOLDIERS staring, the room flashing with blue light, the awful rupturing sound. JOE stays in human form, grinning, as something huge struggles out of the neck of GENERAL ASQUITH's shape.

98 INT. TYLERS' FLAT NIGHT 5 0113

JACKIE walks out of the kitchen, and the CREATURE rears above her. It's 8 ft tall, a thick tube of solid, wet, green flesh, all bristling with spikes and spines. The whole thing curves over at the top, like an upright prawn, so its head leers down. A face like a big, sweet, bloated green baby, with jet-black eyes. Green slime trickling from its terrible smile.

99 INT. CABINET ROOM NIGHT 5 0113

An identical CREATURE rears above INDRA, ROSE and HARRIET, shucking off its Margaret-suit, its carapace widening. A powerful claw shoots out, grabs Indra by the neck.

100 INT. DOWNING STREET CONFERENCE ROOM NIGHT 5 0113

THE DOCTOR, ACADEMICS, UN SOLDIERS awestruck, as the General Asquith version of the CREATURE stands proud. All the creatures have an electronic gizmo, roughly where a throat would be. Lights blink on the box – like a translator – as it speaks. A guttural, bubbling distort:

SLITHEEN/ASQUITH We ... are ... Slitheen ...

JOE holds up a little black box, with a button on top.

JOE And thank you for wearing your ID cards. They will help to identify the bodies.

He presses the button. The ID cards electrify! The Doctor grabs the card on his chest, racked with pain. Miniature lightning shoots out from the card, zig-zags across his body, electrifying him. The ACADEMICS and UN SOLDIERS arch, in pain – they're dying, as lightning zaps across them.

101 INT. CABINET ROOM NIGHT 5 0113

The claw tightens, INDRA screams, dying – ROSE and HARRIET in terror ...

102 INT. TYLERS' FLAT NIGHT 5 0113

The SLITHEEN lurches forward, looming over JACKIE – she screams and screams and screams –

103 INT. DOWNING STREET NIGHT 5 0113

THE DOCTOR yells in pain, falls to his knees.

JOE laughs, and the SLITHEEN shudders.

CU the vile, green baby face. Giggling with delight.

Episode 5

World War Three
By Russell T Davies

1 INT. DOWNING STREET CONFERENCE ROOM NIGHT 5 0113

(RECAP OF EPISODE 4.)

THE DOCTOR, on his knees, grits his teeth, grabs the ID card, yanks it off – the chain snaps. Hero shot: the Doctor rising into frame, a living fury, holding the card, still electrified, lightning zig-zagging over his fist. He's the most scary thing in the room.

THE DOCTOR Deadly to humans, maybe.

He shoves the card into the gizmo on the SLITHEEN's throat. The miniature lightning bolts zig-zag over the Slitheen; it screams, warps – its entire body distorting –

2 INT. CABINET ROOM NIGHT 5 0113

ROSE and HARRIET gobsmacked, as the SLITHEEN screams! It drops INDRA's body, clutches the gizmo at its throat. The warp transmits across all the creatures, its body rippling, shuddering –

3 INT. TYLERS' FLAT NIGHT 5 0113

JACKIE staring, terrified, as the SLITHEEN screams, its body buckling, warping –

4 INT. DOWNING STREET CONFERENCE ROOM NIGHT 5 0113

JOE GREEN's also screaming, warping, clutching his throat. The Doctor pushes past him – runs out of the room –

5 INT. CABINET ROOM NIGHT 5 0113

The SLITHEEN's still screaming. ROSE grabs HARRIET, pulls her past the creature, to the door, out –

6 INT. TYLERS' FLAT NIGHT 5 0113

MICKEY Jackie!

MICKEY's in the doorway, he picks up a wooden chair, slams it against the Slitheen. The chair splinters into pieces, the creature staggers. Mickey grabs JACKIE, pulls her out, into the hall. Then Mickey turns back, faces the creature – brave, as it rights itself. He holds up his mobile. Takes a photo. Then he runs –

7 EXT. TYLERS' FLAT NIGHT 5 0113

MICKEY and JACKIE run out of the flat, belt along, terrified –

8 INT. CABINET ROOM CORRIDOR NIGHT 5 0113

ROSE and HARRIET running; but Harriet stops, pulls back –

HARRIET No, they're still in there – the Emergency Protocols, we need them –

9 INT. DOWNING STREET CONFERENCE ROOM NIGHT 5 0114

The SLITHEEN rips off the ID card, throws it away. The zig-zags of lightning stop dead.

10 OMITTED

11 INT. 10 DOWNING STREET RECEPTION NIGHT 5 CONTINUOUS

ARMED POLICE on duty, as THE DOCTOR runs in –

THE DOCTOR Oy! You want aliens, you've got them – they're inside Downing Street, come on – !

He runs back, the armed police run after him –

12 OMITTED

13 INT. DOWNING STREET UPSTAIRS CORRIDORS NIGHT 5 0114

A fast, wild chase: ROSE and HARRIET burst through a door, slam it shut. They run to the next door –

Slam! The SLITHEEN knocks the first door down flat, rampages over it –

14 INT. DOWNING STREET CONFERENCE ROOM NIGHT 5 0115

THE DOCTOR runs in with ARMED POLICE . . .

Nothing alien! JOE GREEN's acting flabbergasted, and GENERAL ASQUITH is facing away, tugging on his sleeve, hiding his final adjustment into his Asquith-suit. The police spread out into the room.

The armed police sergeant – SERGEANT PRICE, 35, Welsh – goes to check the bodies, as Joe flusters:

JOE Where've you been? I called for help, I sounded the alarm – there was this lightning, this sort of electricity, and they all collapsed . . .

Sgt. Price checks the FEMALE GENERAL, she just slumps back.

SGT. PRICE I think they're all dead.

JOE That's what I'm saying –
(points at the Doctor)
He did it! That man there!

THE DOCTOR I think you'll find, the Prime Minister is an alien in disguise –

Stops. Looks at the POLICEMAN next to him.

THE DOCTOR That's never gonna work, is it?

POLICEMAN Nope.

THE DOCTOR Fair enough.

And the Doctor runs out again –

15 INT. CORRIDOR OUTSIDE CONFERENCE ROOM NIGHT 5 CONTINUOUS

THE DOCTOR runs out – more ARMED POLICE are running down the corridor, trapping him. The others run out of the Conference Room. All train their guns on the Doctor. He's surrounded.

He holds up his hands; slowly backs up against the wall. JOE and GENERAL ASQUITH appear in the Conference Room doorway.

GENERAL ASQUITH Under the jurisdiction of the Emergency Protocols, I authorise you to execute that man.

THE DOCTOR Well, now, yes, y'see, the thing is. If I were you, if I was gonna execute someone, by backing him up against the wall, then, between you and me, little word of advice . . .
(big smile)
Don't stand him against the lift.

Ping! The lift behind him (only in vision now, a small, one-door, two-person lift) slides open. The Doctor hops in. The armed police run forward. The Doctor whirrs the sonic screwdriver against the panel. The lift door slams shut, much faster than normal.

16 INT. DOWNING STREET UPSTAIRS CORRIDOR NIGHT 5 0116

ROSE and HARRIET run down a corridor. Suddenly, one of the side doors ahead of them bursts open. The SLITHEEN barges out, rears up – Rose and Harriet terrified . . .

Ping! The lift (only in vision now) opens, right next to the Slitheen, THE DOCTOR standing there, cheery.

THE DOCTOR Hello!

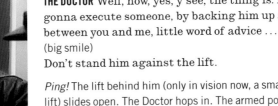

The Slitheen heaves towards him, the Doctor whirrs the screwdriver against the panel, the lift doors shut, fast. Rose and Harriet use the distraction to run on –

17 INT. UPSTAIRS STATE ROOM NIGHT 5 CONTINUOUS

A formal room, fireplace, curtains, plush furniture. ROSE and HARRIET run in, hurry to a second door on the far side. It's locked. They can hear the Slitheen, approaching . . .

ROSE Hide!

18 INT. DOWNING STREET THIRD FLOOR CORRIDOR NIGHT 5 0117

Ping!, door opens, THE DOCTOR looks round – safe – runs out ...

19 INT. DOWNING STREET STAIRCASE NIGHT 5 0117

THE DOCTOR runs down –

20 INT. CORRIDOR OUTSIDE CONFERENCE ROOM NIGHT 5 0117

GENERAL ASQUITH has taken charge, issuing orders:

GENERAL ASQUITH I repeat, the upper floors are under quarantine. You will stay where you are, disregard all previous instructions, and take your orders directly from me.

Ping! The lift arrives back, JOE and General Asquith head for it. SERGEANT PRICE steps forward.

SGT. PRICE Mr Green, sir, I'm sorry, but you've got to come with me, we should evacuate the entire building –

JOE Excuse me, Sergeant, have you read the Emergency Protocols?

SGT. PRICE No, sir.

JOE Then don't question me. Seal off Number Ten, secure the ground floor, and if the Doctor makes it downstairs, shoot on sight.

The lift doors close on him.

21 INT. DOWNING STREET LIFT NIGHT 5 0117

Lift ascending, JOE and GENERAL ASQUITH grinning.

GENERAL ASQUITH Let the sport begin.

JOE (burps)
I'm getting poisoned by the gas exchange, I need to be naked.

GENERAL ASQUITH Rejoice in it. Your body is magnificent.

Joe lifts up his hair. Zip, undoes his head.

22 INT. DOWNING STREET UPSTAIRS CORRIDOR NIGHT 5 0118

THE DOCTOR sneaks down the corridor, wary, when – *Ping!* He leaps into an alcove as the lift opens.

Two SLITHEEN – formerly Joe and the General – squeeze out, gurgling. They sling their Joe and Asquith flimsy-skins over a chair.

The Doctor presses himself into the wall, as they lurch past ...

23 INT. UPSTAIRS STATE ROOM NIGHT 5 0118

ROSE is hiding behind the curtain. Holding her breath. CUT TO the SLITHEEN, its baby-face giggling as it looks round the room. A guttural version of its human voice:

SLITHEEN/MARGARET Oh such fun. Little human children, where are yoooou ...?

CUT TO HARRIET, crouched behind the settee, terrified.

SLITHEEN/MARGARET Sweet little humeykins. Come to me. Let me kiss you better. Kiss you with my big green lips.

SLITHEEN/JOE and SLITHEEN/GENERAL enter (the three Slitheen baby-faces are all slightly different; just like people).

SLITHEEN/JOE Happy hunting?

SLITHEEN/MARGARET It's wonderful, the more you prolong it ... the more they *stink*.

They all breathe deeply.

SLITHEEN/GENERAL Sweat and fear!

SLITHEEN/JOE I can smell an old girl. Stale perfume and brittle bones.

On Harriet, outraged: the cheek!

SLITHEEN/MARGARET And a ripe youngster, all hormones and adrenalin ...

SLITHEEN/MARGARET turns towards the curtains ...

SLITHEEN/MARGARET Fresh enough to bend before she snaps.

On Rose, terrified. Slitheen/Margaret pulls the curtain aside, a hiss of victory –

SLITHEEN/MARGARET Precious child!

HARRIET stands up, waves her arms –

HARRIET No, take me first, take me!

The Slitheen swing towards Harriet, hissing. Rose grabs the curtain, and *heaves* – the curtain-rod and curtain fall over Slitheen/Margaret. The door's kicked open – THE DOCTOR's there. He blasts a big red fire-extinguisher at Slitheen/Joe and Slitheen/General. They scream, fall back –

THE DOCTOR Out! With me!

Rose runs to him. Harriet runs, joins the Doctor and Rose in the doorway as he blasts the extinguisher again:

THE DOCTOR Who the hell are you?

HARRIET Harriet Jones, MP for Flydale North.

THE DOCTOR Nice to meet you.

HARRIET Likewise.

A final blast, and they run –

24 AND 25 OMITTED

26 INT. DOWNING STREET UPSTAIRS CORRIDOR NIGHT 5 CONTINUOUS

Long corridor. THE DOCTOR, ROSE and HARRIET run.

THE DOCTOR Got to get to the Cabinet Room —

HARRIET That's what I said, the Emergency Protocols are in there — they give instructions, about aliens.

THE DOCTOR Harriet Jones, I like you.

HARRIET I like you too, I think.

27 INT. DOWNING STREET UPSTAIRS CORRIDOR NIGHT 5 0121

The reverse of sc.13, THE DOCTOR, ROSE and HARRIET running back through the doorway (the door now flat on the floor). The three SLITHEEN gallop along, behind —

28 INT. CABINET ROOM AND ADJOINING ROOM NIGHT 5 CONTINUOUS

(The next door is part of an adjoining room, which leads to the Cabinet Room from a different direction, via the side door which Harriet found locked in ep.4/58.) THE DOCTOR, ROSE and HARRIET run up to the door. It's locked. The Doctor whirrs at it with the sonic screwdriver, fast. Click, it opens; they pile into the Cabinet Room.

The three SLITHEEN barge into the adjoining room, screeching – in the Cabinet Room, the Doctor picks up a decanter of port, spins back round, stands confident in the doorway, facing the Slitheen, holding the sonic screwdriver up against the decanter: a threat, like he's holding a bomb.

THE DOCTOR One more move and my sonic device will triplicate the flammability of the alcohol. Woomph, we all go up. So back off.

Pause. Stand-off. The Slitheen face the Doctor, with Rose behind the Doctor, to his left; Harriet to the right.

THE DOCTOR Right then. Question time. Who exactly are the Slitheen?

HARRIET They're aliens.

THE DOCTOR Yes I got that, thanks.

SLITHEEN/JOE And who are you? If not human?

HARRIET Who's not human?

ROSE He's not human.

HARRIET He's not human?

THE DOCTOR Could I have a bit of hush?

HARRIET Sorry.

THE DOCTOR So what's the plan?

HARRIET But he's got a northern accent.

ROSE Lots of planets have a north.

THE DOCTOR I said hush!

He turns back to the Slitheen, holds up the decanter, whirrs the sonic screwdriver, threateningly.

THE DOCTOR Come on! You've got a spaceship hidden in the North Sea. It's transmitting a signal. And you've murdered your way to the top of the government, what for? Invasion?

SLITHEEN/JOE Why would we invade this godforsaken rock?

THE DOCTOR Then something's brought the Slitheen race here, what is it?

But the Slitheen just laugh.

SLITHEEN/MARGARET The Slitheen race?

SLITHEEN/JOE Slitheen is not our species.

SLITHEEN/MARGARET Slitheen is our surname.

SLITHEEN/JOE Jocrassa Fel Fotch Pasameer-Day Slitheen. At your service.

THE DOCTOR So ... you're a family?

SLITHEEN/JOE A family business.

THE DOCTOR Then you're out to make a profit. How d'you do that, on a godforsaken rock ...?

SLITHEEN/GENERAL has been quiet, now edges forward.

SLITHEEN/GENERAL Excuse me. Tell me again, your sonic device will do what? 'Triplicate the flammability'?

THE DOCTOR Is that what I said?

SLITHEEN/GENERAL You're making it up.

THE DOCTOR Oh well. Nice try.
(passes the decanter)
Harriet, have a drink, you're going to need it.

HARRIET You pass it to the left.

THE DOCTOR Sorry –
(passes it to Rose)

ROSE Thanks.

SLITHEEN/GENERAL Now we can end this hunt. With a slaughter.

The Slitheen inch forward, claws lifting. Rose and Harriet back off, the Doctor just stands there, confident.

ROSE Don't you think we should run ...?

THE DOCTOR Fascinating history, Downing Street. Two thousand years ago, this was marshland, it was called the Island of Thorns. 1730, it was occupied by a Mr Chicken. Nice man. And since 1796, this has been the Cabinet Room. If the Cabinet's in session, and in danger, then these four walls are just about the safest place in the whole of Great Britain.

His hand goes to the light switch by the door; it's hinged, the whole switch flips up, revealing a red button.

THE DOCTOR End of lesson.

He presses the button. *Sssshunk!* Battleship-grey riveted metal panels slam down.

In the doorway, the main doors, the windows – window after window – *Shunk! Shunk! Shunk! Shunk! Shunk!* The entire room is sealed off.

THE DOCTOR Installed in 1991. Three inches of steel, lining every single wall. They'll never get in.

ROSE And ... how do we get out?

Pause.

THE DOCTOR Ah.

29 INT. ADJOINING ROOM NIGHT 5 0125

The SLITHEEN back away from the door.

SLITHEEN/JOE He's safely contained, now cut off communications inside that room. Then summon the family! It's time we finished with this insane planet for good.

30 OMITTED

31 EXT. 10 DOWNING STREET NIGHT 5 0140

TV FOOTAGE: branded with graphics, *Alien Emergency*, etc.

REPORTER #2 is still on duty.

REPORTER #2 And there's still no word from inside Downing Street, but we're getting even more new arrivals –

CUT TO a 50-year-old MAN getting out of a black car – RAF uniform, GROUP CAPTAIN JAMES. He's noticeably fat.

REPORTER #2 That's Group Captain Tennant James of the Royal Air Force, we don't know why he's been summoned –

CAMERA whips to another car, 50-year-old MAN IN SUIT getting out – again, fat, and sweating, mopping his brow.

REPORTER #2 And that's Ewan McAllister, Deputy Secretary for the Scottish Assembly –

CAMERA whips to a 40-year-old WOMAN – again, large, puffing.

REPORTER #2 And this is really quite unusual, I'm being told that's Sylvia Dillane, director of the North Sea Boating Club. Quite what connects these people, we don't know –

32 INT. 10 DOWNING STREET RECEPTION NIGHT 5 0141

ARMED POLICE lining the hall. MARGARET steps forward, greets GROUP CAPTAIN JAMES as he walks in.

MARGARET Group Captain. Delighted you could make it, we're meeting upstairs –

The Group Captain farts.

MARGARET That's the spirit, off you go –

EWAN MCALLISTER and SYLVIA DILLANE arrive, sweating.

MARGARET Good to see you, come on through.

CUT TO GENERAL ASQUITH, approaching SERGEANT PRICE.

GENERAL ASQUITH Now that the Doctor's been neutralised, the upper levels are out of bounds. To everyone.

SGT. PRICE Then who are they?

Indicates the Group Captain, heading up, followed by Ewan.

GENERAL ASQUITH Need to know, Sergeant, out of bounds. I need you to liaise with Communications, the Acting Prime Minister will be making a public address. He will speak to the nations of the world!

33 INT. DOWNING STREET UPSTAIRS CORRIDOR NIGHT 5 0142

MARGARET ushers SYLVIA DILLANE through a door.

MARGARET There you are, if you'd just like to go through and get changed . . .

Sylvia heads in, Margaret walks on – a glimpse of the room, flickering with blue light, squelching sounds – to a second door, same wall, from which a SLITHEEN emerges. It hands Margaret its body-suit (patterned with RAF uniform). Margaret folds it over her arm like a changing-room attendant, indicates politely:

MARGARET Now, if you'd like to head down there, it's first on the left . . .

34 INT. CABINET ROOM NIGHT 5 0145

THE DOCTOR at the adjoining-room door, his hand poised over the shutter-switch. ROSE and HARRIET at the main doors (which are open, inwards, only the steel shutter barring the way). All tense, like they're about to race:

THE DOCTOR Three Slitheen. Two doors. They can't stop all of us, first one out, hit the fire alarm. Ready?

HARRIET God speed.

THE DOCTOR Three, two, one, go – !

He slams the button – *shunk, shunk, shunk* – shutters slide up. The Doctor freezes, his door filled with FIVE HUGE SLITHEEN. Rose and Harriet freeze, their door filled with FIVE HUGE SLITHEEN. The Doctor slams the button – *shunk!* – the shutters slam back down.

THE DOCTOR Then again, maybe not.

34A INT. MICKEY'S FLAT NIGHT 5 0200

JACKIE sitting, shaken, as MICKEY brings her a cup of tea.

JACKIE Got anything stronger?

MICKEY No chance, I've seen you when you've had a few. This isn't the time for a conga.

JACKIE We've got to tell someone.

MICKEY Who do we trust, though? For all we know, they've all got great big bog-monsters hidden inside.
(squats beside her, serious)

This is what he does, Jacks. That Doctor bloke. Everywhere he goes, it's death and danger, and he's got Rose in the middle of it.

JACKIE Has he got a great big green thing inside him, then?

MICKEY Wouldn't put it past him. But like it or not, he's the only one who knows how to fight 'em.

JACKIE (starts to cry)
I thought I was gonna die.

She's about to lose it; Mickey hugs her.

MICKEY Come on, now. If anyone's gonna cry, it's me, yeah? You're safe now, Jacks, no one's gonna look for you in my flat. Since you hate me so much.

JACKIE You saved my life. God, that's embarrassing.

MICKEY Telling me.

But both smile. Pause, then:

JACKIE But he wanted me dead. And he's still out there, Mickey. That policeman. That ... *thing.*

34B EXT. TYLERS' ESTATE NIGHT 2 0205

ASSISTANT COMMISSIONER STRICKLAND stands beside a police car, with PCs and WPCs. And he *sniffs*. Catching the scent, delighted. To his officers:

STRICKLAND You head off – inform Control, I've got one or two things still need doing.
(stomach rumbles)
I haven't quite finished with Mrs Tyler.

And sniffing the air, Strickland walks away, hunting ...

34C, 35 AND 36 OMITTED

37 INT. CABINET ROOM NIGHT 5 0230

Settling down for a siege: THE DOCTOR's putting INDRA's body into the larger cupboard (in which Harriet hid), on top of the BODY of the Prime Minister. ROSE is checking the drawers, panels, etc. HARRIET's reading the Emergency Protocols.

THE DOCTOR What was his name?

HARRIET (looks up)
Who?

THE DOCTOR This one.
(i.e. Indra)
The secretary, or whatever he was.

HARRIET I don't know. I spoke to him. I brought him a coffee. I never asked his name.

CUT TO INT. CUPBOARD. The Doctor just touches Indra's face. Quiet, private:

THE DOCTOR Sorry.

He goes back out, loses the quiet, clicks to energy:

THE DOCTOR Right then, what have we got? Any terminals, anything?

ROSE Nope, this place is antique. What I don't get is, when they killed the Prime Minister, why didn't they use him as a disguise?

THE DOCTOR He's too slim. They're big old beasts, they've got to fit inside big humans.

ROSE But the Slitheens are about eight feet, how do they squeeze inside?

THE DOCTOR That's the gadget round their necks, a compression field. Literally, shrinks them down a bit. That's why there's all that gas, it's a big exchange.

ROSE I wish I had a compression field, I could fit a size smaller.

HARRIET Excuse me! People are dead, it's not the time for making jokes.

ROSE Sorry. You get used to this stuff, when you're friends with him.

HARRIET Well that's a strange friendship.

THE DOCTOR Harriet Jones. I've heard that name before, Harriet Jones, you're not famous for anything, are you?

HARRIET Hardly!

THE DOCTOR Rings a bell. Harriet Jones . . . ?

HARRIET Lifelong backbencher, I'm afraid.
(helpless)
And a fat lot of good I'm being now. The Protocols are redundant. They list people who could help, but they're all dead downstairs.

ROSE Hasn't it got like, defence codes and things? Couldn't we launch a nuclear bomb at them?

HARRIET You're a very violent young woman.

ROSE I'm serious, we could!

HARRIET There's nothing like that in here. Nuclear strikes do need a release code, yes, but they're kept secret by the United Nations.

The Doctor's suddenly fascinated, fixes on her, intense:

THE DOCTOR Say that again.

HARRIET What, about the codes . . . ?

THE DOCTOR Anything, all of it.

HARRIET Um, well. The British Isles can't gain access to atomic weapons without a Special Resolution from the UN.

ROSE Like that's ever stopped them.

HARRIET Well exactly, given our past record – and I did vote against that, thank you very much – the codes have been taken out of the government's hands and given to the UN ... Is it important?

THE DOCTOR (lost in thought)
Everything's important.

HARRIET It would help if we knew what the Slitheen wanted. Look at me! I'm saying 'Slitheen' like it's normal.

ROSE (to the Doctor)
But what do they want, though?

THE DOCTOR Well they're just one family, so it's not an invasion, they don't want Slitheenworld. They're out to make money. That means they're going to *use* something. Something here on Earth. Some sort of asset ...

HARRIET What, like gold? Oil? Water?

THE DOCTOR (sudden smile)
You're very good at this.

HARRIET Thank you.

THE DOCTOR Why do I know the name Harriet Jones ...?

Rose's mobile beeps, message. As she gets it out:

ROSE Oh, that's me –

HARRIET But – we're sealed off, how d'you get a signal?

ROSE He zapped it. Superphone.

HARRIET Then we can phone for help – you must have contacts!

THE DOCTOR Dead downstairs, yeah.

ROSE It's from Mickey.

THE DOCTOR Tell your stupid boyfriend we're busy.

ROSE He's not so stupid after all.

She slides the mobile right across the table, to the Doctor. He looks:
on screen, Mickey's photo of the Slitheen.

38 INT. MICKEY'S BEDROOM NIGHT 5 0233

The room's become more of a nest since ep.1, like MICKEY's withdrawn into his shell. With elements of Clive's shed from ep.1 – files scattered about, newspaper clippings about the Loch Ness Monster, UFOs, etc, on the wall.

Mickey on his mobile, furious, JACKIE b/g.

MICKEY ... Not just alien, but like, proper alien, like all stinking and wet and disgusting – and more to the point, it wanted to kill us!

JACKIE I could've died!

39 INT. CABINET ROOM NIGHT 5 0233

INTERCUT with sc.38, Mickey and Jackie. ROSE on her mobile, THE DOCTOR and HARRIET close, listening.

ROSE Is she all right though? Don't put her on, just tell me –

THE DOCTOR (takes the phone)
Is that Ricky? Don't talk, just shut up and go to your computer.

MICKEY It's Mickey, why should I?

THE DOCTOR Mickey the idiot. I might just choke before I finish this sentence, but: I need you.

40 INT. MICKEY'S BEDROOM NIGHT 5 0300

CU COMPUTER SCREEN. The website: United Nations Intelligence Taskforce. A box comes up: PASSWORD.

CUT TO MICKEY on keyboard and mobile, a bit in awe.

MICKEY It says password.

41 INT. CABINET ROOM NIGHT 5 0300

INTERCUT with sc.40, MICKEY and JACKIE. THE DOCTOR fiddles with the mobile and the sonic screwdriver. He's just pulled a wire out of the mobile, now plugs it into a speakerphone base on the middle of the table. ROSE listening, HARRIET pouring out three glasses of port.

THE DOCTOR Say again.

MICKEY (on speakerphone)
It's asking for the password.

THE DOCTOR Buffalo. Two Fs, one L.

Mickey types, Jackie brings in mugs of tea, sits with him.

JACKIE So what's that website?

MICKEY All the secret information known to mankind. See, they've known about aliens for years, and they've kept us in the dark.

THE DOCTOR Mickey, you were born in the dark.

ROSE Oh leave him alone.

MICKEY Thank you. Password again.

THE DOCTOR Just repeat it, every time.

Pause, as Mickey hands Jackie the phone, so he can type better. Jackie listens in:

THE DOCTOR Big Ben. Why did the Slitheen go and hit Big Ben?

HARRIET You said, to gather the experts, to kill them.

THE DOCTOR That lot would've gathered for a weather balloon, you don't need to crash-land in the middle of London.

ROSE The Slitheen are hiding, but then they put the entire planet on red alert, what did they do that for?

Jackie can't stay quiet:

JACKIE Oh listen to her!

ROSE Oy! Least I'm trying.

JACKIE Well I've got a question, if you don't mind. Cos since that man walked into our lives, I've been attacked in the street, I've had creatures from the pits of hell in my own living room, and I've had my daughter disappear off the face of the Earth –

ROSE I told you what happened –

JACKIE I'm talking to him! Cos I've seen this life of yours, Doctor, and maybe you get off on it, maybe you think it's all clever and smart, but you tell me, just answer me this. Is my daughter safe?

ROSE I'm fine –

JACKIE *Is she safe?* Will she always be safe, can you promise me that?

Rose, Harriet, eyes on the Doctor; even Rose wondering. Then he looks up, at Rose. She holds his stare. Silence.

JACKIE OOV Well? What's the answer?

Bleep! from the computer.

MICKEY We're in.

Mickey grabs the phone off Jackie. The Doctor focuses on the speakerphone, glad to escape:

THE DOCTOR Now then, on the left, at the top, there's a tab, an icon, little concentric circles – click on that.

Mickey does so. The screen displays an animated wavelength graph, repeating itself, with a weird wowing noise.

MICKEY . . . What is it?

THE DOCTOR The Slitheen have got a spaceship in the North Sea, and it's transmitting that signal, now hush, let me work out what it says.

The Doctor listens hard. Jackie in b/g:

JACKIE He'll have to answer me one day.

MICKEY Hush!

THE DOCTOR . . . It's some sort of message.

Rose and Harriet gather round, to hear the noise.

ROSE What's it say?

THE DOCTOR Don't know, it's on a loop, keeps repeating.

Mickey's doorbell goes.

THE DOCTOR Hush!

MICKEY That's not me!
(to Jackie)
Go and see who it is.

JACKIE It's three o'clock in the morning.

MICKEY Well go and tell them that.

Jackie heads off.

THE DOCTOR It's beaming out into space. Who's it for . . .?

42 INT./EXT. MICKEY'S FLAT NIGHT 5 0303

JACKIE walks down the hall, the bell rings again.

JACKIE All right –

She opens the door: STRICKLAND stands there. Big grin.

STRICKLAND Mrs Tyler.

Jackie slams the door –

43 INT. MICKEY'S BEDROOM NIGHT 5 0304

JACKIE runs into the bedroom, in terror –

JACKIE It's him, it's the thing! It's the Slickeen!

MICKEY (on the phone)
They've found us!

44 INT. CABINET ROOM NIGHT 5 0304

THE DOCTOR, ROSE and HARRIET, alarmed, voices raised:

THE DOCTOR Mickey, I need that signal –

ROSE Never mind the signal, get out of there! Mum, get out!

MICKEY OOV We can't, it's by the front door!

45 EXT. MICKEY'S FLAT NIGHT 5 0304

Mickey's flat is down a secluded, dark walkway; private. STRICKLAND smiles, looks round, yanks his hair – unzips. The discharge of blue light flickers all around –

46 INT. MICKEY'S FLAT NIGHT 5 0304

The blue light flickers round the edge of the door. CUT TO MICKEY and JACKIE at the far end of the hall, staring. Trapped. Mickey holding a baseball bat, and the mobile.

MICKEY It's unmasking. Oh my God. It's going to kill us.

Sc.46 and 47 intercutting *fast* –

47 INT. CABINET ROOM NIGHT 5 0304

THE DOCTOR, ROSE and HARRIET, frantic:

HARRIET There's got to be a way of stopping them! You're supposed to be the expert, think of something!

THE DOCTOR I'm *trying!*

CUT TO the claw, jabbing through the letterbox, savage.

CUT TO MICKEY and JACKIE. Scared and brave:

MICKEY I'll take it on, Jackie, you just run. Don't look back. Just run.

CUT TO ROSE, right up to the Doctor. Deadly quiet:

ROSE That's my mother.

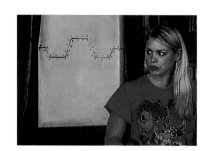

Which galvanises the Doctor – *dialogue top speed, no pauses:*

THE DOCTOR Right! If we're gonna find their weakness, we need to find out where they're from, what planet, so!, judging by their basic shape, that narrows it down to about five thousand planets within travelling distance, what else do we know about them? Information!

ROSE They're green!

THE DOCTOR Yep, that narrows it down –

ROSE Good sense of smell –

THE DOCTOR Narrows it down –

ROSE They can smell adrenalin –

THE DOCTOR Narrows it down –

The claw rips up from the letterbox, through the wood –

HARRIET That pig technology –

THE DOCTOR Narrows it down –

ROSE The spaceship, in the Thames, you said slipstream engine –

THE DOCTOR Narrows it down –

CUT TO Mickey's front door, a huge panel ripping out. The SLITHEEN leers through the gap, bubbling with laughter –

MICKEY It's getting in!

ROSE They hunt, like it's a ritual –

THE DOCTOR Narrows it down –

HARRIET Wait a minute, did you notice, when they … fart, if you'll pardon the word, it doesn't just smell like a … fart, if you'll pardon the word, it's something else, what is it?, it's more like …

ROSE Bad breath!

HARRIET That's it!

THE DOCTOR Calcium decay! Now *that* narrows it down!

ROSE We're getting there, mum!

MICKEY Too late!

The Slitheen's shredding the entire door, splinters flying.

THE DOCTOR Calcium phosphate, organic calcium, living calcium, creatures made out of living calcium, what else, what else? *Hyphenated surname!* YES! That narrows it down to one planet! Raxacoricofallapatorius!

MICKEY Oh great, we can write to them!

THE DOCTOR Get into the kitchen!

The Slitheen pulls out the entire door, bellows with rage, blunders down the hall, huge and wild and strong. Mickey and Jackie fling themselves into the tiny, messy kitchen, slam the door shut – trapped in a tiny space – Mickey shoves a chair against the door handle.

Wham! – the Slitheen hurls itself against the door. All at fever pitch now:

THE DOCTOR Calcium, weakened by the compression field – acetic acid! Vinegar!

HARRIET Just like Hannibal!

THE DOCTOR Just like Hannibal! Mickey, have you got any vinegar?

MICKEY How would I know?!

THE DOCTOR It's your kitchen!

ROSE Cupboard by the sink, middle shelf!

JACKIE Oh give it here –
(grabs the phone)
What d'you need?

CUT TO the hallway, the Slitheen pulling back, then hurling itself at the kitchen door; CUT TO Jackie – phone under her chin – desperate, sloshing a big jar of vinegar into a plastic jug; Mickey stands back, terrified, getting his bat ready to swing; CUT TO the Slitheen, flexing its claw, sliding it forward; CUT TO Jackie, sloshing a jar into the jug –

JACKIE Gherkins!

CUT TO INT. KITCHEN, the claw slices its way through the edge of the door, sliding up; CUT TO Jackie, plucking from the cupboard, in triumph –

JACKIE Pickled onions!

CUT TO the claw sawing roughly through the hinges; CUT TO Jackie, pulling out –

JACKIE Pickled eggs!

THE DOCTOR (to Rose)
And you kiss this man?

CUT TO Jackie sloshing it all into the jug; CUT TO the kitchen door being flung to one side – the Slitheen fills the doorway. Roars! Jackie chucks the contents of the jug – splash – all over the Slitheen. And everything stops.

Mickey and Jackie stare up at the Slitheen. The Slitheen stands there. Stares back.

The Doctor, Rose and Harriet, frozen. Hold.

And then the Slitheen explodes. Great big gobs of green fat and gristle splatter in all directions, covering Mickey and Jackie.

48 INT. CABINET ROOM NIGHT 5 0306

THE DOCTOR, ROSE and HARRIET, a sudden calm. Eventually:

ROSE Hannibal?

HARRIET Hannibal crossed the Alps by dissolving boulders with vinegar.

ROSE Oh. Well there we are, then.

49 INT. 10 DOWNING STREET RECEPTION NIGHT 5 0315

CU JOE GREEN, facing the front door, straightening his tie, preparing for something formal – though he's upset. GENERAL ASQUITH comes up; they're surrounded by ARMED POLICE, so the General has to lean in, mutter:

GENERAL ASQUITH He's dead. Sip Fel Fotch Pasameer-Day Slitheen is dead.

JOE I felt it. How could that happen?

GENERAL ASQUITH Someone must've got lucky.

JOE (quiet anger)
That's the last piece of luck anyone on this rock will ever have.

And they walk forwards, out of the front door –

50 EXT. 10 DOWNING STREET NIGHT 5 0316

JOE and GENERAL ASQUITH step out, flanked by ARMED POLICE. Camera flashes, JOURNALISTS shouting. Joe walks forward to a podium, bristling with microphones, framed against the famous front door.

He holds up his hands, the tumult dies down.

JOE Ladies and gentlemen. Nations of the world. Humankind. The greatest experts in extraterrestrial events came here tonight, they gathered in the common cause. But the news I bring you now is grave indeed.

51 INT. MICKEY'S FLAT LIVING ROOM NIGHT 5 0317

MICKEY towelling green gunge off himself, walking into the living room, just as he hears JOE on TV:

JOE ON TV The experts are dead. Murdered, right in front of me, by alien hands. Peoples of the Earth, heed my words: / these visitors do not come in peace.

At / JACKIE's just walking in – still a bit green-gunged – but Mickey grabs the mobile off her –

MICKEY Listen to this – !

He holds the mobile up to the TV –

52 INT. CABINET ROOM NIGHT 5 0318

THE DOCTOR, ROSE, HARRIET, tight group, listening:

JOE ON TV Our inspectors have searched the sky above our heads. And they have found massive weapons of destruction. Capable of being deployed within forty-five seconds ...

THE DOCTOR *What ...?*

JOE ON TV Our technicians can baffle the alien probes, but not for long, we are facing extinction. Unless! We strike first. The United Kingdom stands directly beneath the belly of the mothership.

53 EXT. 10 DOWNING STREET NIGHT 5 0319

TV FOOTAGE, JOE to CAMERA, impassioned, his finest hour:

JOE I beg of the United Nations. Pass an Emergency Resolution. Give us the access codes. A nuclear strike at the heart of the beast is our only chance of survival. Because as of this moment, it is my solemn duty to inform you, that Planet Earth is at war.

54 INT. CABINET ROOM NIGHT 5 0330

THE DOCTOR storming round the room, like a caged animal.

THE DOCTOR He's making it up! There's no weapons up there, there's no threat, he just invented it!

HARRIET D'you think they'll believe him?

ROSE Well you did last time.

THE DOCTOR That's why the Slitheen went for spectacle – they want the whole world panicking, cos you lot, you get scared, you lash out –

ROSE They release the defence codes –

THE DOCTOR And the Slitheen can go nuclear!

HARRIET But why?

The Doctor slams the button, the shutter *shunks* up. FIVE SLITHEEN swing round, bristling. But he's so angry, they stay back, as he explains at them:

THE DOCTOR You get the codes. Launch the missiles. But not into space, cos there's nothing up there. You attack every other country on Earth. They retaliate. Fight back. World War Three. Whole planet gets nuked.

During this, MARGARET pushes forward through the Slitheen. ROSE and HARRIET join the Doctor, standing back a few steps.

MARGARET And we can sit through it, safe in our spaceship, waiting in the Thames. Not crashed, just parked, barely two minutes away.

HARRIET But you'll destroy the planet. This beautiful place. What for?

THE DOCTOR Profit. That's what the signal is, beaming into space. An advert.

MARGARET Sale of the century! We reduce the Earth to molten slag, then sell it. Piece by piece. Radioactive chunks, capable of powering every cut-price starliner and budget cargo ship. There's a recession out there, Doctor, people are buying cheap. This rock becomes raw fuel.

THE DOCTOR At the cost of five billion lives.

MARGARET Bargain.

And he is so furious now. Very still, calm, controlled:

THE DOCTOR Then I give you a choice. Leave this planet. Or I will stop you.

MARGARET (laughs)
What? You? Trapped in your box?

THE DOCTOR Yes. Me.

And he calmly holds down the button. This time, the shutter descends slowly, and the Doctor holds Margaret's stare all the way. Her smile falters, dies, as he stares her down, even as the shutter slides down over his face, gone.

55 EXT. LONDON DAY 6 0500

Dawn over the city.

56 EXT. EMBANKMENT DAY 6 0501

REPORTER #1 on a deserted Embankment. He's been up all night. Quiet, genuinely scared:

REPORTER #1 Yesterday saw the start of a brave new world, today might see it end. The streets are empty. Everyone's home. Just waiting. As the future is decided in New York . . .

57 EXT. STUDIO NIGHT 5 0001

FEMALE AMERICAN REPORTER to CAMERA, CNN-type graphics on screen reading *The Final Countdown*.

AMERICAN REPORTER It's midnight here, and the United Nations has gathered. England has provided them with absolute proof that the massive weapons of destruction do exist . . .

58 INT. MICKEY'S BEDROOM DAY 6 0502

MICKEY in b/g, at the computer, on the landline, but silent. On JACKIE at the window, sunlight streaming in. She's looking out at the plain, normal world. And she's crying.

In b/g, the distant television OOV:

AMERICAN REPORTER OOV The Security Council will make the Resolution in a matter of minutes. And once the codes are released . . . humanity's first interplanetary war begins.

59 INT. 10 DOWNING STREET RECEPTION DAY 6 0503

A solemn air. ARMED POLICE on duty. JOE GREEN, MARGARET and GENERAL ASQUITH are heading upstairs. Joe stops by SERGEANT PRICE. All in hushed tones, solemn:

JOE We'll take the call in the Prime Minister's office. Maintain your positions . . . and good luck.

Joe shakes his hand, heads upstairs.

60 INT. PRIME MINISTER'S OFFICE DAY 6 0505

A private, wood-panelled room. JOE, MARGARET and GENERAL ASQUITH enter . . . and giggle, excited. Joe lets go with a fart, a ripper. Margaret runs to the desk.

MARGARET Look at that! The telephone is actually red!

JOE How long till they phone?

GENERAL ASQUITH Counting down!

61 INT. MICKEY'S BEDROOM DAY 6 0506

JACKIE now next to MICKEY. She's on the mobile, upset; he's at the computer, repeat-dialling on the landline.

JACKIE All right, Doctor. I'm not saying I trust you. But there must be something you can do.

62 INT. CABINET ROOM DAY 6 0505

ROSE and HARRIET just voices; slow track in to THE DOCTOR.

HARRIET If we could ferment the port, we could make acetic acid.

ROSE Mickey, any luck?

MICKEY OOV There's a hundred emergency numbers, but they're all on voicemail.

HARRIET Voicemail dooms us all.

ROSE If we could just get out of here.

Quietly, almost to himself:

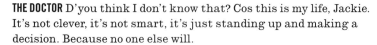

THE DOCTOR There is a way out.

ROSE What?

And he turns, faces them; quiet, dangerous.

THE DOCTOR There's always been a way out.

ROSE Then why don't we use it?

THE DOCTOR Because I can't guarantee your daughter will be safe.

63 INT. MICKEY'S BEDROOM DAY 6 0506

JACKIE horrified:

JACKIE Don't you dare. Whatever it is, don't you dare.

64 INT. CABINET ROOM DAY 6 0506

INTERCUT with sc.63, Jackie and Mickey. ROSE standing to face THE DOCTOR. Frighteningly calm:

THE DOCTOR But that's the thing. If I don't dare, then everyone dies.

ROSE Do it.

THE DOCTOR You don't even know what it is, you'd just let me.

ROSE Yeah.

JACKIE (desperate)
Oh please though. Doctor, she's my daughter, she's just a kid –

THE DOCTOR D'you think I don't know that? Cos this is my life, Jackie. It's not clever, it's not smart, it's just standing up and making a decision. Because no one else will.

ROSE Then what are you waiting for?

THE DOCTOR I could save the world but lose you.

He's never said anything so personal, so intimate. Hold the silence, the Doctor and Rose just look at each other. Helpless. Then, quietly:

HARRIET Except it's not your decision, Doctor. It's mine.

JACKIE And who the hell are you?

HARRIET Harriet Jones, MP for Flydale North.
(stands, magnificent)

The only elected representative in this room. Chosen by the people, for the people, and on behalf of the people, I command you. Do it.

Hold. And then the Doctor *smiles*. Like the devil.

65 EXT. NEW YORK VISTA NIGHT 5 0007

TV FOOTAGE: CU AMERICAN REPORTER.

AMERICAN REPORTER The Council is voting. The result should be known, any second now –

66 INT. CABINET ROOM DAY 6 0507

Action: THE DOCTOR flinging himself across the desk to rifle through the Emergency Protocols; ROSE and HARRIET b/g –

ROSE . . . So how do we get out?

THE DOCTOR We don't. We stay here!

67 INT. PRIME MINISTER'S OFFICE DAY 6 0508

JOE, MARGARET and GENERAL ASQUITH, gathered round the phone.

JOE Victory should be naked!

CU JOE, opening the zip on his forehead.

68 INT. CABINET ROOM DAY 6 0508

THE DOCTOR in command, powerful –

THE DOCTOR Use the buffalo password, it overrides everything –

69 INT. MICKEY'S BEDROOM DAY 6 0508

INTERCUT with sc.68, the Doctor, Rose and Harriet. MICKEY with the mobile under his chin, typing away, sweating, scared. JACKIE just standing back, horrified.

JACKIE . . . But what are you doing?

MICKEY Hacking into the Royal Navy –

On screen, a map of the UK, with red dots indicating –

MICKEY (on the phone)
We're in! Here it is – HMS *Taurean*, Trafalgar Class submarine, ten miles off the coast of Plymouth.

THE DOCTOR Right, we've got to select a missile –

MICKEY We can't go nuclear, we haven't got the defence code –

THE DOCTOR Don't need it, all we need is an ordinary missile, what's the first category?

MICKEY Sub Harpoon, UGM-84A.

THE DOCTOR That's the one! Select!

JACKIE I could stop you.

MICKEY Do it then.

But she doesn't move. Because she knows it's right.

THE DOCTOR Ready for this?

MICKEY Yup.

Hold, all waiting:

THE DOCTOR Mickey the idiot, the world is in your hands. Fire!

Mickey stabs ENTER –

70 EXT. OCEAN DAY 6 0509

The slate-grey ocean ruptures – a burst of smoke and water, a non-nuclear Cruise missile shoots up –

71 INT. MICKEY'S BEDROOM DAY 6 0509

CU JACKIE, horrified.

JACKIE . . . Oh my God.

72 INT. CABINET ROOM DAY 6 0509

HARRIET bangs a shutter; to THE DOCTOR:

HARRIET How solid are these?

THE DOCTOR Not solid enough. Built for short-range attack, nothing this big.

But ROSE is invigorated:

ROSE All right, now I'm making the decision. I'm not gonna die. We're gonna ride this one out!

She's invigorated, runs to the smaller cupboard, where the Prime Minister's body was originally held. She starts pulling out books, files, everything, throwing them out.

ROSE It's like they say about earthquakes, you can survive them by standing under the doorframe – this cupboard's small, so it's strong, come and help me, *come on!*

Harriet runs to help.

73 EXT. FX SHOT MISSILE DAY 0510

Image rattling with sheer velocity – superheated air streaming over the nose of the missile as it hurtles along.

74 EXT. NEW YORK VISTA NIGHT 5 0010

TV FOOTAGE: BCU AMERICAN REPORTER.

AMERICAN REPORTER The vote is in, the Council says yes! They're releasing the codes . . .

75 INT. PRIME MINISTER'S OFFICE DAY 5 0511

All the SLITHEEN – including those from the corridor – are gathered round SLITHEEN/JOE, as he leers at the red phone:

SLITHEEN/JOE Ring, damn you!

76 INT. MICKEY'S BEDROOM DAY 5 0511

CU MICKEY, transfixed by his computer screen.

MICKEY It's on radar!

77 INT. CABINET ROOM DAY 5 0511

B/g, fast, frantic, ROSE and HARRIET are gutting everything out of the smaller cupboard. THE DOCTOR on the mobile:

THE DOCTOR Stop them intercepting it!

MICKEY Doing it now!

MICKEY rattles away on the keyboard.

78 INT. DOWNING STREET CONFERENCE ROOM DAY 5 0512

SERGEANT PRICE leaning over the shoulder of a computer MINION, to look at the screen, incredulous –

SGT. PRICE What do you mean, *incoming*?!

79 EXT. FX SHOT: MISSILE DAY 5 0512

The missile reaches its apogee, starts to curve down –

80 INT. 10 DOWNING STREET RECEPTION DAY 5 0512

SERGEANT PRICE races through, smashes the fire alarm –

SGT. PRICE Everybody out! NOW!

ARMED POLICE run for the door, the Sergeant runs upstairs.

81 INT. PRIME MINISTER'S OFFICE DAY 5 0512

The alarm sounding, the SLITHEEN panicking –

SLITHEEN/JOE What the hell is that for?

Door bursts open, SERGEANT PRICE runs in.

SGT. PRICE Sir, there's a missile . . .

He stops dead. Looks at the Slitheen. Pause. Then:

SGT. PRICE Sorry!

He runs out, slams the door –

82 EXT. FX SHOT: MISSILE DAY 5 0513

Shot from the base of the missile, the cone arrowing down. Below: the South of England, the City of London . . .

83 MICKEY'S FLAT DAY 5 0513

JACKIE runs out, distraught, to the balcony. Far off, in the sky, a thin trail of white smoke.

84 INT. PRIME MINISTER'S OFFICE DAY 5 0513

CU the red telephone, ringing. But all the SLITHEEN are panicking, grabbing body-suits –

SLITHEEN/GENERAL Disguise me, disguise me!

SLITHEEN/MARGARET That's mine, you've got mine!

85 EXT. 10 DOWNING STREET DAY 5 0513

Foreground, a blur of ARMED POLICE clearing JOURNALISTS as SERGEANT PRICE runs out, fires his carbine into the air –

SGT. PRICE Everybody, RUN!

They scatter, panicking. He looks up – in the sky, the trail of white smoke, racing down –

86 EXT. FX SHOT: MISSILE DAY 6 0513

Hurtling downwards, London zooming up –

87 INT. CABINET ROOM DAY 6 0513

ROSE pulls THE DOCTOR into the cupboard, slams the door.

CUT TO INT. CUPBOARD, the Doctor, Rose and HARRIET scrambling to sit down, tight. They hold hands.

ROSE Here we go.

HARRIET Nice knowing you both. Hannibal!

And they all clench fists, brace themselves.

88 INT. PRIME MINISTER'S OFFICE DAY 6 0513

TOP SHOT, looking down on SLITHEEN/JOE looking up –

SLITHEEN/JOE Ohhh, bol-

89 EXT. FX SHOT: EXPLOSION DAY 6 0513

An almighty explosion!

A storm of flame and bricks – the black front door, tumbling: window-frames and brickwork being blasted away from a Cabinet Room outer wall, exposing grey metal underneath.

90 INT. CABINET ROOM DAY 6 0513

THE DOCTOR, ROSE and HARRIET cling on – the entire cupboard slamming and shuddering.

91 EXT. FX SHOT: EXPLOSION DAY 6 0513

The storm of fire and bricks rolls on – the exterior of the Cabinet Room is now a rectangular grey metal box, the whole thing staying level but falling *down*, the floors beneath it no longer existing. It plummets down through the flames –

92 INT. CABINET ROOM DAY 6 0513

Everything in freefall, THE DOCTOR, ROSE and HARRIET flying *up*, still holding hands, in the heart of the storm –

93 EXT. FX SHOT: EXPLOSION DAY 6 0513

And the metal box slams to the ground –

94 EXT. 10 DOWNING STREET RUIN DAY 6 0514

Silence.

The air thick with dust, papers gently floating down to earth. Framed by a valley of bricks: a buckled, scorched, riveted metal wall – the Cabinet Room. The door creaks, then falls down flat – *clang* – revealing THE DOCTOR, ROSE and HARRIET, peering out. Battered, cuts and bruises, shocked. But alive.

HARRIET Made in Britain!

95 EXT. WESTMINSTER STREET DAY 6 0516

Dust, papers blowing, bricks strewn all about. THE DOCTOR, ROSE and HARRIET emerge, dusty, dazed, but smiling. SERGEANT PRICE runs towards them.

SGT. PRICE Oh my God. Are you all right?

HARRIET (shows her card)
Harriet Jones, MP for Flydale North. You must contact the UN immediately, tell the ambassadors, the crisis has passed, they can stand down. Tell the news, go on!

SGT. PRICE Yes ma'am.

He runs off – reveal, behind him, the street sealed off with AMBULANCES, ARMY VANS, POLICE VANS, MEDIA TRUCKS. JOURNALISTS clamouring, being held back by POLICE.

HARRIET Someone's got a hell of a job, sorting this lot out – oh my Lord, we haven't even got a Prime Minister.

THE DOCTOR Maybe you should have a go.

HARRIET Me! I'm just a backbencher.

ROSE I'd vote for you.

HARRIET Now don't be silly – look, I'd better go and help, hold on –

She runs off, calling out to the Journos:

HARRIET We're safe! The Earth is safe!

On the Doctor, smiling, quiet:

THE DOCTOR I thought I knew the name. Harriet Jones. Future Prime Minister, elected for three successive terms, the architect of Britain's Golden Age.

CUT TO Harriet, facing the Journos, in her element.

HARRIET Ladies and gentlemen, spread the word, tell your neighbours, tell your children, tell your friends, the crisis has passed! Mankind stands tall! Undefeated and proud! God bless the Human Race!

95A INT. TYLERS' FLAT DAY 6 1400

ROSE – dishevelled, tired, but smiling – arrives back home. JACKIE – still in last night's clothes, just as tired herself – comes running out of the kitchen. Hugs Rose, tight, and keeps hold of her, tearful, overjoyed. They've been to the end of the world and back, together.

95B INT. TARDIS DAY 6 1400

THE DOCTOR walks in. A smile; he's come back home. He goes to the console, presses this switch, that switch, just pottering, happy.

95C INT. TYLERS' FLAT DAY 6 1420

ROSE sitting, JACKIE complaining at the TV. OOV REPORTER on TV, burbling about:

JACKIE Harriet Jones, who does she think she is? Look at her, taking all the credit, it should be you on there! My daughter saved the world!

ROSE I think the Doctor helped a bit.

JACKIE All right then, him too. You should be given knighthoods.

ROSE That's not the way he does things. No fuss, he just ... moves on. He's not that bad, if you give him a chance.

JACKIE He's good in a crisis, I'll give him that.

ROSE Oh, now the world *has* changed. You're saying nice things about him.

JACKIE (grudging)
Well. Reckon I've got no choice. There's no getting rid of him, since you're infatuated.

ROSE I am not infatuated!

JACKIE What does he eat?

ROSE How d'you mean?

JACKIE I was gonna do shepherd's pie. All of us, a proper sit-down, cos I'm ready to listen. I want to learn about you and him and that life you lead. But I dunno, he's alien, for all I know he eats grass and safety pins and things.

ROSE He'll have shepherd's pie.
(smiling)
You're gonna cook for him?

JACKIE What's wrong with that?

ROSE He's finally met his match.

Jackie heads out to the kitchen:

JACKIE You're not too old for a slap.

Rose, settled down to watch TV, but her mobile rings. She gets it out, Jackie just a voice b/g:

JACKIE We can go and visit your gran tomorrow. Better learn some French, cos I told her you were in France, I said you were au-pairing.

Rose puzzled. On her phone display, instead of caller ID: a simple block-drawing of the TARDIS.

ROSE ... Hello?

95D INT. TARDIS DAY 6 1422

THE DOCTOR on the phone – it's an old-fashioned trimphone-type receiver, complete with curly phone wire, plugged into the console itself.

THE DOCTOR Right, I'm gonna be a couple of hours, then we can go.

ROSE You've got a phone!

THE DOCTOR What, d'you think I can travel in time and space but haven't got a phone? Like I said, couple of hours – I've just got to send out a dispersal –

Pulls down a lever – bleeping noise emits.

THE DOCTOR There you go! That's cancelling out the Slitheen's advert. Just in case any bargain hunters turn up.

ROSE hushed, so Jackie can't hear:

ROSE Um. My mother's cooking.

THE DOCTOR Good, put her on a low heat and let her simmer.

ROSE She's cooking tea, for us.

THE DOCTOR I don't do that.

ROSE She wants to get to know you.

THE DOCTOR Well, tough, I've got better things to do.

ROSE It's just tea.

THE DOCTOR Not for me, it isn't.

ROSE She's my mother.

THE DOCTOR She's not mine.

ROSE That's not fair.

THE DOCTOR You can stay, if you want.

Pause. Both hold the silence. And the Doctor's aware he's been too blunt with her. Softens, more enticing:

THE DOCTOR But right now, there's this plasma storm brewing, in the Horsehead Nebula. Fires are burning, ten million miles wide. I could fly the TARDIS right into the heart of it. Then ride the shockwave all the way out, hurtle right across the sky and end up . . . anywhere. (pause)
Your choice.

He hangs up.

95E INT. TYLERS' FLAT DAY 6 1425

JACKIE walks in with a cup of coffee, sees that Rose is no longer there, walks through.

JACKIE Rose? I was thinking, I've got that bottle of Amaretto from New Year's Eve, does he drink?

95F INT. ROSE'S BEDROOM DAY 6 1425

JACKIE enters. Stops dead. ROSE is packing her big holdall. Looks guilty. But keeps packing. Both keep going on automatic:

JACKIE I was just wondering. Whether he drinks or not.

ROSE He does, yeah.

Silence, as Rose keeps shoving tee-shirts in, lots of stuff, like she's going to be away for a long time. Then, Jackie just stays where she is, says quietly:

JACKIE Don't go sweetheart. Please don't go.

Rose hates this; but she keeps on packing.

96 EXT. TYLERS' ESTATE NIGHT 6 2030

All back to normal, the ordinary world. MICKEY SMITH's sitting on a low wall, with a folded newspaper, waiting. The 10-year-old SKINHEAD KID is on his knees, with brush and bucket, scrubbing his graffiti off the TARDIS. THE DOCTOR steps out, inspects it.

THE DOCTOR Good lad. Graffiti that again and I'll get you, now beat it.

Kid races off, the Doctor wanders over to Mickey.

MICKEY I went down the shop. And I was thinking, y'know, the whole world's changed. Spaceships and aliens, all in public, and there it is –

Holds up the *Evening Standard*. The headline: *ALIEN HOAX?*

MICKEY How can they do that? They saw it!

THE DOCTOR You're just not ready. You're happy to believe in something invisible, but if it's staring you in the face – nope, can't see it! There's a scientific explanation for that: you're thick.

MICKEY (laughs)
We're just idiots.

THE DOCTOR (grudgingly)
Not all of you.

MICKEY Yeah?

The Doctor smiles, digs in his pocket, gets out a disc.

THE DOCTOR Present for you, Mickey. That's a virus, put it online, it'll destroy every mention of me. I'll cease to exist.

MICKEY What d'you wanna do that for?

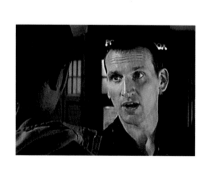

THE DOCTOR Cos you're right. I am dangerous. I don't want anyone following me.

MICKEY How can you say that, then take her with you?

Indicates: ROSE and JACKIE, a distance away, approaching.

THE DOCTOR You could look after her. Come with us.

MICKEY (quiet)
I can't. That life of yours ... it's too much, I couldn't do it.
(pause, ashamed)
Don't tell her I said that.

CUT TO Rose and Jackie. Rose has got one of those huge piled-high travelling-across-Europe backpacks on.

JACKIE I'll get a proper job, I'll work weekends. I'll pass my test. And if Jim comes round again, I'll say no, I really will.

ROSE I'm not leaving cos of you. I'm travelling, that's all, and then I'll come back.

JACKIE But it's not safe.

ROSE Mum. If you saw it out there. You could never stay home.

Just reaching the Doctor and Mickey, Rose shucks off the heavy backpack, slings it to the Doctor, smiling:

THE DOCTOR Got enough stuff?

ROSE First time I stepped in there, it was spur of the moment. Now I'm signing up. You're stuck with me.

She goes to Mickey:

ROSE There's plenty of room, come with us.

THE DOCTOR No chance, he's a liability, I'm not having him on board.

ROSE We'd be dead without him –

THE DOCTOR My decision's final.

ROSE (to Mickey)
Sorry.

MICKEY Good luck.

He kisses her. But Jackie can't keep quiet. At the Doctor:

JACKIE You still can't promise me. What if she gets lost? What if something happens to you, Doctor, and she's left all alone, standing on some moon, a million light years away? How long do I wait then?

The Doctor's awkward, but Rose goes to Jackie.

ROSE Mum, you're forgetting, it's a time machine. I could go travelling round suns and planets and all the way out to the edge of the universe, and by the time I get back here, ten seconds would've passed. Just ten seconds. So stop worrying. I'll see you in ten seconds' time.

She gives Jackie a kiss, quick hug. The Doctor avoids this, goes inside the TARDIS. Rose separates from Jackie, goes to the TARDIS. A smile at them both, then she goes inside.

The ancient engines creak and groan into gear. Jackie and Mickey watch as the TARDIS melts away. Both keep watching the empty space, as Mickey goes back to sit on the wall. Then Jackie looks at her watch, bleak:

JACKIE Ten seconds.

And no sign of Rose.

WIDE SHOT of the estate. Jackie turns, walks away, in tears. Mickey just sitting on the wall. Waiting.

Episode 6

Dalek
By Robert Shearman

2 November 2004. I get on a train at London Paddington, very adult, very solemn, every inch the Serious BBC Writer. But by the time we pull into Cardiff I'm an excitable fan, about to visit the set of Doctor Who — DOCTOR WHO! — and meet my very own Dalek. I keep humming the theme tune and the woman opposite looks at me as if I'm mad. Give it six months and she'll probably be humming along too …

I wasn't a brave kid, and even the sound of *Doctor Who*'s theme music sent me scurrying from the sitting room. The glimpses I caught of Daleks – and my sister's lurid descriptions of them – were enough to give me nightmares. I didn't even like going too close to the rubbish bin in the porch, for fear it'd suddenly sprout a gun and spit laser bolts at me. When I was commissioned to write the Daleks' introductory story for the new series, I was surprised to find that my wife hadn't shared my childhood fears. 'They rant too much,' she said. 'They've got sink plungers and can't get up stairs.' In the forty years since they'd first appeared on our screens, the Daleks had become genuinely iconic – that knobbly pepperpot shape is the most memorable image of the series. But there's something very safe about icons. We take them for granted.

I had the choice. I could either divorce my wife on the spot, or I could try to write the Daleks as I saw them twenty-five years ago, and make a whole new generation of children scared of their dustbins too. The divorce would have been quicker, perhaps, but much less satisfying.

Russell T Davies agreed that rather than reinvent the Daleks, which smacked a little of apology, I should go back to basics and show the cunning manipulators that Terry Nation had created in the sixties. The Doctor needs a nemesis who is as intelligent and persuasive as he is – the monotonous robot of legend diminishes the Doctor too. I decided to use one single Dalek, fighting for survival with the same tenacity and ingenuity that the Doctor showed every week. Rather than have him face an entire army, I wanted the Doctor to face his enemy as an individual. Chris brilliantly portrayed a Doctor on the edge, scarred by the loss of his home world. At the same time Billie's Rose was fast adapting to alien races and putting aside her human prejudices. Her selfless sympathy for the 'unlike' would show how great a journey she's made . . . and how far she still needs to travel.

A few unsung heroes: Joe Ahearne, a brilliant writer himself, directed with a writer's understanding of what I was trying to achieve. My old friend Nick Briggs shouted himself hoarse into a ring modulator and with his voice alone gave a metal box an emotional depth I would never have believed possible. And script editor Helen Raynor was unfailingly encouraging through the rewrites and missed deadlines. I dread to think what 'Dalek' would have looked like without any of them.

I'm taken to the Millennium Stadium, temporarily transformed into the underground base of alien collector Henry Van Statten. I pick my way over the rubble – his prize exhibit was obviously too much to handle – and I'm standing right next to the Dalek. It's so beautiful, so gold and robust and alien. I've spent months with this Dalek in my head, and now I'm up close I just want to give it a hug . . . but worry that I'll look silly in front of the crew. Then I think 'What the hell ' and give it a hug anyway.

Robert Shearman

1 INT. EXHIBIT ROOM NIGHT 7

Darkness. And then, a flash of light, getting more defined, from the lamp on top of the TARDIS as it materialises.

THE DOCTOR steps out. Looks round, alert, treading carefully in the dark.

ROSE appears in the TARDIS doorway.

ROSE So what is it, what's wrong?

THE DOCTOR I don't know. Some sort of signal, drawing the TARDIS off course ...

ROSE Where are we?

THE DOCTOR Earth. Utah, North America. About half a mile underground.

ROSE And, *when* are we?

THE DOCTOR Two thousand and twelve.

ROSE Oh that's weird. God, that's so close. I should be twenty-six!

The Doctor throws a switch. *Chunk! Chunk! Chunk!* Overhead lights slam on! The room is full of large glass cabinets, receding into the distance. It's a huge, stylish museum hall.

ROSE Blimey. Like a great big museum.

THE DOCTOR An alien museum. Someone's got a hobby, must've paid a fortune for all this. Chunks of meteorite. Moondust. That's the milometer from the Roswell spaceship –

ROSE That's a bit of Slitheen, that's a Slitheen arm. It's been stuffed!

She crosses to the Slitheen arm, revealing behind her the head of a Cyberman. Ganglia dangle from the neck.

The Doctor's quiet, even a bit emotional; so many lifetimes.

THE DOCTOR Look at you. That takes me back.

ROSE What is it ...?

THE DOCTOR Old friend of mine. Old enemy. The stuff of nightmares, reduced to an exhibit. I'm getting old.

ROSE So is that where the signal's coming from? It could be transmitting.

THE DOCTOR Naah, it's stone dead. The signal's alive. Something's reaching out. Calling for help ...

Smiling, gentle, he lifts up his hand, touches the case ...

Alarms! Klaxons! Doors open, on all sides, black-uniformed GUARDS pour in. *Click-click-click* of safety catches as they raise rifles. The Doctor and Rose raise arms. Muttered, under the alarms:

ROSE If someone's collecting aliens, that makes you Exhibit A.

2 INT. CORRIDOR NIGHT 7

Doors fly open, SOLDIERS in black, gleaming uniforms run through.
(They all have the year 2012 equivalent of a bluetooth earpiece attached.)
They flank the walls, take positions, guns raised. Military precision.

TANNOY VOICE *Attention all personnel, Bad Wolf One arriving, Bad Wolf One arriving.*

3 INT. OUTSIDE THE DALEK CELL NIGHT 7

An anteroom built around the heavy, fearsome cell door. All around, computer screens and terminals. A guard, DE MAGGIO – American, female – is on her feet, panicked, gathering coffees and pizza boxes, as another guard, BYWATER – American, male – runs in –

BYWATER It's the boss! Surprise visit!

DE MAGGIO I know, I saw it, he's diverted from LAX – God, we're in trouble!

BYWATER (stabs intercom)
Simmons! He's back! I don't care what you have to do, get that creature talking!

4 AND 5 OMITTED

5A INT. DALEK CELL NIGHT 7

(B/g irrelevant for now; a grim mechanistic torture chamber.) MID-SHOT: SIMMONS – American, 30, heartless – is on the intercom. He's dressed in a radiation suit.

SIMMONS You can tell our esteemed employer that the art of getting an alien entity to communicate with the human race is a slow, and delicate, and infinitely subtle process.

He turns round, pulls his radiation hood down. Lifts up a NASTY BIG HEAVY TWO-HANDED WHIRRING DRILL!

SIMMONS Talk, you sucker!

And he advances, with a grin.

6 INT. CORRIDORS NIGHT 7

SOLDIERS line the corridor, stand to attention as HENRY VAN STATTEN strides through. He's 40, effortlessly powerful, always with a glint in his eye; the sort of man who won't allow himself to be bored for a single second. MINIONS – lawyers, accountants, PR – run after him. At the head, Van Statten's chief aide, POLKOWSKI, male, 30. This whole thing on the move, fast, striding down corridors:

POLKOWSKI On behalf of all of us, I'd like to wish you a very happy birthday, sir. And the President phoned to convey his personal best wishes.

VAN STATTEN The President is ten points down, I want him replaced.

POLKOWSKI Um, I don't think that's wise, sir –

VAN STATTEN Thank you so much for your opinion, you're fired, get rid of him –

SOLDIERS reach out, pluck Polkowski out of the entourage, pull him back down the corridor. A severe, prim woman, GODDARD, runs forward, takes Polkowski's place. Nervous – her big chance!

VAN STATTEN Wipe his memory and leave him by the road someplace, Memphis, Minneapolis, somewhere beginning with **M** – so, the next President, what d'you think? Republican or Democrat?

GODDARD Democrat, sir.

VAN STATTEN For what reason?

GODDARD They're just so funny, sir.

VAN STATTEN What's your name?

GODDARD Goddard, sir, Diana Goddard.

VAN STATTEN I like you, Diana Goddard, now where's the English kid?

ADAM runs forward, catches up. He's 20, English, clever.

ADAM Sir! I bought ten more artefacts at auction, Mr Van Statten.

VAN STATTEN Bring them on, let's see 'em –

GODDARD Sir, with respect, there's something more urgent. We arrested two intruders, fifty-three floors down, we don't know how they got in.

VAN STATTEN I'll tell you how they got in. Intruder window.
(keeps walking)
Intruder window, that was *funny*!

And everyone laughs!

VAN STATTEN Bring them in, let's see them. And tell Simmons I want to visit my little pet, get to it!

The parade charges on, leaving Goddard. She talks into her earpiece-communicator.

GODDARD Simmons, you'd better give me good news! Is it talking?

7 INT. DALEK CELL NIGHT 7

An ALIEN POV: A circular lens, overlaid with cross-hairs and scrolling alien text. It's watching SIMMONS. He's still in his radiation suit (hood on, but his earpiece relays messages from Goddard).

SIMMONS Not exactly talking, no.

GODDARD Then what's it doing?

SIMMONS Screaming. That any good?

And he rams the drill under the ALIEN POV. A terrible, metallic scream!
He pulls the drill out. Smiling, vile, quiet:

SIMMONS This hurts me just as much as it hurts you.
(beat; smile)
Okay, that's a lie. *Talk!*

He shoves the drill in again – the scream!

8 INT. VAN STATTEN'S EXECUTIVE OFFICE NIGHT 7

VAN STATTEN's private office – smart and stylish. Works of fine art line the room,
plus monitor screens, glowing, or scrolling with complicated (and not necessarily
legible) 2012 text. An ornate oak desk, centre. GODDARD ushers in THE
DOCTOR and ROSE, TWO ARMED GUARDS at their side. VAN STATTEN ignores
them, talking to ADAM. A collection of metal alien artefacts is on the desk.

ADAM And this is the last. Paid eight hundred thousand dollars for it.

And he hands Van Statten an ugly, misshapen piece of soft metal. Van Statten
studies it, shrewd.

VAN STATTEN What does it do?

ADAM You see these tubes on the side? Must be to channel something,
I think maybe fuel. I think it's part of a spaceship engine.

VAN STATTEN And it's unique, isn't it? The only one in the world.

THE DOCTOR I really wouldn't hold it like that.

GODDARD Keep it shut –

THE DOCTOR Really though, that's wrong.

ADAM Is it dangerous?

THE DOCTOR No, it just looks silly.

He steps forward. The GUARDS raise guns, the click of safety catches,
but Van Statten's fascinated by the Doctor, signals for them to stand down.
Gives the object to the Doctor.

THE DOCTOR You just have to be delicate.

He strokes it. And the metal glows. A beautiful sound shivers out, unearthly
chords. Music of the spheres. Van Statten is enraptured.

VAN STATTEN It's a musical instrument?

THE DOCTOR (affectionately)
Yep. And a long way from home.

VAN STATTEN Let me . . .

Van Statten reaches out, takes it. Discordant sounds.

THE DOCTOR I did say delicate. Careful now, it reacts to the smallest
fingerprint, it needs precision . . .

VAN STATTEN What, like this?

And he strokes it, gently. It sings. Ethereal music. In seconds, Van Statten's learnt how to manipulate it. As the notes sustain, both men smile at each other; that macho sizing-each-other-up smile.

THE DOCTOR Very good.

VAN STATTEN Thank you.

THE DOCTOR Quite an expert.

VAN STATTEN As are you.

And Van Statten slings the object into the bin.

VAN STATTEN Who exactly are you?

THE DOCTOR I'm the Doctor, and who are you?

VAN STATTEN Ohh, like you don't know. We're hidden away, underneath the salt deserts of Utah, with the most valuable collection of extra-terrestrial artefacts in the world. And you just stumbled in by mistake!

THE DOCTOR Just about sums me up, yeah.

Van Statten wanders round, calm, circling towards Rose.

VAN STATTEN Question is, how did you get in? Fifty-three floors down?
(of Rose)
With your little cat burglar accomplice. Quite a collector yourself, she's kinda pretty.

ROSE And she's gonna smack you if you keep calling her 'she'.
You didn't give us an answer, who are you?

VAN STATTEN She's English too.
(to Adam)
Hey, Little Lord Fauntleroy, got you a girlfriend.

ADAM This is Mr Henry Van Statten.

ROSE And who's he when he's at home?

ADAM Mr Van Statten owns the internet.

ROSE Don't be stupid, no one owns the internet.

VAN STATTEN And let's just keep the whole world thinking that way, right kids?

The Doctor steps forward; he and Van Statten challenging each other, both smiling, cool, ready to pounce.

THE DOCTOR So you're just about an expert in everything, except for the things inside your museum. Anything you don't understand, you lock up.

VAN STATTEN Are you claiming greater knowledge?

THE DOCTOR I don't need to make claims. I know how good I am.

VAN STATTEN And yet I captured you. Right next to the Cage. What were you doing down there . . . ?

THE DOCTOR You tell me.

VAN STATTEN The Cage contains my one living specimen.

THE DOCTOR And what's that ...?

VAN STATTEN Like you don't know.

THE DOCTOR Then show me.

VAN STATTEN You want to see it?

ROSE Blimey, you can smell the testosterone.

VAN STATTEN Goddard, inform the Cage, we're heading down. You, English, look after the girl, go and canoodle or spoon or whatever it is the British do. And you, Doctor-with-no-name –
(great big smile)
Come and see my pet!

9 INT. OUTSIDE THE DALEK CELL NIGHT 7

BYWATER and DE MAGGIO run to positions, stand to attention – VAN STATTEN, THE DOCTOR, and GODDARD walk in.

VAN STATTEN We've tried everything. The creature has shielded itself, but there's definite signs of life inside.

THE DOCTOR What d'you mean, inside? Inside what?

But SIMMONS comes out of the door, pulling off his hood.

SIMMONS Mr Van Statten, sir, welcome back! I've had to take the power down, the Metaltron is resting.

THE DOCTOR Metaltron?

VAN STATTEN Thought of it myself, good, isn't it? Although I'd much prefer to find out its real name ...

Van Statten operates the lock on the door, it swings open.

SIMMONS (offers gloves)
Better put these on. The last man who touched it burst into flames.

THE DOCTOR (refuses gloves)
I won't touch it, then.

VAN STATTEN Go on, Doctor. Impress me.

And the Doctor walks into the cell ...

10 INT. DALEK CELL NIGHT 7

THE DOCTOR walks into the darkened room. Slam! The cell door slams shut behind him –

11 INT. OUTSIDE THE DALEK CELL NIGHT 7

VAN STATTEN runs to watch (on screen or through a window).

VAN STATTEN Don't open that door till we get a result –

12 INT. DALEK CELL NIGHT 7

THE DOCTOR's unperturbed, calls out in the dark –

THE DOCTOR Listen, I'm sorry about this, Mr Van Statten might think he's clever, but never mind him. I've come to help. I'm the Doctor.

And out of the darkness, a terrible, rusting voice. Two small lights blink in unison with the words ...

DALEK Doc ... tor ...?

On the Doctor. Sudden, profound terror.

DALEK Doctor?

THE DOCTOR ... Impossible!

DALEK *The* Doctor?

CHUNK! Lights slam on – revealing a DALEK. This is an old, war-torn creature. Casing cracked, some flanks peeled back; it's been experimented upon. No sign of the alien inside, just flashes of strange alien circuitry. Taut chains and wires and tubes hold the body in position. But for all that, it's still armed, and its gun is pointing right at the Doctor.

DALEK Exterminate! *Exterminate! EXTERMINATE!*

And the Doctor runs for the door –

THE DOCTOR Let me out!

13 INT. OUTSIDE THE DALEK CELL NIGHT 7

VAN STATTEN remains impassive.

VAN STATTEN It's *talking*!

GODDARD Sir, it's going to kill him!

14 INT. DALEK CELL NIGHT 7

(ALL INTERCUT with EXT. DALEK CELL: VAN STATTEN watching, enraptured by the confrontation with the DALEK.)

The Dalek's gun jerks –

DALEK You are an enemy of the Daleks, you must be destroyed!

But the gun is clicking, grinding, useless. THE DOCTOR turns. Realising. Smiles.

THE DOCTOR . . . It's not working . . .

Then he walks forward. Wild, energised, he starts to laugh, *vicious*. For once, with no compassion, no joy.

THE DOCTOR Fantastic. Ohh, fantastic. Powerless. Look at you. The great space dustbin. How does it feel? You piece of junk.

DALEK Keep back!

THE DOCTOR Or what? Whatcha gonna do to me? If you can't kill, then what are you good for, Dalek, what's the point of you? You're *nothing*.
(quietly, up close:)
What the hell are you doing here?

Beat.

DALEK I am . . . waiting for orders.

THE DOCTOR What does that mean?

DALEK I am a soldier. I was bred to receive orders.

THE DOCTOR You won't be getting any. Not ever.

DALEK I demand orders!

THE DOCTOR They're never gonna come. Your race is dead. You burnt. All of you. Ten million ships on fire. The entire Dalek species wiped out, in one second.

DALEK You lie!

THE DOCTOR I watched it happen. I *made* it happen.

DALEK You destroyed us?

THE DOCTOR I had no choice.

DALEK And what of the Time Lords?

THE DOCTOR Dead. They burnt with you. The end of the last great Time War; everyone lost.

DALEK And the coward survived.

THE DOCTOR Ohh, and I caught your little signal. Help me. Poor little thing. But there's no one else coming cos there's no one else left.

DALEK I am alone in the universe.

THE DOCTOR Yep.

DALEK So are you. We are the same.

THE DOCTOR (furious)
We're not the same! I'm not –

But he stops. Dangerous. Grins. Back in control, burning with contempt, as he crosses to the wall.

THE DOCTOR No, wait a minute. Maybe we are. Maybe, yeah. Okay. You've got a point. Cos I know what to do. I know what should happen. I know what you deserve.
(pause)
Exterminate.

And he slams down a huge metal lever on the wall. The Dalek is electrified! Lightning bolts zig-zag and scatter across its surface. It screams. The lever's heavy, but the Doctor rams it down –

DALEK Have pity! Have pityyyy!

THE DOCTOR Why should I? You never did!

DALEK Help meeee – !

15 INT. OUTSIDE THE DALEK CELL NIGHT 7

VAN STATTEN yells at BYWATER, DE MAGGIO and SIMMONS –

VAN STATTEN Get him out!

16 INT. DALEK CELL NIGHT 7

THE DOCTOR's still holding the lever down as BYWATER and DE MAGGIO rush in, pull him away. SIMMONS runs to the lever, slams it back up. The electrification stops. The DALEK's cries fade. VAN STATTEN hurries in, runs to it –

VAN STATTEN I saved your life, now talk to me, godammit, talk to *me*!

THE DOCTOR You've got to destroy it!

But Bywater and De Maggio shove the Doctor out, as Van Statten stands, unafraid, in front of the Dalek.

VAN STATTEN The last in the universe. And now I know your name. Da-lek! Speak to me, Da-lek! I am Henry Van Statten, now recognise me!

The eyestick just stares back; unnerving silence.

VAN STATTEN Make it talk again, Simmons. Whatever it takes.

17 INT. ADAM'S WORKSHOP NIGHT 7

It's a mess – tables filled with bits of metal, rock, all strewn higgledy-piggledy. A TV screen is buried beneath papers, and ADAM starts moving them to clear it.

ADAM Sorry about the mess. Mr Van Statten sort of leaves me to do my own thing, so long as I deliver the goods. Like this . . .

He hands her a piece of grooved metal.

ADAM What do you think that is?

ROSE Dunno. Lump of metal.

ADAM Well, yeah, but I think, well, I'm almost certain, it's from the hull of a spacecraft.
(close, inspired)
Thing is, it's all true, everything the United Nations tries to keep quiet. Alien, spacecraft, visitors to the Earth. They really exist.

ROSE That's . . . amazing.

ADAM I know it sounds incredible. But I honestly believe the whole universe is just teeming with life.

ROSE I'm gobsmacked, yeah. And you do what? Sit here and catalogue it?

ADAM Best job in the world!

ROSE Could be better. Imagine if you could get out there. Travel amongst the stars and see it for real.

ADAM I'd give anything. But I was born too soon, I don't think it's ever gonna happen. Not in our lifetimes.

ROSE Oh, you never know. What about all those people who say they've been inside spaceships and things, and talked to aliens?

ADAM I think they're nutters.

ROSE Yeah. I think so too.
(kind, not wanting to take the piss)
So how d'you end up here?

ADAM I was headhunted. Van Statten has agents all over the world, looking for geniuses to recruit.

ROSE Oh right, you're a genius.

ADAM Sorry, but . . . yeah! Can't help it, I was born clever!
(smiling)
When I was eight, I logged into the Pentagon defence system, nearly caused World War Three.

ROSE What, and that's funny, is it?

ADAM You should've been there. Just to see them, running about, fantastic!

ROSE You sound like the Doctor.

ADAM So who is he? I mean, to you, I mean, are you and him, sort of . . . ?

ROSE No, just friends.

ADAM Right, good.

ROSE Why's it good?

ADAM I dunno, it just is.

Both smiling. Big fancying going on. ROSE breaks the moment, steps back, makes light:

ROSE But wouldn't you rather be downstairs? You've got all these bits of metal and stuff, but Mr Van Statten's got a living creature down there.

ADAM I did ask, but Van Statten keeps it to himself. Although . . . (cheeky)
if you're a genius, it doesn't take long to patch through on the comms system.

ROSE Well let's have a look then!

Adam operates a keyboard, a screen blinks into life.

ADAM It doesn't do much, the alien, it's weird, it's a bit useless, it's like this great big pepperpot –

Stops dead, seeing on the computer screen –

17A INT. DALEK CELL NIGHT 7

SECURITY CAMERA SHOT: SIMMONS digs his drill into the DALEK, which is screaming.

17B INT. ADAM'S WORKSHOP NIGHT 7

ROSE watching, horrified. ADAM ashen.

ROSE You sit and watch *that?*

ADAM No, I don't know what they're doing, it's nothing to do with me –

ROSE It's being tortured. Where's the Doctor?

ADAM I don't know –

ROSE Take me down there. Right now.

18 INT. LIFT NIGHT 7

THE DOCTOR talks urgently to VAN STATTEN and GODDARD.

THE DOCTOR That metal's just battle armour. The real Dalek creature is inside.

VAN STATTEN What does it look like?

THE DOCTOR A nightmare. It's a mutation. The Dalek race was genetically engineered, every single emotion was removed. Except hate.

VAN STATTEN Genetically engineered by whom?

THE DOCTOR By a genius, Van Statten. By a man who was king of his own little world, you'd like him.

GODDARD It's been on Earth for over fifty years. Sold at private auctions, moving from one collection to another, why should it be a threat now?

THE DOCTOR (quietly)
Because I'm here. How did it get to Earth, does anyone know?

GODDARD The records say it came from the sky. Like a meteorite. No ship, just the Dalek itself. It fell to Earth on the Ascension Islands. Burnt in its crater for three days before anyone could get near. And all that time, it was screaming. It must have gone insane.

THE DOCTOR It's stronger than that.

GODDARD It was taken by the military and hidden away, until certain interested parties ... acquired it.

THE DOCTOR It must have fallen through time. The only survivor.

GODDARD Of what ...? You talked about a war.

THE DOCTOR The Time War. The final battle between my people and the Dalek race.

VAN STATTEN But you survived too.

THE DOCTOR Not by choice.

VAN STATTEN But this means the Dalek isn't the only alien on Earth, Doctor. There's you. Which makes you unique, the only one of your kind in existence.

CU on the Doctor: horrified, realising what this means –

DISSOLVE TO:

19 INT. EXAMINATION ROOM NIGHT 7

Clamp! One wrist. *Clamp!* A second wrist. GUARDS stand back, reveal THE DOCTOR standing, manacled, his shirt off. VAN STATTEN is standing at a laser machine.

VAN STATTEN Now smile!

Van Statten operates the laser, a beam of light slices across the Doctor's chest. He yells, in pain. Van Statten studies the machine read-out, gleeful.

VAN STATTEN Two hearts. Fascinating! A binary vascular system, with, what ...? Respiratory bypass! That's amazing. Oh, I'm so gonna patent this!

THE DOCTOR Patent? Right, so that's your secret. You don't just collect this stuff, you scavenge it.

VAN STATTEN How d'you think I built all this? My own intelligence aside, of course. But this technology has been falling to Earth for centuries, all it took was the right mind, to use it properly. Oh, the advances I've made from alien junk, you wouldn't believe it, Doctor! Broadband? Roswell. Just last year, my scientists cultivated bacteria from the Russian Crater, and what did we find? The cure for the common cold. Of course, we've kept it strictly within the laboratory, there's no need to get people excited. Why sell one cure when I can sell a thousand palliatives?

THE DOCTOR D'you know what a Dalek is, Van Statten? A Dalek is honest. It does what it was born to do, for the survival of its species. While you just pervert things. That creature in your dungeon is better than you.

VAN STATTEN In that case, I will be true to myself. And continue.

He twists the dial, the laser intensifies.

THE DOCTOR (in pain)
Listen to me! That thing downstairs is gonna kill every last one of us –

VAN STATTEN Nothing can escape the Cage.

He turns up the laser. The Doctor keeps going, in pain –

THE DOCTOR But it's woken up! It knows I'm here! It's gonna get out, Van Statten, I swear to you, no one on this base is safe, no one on this planet!

20 INT. OUTSIDE THE DALEK CELL NIGHT 7

ROSE runs to the cell, furious – BYWATER and DE MAGGIO are there, with SIMMONS wiping his drill clean. Bywater steps forward –

BYWATER Hold it right there –

ADAM, following Rose, holds up his ID –

ADAM Level three access. Special clearance from Mr Van Statten.

Adam and Rose head inside. Simmons mocks the English accent:

SIMMONS 'Special clearance from Mr Van Statten!' Oh I say!

And they laugh, relaxed.

21 INT. DALEK CELL NIGHT 7

ROSE and ADAM are staring at the DALEK. Horror and pity from Rose; scientific fascination from Adam.

ADAM Don't get too close.

But she ignores him, walks forward.

ADAM Rose, I said don't –

ROSE It's an alien. And I know a lot more about aliens than you do.
(to the Dalek)
Hello? Can you hear me?

The eyestalk lifts, feeble.

ROSE Are you in pain? My name's Rose Tyler. I've got a friend, he can help you, he's called the Doctor. What's ... what's your name?

A croak from the Dalek which might be a laugh.

DALEK Yes.

ROSE What?

DALEK I am in pain. They torture me, but still they fear me. Do you fear me?

ROSE ... No.

DALEK I am dying.

ROSE No, we can help ...

DALEK I welcome death. But I am glad. That before I die. I met a human who was not afraid.

ROSE Isn't there anything I can do?

DALEK Nothing. My race is dead. I shall die alone.

ROSE (soft, uselessly)
I'm sorry.

Silence. Rose hesitates. Then reaches out her hand.

ADAM Rose, don't ...

She touches the Dalek dome. Her hand flat upon it. And then suddenly, she pulls away, as if it's hot. Her handprint is marked upon the Dalek metal, glowing, then fading, as though sinking into the metal, becoming part of it. And the Dalek is triumphant.

DALEK Genetic material extrapolated! Initiate cellular reconstruction!

ROSE steps back, horrified ... the DALEK hums with power. Straining against its chains. *Ssschunk!* Cables break!

ADAM (calls to guards)
Um. 'Scuse me. Hello? Um, help? I think something might have gone a little bit wrong ...

Ssschunk! Chains snap! *Schunk – schunk – schunk*, wires snap –

SIMMONS strides in –

SIMMONS What the hell have you done?
(sees the Dalek; grins, loves it)
Ohh, at last! Come alive, have you? Now watch it there, you with your egg whisk and sink plunger, oh that's scary, look at me shaking! Oh baby, don't tell me, after all this time, are you finally ready to talk?
(lifts his drill!)
Well that's tough, cos I haven't finished with the screaming!

The Dalek sucker arm moves towards him –

SIMMONS Whaddya gonna do? Sucker me to de –

Whap! Terrifying speed, the sucker arm shoots out, onto his face. Adam grabs hold of Rose –

ADAM Come on!

He pulls her out of the room. SIMMONS sinks to his knees, head held fast. The rubber spreads, oozing over Simmon's face . . .

22 INT. OUTSIDE THE DALEK CELL NIGHT 7

BYWATER is talking to camera, as DE MAGGIO trains a gun on the door. ADAM and ROSE helpless –

ROSE It's killing him, do something!

BYWATER Condition red! Repeat, condition red! This is not a drill!

Alarms begin to ring.

23 INT. EXAMINATION ROOM NIGHT 7

Alarms sounding. THE DOCTOR is still manacled. He's exhausted, but his eyes are burning as he looks up:

THE DOCTOR Release me if you want to live.

And for the first time, VAN STATTEN is scared.

24 INT. VAN STATTEN'S EXECUTIVE OFFICE NIGHT 7

BYWATER's face fills the monitor screen, GODDARD standing before it. THE DOCTOR rushes into the room, still putting on his jacket, followed by VAN STATTEN.

THE DOCTOR You've got to keep it in that cell!

25 INT. OUTSIDE THE DALEK CELL NIGHT 7

ROSE Doctor, it's all my fault!

BYWATER I've sealed the compartment, it can't get out, that lock's got a billion combinations –

26 INT. VAN STATTEN'S EXECUTIVE OFFICE NIGHT 7

THE DOCTOR A Dalek is a genius – it can calculate a thousand billion combinations in one second flat!

27 INT. DALEK CELL NIGHT 7

The DALEK's sucker arm extends. Covers the lock. Hum, click, and the door slides open.

28 INT. OUTSIDE THE DALEK CELL NIGHT 7

The DALEK emerges from the cell.

BYWATER Open fire!

BYWATER and DE MAGGIO shoot, ROSE and ADAM terrified. Bullets ricochet off the Dalek's casing, sending sparks flying –

29 INT. VAN STATTEN'S EXECUTIVE OFFICE NIGHT 7

VAN STATTEN Don't shoot! I want it unharmed!

THE DOCTOR Rose, get out of there!

30 INT. OUTSIDE THE DALEK CELL NIGHT 7

BYWATER keeps firing, yelling above the noise:

BYWATER De Maggio, take the civilians. Get them out alive, that's your job, got that?

DE MAGGIO Understood, sir. You! With me!

ROSE grabs ADAM, they run off, DE MAGGIO following. The DALEK, unaffected by the gunfire, advances on Bywater who stands back, gun still firing. It disregards him, looking instead at the screen ...

31 INT. VAN STATTEN'S EXECUTIVE OFFICE NIGHT 7

The DOCTOR, GODDARD and VAN STATTEN watch the DALEK on the screen. The sucker arm shoots out towards them ...

32 INT. OUTSIDE THE DALEK CELL NIGHT 7

The sucker arm smashes through the screen – BYWATER stops shooting, stares. Energy feeds into the DALEK. Its entire casing begins to shudder, glow with power. The Dalek cries out in ecstasy!

33 INT. VAN STATTEN'S EXECUTIVE OFFICE NIGHT 7

The lights dip, some screens blink off, the rest flicker.

GODDARD We're losing power! It's draining the base. Oh my God. It's draining the power supplies of the whole of Utah.

Graphics on screen: grid-map of Utah, lights blinking off.

THE DOCTOR It's downloading.

VAN STATTEN Downloading what?

Computer graphic: California blinks off.

GODDARD Sir! The entire West Coast has gone down!

THE DOCTOR It's not just energy. That Dalek has just absorbed the entire internet. It knows everything!

34 OMITTED

35 INT. OUTSIDE THE DALEK CELL NIGHT 7

The DALEK is alive with energy, rebuilding itself. The cracks in its casing are sealing up, the dents are shining.

BYWATER (holds earpiece)
Abandoning the Cage, sir!

BYWATER turns and runs as the Dalek pulls itself free. There is a residue of electricity, dancing around its body.

DALEK The Daleks survive in me!

And it fires its gun, a white bolt of vicious energy – explosions, glass shattering, consoles erupt in flame. The Dalek spins on the spot, firing non-stop, all its mechanisms at full power, elegant, unstoppable. The whole room's shattering under the onslaught of laser bolts. The Dalek at the centre, surrounded by destruction!

36 INT. VAN STATTEN'S EXECUTIVE OFFICE NIGHT 7

THE DOCTOR stands over the flickering computer screen.

GODDARD We've lost visual, the cameras in the Vault have gone down –

THE DOCTOR We've only got emergency power, it's eaten everything else. You've got to kill it, now!

GODDARD pushes past VAN STATTEN, to the intercom –

GODDARD All guards to converge on the Metaltron Cage! Immediately!

37 INT. VAULT CORRIDORS NIGHT 7

A dozen GUARDS running, armed with machine guns – ROSE, ADAM and DE MAGGIO run from the opposite direction –

DE MAGGIO Civilians! Let them through!

De Maggio charges on; Rose and Adam run with her, out. BYWATER appears, running from the cell, takes charge –

BYWATER Cover the north wall: Red Division, maintain suppressing fire along the perimeter, Blue Division, hold –

And then, he simply freezes. For a second, his skeleton is visible through his skin. Then Bywater falls dead, revealing: the DALEK, advancing. The guards open fire. CU Dalek casing – bullets stop, glow, melt, one inch away. The Dalek fires back. Laser bolts sizzle out – guards are blasted down! Others keep firing madly –

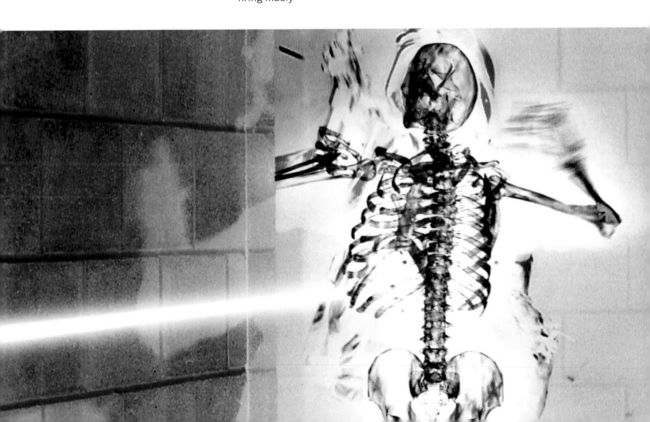

More guards appear at the far end of the corridor, behind the Dalek. They open fire. The Dalek is caught in the middle. The Dalek dome, with eyestalk, swivels 180 degrees to face this new threat, fast as lightning, elegant, fluid. Then the Dalek midsection, containing the gun, swivels 180 degrees to match the eyestalk; fires at these new guards. As both sets of guards fire, from both ends of the corridor, the Dalek comes into its own. A perfectly articulated machine – dome, midsection, base, all capable of rotating 360 degrees with smooth swift action, all swivelling independent of each other, whip, whip, whip – and all the time the gun, shooting one way, then the other, non-stop; not a laser bolt wasted, each one finding its target.

38 INT. VAN STATTEN'S EXECUTIVE OFFICE NIGHT 7

All they can hear is gunfire, THE DOCTOR anguished. VAN STATTEN rages at GODDARD –

VAN STATTEN Tell them to stop shooting at it!

GODDARD But it's killing them!

VAN STATTEN They're dispensable – that Dalek is unique!

And he stabs at the intercom –

39 INT. VAULT CORRIDORS NIGHT 7

All the guards are dead – bodies all over the ground, and the DALEK in the middle of them all.

VAN STATTEN V/O Don't hurt it! I don't want a scratch on its bodywork! Can you hear me? Can you hear me?

Underneath this, all three sections of the Dalek realign smoothly. And it glides away.

40 INT. VAN STATTEN'S EXECUTIVE OFFICE NIGHT 7

GODDARD shows THE DOCTOR a graphic of the base, 53 floors. A moving blip of light on the lowest floor – the DALEK.

GODDARD That's us, right below the surface, that's the Cage, that's the Dalek –

THE DOCTOR This museum of yours, have you got any alien weapons?

GODDARD Lots of them, but the trouble is –
(points at map)
– the Dalek's between us and them.

VAN STATTEN We've got to keep that thing alive, we could just seal the entire Vault, trap it down there.

THE DOCTOR Leaving everyone trapped with it. Rose is down there. I won't let that happen, have you got that?
(to Goddard)
It'll have to go through this area, what is that?

GODDARD Weapons testing.

THE DOCTOR Maybe. It's strong, but it's not invulnerable. If we get enough guns, attack in force . . .

GODDARD Mr Van Statten's got the equivalent of a small private army.

THE DOCTOR Small's no good. Give guns to the technicians, the lawyers, anyone, everyone. Only then d'you stand a chance of killing it.

Goddard runs out –

VAN STATTEN I thought you were the great expert, Doctor. If you're so impressive, then why not reason with this Dalek? It must be willing to negotiate. There must be something it needs, everything needs something.

THE DOCTOR What's your nearest town?

VAN STATTEN Salt Lake City.

THE DOCTOR Population?

VAN STATTEN One million.

THE DOCTOR All dead. If the Dalek gets out, it'll murder every living creature. That's all it needs.

VAN STATTEN But why would it do that?

THE DOCTOR Because it honestly believes they should die. Human beings are different, and anything different is wrong. It's the ultimate in racial cleansing, and you, Van Statten, you've let it loose.

41 INT. STAIRCASE NIGHT 7

ROSE, ADAM and DE MAGGIO run up to a metal staircase.

ROSE (laughing with relief)
Stairs! That's more like it! It hasn't got legs, it's stuck!

DE MAGGIO It's coming! Get up!

The DALEK appears at the end of the corridor. Rose, Adam, De Maggio run up the stairs. At the top:

ROSE We made it!

ADAM Great big alien death machine. Defeated by a flight of stairs!

De Maggio looks down, brave, points her gun at the Dalek.

DE MAGGIO Now listen to me. I demand that you return to your Cage. If you want to negotiate, then I can guarantee that Mr Van Statten will be willing to talk. I accept that we imprisoned you, and maybe that was wrong, maybe we can help you. But people have died, and that stops, right now – the killing stops, have you got that? I demand that you surrender. Is that clear?

DALEK El-ev-ate.

And the Dalek rises off the ground!

ROSE Oh my God . . .

And it rises up, over the steps . . .

De Maggio stands her ground.

DE MAGGIO Adam, get her out of here!

ROSE Come with us – you can't stop it –

DE MAGGIO Someone's got to try. Now get out, don't look back, just *run*!

Rose and Adam run. De Maggio turns, as the Dalek rises up in front of her. DALEK POV: closing in, descending upon De Maggio. She fires and fires, terrified, but holding her ground. The sound of a Dalek blaster, and De Maggio screams –

41A INT. CORRIDOR NIGHT 7

ROSE and ADAM running – they hear DE MAGGIO's scream –

ROSE Oh my God . . .

Truly scared now, they run for their lives –

42 INT. KILLING ZONE NIGHT 7

A large concrete room on two levels – an open floor and an upper gantry running all around. It's a weapons testing area, crates piled up with 'GEOCOMTEX' stamped on the side. GUARDS pour in, armed. Alongside them, technicians in white coats, more nervous, but determined . . .

43 INT. VAN STATTEN'S EXECUTIVE OFFICE NIGHT 7

THE DOCTOR speaks into the intercom.

THE DOCTOR The Dalek's surrounded by a forcefield, the bullets are melting before they even hit home. But it's not indestructible, if you concentrate your fire, you might get through –

44 INT. KILLING ZONE NIGHT 7

GUARDS and TECHNICIANS taking up positions –

45 INT. VAN STATTEN'S EXECUTIVE OFFICE NIGHT 7

THE DOCTOR Aim for the dome, the head, the eyepiece, that's the weak spot –

46 AND 47 OMITTED

48 INT. KILLING ZONE NIGHT 7

The COMMANDER – American, 40 – clicks off his bluetooth.

COMMANDER Thank you, Doctor, I think I know how to fight a single tin robot.
(to the troops)
All right, people. On my command!

SOLDIER It's coming!

COMMANDER Positions!

On the SOLDIERS, tense, sweating. And the clicking of a hundred safety catches being released ...

And ROSE and ADAM run out –

COMMANDER Hold your fire! You two, get out of there, clear the zone!

CUT TO Rose, running with Adam to the far side of the room. As they reach the door, Rose looks back – and the DALEK emerges.

A moment of eye-contact. Its eyestick levelled at her. Rose suddenly chilled by the connection. Adam grabs her, pulls her through the door –

48A INT. CORRIDOR OUTSIDE KILLING ZONE NIGHT 7 CONTINUOUS

ADAM pulls ROSE through; a GUARD inside the Zone pulls the door shut, slam, they're alone. Exhausted, heaving for breath. But Rose is disturbed, quiet:

ROSE It was looking at me.

ADAM It wants to slaughter us!

ROSE No, but it was looking right at me.

ADAM So? It's just a sort of metal eye thing, it's looking all round.

ROSE I don't know, it's like there's ... something inside. Looking at me, like ... like it *knows* me.

48B INT. KILLING ZONE NIGHT 7

The DALEK calmly glides to the centre of the room. GUARDS and TECHNICIANS take aim. The COMMANDER's quiet, into his bluetooth.

COMMANDER Hold it. On my mark. Aaaaand ...

The Dalek reaches centre.

COMMANDER Open fire!

All the guards and technicians fire –

49 INT. VAN STATTEN'S EXECUTIVE OFFICE NIGHT 7

One camera monitor blinks on, showing the KILLING ZONE.

GODDARD We've got vision!

THE DOCTOR It wants us to see.

50 INT. KILLING ZONE NIGHT 7

The DALEK simply takes the storm of bullets. Some of the GUARDS are even whooping, enjoying themselves. And then, the Dalek begins to rise. Slow, elegant, majestic. The guards follow it with gunfire. The Dalek now 10 ft off the ground, being shot at from all sides. At its most iconic. Magnificent. The Dalek shoots a single bolt. A GUARD dodges, as the bolt simply hits the fire alarm. Sprinklers in the roof activate. Water showers down.

51 INT. VAN STATTEN'S EXECUTIVE OFFICE NIGHT 7

THE DOCTOR, VAN STATTEN, GODDARD, watching the screen –

52 INT. KILLING ZONE NIGHT 7

The DALEK is still in mid-air. Water falling down around it, bouncing off it. The water is pooling around the guards' feet as they continue their gunfire. Then the Dalek calmly shoots a laser bolt – down. Blue arcs of electricity zig-zag through the water. GUARDS at ground level jerk, shudder, electrocuted – panic in the gantries. Guards and TECHNICIANS crying out, break cover, run. Too late – the Dalek fires – the gantries are electrified, the troops twist and die.

53 INT. VAN STATTEN'S EXECUTIVE OFFICE
INTERCUT WITH KILLING ZONE NIGHT 7

Van Statten stares at the screen, stunned.

VAN STATTEN I think, perhaps, it's time for a new strategy. Maybe we should consider abandoning this place.

GODDARD Except there's no power to the helipad, sir. We can't get out.

THE DOCTOR You said we could seal the Vault?

VAN STATTEN It's designed as a bunker in the event of nuclear war.
(taps computer)
Steel bulkheads close off the area –

On screen, red lines appear around the Vault diagram.

THE DOCTOR That should contain it, till I can think of something better.

GODDARD But there's not enough power, those bulkheads are massive.

DOCTOR We've got emergency power, we can reroute that to the bulkhead doors.

GODDARD We'd have to bypass the security codes, it would take a computer genius ...

VAN STATTEN Good thing you've got me, then.

THE DOCTOR What, you want to help?

VAN STATTEN I don't want to die, Doctor. Simple as that. And no one knows this software better than me.

GODDARD Sir! It's the Dalek –

They turn to look. One by one, the wall of monitors are turning on, all showing the DALEK. Rain still pouring down around it, soaking. Hundreds of Dalek images.

54 AND 55 OMITTED [53 CONTINUES]

DALEK I shall speak only to the Doctor.

THE DOCTOR You're gonna get rusty.

DALEK I fed off the DNA of Rose Tyler. Extrapolating the biomass of a time-traveller regenerated me.

THE DOCTOR So what's your next trick?

DALEK I have been searching for the Daleks.

THE DOCTOR Yeah, downloaded the internet, I saw, what did you find? Lots of naked bodies and people arguing about the revival of Buffy, did that help? Did you go in the chatrooms? Find a date? Gonna hook up with a coffee machine?

DALEK I searched for my species. I scanned your satellites and radio telescopes.

THE DOCTOR And?

DALEK Nothing.
(a sudden cry)
Where shall I get my orders now?

THE DOCTOR So much for intelligence. You're just a soldier with no commands.

DALEK Then I shall follow the Primary Order. The Dalek Instinct. To destroy. To conquer!

THE DOCTOR But what *for*? What's the *point*?! Don't you see, it's all gone, everything you were, everything you stood for. Gone.

DALEK Then what should I do?

THE DOCTOR (incredulous)
... You're asking me?

DALEK You have ... intelligence.

THE DOCTOR All right. If you want an order, then accept this one: kill yourself.

DALEK The Daleks must survive!

THE DOCTOR The Daleks have failed! So finish the job, make the Daleks extinct. Rid the universe of your filth. Why don't you just *die*?

THE DOCTOR shaking with anger; the DALEK considers:

DALEK You would make a good Dalek.

And the screen goes dead. Silence. The Doctor burning with anger, then quietly:

THE DOCTOR Seal the vaults.

56 INT. KILLING ZONE NIGHT 7

The DALEK elevates, arcs round elegantly and flies off.

57 INT. VAN STATTEN'S EXECUTIVE OFFICE NIGHT 7

The DOCTOR and VAN STATTEN sit side by side, tapping furiously at the keyboard. On the map, we can see that the DALEK is on the move, rising to another level.

VAN STATTEN I can leech power off the ground defences, feed it to the bulkheads,
(grins)
God, it's years since I had to work this fast!

THE DOCTOR Are you enjoying this?!

GODDARD Doctor. She's still down there.

THE DOCTOR ... I know.

58 INT. STAIRWELL NIGHT 7

ROSE and ADAM are running up a staircase. Rose's mobile phone rings – she fumbles for it, still running –

ROSE This isn't the best time ...!

THE DOCTOR V/O Where are you?

ROSE Level 49 –

59 INT. VAN STATTEN'S EXECUTIVE OFFICE NIGHT 7

THE DOCTOR keeps typing, fast – talks to ROSE on a headset:

THE DOCTOR You've got to keep moving! The Vault's being sealed off, up at level 46.

ROSE Can't you stop them closing?

THE DOCTOR I'm the one who's closing them. I can't wait. And I can't help you. Now for God's sake, *run*!

60 INT. STAIRWELL NIGHT 7

ROSE and ADAM race up the stairs, in panic . . .

61 INT. VAN STATTEN'S EXECUTIVE OFFICE NIGHT 7

GODDARD follows the DALEK's progress on the map anxiously.

GODDARD The Dalek's right behind them!

VAN STATTEN Done it! We have power in the bulkheads!

62 INT. STAIRWELL NIGHT 7

The stairs opening out onto a floor displaying '46'; large metal bulkheads raised. ROSE, running towards them, a little behind ADAM, shouting into the phone:

ROSE We're there, give's two seconds –

63 INT. VAN STATTEN'S EXECUTIVE OFFICE NIGHT 7

VAN STATTEN We haven't got two seconds, we're losing it – Doctor, I can't sustain the power, the whole system is failing, if you want to close the bulkheads, you've got to do it now –

ROSE V/O Wait for me!

VAN STATTEN Doctor, we've got to close –

THE DOCTOR (softly)
I'm sorry.

And he stabs the button –

64 INT. STAIRWELL NIGHT 7

The bulkhead door begins to lower: ADAM is nearly there – he dives underneath –

65 INT. VAN STATTEN'S EXECUTIVE OFFICE NIGHT 7

VAN STATTEN The Vault is sealed.

THE DOCTOR, standing, desperate, only caring about:

THE DOCTOR Rose? Where are you? Rose, did you make it?

66 INT. STAIRWELL NIGHT 7

ROSE stands against the bulkhead. On her mobile. Quiet:

ROSE Sorry. I was a bit slow.

Slowly, in dread, she looks round . . .

The DALEK is gliding towards her. Rose is close to tears, but so brave.

ROSE See you then, Doctor. It wasn't your fault. Remember that, okay, it wasn't your fault. And d'you know what? I wouldn't have missed it for the world.

67 INT. VAN STATTEN'S EXECUTIVE OFFICE NIGHT 7

Over the phone, a cry of 'Exterminate' from the DALEK, the sizzle of a laser bolt, a scream – cut off as the phone goes dead.

THE DOCTOR pulls off his headphones. Stands there, blank.

THE DOCTOR I killed her.

VAN STATTEN . . . I'm sorry.

Slowly, the Doctor turns to look at him.

THE DOCTOR I said I'd protect her. She was only here, because of me. And you're *sorry* . . .? I could have killed the Dalek inside its cell. But you stopped me.

VAN STATTEN It was the prize of my collection . . .

And the Doctor loses it! A titan of fury. VAN STATTEN backs away, scared.

THE DOCTOR Your collection?! Was it worth it? Worth all those men dying? Worth Rose?

Van Statten backs away as the Doctor advances on him.

THE DOCTOR Let me tell you, Van Statten. Mankind goes into space to explore. To be part of something greater –

VAN STATTEN Exactly! I wanted to touch the stars –

THE DOCTOR You just want to drag the stars down. Stick them underground. Beneath tons of sand. And dirt. And label them. You're about as far from the stars as you can get.

But then he falters, upset, hollow:

THE DOCTOR And you took her down with you. She was nineteen years old.

68 INT. BULKHEAD NIGHT 7

ROSE looks up. Wonders why she's still alive. Her POV: the DALEK, staring down, gunstick ready.

ROSE Go on then. Kill me.

DALEK . . . Rose Tyler.

ROSE Why are you doing this?

DALEK I am armed, I will kill. It is my purpose.

ROSE They're all dead because of you!

DALEK They are dead because of us.

Beat. ROSE is shaken by this.

ROSE And now what? What are you waiting for?

DALEK (uneasily)
I feel your fear.

ROSE What did you expect?

DALEK Daleks do not fear. Must not fear!

He shoots at her twice. The laser bolts pass close by her, either side.
Rose breathes, frightened.

DALEK You gave me life. What else have you given me? I have been contaminated.

69 INT. VAN STATTEN'S EXECUTIVE OFFICE NIGHT 7

ADAM runs into the room. THE DOCTOR's furious.

THE DOCTOR And you were fast on your feet, running away, leaving Rose behind –

ADAM Oy! I'm not the one who sealed the Vault!

The Doctor doesn't know what to say. But a screen comes to life. ROSE and the DALEK stare out.

DALEK Open the bulkhead. Or Rose Tyler dies.

THE DOCTOR You're alive . . .

And he's staggered. Like he's been punched. Joyous, and yet this now makes it *worse*.

ROSE Can't get rid of me.

THE DOCTOR I thought you were dead.

ROSE Day's not over yet.

THE DOCTOR Rose Tyler . . .

DALEK Open the bulkhead!

ROSE Don't do it!

DALEK What use are emotions? If you will not save the woman you love?

70 AND 71 OMITTED [69 CONTINUES]

THE DOCTOR, in agony, looks at VAN STATTEN.

THE DOCTOR I killed her once. I can't do it again.

And he's shaking, actually yells, as he punches the button.

72 INT. BULKHEAD NIGHT 7

ROSE and the DALEK face the bulkhead door as it rises . . .

73 INT. VAN STATTEN'S EXECUTIVE OFFICE NIGHT 7

THE DOCTOR, VAN STATTEN, GODDARD, ADAM watch the lift-light rise.

VAN STATTEN They're in the lift. It's coming up! What do we do, you bleeding heart, what the hell do we do now?

ADAM Well. Kill it when it gets here, sounds like a good plan to me.

GODDARD The guns are useless, and all the the alien weapons are in the Vault.

ADAM Only the catalogued ones.

Beat. And Adam quails, as the Doctor, Van Statten, Goddard, all turn to look at him . . .

74 INT. LIFT SHAFT NIGHT 7

The lift is rising . . .

75 INT. LIFT NIGHT 7

ROSE tries to reason with the DALEK.

ROSE I'm begging you. Don't kill them. You didn't kill me –

The Dalek is agitated, twitching – some words are sounding more human, more inflected, real emotion breaking through.

DALEK But why not? Why are you alive? My function is to kill. What am I? *What am I?*

76 INT. ADAM'S WORKSHOP NIGHT 7

THE DOCTOR pulling guns out of boxes, inspecting them, then tossing them aside. ADAM winces as he does so.

THE DOCTOR Broken. Broken. Hairdryer.

ADAM Mr Van Statten tends to dispose of his staff, and when he does, he wipes their memory – I kept this stuff, in case I needed to fight my way out one day –

THE DOCTOR What, you, in a fight? I'd like to see that!

ADAM I could do!

THE DOCTOR What you gonna do, throw your A-Levels at 'em?
(finds)
Ohhh yes!

And he lifts up a GREAT BIG BRUTE OF A SPACE-GUN!

THE DOCTOR Lock and load!

77 INT. VAN STATTEN'S EXECUTIVE OFFICE NIGHT 7

GODDARD and VAN STATTEN terrified –

VAN STATTEN Do something, Goddard, you're supposed to protect me!

The lift door opens. The DALEK glides out. But ROSE is at its side –

ROSE Don't move, don't do anything! It's beginning to question itself –

The Dalek glides towards Van Statten. He backs away, against the wall, slides down to the floor, gibbering. A child cowering before the bogeyman.

DALEK You. Van Statten. You tortured me. Why?

VAN STATTEN I wanted to help you, I just – I don't know, I was trying to help, I thought, if we could get through to you, if we could mend you, that's all I wanted, I just wanted you better, oh I'm sorry, I'm so sorry, I swear, I just wanted you to talk –

DALEK Then hear me talk now. Exterminate! *Exterminate! EXTERMINATE!*

ROSE Don't do it, don't kill him!

The dome and eyestalk swivel to face Rose.

ROSE You don't have to do this any more. There must be something else, not just killing, what else is there, what do you want?

DALEK I want ... freedom.

78 INT. CORRIDOR NIGHT 7

THE DOCTOR running, carrying his lethal cannon gun –

79 INT. CORRIDOR DAY 8

The DALEK enters, ROSE following. The Dalek fires upwards. The roof explodes out. For the first time, sunlight: it is dazzling. Shafts of light surrounding the Dalek; almost holy.

ROSE You made it. You're out. I never thought I'd feel sunlight again.

DALEK How does it ... feel ...?

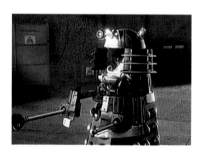

And, slowly, the Dalek's casing opens. The metal panels slide back, layer by layer, revealing a deformed, wizened little creature, held into position by metal clamps. Pistons cut into the flesh. Its tentacles, like arms, reach out to the sunlight, basking in it in wonder. *Ka-chik!* The sound of a huge metal safety catch. Rose turns. At the far end: THE DOCTOR. Gun raised. Murder in his eyes. But Rose stands between him and the Dalek.

THE DOCTOR Get out of the way.

ROSE Put the gun down.

THE DOCTOR Rose, get out of the way, right now.

ROSE No. Cos I won't let you do this.

THE DOCTOR That thing's killed hundreds of people.

ROSE It's not the one pointing a gun at me!

Beat. The Doctor is shaken by this.

THE DOCTOR I've got to do this. I've got to end it. The Daleks destroyed my home. My people. I've got nothing left.

ROSE But look at it.

And Rose steps out of the way. The Dalek turns; the Doctor sees the creature inside.

THE DOCTOR What's it doing . . .?

ROSE It's the sunlight. That's all it wants.

THE DOCTOR But it can't . . .

ROSE It couldn't kill Van Statten, it couldn't kill me. It's changing. And what about you, Doctor, what the hell are you changing into?

The Doctor, dazed, appalled. He lowers the gun.

THE DOCTOR I couldn't . . . I wasn't . . . Ohh, Rose. They're all dead.

Silence. Then, quiet:

DALEK Why do we survive?

THE DOCTOR I don't know.

DALEK I am the last of the Daleks.

THE DOCTOR (sadly)
You're not even that. Rose did more than regenerate you. You've absorbed her DNA, you're mutating.

DALEK Into what . . .?

THE DOCTOR Something new. I'm sorry.

ROSE But . . . isn't that *better*?

THE DOCTOR Not for a Dalek.

DALEK I can . . . feel. So many ideas. So much darkness. Rose. You contaminated me. Now give me orders. Order me to die.

ROSE I can't do that.

DALEK This is not life. This is sickness. I shall not be like you! Order my destruction! Obey! Obey! Obey!

ROSE (softly)
Do it.

The Dalek falls silent. Then:

DALEK Are you frightened, Rose Tyler?

ROSE Yes.

DALEK So am I.
(almost a whisper)
Exterminate.

And the Dalek begins to glow. The Doctor runs forward, grabs hold of Rose –

THE DOCTOR Get down!

And he pulls her to the side, shields her, as the Dalek explodes.

79A INT. CORRIDOR DAY 8

VAN STATTEN's parade – but in reverse, he's now being dragged along by four GUARDS, GODDARD marching after him.

VAN STATTEN What the hell are you doing?

GODDARD Two hundred personnel dead, and all because of you, sir –
(to the guards)
Take him away. Wipe his memory, and leave him by the road someplace –

VAN STATTEN You can't do this to me, I am Henry Van Statten!

GODDARD And by tonight, Henry Van Statten will be a homeless, brainless junkie, living on the streets of San Diego, Seattle, Sacramento, somewhere beginning with S.

And Van Statten is dragged away.

80 INT. EXHIBIT ROOM DAY 8

THE DOCTOR walks up to the TARDIS, ROSE behind him. Just touches it.

THE DOCTOR Little piece of home. Better than nothing.

ROSE Is that the end of it? The Time War.

THE DOCTOR I'm the only one left.
(bleak)
I win. How about that?

ROSE The Dalek survived. Maybe some of your people did too.

THE DOCTOR I'd know. In here.
(his head)
Feels like there's no one.

ROSE Well then. Good thing I'm not going anywhere.

THE DOCTOR Yeah.

Sad smile between them.

ADAM comes running in, changed clothes, carrying holdalls –

ADAM We'd better get out, Van Statten's disappeared, they're closing down the base, Goddard says they're gonna fill it in with cement. Like it never existed!

ROSE About time.

ADAM I'll have to go back home.

THE DOCTOR Better hurry up then, next flight to Heathrow leaves at fifteen hundred hours.

ROSE (to the Doctor)
Adam was saying. All his life, he's wanted to see the stars.

THE DOCTOR Tell him to go and stand outside, then.

ROSE He's all on his own, Doctor. And he did help.

THE DOCTOR He left you down there!

ROSE So did you.

ADAM What are you on about? We've got to leave, come on!

THE DOCTOR Plus, he is a bit pretty.

ROSE I hadn't noticed.

THE DOCTOR On your own head . . .

The Doctor and Rose walk into the TARDIS.

ADAM What are you doing? . . . She said cement, she wasn't joking, we're gonna get sealed in! Rose? Doctor? What are you doing, standing inside a box? Rose?

Adam goes to the TARDIS door. Steps inside. The dematerialisation noise starts; his voice floats out:

ADAM OOV Oh . . . My . . .

And the TARDIS fades away.

Episode 7
The Long Game
By Russell T Davies

Poor 'The Long Game'. As a story, it's torn in all directions.
I really should've made my mind up. To tell this tale
properly, it should have been a version of 'Rose', this time
called 'Adam'. The story of an ordinary lad in outer space,
with the mysterious Doctor and the enigmatic Rose in
peripheral roles, seen only through his eyes.

But by the time I'd started writing, we'd started filming.
And everyone, but everyone, could see the absolute magic of
Christopher Eccleston and Billie Piper together. For the first
time, we could see the glimmer of hope, the honest chance of
this being a truly special show. And yet I was proposing to reduce
their roles, only seven weeks into a risky new series. Instead, the
Doctor and Rose had to increase in status – though their half-life
still persists, it's probably the most ordinary dialogue I've ever
given them. (I even apologised to Billie for giving her plain
'What's happening, Doctor?' speeches. She said she liked it cos
it was less to learn!) Meanwhile, on the other side of the see-saw,
Adam never quite achieves a proper, independent life. If ever I get
One Character In Search of an Author, Adam will be chasing me.
(I'm not complaining.)

But the split focus rips the whole thing in half. And while this
is pure hindsight, after many months – you never stop thinking
about scripts, they linger for decades – I'm still not sure how

I'd fix it, even if I had all the time in the world. I'd still want more Adam, I'd still want more Doctor and Rose. Some problems are so fundamental that they always show, bleeding through the wallpaper.

Thank God then, for a great cast and great director; Bruno Langley, Simon Pegg, Tamsin Greig and Brian Grant conspired to make this much, much better than it is on the page. Maybe that's true of all these episodes, but here, specifically, I want to say: thank you.

This episode also had a few practical tasks: the Writer's Checklist. (I never believe writers who say 'I was writing about betrayal/redemption/love/whatever' – it's more likely they're writing about forty-five minutes with six actors, five sets and a couple of good gags. The Checklist rules; themes just happen.) Here, in 'The Long Game', I had to give us the studio sets and the CGI Space Station which could house the season finale. With Floor 500, I had to calculate ahead and work out how the same set could stage the final battle of the Time War, in six weeks' time. In fact, this episode was meant to be comparatively cheap, to balance costs across the series. I'd blown up Big Ben, and the Earth itself, so it was only fair that I should save a few pennies and deliver a more standard adventure. Oh, but I needed a monster! That's why another half-born idea creeps in. The Jagrafess never becomes the full-blown nightmare that it should be, because the episode should never have afforded a Jagrafess in the first place. It only exists at all because Phil and the Mill (our FX house) worked miracles, again. The creature hangs there but never quite attacks, cos we simply couldn't afford the shot. But it's weird – and shows how good the direction and the FX are – cos the Jagrafess turned out to be one of my favourite monsters. Oh, it's all one long accident. Don't let anyone tell you otherwise.

Russell T Davies

1 INT. FLOOR 139, CORRIDOR DAY 8 1805

Ancient engines grind and lurch; the TARDIS appears. It's tucked away, in an alcove of a wide corridor – genuinely wide, like a road. The floor's smooth, but the walls are busy, high, metal, cluttered; shutters, junction boxes, pipes, very industrial. Fans turning. Looming above, painted letters, a massive 139 (so large, they're seen only on a wide matte-shot). The hum of engines.

THE DOCTOR and ROSE hurry out of the TARDIS, quick, secretive:

THE DOCTOR So, it's two hundred thousand; it's a spaceship, no, wait a minute – space station! And, um – try that gate over there, off you go!

ROSE Two hundred thousand?

THE DOCTOR Two hundred thousand.

Rose acts confident, the Doctor just steps back, amused.

ROSE Right. Adam! Out you come.

Adam appears in the TARDIS doorway. Terrified. Boggling!

ADAM . . . Oh my God . . .

ROSE Don't worry, you'll get used to it.

ADAM Where are we ...?

ROSE Good question, let's see. Um, judging by the architecture, I'd say we're round about the year two hundred thousand. And if you listen ... yep, engines, we're on some sort of spaceship – no, hold on, feels like we're in orbit, maybe a space station? Yeah, definitely, space station. Bit warm, they could turn the heating down. Tell you what, let's try this gate, come on –

She opens the metal trellis-gate (like those on old lifts) –

2 INT. OBSERVATION DECK DAY 8 CONTINUOUS

The gate opens onto a short flight of plain metal steps. ROSE heads up, followed by ADAM, then THE DOCTOR.

ROSE Here we go, and this is ...

She stops, gobsmacked, reaching a small metal platform – functional and factory-like – with a glass wall, overlooking –

FX VIEW: the Earth, bristling with technology. The poles have melted away. Intricate metal crests circle the entire planet, and cities have spired up, through the clouds, into space. Five moons. Spaceships buzz like fireflies.

Rose can't stop smiling, still impressed by this stuff.

ROSE I'll let the Doctor describe it.

The Doctor steps forward: Rose and him in front, Adam between and behind them, all facing out. Loving the view:

THE DOCTOR The Fourth Great and Bountiful Human Empire. And there it is. Planet Earth, at its height. Covered with mega-cities, five moons, population ninety-six billion, the hub of a galactic domain stretching across a million planets, a million species, with mankind right in the middle.

Adam faints, gently, just slumps OOV. The Doctor and Rose just keep facing front.

THE DOCTOR He's your boyfriend.

ROSE Not any more.

CUT TO OPENING CREDITS.

3 EXT. FX SHOT: SATELLITE FIVE DAY 8 1810

Satellite Five hangs above the future Earth. A vertical tube, ringed with hoops, glinting in sunlight. Busy design – a workplace, not a home. Clusters of transmitters and pylons.

Huge lettering on the side: SATELLITE FIVE. Little buggy-spaceships beep horns and whizz past, like cars.

4 INT. FLOOR 139, CORRIDOR DAY 8 1810

THE DOCTOR, ROSE and ADAM walk back into the corridor.

THE DOCTOR You're gonna like this. Fantastic period of history, the Human Race at its most intelligent. Culture! Art! Politics! This era, it's got fine cuisine, the great philosophers, good manners, the works –

Klaxon hoots; big, chunky red lights flash on and off. Noise, doors, PEOPLE. Doors shoot open, WORKERS pour out. Hundreds of them! Male and female, mostly 20–30s, simple clothes – jeans, boots, tee-shirts, plain colours, workmanlike.

Clamour, some people running – the Doctor, Rose and Adam are shoved aside, as workers run to partitions in the central booths. These swing open, shutters clatter up – revealing fast-food booths. Nothing swanky, all greasy-spoonish – burgers, sausages, tubs of noodles, hissing grills, hobs, steaming tea urns, served up by big sweaty GRIMY MEN in aprons. (Some booths in b/g are even taking in laundry.) It's chaos around the booths, as workers grab food, shovel it down.

The GRIMY MAN yells throughout:

GRIMY MAN One at a time, what was it? Kronkburger with cheese, kronkburger with pajato, stop pushing, oy – you, mate, stop pushing, get back, I said, *back* –

Etc. During this, workers – rushing, always rushing – grab plain fold-up chairs and tables from storage bays, spread them out, so the corridor instantly feels like a street, a busy market. Although it's the opposite of a sterile space station – the place is alive! – it doesn't feel happy. It's all frantic, rushed.

And *hot*: always, fans spinning, sweat.

Adam's gobsmacked, Rose loving it, the Doctor puzzled.

ROSE Fine cuisine . . . ?

THE DOCTOR My watch must be wrong.
(taps wristwatch)
No, s'fine. Weird.

ROSE That's what comes of showing off. Your history's not as good as you thought it was.

THE DOCTOR My history is perfect.

ROSE Well, obviously not.

ADAM What is this place, a factory . . . ?

ROSE Must be. There's always gonna be factories. Even in paradise, there's got to be a sweatshop somewhere behind the scenes.

ADAM But . . . they're all human, what about the million planets, the million species, where are they?

THE DOCTOR Good question. Actually, that *is* a good question.
(suddenly friendly)
Adam, me old big fella, you must be starving!

ADAM No, I think I'm a bit timesick –

THE DOCTOR Naah, you just need some grub –
(yells across)
Oy mate, how much for a kronkburger?

GRIMY MAN Two credits twenty, sweetheart, join the queue!

The Doctor crosses to a panel in the wall, whirrs the sonic screwdriver against it.

THE DOCTOR Money! We need money. Hold on, let's use the cashpoint . . .

A grey metal pencil slides out, he gives it to Adam.

THE DOCTOR There you go, pocket money. Don't spend it all on sweets.

ADAM How does it work?

THE DOCTOR Go and find out, stop nagging me! Thing is, Adam – time travel, it's like visiting Paris. You can't just read the guidebook, you've got to throw yourself into it, eat the food, use the wrong verbs, get charged double and end up kissing complete strangers, or is that just me? Stop asking questions, and do it!

He shoves Adam towards a burger counter. Turns to Rose:

THE DOCTOR Off you go then. Your first date.

ROSE You're gonna get a smack, you are. And maybe it is, yeah.

Cheeky smile between them, she goes to join Adam.

Alone, the Doctor's face falls. Suspicious, looking round, he sees two women – CATHICA, 30, black, tough, wry, and SUKI, 25, shy, smiling.

THE DOCTOR Um, this is gonna sound daft, but . . . can you tell me where I am?

CUT TO SECURITY CAMERA FOOTAGE: HIGH ANGLE of the Doctor, Cathica and Suki. Sinister. Someone watching ...

CATHICA Floor One Three Nine, could they write it any bigger?

THE DOCTOR Floor One Three Nine of what?

CATHICA That must've been a hell of a party.

SUKI You're on Satellite Five.

THE DOCTOR And what's Satellite Five?

CATHICA Oh come on, how could you get on board without knowing where you are?

THE DOCTOR Look at me, I'm stupid!

CUT OUT OF SECURITY FOOTAGE, back to normal:

SUKI Hold on, wait a minute – are you a test? One of those management test sort-of-things?

THE DOCTOR You've got me! Good guess, well done, you're too clever for me.

The Doctor flashes his blank wallet-card from ep.2, as ID.

SUKI (to Cathica)
They warned us about this in basic training. All workers have to be versed in company promotion.

CATHICA All right then, ask your questions, fire away – if it gets me to Floor 500, I'll do anything.

THE DOCTOR Why, what happens on Floor 500?

CATHICA The walls are made of gold! And you should know, Mr Management. Right, so, this is what we do –

Cathica crosses to the wall, where at least six TV screens are installed, all displaying different footage. SCREEN 1: STOCK FOOTAGE, a desert sandstorm. Logo: *BADWOLF TV*; headline: *Sandstorm chaos on NVA:27.*

CATHICA Latest news! Sandstorms on the New Venus Archipelago, 200 dead –

SCREEN 2: STOCK FOOTAGE, city riot at night. Logo: *CHANNEL McB*; headline: *Water riots in Caledonia Prime.*

CATHICA The Glasgow water riots are now into their third day, and –

SCREEN 3: the sc.2 FX SHOT of Future Earth. Logo: *CHANNEL [smiley face]*; headline: *Solar flares rage at 5.9.*

CATHICA Spacelane 77 closed by sunspot activity, and –

SCREEN 4: THE FACE OF BOE, burbling away. Logo: *BOEWATCH*; headline: *Face of Boe expecting Baby Boemina.*

CATHICA The Face of Boe has announced that he's pregnant –

THE DOCTOR I get it, you broadcast the news.

CUT TO SECURITY CAMERA FOOTAGE (play below into sc.5):

CATHICA We *are* the news, we're the journalists, we write it, package it and sell it. Six hundred channels, all coming out of Satellite Five, broadcasting everywhere. Nothing happens, in the whole Human Empire, without it going through us.

5 INT. CONTROL ROOM DAY 8 1813

CU SCREEN, Cathica's speech, end of sc.4.

CUT TO a man, leaning in, profile. The EDITOR, 30, smart, sharp. Black suit. Eyes bright, watching. He's quiet, intense, but almost delighted:

EDITOR Something . . . is wrong. Something fictional.

Reaches forward, taps the screen.

EDITOR Those people. Security check. Go deep.

6 INT. FLOOR 139, CORRIDOR DAY 8 1814

ADAM sits with ROSE, at a table, surrounded by WORKERS. They've got recognisable fast food, burgers and cups with straws. Adam's hot, fanning himself with a laminated menu.

ADAM This place, d'you think it's got, like . . . artificial gravity?

ROSE Dunno. Must have, yeah.

ADAM Oh blimey. 'Scuse me.

He lowers himself off his seat, sits against the wall.

ADAM One flick of a switch, and gravity's gone. Kaput! It's ... strawberry jam on the tarmac, sort of thing.

Rose, patient, comes down to sit with him, offers a cup:

ROSE Try this, he called it 'zaffic', it's nice, it's like a slush-puppy.

ADAM What flavour?

ROSE Um. Sort of, beef.

ADAM Oh my God.

She laughs, and he laughs at himself, feeble.

ADAM Look at you. We come all this way, and you just stroll through it, like it's nothing.

ROSE I dunno, suppose I'm a bit thick. All that stuff you're going on about, it never even occurs to me.

ADAM But it's like everything's gone. Home and family and ... everything.

Rose quiet, kind, gets out her mobile.

ROSE This helps. The Doctor gave my mobile a bit of a top-up. Who've you got back home, mum and dad?

ADAM Yeah, they live just outside Manchester.

ROSE Phone 'em up.

ADAM But that's one hundred and ninety-eight thousand years ago.

ROSE Honestly, go on, try it.

He takes it, smiling, in awe.

ADAM Is there a code for planet Earth?

ROSE Just dial.

He enters the number –

7 INT. SUBURBAN HOUSE, MANCHESTER DAY 8 1400

CU answerphone. (INTERCUT with Adam, INT. SATELLITE FIVE.)

ADAM'S MUM V/O Sorry, we're not in, so leave a message, bye! [BEEP]

ADAM V/O Um, hello. It's me, um. I can't believe you're out! I've just, um, sort of gone travelling ...

CUT TO a scottie-dog, coming through the kitchen cat-flap. As it trots through, reveal the most ordinary house. Sunlight, big bay window, high ceiling; comfy middle-class, but not too posh – if there's a piano, it's only an upright. [NB, technically, this is the year 2012, but nothing's futuristic. Maybe the plasma telly looks old.]

ADAM V/O I met these people, and we're travelling together, no, that makes it sound weird, well, it is a bit weird, I just mean – I don't know what I mean, but I'm fine. I'll call again later. Love you. Bye.

8 INT. FLOOR 139, CORRIDOR DAY 8 1816

ADAM hangs up, laughing, exhilarated. ROSE smiling.

ADAM That's just so mad!

ROSE 'Love you'!

ADAM Oh shut up.
(more serious)
But that means you've got constant contact with back home. You could tell them anything.

ROSE You should hear my mother panicking, she always thinks I'm floating round on asteroids and things.

ADAM No, but you could *use* it. Think about it! Like, my dad's got arthritis, but right now, two hundred thousand years later, they must have cured it. I could find it out and phone him up.

Rose's smile stops dead.

ROSE Except, you can't.

ADAM Says who?

ROSE Says, the Doctor.

ADAM Did he actually say it? Is that what he actually said, in words?

ROSE No. Cos he doesn't need to.

ADAM Try explaining that to my dad.

ROSE (flustered)
Look, I know you're all clever and that. And I'm not an expert, but … it can get dangerous, out here. Don't go round thinking you're smarter than anyone else, all right?

The klaxon hoots! Red lights flash (not constantly, just six good blasts, each time). Breaking the tension between Rose and Adam – the WORKERS around them huff, complain, but stand, wolfing down food, going back to work.

THE DOCTOR, CATHICA and SUKI at a distance, shouts across:

THE DOCTOR Oy, Mutt and Jeff! This way!

Big smile from Rose, she stands, follows.

Stay on Adam. He's still got the mobile phone. He hesitates, then slips it into his pocket, then follows.

CUT TO SECURITY CAMERA FOOTAGE: Rose running over to the Doctor, then Adam, all following Cathica and Suki –

9 INT. CONTROL ROOM DAY 8 1817

CU SCREEN: SECURITY CAMERA FOOTAGE, sc.8, playing – the Doctor, Rose, Adam, Cathica, Suki, heading off.

CUT TO THE EDITOR, watching. Over this, a female, gentle voice:

COMPUTER VOICE Security check cleared.

EDITOR No, something's wrong, I can taste it. A tiny little shift in the information. Someone down there shouldn't be here. Double check, triple check.

He moves round. CU DRONE, sitting, enslaved to the computer screen. White-faced, blank, unthinking. Eyes pitch black. The Editor mutters in his ear:

EDITOR Follow them.

10 INT. SPIKE ROOM, FLOOR 139 DAY 8 1820

A functional metal room: eight desks, with chairs, with a simple computer screen on each desk. All arranged in a circle, with a smart starship-captain's-type chair centre. SUKI and SEVEN WORKERS sit at the desks, face inwards, facing CATHICA; she's centre of the circle, not sitting yet.

Cathica addresses THE DOCTOR, ROSE and ADAM; they're on a small raised level to one side.

CATHICA (to the workers)
Now everyone behave, we have a management inspection.
(to the Doctor)
How d'you want it, by the book?

THE DOCTOR Right from scratch, thanks.

CATHICA Okay. So! Ladies, gentlemen, multisex, undecided or robot, my name's Cathica Santini Khadeni, that's Cathica with a C, just in case you want to write to Floor 500, praising me. And please do. Now, you're free to ask questions – the process of newsgathering must be open and honest and beyond bias, that's company policy.

SUKI Actually, it's the law.

CATHICA Thank you, Suki. The info-spike will begin in thirty seconds.

She presses a switch on the arm of the central chair. Lights come down, focus on the circle. The eight place their hands flat in front of their screens – power, building.

Cathica goes round her team, a quiet word for each; b/g, hushed and tense. The Doctor, Rose and Adam huddle, quiet:

THE DOCTOR Think of it, even in your time, the amount of news in the world is massive – a flood in China, an assassination in Brazil, a skateboarding duck in Aberdeen –

ROSE So on this scale, a million planets, the sheer amount of news …

THE DOCTOR Exactly. Tons of it. How d'you gather it together? The info-spike.

And he indicates the circle. Cathica sits in her chair. The workers place hands flat on the desk, in front of their computer screens; this connects them to the machine.

CATHICA Keep it calm, now. Don't show off for the guests. Here we go.

The chair tilts back, like a dentist's chair, so Cathica's lying back, looking up at the roof. She's nervous, now:

CATHICA And, engage safety.

She lifts her hand. Deep breath. Clicks her fingers.

And her head opens. Cathica's forehead opens up. A skin-and-bone door opens, hinging upwards. A little whine of servos. Her brain is visible. And she stays completely calm.

Rose, Adam, boggling. The Doctor's fascinated. But also suspicious . . .

CATHICA And three, and two, and . . . spike!

In the ceiling above her head, is a metal disc. A surge of power, it shines white [practical light]. Cathica glows. Hot! She's frozen, wide-eyed, mouth open, a conduit –

The eight workers sit bolt upright – rigid, flooded with power. Staring straight ahead, robotised – their hands flexed, stiff, flat on their desks. Their eight screens blaze white.

[If possible: the white light between Cathica's open skull and the ceiling-disc seems to solidify, becomes FX light. Beautiful streaming wisps of white, burning at the edges with fleeting reds and oranges – volcanic. Curling and sinuous, the information trails down into Cathica's head. If not possible, then it remains as a white practical light, shining down.]

The Doctor, Rose and Adam awestruck, hushed:

THE DOCTOR Compressed information. Streaming into her! Reports from every city, every country, every planet, they all get packaged, inside her head. She becomes part of the software. Her brain *is* the computer!

ROSE If everything goes through her, she must be a genius.

The Doctor stands, walks round the circle, transfixed.

THE DOCTOR Nah, she wouldn't remember any of it, there's too much. Her head would blow up! The brain's just a processor. Soon as it closes, she forgets.

ROSE What's the people round the edge?

THE DOCTOR They've all got tiny little chips in their head, connecting them to her. And they transmit! Six hundred channels. Every single fact in the Empire beams out of this place. Now that's what I call power.

10 A INT. CONTROL ROOM DAY 8 1822

SECURITY CAMERA FOOTAGE, WIDE SHOT of sc.10 on screen.
The EDITOR stares, riveted; the DRONE blind.

COMPUTER VOICE Analysis confirmed. Security breach.

EDITOR I knew it! Which one? It's someone inside that room, which one?

COMPUTER VOICE Isolating breach.

EDITOR Come on. Show me! Who is it?

The SECURITY CAMERA darts about, zooming on, zooming out: Cathica, Rose, Suki, Adam, a worker, the Doctor . . .

10B INT. SPIKE ROOM, FLOOR 139 DAY 8 1823

ROSE moves over to ADAM, who's queasy.

ROSE You all right?

ADAM . . . I can see her brain.

ROSE D'you want to get out?

ADAM No, but . . . look at her. This technology, it's . . . amazing.

THE DOCTOR No, this technology is *wrong*.

A look between the Doctor and Rose, recognising:

ROSE Trouble?

THE DOCTOR Oh yes.

Pause. And they both smile.

11 INT. CONTROL ROOM DAY 8 1824

CUT TO the screen: SECURITY CAMERA zooms in, going past the Doctor, ignoring him, focusing instead upon Suki.

EDITOR That's it! Oh yes! She's the liar! Intercept and scan –

The DRONE flexes his palm, the computer burbles –

12 INT. SPIKE ROOM, FLOOR 139 DAY 8 1824

CU SUKI. A twitch, sharp breath, pain –

13 INT. CONTROL ROOM DAY 8 1824

The EDITOR smiles, delighted.

EDITOR Gotcha!

14 INT. SPIKE ROOM, FLOOR 139 DAY 8 1824

CU SUKI: pain, she jerks her hands up, breaks contact. The power dies, the white light fades, the session ends. CATHICA's forehead closes (it's invisible, when shut). Then she sits up, angry:

CATHICA Oh come off it Suki, I wasn't half way, what was that for?

SUKI Sorry. Must've been a glitch ...

15 INT. CONTROL ROOM DAY 8 1825

The EDITOR leans past the DRONE, studies the screen.

EDITOR Her information's been tampered with, there's a second biography hidden underneath ...

A VOICE: a deep, wet rumble, from above. The Editor turns. HIGH ANGLE, looking down on the Editor, a lofty POV. And the Editor's suddenly nervous.

EDITOR Oh yes sir. Absolutely sir.
(rumble)
No sir, her data was encrypted, there's no way we could have found it sooner. I'm sorry sir.
(rumble!)
Yes sir, of course sir.

CUT TO NORMAL ANGLE: Editor turns to Drone, a little panicked, now.

EDITOR Get her up here!

16 INT. SPIKE ROOM, FLOOR 139 DAY 8 1826

A chime, the signal for an announcement, everyone turns –

CATHICA Oh, here we go –

THE DOCTOR, ROSE, ADAM, CATHICA, SUKI, WORKERS all look; the entire wall opposite the raised area blinks, fizzes; it's a giant screen [or, on a monitor]: simple, bold lettering. The cursor blinks out: *PROMOTION.*

Excitement from the workers!

CATHICA Oh yes, come on, my turn, come on –

Cursor blinks out: *FLOOR 500.*

CATHICA Oh my God, it's the big one, come on, say my name, make it me –

Cursor blinks out: *SUKI MACRAE CANTRELL.*

Delight! The workers overjoyed, clap.

SUKI I don't believe it! Floor 500!

CATHICA How the hell did you get that? I'm above you!

SUKI I don't know, I just applied on the off chance – and they've said yes!

CATHICA That is so not fair, I've been applying to 500 for three years!

CUT TO the Doctor, Rose and Adam, left out of this.

ROSE What's on Floor 500?

THE DOCTOR The walls are made of gold.

17 INT. FLOOR 139, CORRIDOR DAY 8 1830

Breaktime again, a few workers having a quiet break. A small CROWD's saying goodbye to SUKI, who's waiting with a packed holdall and shoulder bag. THE DOCTOR, ROSE and CATHICA amongst them. ADAM sits in b/g, hot and bothered.

SUKI Cathica, I can't thank you enough, you've been so brilliant.

CATHICA Hurry up and go, we've only got a ten-minute break –

SUKI Ohh Jackson, I'm gonna miss you –
(goes to the Doctor)
And you! Floor 500! Thank you!

THE DOCTOR I didn't do anything!

SUKI You're my lucky charm!

THE DOCTOR All right then, I'll hug anyone!

And they hug, laughing.

Laughter, etc, now b/g, as Rose goes to sit opposite Adam.

ROSE Come on, it's not that bad.

ADAM What? With that head-thing?!

ROSE She's closed it now.

ADAM Yeah, but ... it's everything, I keep thinking, we're in space, there's no air! All the oxygen must be artificial, it's all recycled and stuff. Freaks me out.
(pause; quiet)
I don't know if I can do this.
(looks across)
Don't tell the Doctor.

ROSE I think he's noticed.

ADAM All my life, I've wanted this. Then I get here, and I can't ...
If I could just ... cool down. Sort of, acclimatise.

ROSE How d'you mean?

ADAM Maybe I could just go and sit on that observation deck, would that be all right? Soak it in, y'know. Pretend that I'm a citizen of the year two hundred thousand.

ROSE D'you want me to come with you?

ADAM No, stick with the Doctor.
(sad smile)
You'd rather be with him. It's gonna take someone better than me, to get between you.

Awkward pause, because it's true. Then he stands.

ADAM Anyway. I'll be on the deck.

ROSE Here you go, have the TARDIS key. Just in case it all gets too much.

ADAM Yeah, like it's not weird in there.

ROSE (calls across)
Doctor?

And she holds up the key, indicates Adam, meaning, is it all right to give him the key? The Doctor just indicates yeah, not bothered, gets back to talking to the others.

Rose hands Adam the key. He takes it, heads off. Follow him (Rose going to the Doctor, Cathica, Suki, etc, b/g). He walks faster. And slowly, he smiles; hurries along. A man with a plan . . .

Beep beep! A zippy little scooter beetles past him. Follow the scooter. The COURIER – black helmet, face OOV – nips up to Suki –

SUKI It's for me, oh my God, this makes it really real!

The courier gives her an envelope, and zooms away.

SUKI This is it, I've got it, look –

Suki rips it open, pulls out a rectangular gold tab.

SUKI It's the key to the lift! It's really happening, I'm on 500! Oh my God, I've got to go, I can't keep them waiting, I'm sorry, say goodbye to Steve for me –

She steps into the lift, uses the key, it *pings*!

SUKI Look at that, it works! Bye!

CATHICA Good riddance!

'Bye!', doors close, she's gone. The crowd disperses.

THE DOCTOR She's only going upstairs, you're talking like you'll never see her again.

CATHICA We won't. Once you go to 500, you never come back.

18 INT. SATELLITE FIVE LIFT DAY 8 1832

SUKI in the high-velocity lift, lights whizzing past. The counter lists the floors, fast: 299, 300, 301, 302, 303 – Suki's excited, nervous.

19 INT. FLOOR 139, CORRIDOR DAY 8 1832

CATHICA with THE DOCTOR and ROSE.

CATHICA Floor 500 is editorial. Marble toilets, double beds, fifteen different menus, and all the big decisions. Paradise.

20 INT. SATELLITE FIVE LIFT DAY 8 1832

SUKI watches the counter: 456, 457, 458, 459, 460 . . .

21 INT. FLOOR 139, CORRIDOR DAY 8 1832

CATHICA with THE DOCTOR and ROSE.

THE DOCTOR Have you ever been up there?

CATHICA Can't, you need a key for the lift, and you only get a key with promotion. No one gets to Floor 500, except the chosen few.

22 INT. SATELLITE FIVE LIFT DAY 8 1833

Ping! 500. The lift door opens, SUKI steps out –

23 INT. FLOOR 500, CORRIDOR DAY 8 CONTINUOUS

SUKI steps out, and she's *cold*. Exactly the same as Floor 139 – the floor, busy walls, doors, a massive 500 sign. But a very different world. Deserted. Abandoned. Icy. Shafts of moonlight slanting across. The moan of wind in the rafters; ominous metal creaks from above, like the whole place might collapse.

Suki looks round. Cold, lost, scared. The lift door closes behind her. Too late – she stabs the button, then hits it, but no response. She turns to face the corridor.

SUKI Hello . . . ?

Braver than she seems at first, she ditches the holdall and bag, pulls out a torch. Shines it round. Her footsteps crunch, a light frost on the floor. She heads for the nearest SPIKE ROOM. Opens the door ...

24 INT. SPIKE ROOM, FLOOR 500 DAY 8 CONTINUOUS

The same as the FLOOR 139 SPIKE ROOM, but in darkness, derelict. SUKI shines her torch. The computer seats are occupied by SKELETONS. Ragged clothes. Torchlight hollowing round the empty eye-sockets.

25 INT. FLOOR 500, CORRIDOR DAY 8 CONTINUOUS

SUKI backs away from the SPIKE ROOM. Really scared, now.

At the far end – *schunk*! – a shaft of blue light falls across the floor. Like a door has been opened. An invitation.

26 INT. CONTROL ROOM DAY 8 1835

SUKI walks in slowly; scared, but determined.

The heart of the satellite. A techno-room – circular, ringed with glowing computer screens. Each desk is attended by DRONES, staring mindlessly at their screens, hands flat on the worktop; like this room is staffed by the dead. Above, more screens suspended in the air, stacking upwards; metal struts and rafters above, ascending into absolute blackness. Small icicles hanging from the metal struts.

Centre, a raised metal platform; the EDITOR stands, smiling.

SUKI ... Who are you?

EDITOR I'm the Editor.

SUKI But ... what's happened? There are bodies out there, what's going on?

EDITOR While we're asking questions, can you confirm your name?

He clicks his fingers. A huge graphic projects into the air above the DRONES. An ID card: Suki's face, number, signature. The photo talks:

SUKI PROJECTION My name is Suki Macrae Cantrell, I was born one-nine-nine-apostrophe-eight-nine, in the Independent Republic of Morocco –

The Editor clicks his fingers, jump-cuts the recording –

EDITOR Liar.

SUKI PROJECTION Hobbies include reading, and archaeology, I'm not an expert or anything, I just like digging –

EDITOR Liar!
(click)

SUKI PROJECTION I want to work for Satellite Five cos my sister can't afford university, and the pay-scheme is –

EDITOR *Liar!*

The Editor clicks, the image freezes.

EDITOR Let's have the facts!

Another click. The projected image blinks, changes to a different Suki – a juddering, grabbed photo of a tough, angry woman in battle-fatigues, yelling as she fires a gun.

EDITOR Hidden behind a genetic graft, but that's still you. Eva Saint Julienne, last surviving member of the Freedom Fifteen, self-declared anarchist, is that right?

And Suki drops the act. Tough as nails, she reaches behind, pulls a gun – a small blaster – out of her waistband, holds it with both hands, aimed at him.

SUKI Who controls Satellite Five?

EDITOR Now there's the truth!

SUKI The Freedom Foundation has been monitoring Satellite Five's transmissions, we have absolute proof that the facts are being manipulated. You're lying to the people!

EDITOR Oh I love it, say that again!

SUKI This whole system is corrupt, who do you represent?

EDITOR I'm just a humble slave. I answer to the Editor-in-Chief.

SUKI Then who's he, where is he?

EDITOR Oh, he's overseeing everything. Literally, everything. If you don't mind, I'll have to refer this upwards . . .

He clicks his fingers. Concealed lights around the base of the room slam on, *CHUNK*! Spotlights beaming upwards. Suki looks up . . .

CUT TO HIGH ANGLE POV, something in the roof, right above them, looking down on Suki. She looks up, into CAMERA. Her terror.

SUKI What is that . . . ?

CUT TO the Editor, smiling.

EDITOR Your boss. This has always been your boss. Since the day you were born.

CUT TO HIGH ANGLE POV, starting to descend upon her . . .

Suki's terrified, fires – plain bullets – again and again and again, but the HIGH ANGLE POV keeps lowering, lowering. And as Suki Macrae Cantrell screams, CUT TO:

27 INT. OBSERVATION DECK DAY 8 1840

ADAM alone, and furtive. The waist-height wall facing the view has a computer screen built into it. Adam tentatively holds out his palm, just as he saw the workers do. He moves his hand, right, left . . . tiny movements. Result! The screen burbles, alien letters flows across it.

ADAM Slowly. Give me access, give me –

Burble increases, text flows faster, too fast – Adam whips his hand away, the screen stops. But Adam's smiling.

ADAM I can learn anything.

And he holds out both hands, keeps going. Text scrolls on screen. Adam smiles, getting the hang of it.

28 INT. SPIKE ROOM, FLOOR 139 DAY 8 1845

Empty, downtime, THE DOCTOR and ROSE with CATHICA. She's got a clipboard, checking the screens, her usual routine.

CATHICA Look, they only give us twenty minutes for maintenance, can't you give it a rest?

THE DOCTOR But you've never been to another floor? Not even one floor down?

CATHICA I went to Floor 16 when I first arrived, that's Medical, that's where I got my head done, then I came straight here. Satellite Five, you work, eat and sleep on the same floor, and that's it, that's all. (wary)
You're not management, are you?

THE DOCTOR At last, she's clever!

CATHICA Whatever this is, don't involve me. I don't know anything.

THE DOCTOR Don't you even ask?

CATHICA Why would I?

THE DOCTOR Because you're a journalist!
(harder)
Why's all the crew human?

CATHICA What's that got to do with it?

THE DOCTOR There's no aliens on board, why?

CATHICA I dunno, no real reason. They're not banned or anything.

THE DOCTOR Then where are they?

CATHICA I suppose immigration's tightened up – it had to, what with all the threats.

THE DOCTOR What threats?

CATHICA I dunno, all of them, the usual stuff. And then price of spacewarp doubled, that kept visitors away. Oh, and the

government collapsed on Chavic Fice, so that lot stopped coming, y'see? Lots of little reasons, that's all.

THE DOCTOR Adding up to one great big fact. And you didn't even notice.

CATHICA Doctor, if there was any sort of conspiracy, Satellite Five would have seen it, we see everything.

THE DOCTOR I can see better. This society is the wrong shape, even the technology –

CATHICA It's cutting edge!

THE DOCTOR It's backwards! There's a great big door in your head! You should've chucked this out years ago!

ROSE So what d'you think's going on?

THE DOCTOR It's not just this space station, it's the whole attitude, it's the way people *think*. The Great and Bountiful Human Empire is stunted, something's holding it back.

CATHICA And how would you know?

THE DOCTOR Trust me. Humanity's been set back about ninety years. When did Satellite Five start broadcasting?

Pause.

CATHICA ... Ninety-one years ago.

29 INT. OBSERVATION DECK DAY 8 1850

ADAM's becoming more confident, hands on controls.

ADAM Accept vocal command. Hello?
(bleep, negative)
Hold on. There, s'that better?
(bleep, positive)
Give me, um ... arthritis, history of, treatment and care.

Screen burbles, scrolls.

ADAM Okay. There's got to be better stuff than that, let's try, um ... computers. From the twenty-first century to the present day. Give me the history of the microprocessor.

Screen burbles, text scrolls.

ADAM Oh my God. Um ... pause, hold on –

Screen pauses. Keeping one hand on the keyboard, Adam gets out the mobile, clicks redial. Tense, excited:

ADAM Here we go.

ADAM'S MUM V/O Sorry, we're not in, but leave a message, bye! [BEEP]

ADAM Right, mum, dad, keep this message, okay, whatever you do, don't wipe it, save it, got that? Okay?
(reads the screen)

The microprocessor became redundant in the year 2019, replaced by a process called SMT, that's Single Molecule Transcription . . .

30 INT. SUBURBAN HOUSE, MANCHESTER DAY 8 1435

The answerphone blinks away. On a normal, sunny Earth day, the dog looks up at the device. Gives a single bark. Over this:

ADAM V/O . . . Developed by the Butler Corporation, first registered in Cincinatti. SMT is a means of indenting the wall of a hydrogen molecule with code which responds to the physical excitation of the surrounding space – no no no – !

31 INT. OBSERVATION DECK DAY 8 1851

The screen flares white, information disappears.

ADAM Come back, come back, come back –
(thumps it)
Why d'you keep doing that – ?

The screen displays, big letters: *FLOOR 16.*

ADAM What's Floor 16, what's down there?
(screen burbles)
Is that like the IT department? D'you want me to go to Floor 16?

The computer *pings*!, a positive yes.

32 INT. SATELLITE FIVE LIFT DAY 8 1855

The counter reads: 23, 22, 21, 20, 19, 18, 17. . . ADAM watches the counter tick down, nervous.

Ping! 16. The door opens –

33 INT. FLOOR 16, CORRIDOR DAY 8 CONTINUOUS

ADAM steps out into another version of the same corridor. Emptier, more sterile – though still warm, with fans turning. Desks are installed at intervals, in front of doors, and at each desk, a NURSE, in plain white uniform. Adam heads for the Nurse. She's late 30s, efficient, dry.

ADAM Sorry, um . . . Floor 16, that's, um . . . what sort of thing do you cover . . . ?

NURSE Medical non-emergency.

ADAM Right! Wrong floor. I'm just having technical problems, my screen keeps freezing and locking me out.

NURSE No, that's medical, there must be something wrong with your chip.

ADAM Right, and, what chip's that?

NURSE The chip in your head.

ADAM Right, that's it, yeah. Haven't got one.

NURSE No wonder you can't get a screen to work, what are you, a student?

ADAM Yeah, I'm on a research project, from the University of … Mars.

NURSE Oh, the Martian boondocks, typical. Well, you still need chipping.

ADAM But does that mean, like, brain surgery …?

NURSE That's an old-fashioned phrase, but it's the same thing, yes.

ADAM (backing off)
Okay. Never mind. Thanks then.
(stops)
But, if I get a chip, then I can use *any* computer?

NURSE Absolutely. You'll have to pay for it, they've stopped subsidising.

ADAM (backing off)
Right, yeah, sorry, of course. Anyway. Wasting your time –
(stops)
Hold on! Can I use this?

And he holds up his metal money-pencil. She smiles:

NURSE That'll do nicely.

34 INT. MEDICAL ROOM DAY 8 1900

A sterile white-tiled windowless box. Walls shining with x-ray-type light-boxes. Banks of steel instruments.

The NURSE spins ADAM round in a high-tech dentist's-type chair, to face technical diagrams. He's nervous.

NURSE It all comes down to two basic types. Type One, the head-chip, inserted into the back of the skull, one hundred credits. There's the chip –

She holds up a small, 1-mm microcircuit.

NURSE Tiny, invisible, no scarring. Type Two is the full info-spike.

ADAM That's the …?

He mimes, a door in his forehead.

NURSE That's the one. It does cost ten thousand.

ADAM Oh, well I couldn't afford it, then.

NURSE Not at all.
(holds up pencil)
Turns out, you've got unlimited credit.

ADAM No, but I couldn't have it done, I mean, that's gotta hurt, hasn't it?

NURSE Painless. Contractual guarantee.

ADAM No, but, my mate's waiting upstairs, I can't have major surgery.

NURSE Takes ten minutes. That sort of money buys a very fast picosurgeon.

ADAM ... No, but I couldn't though, no.

The nurse leans in. A fine saleswoman.

NURSE Type One, you can interface with a simple computer. Type Two, you are the computer. You can transmit any piece of information from the archive of Satellite Five, which is just about the entire history of the Human Race. Now, which one's it going to be ...?

35 INT. FLOOR 139, CORRIDOR DAY 8 1905

THE DOCTOR's whirring the sonic screwdriver against a big, door-sized metal panel in the wall. (The corridor deserted behind them.)

CATHICA We're so gonna get in trouble. You're not allowed to touch the mainframe, we'll get told off –

THE DOCTOR Rose, tell her to button it.

CATHICA You can't just vandalise the place, someone's gonna notice!

CUT TO SECURITY CAMERA FOOTAGE, as the Doctor lifts the entire panel away from the wall.

35A INT. CONTROL ROOM DAY 8 1905

SECURITY CAMERA FOOTAGE from sc.35 playing on screen. The EDITOR studying the screen – the Doctor.

EDITOR I don't understand. We did a full security scan, that man was there when we found Suki MacRae Cantrell.

He moves round. And the nearest DRONE is actually SUKI.

She's sitting at a terminal, palms flat out, skin a terrible white, eyes black. Impassive, unflinching, enslaved.

EDITOR Nothing was indicated about him. Yet here he is, clearly acting outside the parameters.
(big smile)
Fascinating!

A rumble from above, the Editor loses his smile.

EDITOR Absolutely! At once!
(to the Drone)
Check him. Double check, triple check, quadruple it!

35B INT. FLOOR 139, CORRIDOR DAY 8 1906

THE DOCTOR's gutting the space behind the removed panel, yanking out huge swathes of cables, all strewn across the corridor; ROSE helping him pull more out. CATHICA stands back.

CATHICA This is nothing to do with me, I'm going back to work.

THE DOCTOR Go on then, see ya.

She hesitates, but she stays.

CATHICA Well I can't just leave you, can I?

ROSE If you want to be useful, get them to turn the heating down, it's boiling. What's wrong with this place, can't they do something about it?

CATHICA I dunno, we keep asking. It's something to do with the turbines.

THE DOCTOR 'Something to do with the turbines'.

CATHICA Well I don't know!

THE DOCTOR Exactly! I give up on you, Cathica. Now Rose, look at Rose, Rose is asking the right sort of question –

ROSE I thank you.

THE DOCTOR Why is it so hot?

CATHICA One minute you're worried about the Empire, next minute, it's the central heating!

THE DOCTOR Oh, plumbing's important. Never underestimate plumbing.

35C INT. CONTROL ROOM DAY 8 1907

The EDITOR poised, alert –

COMPUTER VOICE Security scan complete.

EDITOR And? Who is he?

COMPUTER VOICE He is no one.

EDITOR ... What does that mean?

COMPUTER VOICE He is no one.

EDITOR D'you mean he's got a fake ID?

COMPUTER VOICE He has no identification.

EDITOR But everyone's registered, we've got a census of the whole Empire!

COMPUTER VOICE He is no one

EDITOR He doesn't exist ...? Not anywhere? What about the blonde?

COMPUTER VOICE She is no one.

EDITOR Both of them . . .
(big grin)
Well, we all know what happens to non-entities. They get promoted.
Bring them up!

35D INT. FLOOR 139, CORRIDOR DAY 8 1908

THE DOCTOR has now pulled a computer screen out of the wall, still attached by hundreds of wires. He holds it like a portable DVD player, demonstrates to ROSE and CATHICA:

THE DOCTOR Here we go. Satellite Five. Pipes and plumbing! Look at the layout –

A screen shows an animated schematic of Satellite Five.

CATHICA This is ridiculous. You've got access to the computer core, you could look up the archive, the news, the stock exchange . . . and you're looking at pipes!

THE DOCTOR But doesn't it look wrong . . . ?

Cathica's fascinated, despite herself.

CATHICA I suppose . . .

ROSE Why, what is it . . . ?

CATHICA The ventilation system. Cooling ducts. Ice filters. All working flat out. They're chanelling massive amounts of heat *down* . . .

THE DOCTOR All the way from the top.

ROSE Floor 500.

THE DOCTOR Something up there is generating tons and tons of heat.

ROSE Dunno about you, but I feel like I'm missing a party. It's all going on upstairs, fancy a trip?

CATHICA But you can't, you need a key.

THE DOCTOR A key's just a code. And I've got the codes, right here . . .

A display inside the wiring whizzes through numbers, like a fruit machine, numbers stopping one by one, left to right.

THE DOCTOR Here we go, bypass code two . . . one . . . five . . . point . . . nine . . .

Beep beep! They look round, hearing a familiar buzzing. From the far end of the corridor, the COURIER beetles along on his zippy little scooter. Face helmeted, inscrutable. He stops some distance away. Engine purring. Threatening.

The courier throws an envelope, the Doctor catches it – and the scooter does a quick circle, buzzes away, gone. The Doctor rips open the envelope, a gold tab falls out.

THE DOCTOR We've been invited.

CATHICA But . . . how come you get a key?

CUT TO SECURITY FOOTAGE: CU Doctor, looking into CAMERA.

THE DOCTOR Someone up there likes me.

36 INT. CONTROL ROOM DAY 8 1910

The EDITOR, watching the Doctor on screen, laughs.

37 INT. FLOOR 139, CORRIDOR DAY 8 1910

THE DOCTOR and ROSE head for the lift, CATHICA on edge.

ROSE Come on, come with us.

CATHICA No way! You only get one shot at Floor 500. When I go up, I'm gonna get there as a proper journalist.

THE DOCTOR No offence, but calling yourself a journalist is like an abacus calling itself a mathematician.

ROSE That's a whole new definition of 'no offence'.

THE DOCTOR (big smile at Cathica)
See ya!

CATHICA Don't mention my name. When you get in trouble, don't involve me.

And Cathica walks off, furious. As they get in the lift:

THE DOCTOR That's her gone. Adam's given up. Looks like it's just you and me.

ROSE Yup.

THE DOCTOR Good.

ROSE Yeah.

He inserts the key. And as the doors close, he takes Rose's hand, both smiling.

38 INT. SPIKE ROOM, FLOOR 139 DAY 8 1911

EIGHT WORKERS sit waiting, as CATHICA storms in, foul mood.

CATHICA All right, I'm sorry, my fault, you won't lose any pay, let's get on with it.
(sits)
Anyone gonna ask where I've been?

No one does, busy at their screens. She presses the chair-arm switch, lights lower. But Cathica's lost in thought.

39 INT. FLOOR 500, CORRIDOR DAY 8 1911

Ping! 500. The lift doors open – THE DOCTOR and ROSE step out carefully. The cold, the dark, the emptiness. Quiet:

THE DOCTOR The walls are not made of gold.
(pause)
You should go back downstairs.

ROSE Tough.

And that's a fact. They walk on. The crunch of frost.

40 INT. MEDICAL ROOM DAY 8 1912

ADAM's in a white dressing gown – staring at himself in a mirror – the NURSE beside him. He's stunned, scared.

NURSE Told you it was painless. No scarring, you see? Perfect success.

ADAM How do I ... activate it ...?

NURSE It's a personal choice, some people whistle. I know one man who triggers it with 'Oh Danny Boy'. But you're set on default for now, that's a click of the fingers.

ADAM You mean I just ...?

NURSE Click.

He holds up his hand. Terrified. Steels himself. The nurse smiling. And then, deep breath – he clicks – and his head opens. The little door in his forehead whines, lifts, and there's his brain. Adam breathing fast, eyes wide. In shock! He clicks again, the door closes.

ADAM Oh my God, I'm gonna be sick –

He heaves. His cheeks puff. Then he stops. He frowns. Puzzled. Strangely calm, he reaches into his mouth. Plucks out a sick-coloured lozenge.

NURSE Special offer, we installed the vomit-o-matic at the same time.

Nano-termites have been placed in the lining of your throat.
In the event of sickness, they freeze the waste. No extra charge!

ADAM Oh my God . . .

He heaves again; mouth fills, then stops. He reaches up, plucks out another lozenge.

41 INT. CONTROL ROOM DAY 8 1913

SECURITY CAMERA FOOTAGE of THE DOCTOR and ROSE, being projected into the air, huge. NEW ANGLES on sc.28, 35B, 35D, the Doctor voicing his suspicions, etc.

The EDITOR stands centre, watching it. Clicks his fingers, jumps the footage; does so again, completely in charge. Then, almost lazy, he turns.

EDITOR I started without you.

The Doctor and Rose are standing in the doorway. Gobsmacked, taking it all in. As they walk forwards, slowly, they keep looking round. The Editor keeps going, regardless.

EDITOR Now you see, this is fascinating. Satellite Five contains every piece of information contained in the Fourth Great and Bountiful Human Empire. Birth certificates, shopping habits, bank statements, but you two . . . don't exist. Not a trace. No birth, no job, not the slightest kiss. How can you walk through the world without leaving a single footprint?

ROSE Suki, that's Suki –

She runs over – SUKI stays at her desk, keeps working. No reaction.

ROSE Hello? Can you hear me? Suki?
(to the Doctor)
What have they done to her?

THE DOCTOR I think she's dead.

ROSE But she's . . . working.

THE DOCTOR They've all had their heads chipped. The chip keeps going. Like puppets.

EDITOR You're full of information, it's only fair that we get information back. Because you, apparently, are no one. Ohh, and it's so rare, to not know something. Who are you?

THE DOCTOR Doesn't matter, cos we're off, nice to meet you, come on –

Rose takes a step towards the Doctor; the Editor clicks his fingers; a hand grabs Rose's forearm; she turns. Suki stands, gripping Rose's arm – impassive, strong, not flinching. Rose struggles. The Doctor runs forward – two other DRONES grab him, pin his arms back.

EDITOR Tell me who you are!

THE DOCTOR Since that information's keeping us alive, I'm hardly gonna say, am I?

EDITOR Perhaps the Editor-in-Chief can convince you otherwise.

THE DOCTOR And who's that?

EDITOR It might interest you to know that this is *not* the Fourth Great and Bountiful Human Empire. It's not human at all, it's merely a place where humans happen to live.

A deep, angry rumble, from above. The Editor looks up.

EDITOR Yes of course, I'm sorry: a place where humans are *allowed* to live, by kind permission of my client.

He clicks his fingers. At floor level, the concealed spotlights slam on, with the *chunk!* of massive lights – beams shooting up, to the roof. The Doctor and Rose look up in horror ... seeing ... a wet, red, quivering mountain of meat, suspended right above them, so that it *is* the ceiling. A vast expanse of raw steak, stringed with white fat. Water trickling down it. Faceless, pulsating, breathing. It hangs above, pipes and wires plumbed into its mass.

The Doctor and Rose awestruck.

ROSE What is it ...?

THE DOCTOR D'you mean, that thing's in charge of Satellite Five?

EDITOR No, that 'thing', as you put it, is in charge of the Human Race. For almost a hundred years, mankind has been guided and shaped. Its knowledge and ambition, strictly controlled, through its broadcast news. Edited by my superior, your master, and

humanity's guiding light: the Mighty Jagrafess of the Holy Hadrojassic Maxarodenfoe.

And the meat flexes, bulges – an awful, huge bellow, rage and triumph, thundering throughout the room.

42 INT. FLOOR 139, CORRIDOR DAY 8 1915

The klaxon hoots, red lights flash, WORKERS emerge.

ADAM watches. Gingerly, he touches his head, but it's normal, fine.
He heads towards the Spike Room as CATHICA comes out (ignoring Adam).

Follow her; worried, she crosses to the panel which the Doctor gutted. The piles of cables and wires are still strewn everywhere. She stops. Looks at the wiring. Steps into it. The code is now complete, still on display: 215.9976/3.

43 INT. SATELLITE FIVE LIFT DAY 8 1916

CU numbers written on the back of CATHICA's hand: 215.9976/3. She's in the lift. She's removed a panel from the lift controls. Behind it, a small keyboard, allowing her to tap in the code. *Ping!* The lift door closes, she's off.

44 INT. SPIKE ROOM, FLOOR 139 DAY 8 1916

The lights are down; the noise of power building. ADAM sits in the central chair, psyching himself, scared. And he gets out the mobile phone, holds it tight.

45 INT. CONTROL ROOM DAY 8 1918

THE DOCTOR and ROSE are prisoners, wrists sealed in clunky, heavy electro-manacles, fastened to a horizontal bar. Wrists at head-height. The DRONES are back at their desks. The EDITOR's centre, the huge JAGRAFESS looming above him.

EDITOR Create a climate of fear, and it's easy to keep the borders closed. It's just a matter of emphasis. The right word in the right broadcast, repeated often enough, can destabilise an economy. Invent an enemy. Change a vote.

ROSE So all the people on Earth, they're like … slaves.

EDITOR Well now, there's an interesting question. Is a slave a slave if he doesn't know he's enslaved?

THE DOCTOR Yes.

EDITOR Oh, and I was hoping for a philosophical debate, is that it, just 'yes'?

THE DOCTOR Yes.

EDITOR You're no fun.

THE DOCTOR Let me out of these manacles. Then you'll find out how much fun I am.

EDITOR Ohh, he's so tough! But come on! Isn't it a good system? You've got to admire it, just a little bit. No warfare needed. No guns, no soldiers, no blood, just a slow and silent occupation. It's not only effective, but cheap!

ROSE You can't hide something on this scale, someone must've noticed.

EDITOR Oh, now and again, someone, yes. But the computer-chip system gives me access inside their heads. I can see the smallest doubt. And crush it. So the people just carry on, living the life, strutting about downstairs and all over the surface of the Earth, thinking that they're so individual. When in fact, they're just cattle. In that sense, the Jagrafess has hardly changed a thing.

ROSE But what are you doing it for, why the human race?

EDITOR Earth was expanding, the Jagrafessfold breeding grounds would have been next. My client prefers mankind small.

ROSE But what about you? You're not a Jagra, belly, thing –

THE DOCTOR Jagrafess.

ROSE Jagrafess, you're not a Jagrafess. You're human.

EDITOR Yes, but simply being human doesn't pay that well.

ROSE But you can't have done all of this on your own.

EDITOR Course not! I represent a consortium of banks. Money prefers a long-term investment. And the Jagrafess did need a hand, to install itself.

THE DOCTOR No wonder, creature that size, what's its lifespan?

EDITOR Three thousand years.

THE DOCTOR That's one hell of a metabolism. Generating all that heat. That's why Satellite Five is so hot, you pump it out of the creature, channel it downstairs – the Jagrafess stays cool, it stays alive. / Satellite Five is one great big life-support system.

Said with calm emphasis. At / he glances to the side – his POV: a panel of metal, and reflected in that metal, a figure, in the background, hiding by the door:

Cathica crouching, terrified. Listening.

46 INT. SPIKE ROOM, FLOOR 139 DAY 8 1919

Power building. ADAM scared, but determined. He tilts the chair so that he's lying back, staring up at the ceiling. Deep breath:

ADAM Engage safety.

Then he lifts up his hand, clicks his fingers. His forehead opens. Adam breathing hard, but excited. He redials the mobile –

ADAM'S MUM V/O Sorry, we're not in, but leave a message, bye! [BEEP]

ADAM Me again, don't wipe this message, it's just gonna sound like white noise, but save it, cos I can translate it, okay?
(looks up)
Three, two, one, and ... spike!

The disc above shines white, Adam glows! [Practical light.]

47 INT. CONTROL ROOM DAY 8 1919

CATHICA, still hiding, watching. Her POV: the EDITOR walking up to THE DOCTOR and ROSE.

EDITOR But that's why you're so dangerous. Knowledge is power, but you remain unknown.

He clicks his fingers. A [practical] light on the manacles burns red. The Doctor and Rose in pain. Spasming, gasping.

EDITOR *Who are you?*

48 INT. SPIKE ROOM, FLOOR 139 DAY 8 1920

ADAM wide-eyed, open-mouthed. The white curls of light [FX light?] pour down from the disc, into his head. Beautiful, shining, incandescent.

And Adam holds out his arm – rigid, shaking the mobile phone –

49 INT. SUBURBAN HOUSE, MANCHESTER DAY 8 1505

The dog's going mad, barking like crazy – the answerphone is glowing! Streams of beautiful white [FX light?] pour out of the device, channelling up, a column of light, fringed with burning red and gold. The most ordinary room, with a fantastic light burning away.

50 INT. SPIKE ROOM, FLOOR 139 DAY 8 1920

CU ADAM: shining with power. And he *grins.*

51 INT. CONTROL ROOM DAY 8 1920

THE DOCTOR and ROSE flinching, the manacles electrified. But the Doctor can't bear to see her in pain:

THE DOCTOR Leave her alone! I'm the Doctor, and she's Rose Tyler – we're nothing, we're just wandering, let her go.

EDITOR But who are you?

THE DOCTOR I've just said!

EDITOR Who do you work for? Who sent you? Who knows about us? Who exactly do you represent ...

And the EDITOR stops. Sharp breath. Smiles. Enchanted.

EDITOR Time Lord.

THE DOCTOR ... What?

52 INT. SPIKE ROOM, FLOOR 139 DAY 8 1921

ADAM flinches. Pain. Something going wrong. The FX white-light information-flow reverses. Curling, hot light streams out of his head, *up*, into the disc.

53 INT. CONTROL ROOM DAY 8 1921

THE DOCTOR and ROSE lost, unnerved; the EDITOR grinning.

EDITOR Information! Oh yes! The last of the Time Lords. And his travelling machine. With his little human girl from long ago.

THE DOCTOR Don't know what you're talking about –

EDITOR Time travel!

54 INT. SPIKE ROOM, FLOOR 139 DAY 8 1922

ADAM in pain, white FX light boiling out of his head, upwards. He yells! Rage, fear, can't stop it ...

55 INT. CONTROL ROOM DAY 8 1922

THE DOCTOR and ROSE trapped, the EDITOR gleeful. Throughout, the rumble of the JAGRAFESS, heaving in delight.

THE DOCTOR Someone's telling you lies –

EDITOR What, young master Adam Mitchell?

He clicks his fingers. A huge graphic projection in the air: SECURITY CAMERA FOOTAGE, FLOOR 139 SPIKE ROOM; ADAM, trapped in the chair.

ROSE Oh my God, his head ...

THE DOCTOR What's he done ...?
(furious)
What the hell has he gone and done? They're reading his mind, he's telling them everything –

EDITOR And through him, I know all about you. Every piece of information in his head is now mine. And what a prize! Bonanza!

ROSE You're killing him!

EDITOR Small price to pay!

ROSE Let him go!

INTERCUT with CATHICA, still watching.

EDITOR Knowledge is power, and you've got infinite knowledge, Doctor. The Human Empire is tiny, compared to what you've seen. In this T, A, R, D, I, S – TARDIS!

THE DOCTOR Well you're not getting your hands on it, I'll die first —

EDITOR Die all you like, I don't need you! I've got the key!

56 INT. SPIKE ROOM, FLOOR 139 DAY 8 1923

ADAM staring, fearful, as the TARDIS key lifts up in the air. Glowing. It stays suspended, turning in the light.

57 INT. CONTROL ROOM DAY 8 1923

THE DOCTOR outraged:

THE DOCTOR You gave him the key!

ROSE You said yes!

THE DOCTOR You and your boyfriends!

EDITOR Today, we become the headlines. The Mighty Jagrafess and the Holy Hadrojassic Maxarodenfoe can maximise its newsgathering. We can rewrite history. We can prevent mankind from ever developing.

And the Doctor's grim, precise: aims this right at the sheet of metal, at the reflection of CATHICA.

THE DOCTOR And no one will stop you. Cos you've bred a Human Race which doesn't even bother asking questions. Stupid little slaves. Believing every lie. They'll just trot right into the slaughterhouse, if they're told it's made of gold.

On Cathica. Realising . . . she turns, runs —

58 INT. FLOOR 500, CORRIDOR DAY 8 1923

CATHICA runs, heading for the SPIKE ROOM —

JUMP CUT TO:

59 INT. SPIKE ROOM, FLOOR 500 DAY 8 1924

CATHICA shoves the skeleton out of the central chair, assumes her position, presses the chair-arm trigger. The room powers up. And she's invigorated —

CATHICA Disengage safety.

And she clicks her fingers —

60 INT. CONTROL ROOM DAY 8 1924

The glowing screens flicker. The EDITOR turns round, alert —

EDITOR What's happening — ?

61 INT. SPIKE ROOM, FLOOR 500 DAY 8 1924

CATHICA sits, now with her forehead open.

CATHICA Maximum access, override Floor One Three Nine, and . . . *spike!*

The disc above her glows [practical] white.

62 INT. SPIKE ROOM, FLOOR 139 DAY 8 1924

The light cuts off, the spike stops dead – ADAM's frozen, as his forehead gently closes.

CU TARDIS key, clattering to the ground.

63 INT. CONTROL ROOM DAY 8 1925

The EDITOR strides across to the DRONES.

EDITOR Someone's disengaged the safety, who is it – ?

He clicks his fingers. The huge projection in the air: SPIKE ROOM, FLOOR 500, Cathica, with solid FX light curling into her head.

ROSE It's Cathica . . .

THE DOCTOR And she's *thinking*! She's using what she knows.

EDITOR Terminate her access! I said, terminate!

THE DOCTOR Everything I showed her about Satellite Five, the pipes, the filters, she's reversing it! Look at that. It's getting hot.

He nods over at water pouring off the metal struts. Dripping down from the roof. Icicles melting.

EDITOR Burn out her mind!

64 INT. SPIKE ROOM, FLOOR 500 DAY 8 1925

CATHICA fierce – knows they're fighting back – slams her fist on the arm-rest. A savage smile –

CATHICA Ohh no you don't. You should've promoted me years back –

65 INT. CONTROL ROOM DAY 8 1925

A surge of power – two or three computer screens spark, blow up – then more smoke, flame.

The DRONES slump, lifeless. Some stay sitting, heads down; some slide to the floor, including SUKI. She rolls to the ground, unfeeling, just a body, now.

The EDITOR runs from screen to screen, opening his palm over them, trying to control them himself, frantic. The electro-manacles holding THE DOCTOR and ROSE spark! Rose's fly open. As she pulls herself free the JAGRAFESS roars! The Editor looks up, frantic –

EDITOR I'm trying, sir, I don't know how she did it, it's impossible! A member of staff with an idea!

Rose takes the sonic screwdriver out of the Doctor's pocket, whirrs at the electro-manacles –

ROSE What do I do, what setting?

THE DOCTOR Flick the switch on the side up –

And strong JETS OF STEAM erupt through the floor of the raised area. The Doctor grinning:

THE DOCTOR She's venting the heat. Back up to Floor 500! The Jagrafess needs to keep cool, now it's sitting on top of a volcano!

66 INT. FLOOR 139, CORRIDOR DAY 8 1926

Satellite Five shudders, the corridor shakes! Bursts of steam shoot out of the walls, panels of metal go flying – WORKERS running, screaming – chaos. ADAM staggers through it, like he's lost in hell.

67 INT. SPIKE ROOM, FLOOR 500 DAY 8 1927

The room shaking; CATHICA shining now. The light between her and the ceiling-disc is wild and boiling. And she's smiling. Lost in the light, ecstatic.

68 INT. CONTROL ROOM DAY 8 1927

The room shaking, as the JAGRAFESS starts to boil. Parts of it burst open. Steam-jets shoot out of its wet bulk. ROSE pulls THE DOCTOR free. Water's pouring down, steam's jetting up, and smoke – the whole room is shaking. He shouts across to the frantic EDITOR –

THE DOCTOR Oy mate, you want to bank on a certainty? Massive heat, in a massive body, massive bang!

A huge chunk of the Jagrafess bursts open! Chunks of wet, raw meat slap down, around the Editor.

THE DOCTOR See you in the headlines –

And the Doctor and Rose run. The Editor looks up at the Jagrafess.

EDITOR If it's all the same to you, sir. I resign. Bye, then –

And he turns to run – falls flat on the floor. He looks round. SUKI is stretched out, staring with blank, black eyes, expressionless. But she's holding on to his ankle. With the strength of ten. The Editor kicks, writhes –

EDITOR Let go of me! *Let go of me!*

69 INT. FLOOR 500, CORRIDOR DAY 8 1928

Corridor shaking, rubble falling, as THE DOCTOR and ROSE run –

70 INT. CONTROL ROOM DAY 8 1928

The JAGRAFESS is shuddering with steam – blistering. The EDITOR pulls with all his might, but SUKI hangs on –

71 INT. SPIKE ROOM, FLOOR 500 DAY 8 1928

CU CATHICA: forehead open, lost in light. Shining, and burning, about to disappear into sheer whiteness . . . and then calmly, with great strength, THE DOCTOR moves in, at her side. Holds her, gently.

THE DOCTOR Not today.

Smiling, he clicks his fingers.

72 INT. CONTROL ROOM DAY 8 1928

CU the EDITOR, as he screams with rage – and the JAGRAFESS explodes! Water and steam and huge slabs of wet meat, gristle and fat, shoot in all directions – *whoomph* – gone!

73 EXT. FX SHOT SATELLITE FIVE DAY 8 2000

Satellite Five hangs in space, a calm image. Over this:

TANNOY VOICE *Workers of Satellite Five, stay where you are, the authorities have been summoned. Stay where you are, the authorities have been summoned …*

74 INT. FLOOR 139, CORRIDOR DAY 8 2000

Tannoy voice continues b/g. The corridor's a mess, rubble strewn about. WORKERS dazed, but hugging, glad to be alive. CATHICA sits, shattered, smiling, with THE DOCTOR and ROSE.

THE DOCTOR We're just gonna go, I hate tidying up. Too many questions. You'll manage.

CATHICA But you'll have to stay and explain it, no one's gonna believe me.

THE DOCTOR They might start believing a lot of things, now. Human race should accelerate. All back to normal.

CATHICA What about your friend …?

THE DOCTOR He's not my friend.

And he's as dark and tall as a storm as he stands, looks round. Far end of the corridor: ADAM, beside the TARDIS. The Doctor starts to walk towards him – terrifying.

Rose follows, scared.

ROSE Now don't …

He ignores her. Marches on. INTERCUT TRACK IN on Adam, TRACK with the Doctor, as they get closer and closer, and Adam quails –

ADAM I'm all right now. Much better.
(closer)
I've got the key, look, it's fine.
(closer)
And it all worked out for the best, yeah?
(closer)
It wasn't my fault, you left me all alone, you were in charge –

And without stopping, one fluid movement, the Doctor grabs him by the arm, pulls him into the TARDIS.

75 INT. SUBURBAN HOUSE, MANCHESTER DAY 8 XXXX

The dog belts out of the cat-flap, yelping – scared, because of the ancient, groaning engine-noise. CUT TO THE TARDIS, inside the living room, within the bay window. And, like he never stopped moving from sc.74, THE DOCTOR pulls ADAM out of the TARDIS; ROSE following.

ADAM It's my house. I'm home. Oh my God, I'm home. Blimey. I thought you were gonna chuck me out of an airlock.

THE DOCTOR Is there something else you want to tell me?

ADAM No. Um. What d'you mean ...?

The Doctor's crossed to the answerphone, holds it up.

THE DOCTOR The archive of Satellite Five. One second of that message could change the world.

The Doctor puts it down, whirrs the sonic screwdriver over it. The answerphone explodes! Sparks, fizz, smoke, dead.

THE DOCTOR That's it then. See ya.

ADAM How d'you mean, see ya?

THE DOCTOR As in, goodbye.

ADAM But ... what about me? You can't just go, I've got my head. I've got a chip Type Two, my head opens!

THE DOCTOR What, like this?

The Doctor clicks, Adam's forehead opens.

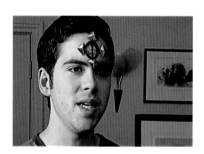

ADAM Don't!

Adam clicks, his forehead closes.

THE DOCTOR Don't do what?

The Doctor clicks, Adam's forehead opens.

ADAM Stop it!

Adam clicks, his forehead closes. Rose stern:

ROSE All right now, Doctor. That's enough. Stop it.

And the Doctor huffs, loses some of his tension. Adam humble, to Rose:

ADAM Thank you.

And Rose clicks her fingers, Adam's forehead opens.

ADAM Oy!!

He clicks, his forehead closes.

ROSE Sorry, couldn't resist.

The Doctor's quiet now, more sad:

THE DOCTOR The whole of history could've changed. Because of you.

ADAM I just wanted to help.

THE DOCTOR You were helping yourself.

ADAM I've said I'm sorry, and I am, I really am. But you can't just leave me like this.

THE DOCTOR Yes I can. Cos if you show that head to anyone, they'll dissect you in seconds. So you'll have to live a very quiet life. Cause no trouble. Stay quiet. Unseen. Good luck.

ADAM But I want to come with you.

THE DOCTOR I only take the best. I've got Rose.

The Doctor goes inside the TARDIS. Adam turns to Rose –

ADAM Can't you tell him?
(hears a key)
Oh my God –

ADAM'S MUM OOV Who's that? Geoff, is that you?

CUT TO THE HALL: ADAM'S MUM walking in, laden with shopping bags. She's 45, friendly, kind. She makes a three-act play of extricating herself from bags and coat.

ADAM OOV It's me, don't come in mum, stay there a minute –

ADAM'S MUM Oh my Lord! You never said you were coming home! Is that your father keeping secrets again, oh how marvellous, hold on, I'm stuck –

CUT TO THE LIVING ROOM, hushed:

ADAM Take me with you.

ROSE Thing is, I know you lied and stole my phone and almost gave the secret of time travel to the Mighty Jagravole –

THE DOCTOR Jagrafess.

ROSE Jagrafess, but d'you know what you *didn't* do? Back there, on Satellite Five, when I said I was thick? You didn't say, no, you're not. (big smile)
Bad move.

And she goes inside the TARDIS, closes the door.

CUT TO THE HALL: mum disentangling herself.

ADAM'S MUM There we go – oh what's that noise?

The groan of ancient engines. The wind sweeps through –

ADAM'S MUM Have you opened that back door? Blimey, that's a draft. Now then, where are you, what a surprise!

She walks into the living room. No Tardis, just Adam, standing way across the room, a scared smile. Mum stays in the doorway, so happy.

ADAM'S MUM Oh, let me look at you, I bought you that shirt! Six months, it's like I saw you yesterday, isn't it funny? The time goes by like that –

And she clicks her fingers!

Episode 8

Father's Day
By Paul Cornell

I once had a dream about my Dad. Men were being drafted into the army again, and Dad told me that he would never let them take me. That I didn't have to go if I didn't want to. That he'd put his life before mine.

I woke up crying, feeling that I'd been told something true about him that he would never have told me himself. He fought in Burma during World War Two, and still has terrible nightmares. I think he would have died for his country, and I know he would die in my place if he ever had the chance. That makes him absolutely special, and completely normal for a father, at the same time.

I wrote about that dream in a fanzine, in the middle of an article about chapter titles in Terrance Dicks' *Doctor Who* novelisations. You're allowed to do that in fanzines. The point I was making then is the one I'd like to make here again, that for me *Doctor Who* has always been about big emotions, and it's always been about my Dad. It's about him reading those books to me when, as a kid, I was ill; books written by someone who much later I was pleased to be able to call a friend.

Terrance called me on the night 'Father's Day' was broadcast, right after my Dad did. Dad said that he could see that the episode had the same basic plot as all my work, which I hadn't realised until then. I'd say that goes something like this: grace gets written into the world, in such a way that it turns out it's always been there, through sacrifice. Dad would say it's always about some poor chap who has to suffer for the sake of everyone else.

I think the most important detail in this current version of my plot is that the driver of the deadly car has now, has always, stopped and tried to deal with what he's done. I also like the fact that the Doctor is prepared to forgive Rose for the end of everything, as long as she understands what she's done and owns it.

One good thing Russell has done with the new *Doctor Who* is something Terrance did with the old. He's made the audience aware of the writers. I remember thumbing through Terrance's *The Making of Doctor Who* when I was a child, and finding that the only credit, for every story, was the writer, big and bold. That's a fiction of course, in television, where there's always joint authorship. I'd be nowhere without Russell, Joe, Elwen, Helen, Chris and, above all, Billie and Shaun. But this emphasis on writing will, hopefully, make small children again start thinking about what being a writer involves. The story of me and my Dad and Terrance will go round again, with the details and the people different.

I also hope this episode causes a few dreams about fathers.

Paul Cornell

1 INT. PHOTO DAY

A photo of Pete Tyler, a man in his early 30s. He looks great: capable and strong.

ROSE V/0 Peter Alan Tyler, my Dad. The most wonderful man in the world. Born 15th September, 1954.

2 INT. JACKIE'S BEDROOM DAY (1992)

This is the mid-1990s. JACKIE, younger than we've seen her, has the photo album out, and calls LITTLE ROSE, who's about 6 years old, over to see it.

JACKIE Come here Rose. Who's that? Yes, that's your Daddy. You weren't old enough to remember when he died. 1987. The 7th of November. D'you remember what I told you? The day Stuart Hoskins and Sarah Clarke got married.

She points to a photo of Pete and her, happy together.

JACKIE We were so happy together, me and him. He was always having adventures. He would have loved to have seen you now.

On Little Rose, taking that in seriously.

3 INT. TARDIS DAY (NOW)

On ROSE, grown up now, explaining to THE DOCTOR.

ROSE That's what my Mum always says. So I was thinking ... could we? Could we go and see my Dad, when he was still alive?

THE DOCTOR Where's that come from, all of a sudden?

ROSE All right, if we can't, if it breaks the laws of time or something, then ... never mind, just leave it.

THE DOCTOR No, I can do anything. I'm more worried about you. Are you sure about this?

ROSE Yeah. I want to see him.

THE DOCTOR Okay.

He slams down a big lever to change course.

THE DOCTOR Your wish is my command. But be careful what you wish for ...

On Rose: kind of nervous.

4 EXT. THE SPACETIME VORTEX

The TARDIS changes course to spin off towards Earth.

CUT TO OPENING TITLES.

5 INT. REGISTRY OFFICE DAY (1982)

PETE is getting married to JACKIE. A REGISTRY OFFICER is officiating.

REGISTRY OFFICER I, Peter Alan Tyler, take you, Jacqueline Andrea Suzette Prentice . . .

PETE I, Peter Alan Tyler, take you, Jacqueline Susan . . . Suzette . . . Anita?

Jackie shakes her head, sighing. Pete looks sheepish.

JACKIE Oh just carry on, it was good enough for Lady Di.

THE DOCTOR and ROSE stand in a quiet corner at the back, the Doctor smiling at Pete's haplessness, Rose a little crestfallen at the first sight of her Dad.

ROSE I thought he'd be taller.

6 AND 7 OMITTED

8 INT. JACKIE'S BEDROOM DAY (1992)

Flashback again. JACKIE is in full flight to LITTLE ROSE about Pete's greatness.

JACKIE He died so close to home. But I wasn't there, nobody was. It was a hit and run driver. We never found out who. I hope he can't sleep at night, I hope he never slept again.

She restrains herself, not wanting to scare Little Rose.

JACKIE Pete was dead when the ambulance got there. By the time I saw him . . .

She decides against filling in those nasty details.

JACKIE I only wish there'd been *someone* there for him.

9 THRU 11 OMITTED

12 INT. TARDIS DAY (1986)

ROSE finishes her request.

ROSE I want to be that someone. So he doesn't die alone.

THE DOCTOR The 7th of November?

ROSE 1987.

THE DOCTOR slams down another lever –

12A EXT. SUBURBAN STREET DAY (1987 FROM HERE ON)

An ordinary tarmac space, no one around. THE DOCTOR and ROSE step out of the TARDIS. She looks around:

ROSE This is so weird. The day my father died. I thought it would be all sort of grim and stormy, it's just an ordinary day.

THE DOCTOR The past is another country. 1987 is just the Isle of Wight.
(pause)
Sure about this?

ROSE Yeah.

And she leads the way.

13 EXT. THE TYLER ESTATE DAY

THE DOCTOR and ROSE walk along. Their POV: the Tyler estate in 1987. *Socialist Worker* posters on the wall saying 'No Third Term For Thatcher' with cartoons of missiles and Ronald Reagan. Rave posters with smiley faces on them. One of them has 'Bad Wolf' written over it. Somebody's talking in a call box, with a queue of two behind them – one in cycling shorts. The hair and the make-up! Somewhere distantly a radio is playing 7th November 1987 pop music.

The Doctor takes Rose's hand as they get closer . . .

ROSE This is it, Jordan Road. He was late, he'd been to get this wedding present, a vase, mum always said – that stupid vase. He got out of his car. Crossed the road . . .

A battered old car pulls up on the other side of the road.

ROSE Oh God. This is it.

The Doctor and Rose stand on the pavement, watching. Still holding hands. PETE leaps out of the car, in an orange tee-shirt, white jacket with rolled-up sleeves and 501s, carrying his wedding gift: a vase. He's intending to run across the road to the Tyler estate. He's not paying attention.

Round the corner, far too fast, skids a stupid 1987 boy-racer car with too many exhausts and go faster stripes. It's right on top of Pete, instantly.

Freeze on Pete, just turning his head, a terrible despair on his face: he's going to die.

Freeze on the driver, just a kid, MATT, staring in horror.

Matt throws an arm up to shield his face. Rose has to look away. We hear the thump. The vase hits the ground and shatters. Matt's car speeds on, departing the scene of the crime.

Rose, turns, looks, bursts into tears and runs.

14 EXT. THE TYLER ESTATE DAY

Nearby. We hear the sounds of an arriving ambulance. ROSE and THE DOCTOR are slumped against a wall, Rose drying her tears.

ROSE It's too late now. By the time the ambulance got there, he was dead.

She looks imploringly at the Doctor.

ROSE He can't die on his own. Can I try again?

The Doctor's heavy-hearted, knows this is trouble, but he's going to say yes.

15 EXT. THE TYLER ESTATE DAY

We see PETE's battered old car arriving once more, as before. THE DOCTOR and ROSE hide around the corner, a short distance behind their selves from the previous visit.

THE DOCTOR Right, that's the first you and me. It's a very bad idea, two sets of us being here at the same time. Just be careful they don't see us, wait till she runs off and he follows, then go to your Dad.

Rose nods, numb, tense, anticipating.

Pete's car comes to a halt on the other side of the road. He unclips his seat belt and starts to open the door.

ROSE I can't do this.

THE DOCTOR You don't have to do anything you don't want to. But this is the last time we can be here.

Rose gets her courage together. Pete gets out of the car. The deadly car races around the corner. All exactly as before.

Rose starts to shake her head. She rushes forward, past her and the Doctor's previous selves, and leaps in front of the speeding car –

MATT throws his arm up, like last time.

THE DOCTOR Rose! No!

Rose shoves Pete backwards. The two of them fall out of the way of the car. The vase rolls, unshattered. The car roars past and away around the next corner.

The previous Doctor and Rose stare, shocked, then . . . they vanish!

The Doctor runs up, horrified now, and then all is quiet. He looks around, knowing that something weird and terrible has happened . . . but what? Everything seems normal. His gaze fixes on Rose, furious.

Rose is oblivious. She's helping Pete up. She can only stare at him.

ROSE I did it. I saved your life!

PETE Blimey, see the speed of him? D'you get his number?

ROSE But I really did it! Oh my God, look at you, you're alive! That car was gonna kill you!

PETE Give me some credit, I did see it coming, I wasn't gonna walk under it, was I? I'm not that daft!

They look at each other, Rose still bouncing with joy.

ROSE I'm Rose.

PETE Oh that's a coincidence, that's my daughter's name.

A big smile from Rose.

ROSE It's a great name. Good choice. Well done.

We see that the Doctor is glaring at them, blazingly angry, containing himself. Pete looks awkward.

PETE Well . . . I better shift. I'm late for a wedding.

ROSE can't let him go. She steps into his way.

ROSE Is that . . . Sarah Clarke's wedding?

PETE Yeah. Are you going?

ROSE . . . Yeah!

PETE Do you and your boyfriend need a lift?

Rose looks happily over to the Doctor, who looks furious.

16 INT. TYLERS' FLAT DAY

PETE lets them in, puts the vase down –

PETE There we go, sorry about the mess, if you want a cup of tea, the kitchen's just down there, on the left, milk's in the fridge, well it would be, wouldn't it, where else would you put milk? Mind you, there's always the windowsill outside, I always thought, if someone invented a windowsill with special compartments, like one for milk, one for yoghurt, you could make money out of that, sell it to students and things. I should write that down – anyway, never mind that, 'scuse me a minute, gotta go and change ...

ROSE stops just inside the room, staring at how different it is. The difference is, Pete lives here. There are bowling trophies on the mantelpiece; half-made DIY projects; piles of unsold health drinks; detergent in boxes.

ROSE All the stuff mum kept. His stuff. She had it all packed away in boxes in the cupboard, she used to show me, when she'd had a bit to drink. And here it is, on display. Where it should be.

She goes and picks up a trophy.

ROSE Third prize at the bowling. First two got to go to Didcot. Health drinks! Tonics, mum used to call them, he made money selling this Vitex stuff, he had all sorts of jobs, he was so clever.

She picks up a rolled sheaf of plans.

ROSE Solar power! Mum said he was going to do that. Now he can!

She looks to THE DOCTOR again, worried that he's so angry.

ROSE Okay, look: I'll tell him you're not my boyfriend.

The following is quiet, both trying not to let PETE overhear.

THE DOCTOR When we first met, I said: 'travel with me in space'. You said no. But when I said 'time machine'! ... Is this why you went with me?!

ROSE This wasn't some big plan. I just saw it happening, and I thought 'I can stop it'.

THE DOCTOR I did it again. I picked another stupid ape. I should have known: it's not about showing you the universe. It never is. It's about the universe doing something for you.

ROSE So it's okay when *you* go to other times and *you* save people, but not when it's me saving my Dad?

THE DOCTOR I know what I'm doing and you don't! Two lots of us being there made that a vulnerable point.

ROSE But he's alive –

THE DOCTOR My entire planet died, my whole *family*, do you think it never occurred to *me* to go back and save them?

ROSE But it's not like I changed history. Not much. I mean, he's never gonna be a world leader, he's not gonna start World War Three or anything.

THE DOCTOR Rose, there is a man alive in the world, who wasn't alive before. An ordinary man. That's the most important thing in creation, an ordinary man. The whole world is different, because he's alive.

ROSE What, would you rather him dead?

THE DOCTOR I'm not saying that –

ROSE Oh, I get it. For once, you're not the most important man in my life!

THE DOCTOR D'you think I'm not? Let's see you do without me, then. Give me the key.

ROSE What key?

THE DOCTOR The TARDIS key. If I'm so insignificant, give it back!

ROSE All right then, I will!

She shoves the key at him –

THE DOCTOR You've got what you wanted, so that's goodbye then –

He makes for the door, she gets between him and it.

ROSE You don't scare me! I know how sad you are! You'll be back in a minute! Or you'll hang around the TARDIS waiting for me, and I'll make you wait a long time!

He just steps past her and out of the door, furious. She stares after him, not quite believing this has happened.

Pete pops his head back in.

PETE Boyfriend trouble?

17 EXT. STREET DAY

A sign on one door says: 'Gone to wedding' – the street empty and quiet, everyone at the ceremony. THE DOCTOR is marching out, furious. We see him from an ALIEN POV, which goes along with a horrible, frightening noise that seems to be hovering just above him.

He remains unaware.

18 INT. THE TYLER'S FLAT DAY

PETE, now in his wedding suit, picks up the vase, ready to head out. ROSE is tidying up old newspapers.

PETE 'Scuse me, d'you mind, what are you tidying up for?

ROSE Sorry, force of habit.

PETE Don't worry about him, couples have rows all the time.

ROSE We're not a couple. Why does everyone think we're a couple?
(slumps)
I think he's left me.

PETE A pretty girl like you? If I was going out with you –

Rose is horrified.

ROSE Stop right there.

PETE I'm just saying –

ROSE I know what you're saying, and we're not going there, at no point are we going anywhere near there. You aren't even aware that there exists. I don't want to think about there, and believe me, neither do you. There, for you, is like the Bermuda Triangle.

PETE Blimey, you know how to flatter a bloke.

ROSE I'm just saying.
(beat)
Are we off then?

Sure of that, she carefully puts her arm through his. He stares at her in surprise.

PETE So one minute I can't come near, next minute we're all pals. Are you ever gonna make sense?

ROSE Doubt it.

PETE I'd take you back to the looney bin where you belong, but it's weird, I keep on thinking, haven't I seen you somewhere before . . . ?

Rose goes back to feeling awkward again as they head for the door.

19 OMITTED

20 EXT. TERRACED STREET DAY

A street near the Tyler estate. A series of quick shots of ordinary people doing ordinary things, viewed from the ALIEN POVs, like they're prey. Their chittering becomes louder.

A wino in an alleyway sips from his can; a teenage mum attaching clothes to a rotary washing line; a man gardening.

21 INT. CAR DAY

PETE is driving ROSE along. The car radio is playing 'The Number One Song in Heaven' by the Sparks. Rose can't help looking at her Dad with interest, just staring at him.

ROSE So what work are you doing now?

PETE (enthused)
Oh, now, brilliant idea, you know Henderson's Tower?

ROSE No.

PETE Exactly! It's going to be the next Rubik's Cube, only this is from Basingstoke. I met this guy at the horses, he's cutting me in on the copyright.

ROSE But I've never heard of Henderson's Tower.

PETE You will do!

ROSE But I haven't, which means . . . it's not gonna work.

PETE If it doesn't, I'm penniless.

ROSE But . . . I thought you were a proper businessman, that's what I was told.

PETE I wish! I do a bit of this and that. I scrape by.

ROSE Right
(realising the truth)
I must've heard wrong. So, really, you're a bit of a Del Boy.
(thinks he won't get the reference)
I mean you're a real chancer –

PETE I *know* who Del Boy is. 'You plonker, Rodney!'

ROSE Anyway, try something else. It isn't going to work.

PETE Oh, shoot me down in flames. You're not related to my wife, by any chance?

Rose hadn't thought.

ROSE Oh. My. God. She'll be at the wedding.

PETE What, Jackie, d'you know her?

ROSE Sort of.

PETE Are you two mates then?

ROSE We . . . talk. Sometimes.

PETE Oh yeah? What's she told you about me?

ROSE She said you were brilliant. That she'd picked the most fantastic man in the world. Someone who made her feel special, every day.

PETE Must be a different Jackie, she'd never say that.

Rose looks awkward again. She knows the reason – that Pete was dead. But she can't say that.

The radio suddenly starts playing 2005 pop, a familiar tune that couldn't be from anywhen else.

PETE That Acid House stuff goes right over my head.

ROSE But . . . that song isn't out yet . . .

PETE Good thing an' all.

She reaches for her mobile.

ROSE I'm ... just going to check my messages.

PETE How d'you mean, messages?

He sees how small the phone is and switches off the radio.

PETE Is that a *phone*?

She hits a button.

ROSE Yeah.

PLUMMY SCOTS VOICE (from phone)
Watson, come here, I want you.

It keeps repeating. Rose stares at the phone, getting worried. Pete looks to her, but we look to the rear-view mirror, where, unseen by him, a car is looming up behind them. It's the boy-racer car that didn't kill Pete.

22 EXT. ROAD DAY

We zoom in on the deadly car, and see, at the wheel, MATT throwing an arm up to shield his face, replaying the action of the accident.

Pete's car, ahead, goes round a corner. And Matt's car vanishes, fading out.

23 EXT. PLAYGROUND DAY

A playground nearby an urban church (we hear bell rehearsals), with a handful of kids playing on swings and roundabouts, including one in wedding clothes, YOUNG MICKEY.

We switch to the invading POV with the alien noise. There are several of them, watching the children from different angles. They start to move in on them.

24 EXT. SUBURBAN STREET DAY

THE DOCTOR heads towards the TARDIS, some way from the Tyler estate. He's observed by the ALIEN POV. He turns, for the first time realising that something is watching him. But it's gone. He gets out his key, goes to the TARDIS and opens the door.

Big shock: he finds nothing inside. It's an empty box. Inside, he looks round desperately, puts his hands on the walls, can't believe it. A moment of sheer horror for him: his home is gone.

And then it sinks in – something is terribly wrong.

THE DOCTOR Rose.

He sprints off back towards the estate.

25 EXT. PLAYGROUND DAY

YOUNG MICKEY is on the swing. Other kids play on the roundabout. An ALIEN POV moves towards the roundabout. Young Mickey looks across and the kids on the roundabout have just gone – vanished.

Young Mickey looks frantically around from where he's swinging. The kid next to him on the swing has vanished.

Young Mickey looks over his shoulder and the kid pushing his swing has gone. Now it's just Young Mickey swinging alone. All the other kids have vanished. He stares in horror, jumps off the swing and runs for his life.

26 EXT. CHURCH DAY

Wedding cars are pulling up outside this urban church with people going inside – and others like BEV and SUZIE. Bev and Suzie are fruity single mums in ra-ra skirts.

SUZIE I'll give it three weeks.

BEV I'm only here for the Babycham. Mind you, weddings, best place to find a husband, it said so in *Cosmopolitan*.

The father of the groom, SONNY – 50-ish, a big, respectable pillar of the community – emerges from the church, talking into a vast mobile phone.

SONNY (into phone)
Don't worry, half the guests haven't turned up! You're better off not being here, it's a disaster in the making.
(listens)
No, in this case 'knocked her up' *is* a phrase I would use!

Static from the phone fades into . . .

PLUMMY SCOTS VOICE (from phone)
Watson, come here, I want you.

SONNY (into phone)
Hello? Who is this?

It keeps repeating. Sonny looks puzzled, starts hitting buttons. STUART, the bridegroom, finds him.

STUART Dad, get inside! We can't see the bride before the wedding. It's bad luck!

SONNY Now you worry. It was bad luck when you met her! Two a.m. outside a nightclub, and this is the longest hangover of your life! I'm telling you, this day is cursed!

27 EXT. TERRACED STREET DAY

We're back with the same quick shots of ordinary people doing ordinary things, viewed from their POVs: the WINO looks up from his can – an ALIEN POV moves towards him, and he's gone. The can rolls along the ground.

The TEENAGE MUM comes out with a new basket of clothes for her washing line, starts to attach them: the alien POV again – and she's gone, the washing line left spinning. The GARDENER trimming the hedge: the POV moves in – and he's gone with a snap of the shears.

28 EXT. CHURCH DAY

SUZIE and BEV are looking towards the road, where a limousine is heading towards the church.

SUZIE Here comes the bride.

BEV Poor thing, imagine marrying Stuart Hoskins.

SUZIE Well we've both been there. And we both thought better of it!

29 EXT. TERRACED STREET DAY

YOUNG MICKEY runs for his life. We hear a quiet chittering in the distance.

30 EXT. CHURCH DAY

SARAH CLARKE, a heavily pregnant young bride, steps out of the car in 1987 wedding regalia: big hair and shoulder pads!

BEV (high praise)
Now that's what I call a meringue!

SARAH It's not too much?

SUZIE 'Too much!'

BEV It's your wedding dress! How could anything ever be too much?

SUZIE Stuart's dad said, go round the block, cos there's people missing, loads of 'em, he said.

SARAH How d'you mean, missing?

BEV There's no Dave, no Sunita, no Bee –

SUZIE There's no one from the Lamb and Flag, and your Aunty Jean hasn't turned up either. It's weird, she's always on time –

SARAH Where are they then? –
(looks round)
Oh my train's detached again, I knew I should have used velcro, Jackie! Give's a hand!

Out of the limo behind Sarah steps JACKIE, in her maid-of-honour gear, and an extraordinary perm.

JACKIE I'm here, stop your bellyaching! Bev, take Rose a sec, will you?

She lifts BABY ROSE, in a carrier, out from the back seat. Big on the baby: it's Rose!

BEV Ohh, isn't she pretty?

JACKIE She's a little madam, that's what she is!
(looks towards road)
I need more hands! Where's her useless article of a Dad got to?

31 INT. CAR DAY

PETE, driving, turns the car into the street where the church is. Pete sees MATT's car heading right for him on a collision course.

Pete spins the wheel in sheer panic.

ROSE Dad!

32 EXT. CHURCH DAY

The car swerves and comes to a stop. PETE and ROSE jump out, looking around. There's nothing there.

PETE It was that car, same one as before, where did it go? It was there, right in front of us, where's it gone . . . ?

ROSE It just sort of . . . vanished.

He stares at Rose.

PETE You called me Dad?! What did you say that for?

Rose can't answer.

JACKIE arrives, carrying BABY ROSE in her carrier.

JACKIE Oh, wonderful!

Rose stares at her as she lays into Pete.

JACKIE Here he is, the accident waiting to happen! You'd be late for your own funeral and it nearly was!

PETE No damage done.

JACKIE Oh, and who's this?
(to Rose)
What are you looking at with your mouth open?!

ROSE can only be honest.

ROSE Your hair.

JACKIE What?

ROSE I've never seen it like –

She corrects herself, not wanting to give herself away.

ROSE I mean – It's lovely, your hair's lovely.
(quiet, amazed)
And that . . . baby. That must be . . . your baby.

PETE She does this a lot.

JACKIE (to Pete)
Another one of yours, is she?

PETE Why do you always think the worst?! She saved my life!

JACKIE That's a new one. What was it last time? –

PETE I didn't even know her! She was a cloakroom attendant!

ROSE is quite surprised.

ROSE What do you mean, a cloakroom attendant, who was?

PETE I was helping her look for my ticket. There were three dufflecoats all the same. Somehow the rack collapsed. We were under all this stuff –

ROSE Were you playing around?!

JACKIE Hoi. What's it got to do with you what he gets up to?

ROSE What *does* he get up to?

JACKIE You'd know!

PETE Because I'm that stupid. I play around, then bring her to meet the missus. You silly cow!

Which makes Rose stare.

JACKIE But you *are* that stupid!

PETE Can we keep this for back home, just for once?

JACKIE What, with the rest of the rubbish? You bring home cut-price detergents and tonic water and Betamax tapes and none of it works, I'm drowning in your rubbish.
(to Rose)
What did he tell you, did he say he's this big businessman? Cos he's not, he's a failure – born failure, that one!

PETE Jackie, I'm making a living. It keeps us fed, doesn't it?

JACKIE Rose needs a proper father, not one who's playing about like a big kid.

This is now turning into a really big row, and ROSE can't stand it any more.

ROSE Stop it. You're not like this. You love each other.

Which makes them both stop and look at her, bemused.

JACKIE You never used to like them mental, Pete. Or I don't know, maybe you did.

She marches off.

PETE Jackie, wait, listen –

JACKIE If you're not careful there'll be a wedding and a divorce on the same day.

She heads back off towards the church. Pete grabs the vase from the car and points at Rose.

PETE Wait here, give me a couple of minutes with the missus – tell you what, straighten the car up. And don't cause any more trouble!

And he's off after Jackie. Leaving Rose looking lost and not sure she should follow.

33 INT. CHURCH DAY

It's a big urban church. We move across the wedding party: AUNTS, UNCLES, REBELLIOUS TEENS, all dressed for a wedding, all big hats and 1987 suits, waiting for the bride.

SONNY stands with STUART.

STUART It's weird, there's so many people missing. Uncle Steven, Aunty Lynn, all of the Baxters, where are they? D'you think something's gone wrong?

SONNY Maybe it's a godsend, gives you time to think. You don't have to go through with it, not these days. Live in sin for a bit, see how it works out – go on, I won't mind.

STUART Dad: married, suitcases, Pontins Camber Sands, all today.

SONNY And in ten years time, you'll say: 'if only I could turn the clock back!'.

He stops, looks nervous for a second.

SONNY Is it me, or did it just get cold?

34 EXT. CHURCH DAY

SARAH is getting a YOUNG VICAR to experimentally tug on her now-refastened train; BEV and SUZIE with her.

SARAH That's it. She'll hold now.

BEV Until tonight. That's when you want it ripping off!

SUZIE Blimey, it's freezing, all of a sudden ...

JACKIE, with BABY ROSE, is still arguing with PETE, who's still got his vase.

JACKIE I'm not listening; it's the dufflecoats all over again.

PETE Sometimes a dufflecoat is just a dufflecoat.

He stops her turning away, and composes himself for a moment then gets to the heart of this.

PETE Jackie. Things will get better. I promise.

She'd like to melt at that. But she can't.

JACKIE I'm just tired, Pete. I've had enough of all your daft schemes. I don't know where the next meal's coming from.

PETE I'll get it right, love. I promise you, one day soon, I'll get it right.

YOUNG MICKEY comes sprinting round the corner.

YOUNG MICKEY Monsters! Gonna eat us!

SUZIE (laughs)
Oh isn't he sweet, what sort of monsters, sweetheart? Is it aliens?

35 EXT. CHURCH DAY

A little distance behind ROSE, we see the figure of THE DOCTOR, running desperately towards her.

THE DOCTOR Rose! Get into the church!

But he's too far away for her to notice him. He manages a big bellow –

THE DOCTOR Rose!

– which she does hear. She turns with a big smile of relief, she knew he'd come after her!

She turns round and sees a floating shape materializing overhead. She stares. And screams.

We see what's looming over her. It's a REAPER. Its shape keeps shifting, juddering, superimposed on itself like something out of *Jacob's Ladder*, shrieking its alien sound.

Rose turns to run.

The Reaper closes in. But then – the Doctor grabs her and carries her along with his momentum, out of the creature's reach.

36 EXT. CHURCH DAY

SUZIE sees THE DOCTOR and ROSE pelting towards them, the impossible figure of the REAPER behind them. The Doctor is yelling at them.

THE DOCTOR Get into the church!

The group look startled. REAPERS swoop down on them and send them running in all directions.

SUZIE My God. What are they?! What *are* they?!

A rout, lots of scrambled shots, handheld chaos.

The Doctor arrives, starts grabbing at people, shoving them towards the church. But people are running in all directions with Reapers picking them off.

THE DOCTOR Inside!

STUART and SONNY appear at the church doorway, along with a few other guests.

STUART Sarah!

He runs to help her, past the Doctor's angry grasp.

THE DOCTOR Stay in there!

Sonny runs out –

SONNY What the hell is going on? –

And a Reaper descends, consumes him, gone.

PETE has grabbed JACKIE, with the baby in her carrier, and, shielding them, is heading for the church doorway. BEV, with YOUNG MICKEY, runs with them.

The YOUNG VICAR has seen a Reaper diving at Stuart and SARAH and leaps into its way, making it turn, letting the couple get inside, the last ones. The Young Vicar is grabbed by the Reaper instead.

The Doctor steps into the church doorway, with everyone else behind him. He's forcing them back inside the church.

THE DOCTOR In!

He swings round to see the Reapers speeding towards the door. Everyone else leaps back. But he stares at the creatures, very afraid, but controlling it, getting a good look at them.

The Reapers arrive at high speed at the doorway. The Doctor slams the door on them.

The Reapers stop at the door, bellowing.

37 INT. CHURCH DAY

THE DOCTOR leans on the door, and turns to face the traumatised wedding party. PETE'S looking after JACKIE and BABY ROSE. He looks at ROSE, astonished. STUART's picked up the mobile phone (which Sonny left in the church) – hits buttons.

All around, noises, everyone clamouring.

JACKIE (in background)
What the hell were those things, what's going on? It's a joke right, someone's playing some sort of joke –

BEV (in background)
They were like –
(pause)
It's Judgement Day, it's the end of the world, that's what it must be –

THE DOCTOR They can't get in. Old walls and doors. If they're from outside time … okay, the older something is, the stronger it is. What else?

The shadow of a REAPER passes a window. And we hear the Reaper – sounds louder. The Doctor springs into action.

THE DOCTOR Check the other doors. Move!

The others do, but Jackie grabs the Doctor.

JACKIE What's happening?! What are they?!

THE DOCTOR There's been an accident with time. A *wound* in time. I think they're like bacteria, taking advantage, streaming in from outside.

JACKIE What's that mean, 'time', what are you jabbering on about, 'time'? –

THE DOCTOR Oh I might've known you'd argue. Jackie, I'm sick of you complaining, I haven't got time for this –

JACKIE What are you on about? How d'you know my name? I've never met you in my life –

THE DOCTOR No, and you never will, if I don't sort this out – now if you don't mind, I've waited a long time to say this –
(right at her, stern)
Jackie Tyler. Do as I say. Go and check the doors!

JACKIE (scared)
Yes sir.

She runs off. The Doctor's a bit chuffed:

THE DOCTOR Should've done that ages back.

STUART steps forward.

STUART My dad was out there, he sort of ... vanished. With those things. Is he ...?

THE DOCTOR I'm sorry.

STUART Oh my God.

THE DOCTOR You can mourn him later. Right now we've got to concentrate on keeping ourselves alive.

STUART My dad –

THE DOCTOR (sharp)
There's nothing I can do for him!

STUART No, but he had this telephone thing, cost him a fortune, I can't get it to work, I keep getting this voice –

He hands the mobile to the Doctor.

PLUMMY SCOTS VOICE (from phone)
Watson, come here, I want you.

THE DOCTOR That's the very first phone call, Alexander Graeme Bell. I don't think the telephone's gonna be much use.

STUART But someone must've called the police!

THE DOCTOR The police can't help you now, no one can.

38 EXT. CHURCH DAY

An empty police car, its doors open, stands in the middle of a road. The streets are empty. A WOMAN and a MAN run from REAPERS.

ALL UNDER THIS:

THE DOCTOR V/O Nothing in this universe can harm those things. Time is damaged, and they've come to sterilize the wound.

Children's bikes, pushchairs, lie unattended in the streets where the children have vanished.

THE DOCTOR By consuming everything inside.

39 INT. CHURCH DAY

ROSE can't stop herself. She goes straight to THE DOCTOR. We see PETE watching her, interested.

ROSE Is this because ...

She can't say it with Pete this close.

ROSE Is this my fault?

The Doctor looks darkly at her. Yes.

On Rose, like she's been slapped in the face.

40 INT. CHURCH ANTEROOM DAY

PETE is barricading a door. THE DOCTOR enters and looks out of a window.

PETE There's smoke coming up from the city. But no sirens. I don't think it's just us, those things must be over the whole city. I dunno. The whole world.

But the Doctor isn't listening. Outside, there's the sound of a car. The Doctor watches as the boy-racer car goes past on the road outside, Matt still at the wheel, still raising and lowering his arm. The Doctor looks horrified, realising something.

Pete's coming over to the window, but the car has vanished.

PETE Was that a car?

THE DOCTOR It's not important. Don't worry about it.

He leaves quickly, leaving Pete puzzled.

41 INT. CHURCH DAY

ROSE sits alone. She shivers as the shadow of a REAPER makes its way past a big old window. PETE approaches her.

PETE (gently)
Rose ... This mate of yours ... what did he mean, this is your fault?

ROSE Dunno. Just ... everything.

PETE I gave you my car keys.

ROSE ... So?

PETE You don't give your keys to a complete stranger. But it's like I trusted you. Moment I met you. I just did. A wound in time he said ...
(pause; closer)
You called me Dad.

All she can do is stare at him; and he's scared too.

PETE I know it's impossible, but ... everything that's happening is impossible. And look at you. I can see it. My eyes. Jackie's attitude. You sound like her when you shout.

He reaches to wipe a hair back from her brow, and stops, not sure if he's allowed to.

She grabs his hand and holds it against her face.

PETE You are! My Rose. Grown up!

ROSE Dad. My Dad. My Daddy!

The last being said in a terrible outpouring of grief and love as she crumples into embracing him.

42 INT. CHURCH DAY

Away from the others, THE DOCTOR is feeling his way along the wall – the noise of Reapers from outside – mind whirring, desperate, trying to work something out, when:

STUART 'Scuse me, Mister, um ...?

STUART and SARAH are standing there, quiet, meek.

THE DOCTOR Doctor.

STUART Sorry to keep bothering, but ... you seem to know what's going on.

THE DOCTOR I give that impression, yeah.

STUART I just wanted to ask, I mean ... I don't know what's happening and I think I'm gonna wake up soon cos it's all just barmy, but the thing is –

SARAH Can you save us?

The Doctor stops, considers them properly, kind:

THE DOCTOR Who are you two, then?

STUART Stuart Hoskins.

SARAH Sarah Clarke. Sarah Hoskins. Almost.

THE DOCTOR And one extra, boy or girl?

SARAH Dunno, I don't want to know. Though everyone says she's a girl, cos of the way she's sitting.

THE DOCTOR So where did you meet, you two, how did all this get started?

STUART Outside the Beatbox Club, down in the precinct, two in the morning.

SARAH Street corner, I'd lost my purse, didn't have money for a taxi.

STUART I took her home.

THE DOCTOR Then what? Asked her for a date?

SARAH Wrote his number on the back of my hand.

STUART Never got rid of her since. My dad said ...
(beat)
My dad said a lot of things.

SARAH I don't know what this is all about, and I know we're not important – Stu just works in the printer's, and I've only got dental nursing –

THE DOCTOR Who said you're not important? Listen to me. I've travelled to all sorts of places, I've done things you can't imagine. But you ... street corner, two in the morning, getting a taxi home – I've never had a life like that. You don't know how important that is.
(big smile)
Yes, I'll try and save you. I'll try my best, okay?

43 INT. CHURCH ANTEROOM DAY

PETE and ROSE are sitting together, in private now. Rose has been crying.

PETE I'm a Dad. I mean, I'm already a Dad, but ... Rose grows up and she's you! That's wonderful. I mean, I suppose I thought ... That you'd be a bit useless. With my useless genes and all. But look at you! I mean, how did you get here?

ROSE D'you really want to know?

PETE Yeah.

ROSE Time machine.

PETE Time machine?

ROSE Cross my heart.

PETE (laughing)
Time machine!

ROSE (laughing)
I know!

PETE Blimey. D'you all have time machines where you come from?

ROSE No. Just the Doctor.

PETE What are you doing here? Did you know those things were coming?

ROSE No.

PETE Then ...? God, I dunno, my head's spinning. What's the future like?

ROSE Not so different.

PETE What am I like? Have I gone grey?

Rose quickly shakes her head.

PETE What, am I bald? Don't tell me I'm bald!

Pete understands now that she's fending off these questions.

PETE Hold on. Something went wrong? And it's your fault?

Rose doesn't know what to say. Pete lets her off the hook.

PETE So, if your mate isn't your boyfriend – and I have to say I'm glad, cos being your Dad an' all, I think he's a bit old for you – have you got a bloke?

ROSE No. I did. But –

YOUNG MICKEY enters, running in pursued by JACKIE.

JACKIE Mickey!

Rose finds herself looking right into the eyes of the younger version of her boyfriend. He suddenly grabs Rose, holds on to her for comfort. Rose is boggled, tries not to touch him.

PETE You know him?

ROSE I just … didn't recognise him in a suit.
(to Mickey)
Now let go of me, sweetheart.
(to herself)
And I'm always saying that.

Jackie eases Mickey away from Rose.

JACKIE He just grabs whatever's passing and holds on for dear life. God help his poor girlfriend if he ever gets one.

PETE (to Jackie)
Me and her were just talking –

JACKIE Oh yeah, talking. World comes to an end, what do you do? Cling to the youngest blonde!

She exits to take Mickey back to BEV. Pete makes a decision and makes to follow at speed, but Rose stops him.

ROSE You can't tell her.

PETE Why?

ROSE I mean: I really don't *want* you to tell her.

PETE Has this got something to do with this mistake of yours? You don't want people to know –

ROSE Where I come from, Jackie doesn't understand the timer on a video recorder.

PETE But I showed her that last week!

Rose gives him a look.

PETE Point taken.

44 INT. CHURCH DAY

THE DOCTOR is talking to BABY ROSE in her carrier.

THE DOCTOR Now then, Rose, you're not going to bring about the end of the world, are you? Are you?

Enter ROSE. The Doctor looks awkwardly at her, a difficult conversation. But both want to talk.

THE DOCTOR Jackie gave her to me to look after. How times change.

ROSE I'd better be careful. I think I just imprinted myself on Mickey like a mother chicken.

She reaches out for the baby, but the Doctor grabs her hand.

THE DOCTOR No!

The sounds of the REAPERS outside suddenly increase.

THE DOCTOR Don't touch the baby, you're both the same person, that's a paradox. And we don't want a paradox, not with those things outside. Anything new, any sort of time disturbance, makes them stronger. A paradox might let them in.

ROSE I can't do anything right, can I?

THE DOCTOR No you can't, since you asked, so –
(like she's thick)
Don't touch the baby!

Rose upset, close to tears, tries not to show it to him.

ROSE I'm not stupid!

THE DOCTOR Could've fooled me.

Silence. Then, calmer, feeling guilty:

THE DOCTOR All right, look. Sorry. I wasn't really going to leave you.

ROSE I know.

THE DOCTOR Between you and me. I haven't got a plan. No idea. No way out.

ROSE You'll think of something.

THE DOCTOR The entire Earth is being sterilised. This, and a few places like it, are all that's left of the human race. We might hold out for a while, but nothing can stop those creatures. They'll get through in the end, the walls aren't that old. And there's nothing I can do to stop them. There used to be laws that stopped this kind of thing from happening. My people would have stopped this. But they're gone. And now I'm going the same way.

ROSE (upset)
I didn't know. If I'd realised ...

THE DOCTOR Just ... tell me you're sorry.

She means it now, all the anger gone.

ROSE I am. I'm sorry.

He puts his hand on her face and breaks into the most wonderful smile, accepting that honest regret completely.

THE DOCTOR Okay.

Rose is bowled over by that. She smiles back.

The Doctor closes his eyes, takes her in his arms. Rose is very happy for a moment to be held. But then she realises that there's something warm in his breast pocket.

ROSE Doctor, have you got ... something hot ...

She reaches inside his jacket and gasps as she throws something very hot out. It skitters across the floor and lands in a corner, glowing red hot.

It's the TARDIS key.

THE DOCTOR The TARDIS key.

The Doctor stares at it for a moment, wondering. Then he realises. He pulls off his jacket, and uses it to grab the key off the floor.

THE DOCTOR It's telling me it's still connected to the TARDIS!

45 INT. CHURCH DAY

THE DOCTOR is pacing up and down in front of the crowd, holding the key in a piece of cloth.

THE DOCTOR The inside of my ship was thrown out of the wound, but we can use this to get it back. And once I've got my ship, I can mend everything! I need a bit of power, anyone got a battery ...?

STUART holds up the chunky mobile phone battery.

STUART This one big enough?

THE DOCTOR Fantastic!

STUART Good old dad. There you go –

The Doctor takes it, holds the sonic screwdriver up against it, whirrs away.

THE DOCTOR Just need to charge up. Then we can bring everyone back. We can save the world!

46 INT. CHURCH DAY

The noise of the REAPERS outside, restless and growing.

Inside, the crowd is intently watching THE DOCTOR as he fiddles – pressing the sonic screwdriver against the key, trying to find the right harmony.

JACKIE is sitting with BEV. She's got BABY ROSE back, and she's glaring across the room at where PETE has just sat down beside ROSE.

PETE You never told me why you came here in the first place. If I had a time machine, I wouldn't think 1987 was anything special. Not in Britain, anyway.

Rose looks instantly guilty and worried.

ROSE We just ended up here.

PETE Lucky for me. If you hadn't been there to save me –

ROSE (fast, bright)
That was just a coincidence, that was just really good luck, it was really amazing, right?

Pete looks disbelieving at her. She looks away. Now he knows he's right.

PETE So, in the future, are me and her indoors still together?

ROSE Yeah.

PETE Do you still live with us?

ROSE Yeah.

PETE Am I a good Dad?

That sounds so plaintive that Rose can't help but lie. It takes her a moment to get her thoughts together to make it all up. But then –

ROSE You ... told me a bedtime story every night, when I was small. You were always there, you never missed one.

She gets into it. Her dreams for years.

ROSE And you took us for picnics. In the country. Every Saturday. You never let us down. You were there for us all the time. Someone I could always rely on.

PETE would love to believe it. But he can't.

PETE That's ... not me.

They hear a slow version of the TARDIS materialisation sound and look across to where the Doctor is now standing holding the key, at the height where the TARDIS lock would be.

The TARDIS interior, and then its exterior, start to form around the key. He lets go and the key hangs there in mid-air, supported by the slowly materialising TARDIS.

THE DOCTOR Right, no one touch the key, have you got that? Don't touch it. Anyone touches that key, they'll be .... well, zap – all right? Just leave it be, and everything's gonna turn out okay. We're getting out of here. All of us. Stuart. Sarah! You're getting married, just like I said!

47 EXT. CHURCH DAY

The emptiness around the church is broken by the sudden fading in of Matt's car. Inside it, MATT is still repeating his gesture. The car vanishes again.

48 INT. CHURCH DAY

THE DOCTOR and ROSE are sitting on chairs with a bottle of communion wine and two glasses, waiting, watching the TARDIS forming. PETE waits also, troubled, with a glass of his own.

ROSE When time gets sorted out –

The Doctor knows Pete can hear, so answers carefully.

THE DOCTOR The wound gets healed, everything back to normal. Everyone will forget this happened. And don't worry, cos the ... thing you changed will still be ... changed, y'know. Just as you wanted it.

Pete raises his voice, without turning to them.

PETE You mean, I'll still be alive. Although I'm meant to be dead.

He turns to them, and sees from the look on their faces that it's true.

PETE That's why I've never done anything with my life. Because it didn't mean anything. It wasn't leading to anything.

THE DOCTOR Doesn't work like that.

PETE Rubbish. I was so useless I couldn't even die properly! And now it's my fault that it's the end of the world!

ROSE It's *my* fault.

The expression on her face brings Pete up short. He doesn't see that JACKIE, carrying the BABY, is approaching behind him.

PETE No, love. I'm your Dad. It's my *job* for it to be my fault.

JACKIE stares.

JACKIE Her *Dad*? How are you her Dad?

Pete turns to her.

PETE It's time you knew, love.

JACKIE You what? Oh that's disgusting! How old were you, twelve?

PETE Jacks, just listen. This is Rose –

JACKIE Rose?! How sick is that?! Did you give my daughter a second-hand name? How many are there, d'you call them all Rose?!

PETE Oh for God's sake, look! When I say Rose –

He plucks Baby Rose out of JACKIE'S arms and shows her to her, then holds her by Rose.

PETE It's the same Rose, don't you see?!

He plonks her down into Rose's arms.

PETE She's the same –

THE DOCTOR No don't! –

But ROSE has automatically caught hold of baby Rose. A REAPER materializes, inside the church, shrieking. The Doctor grabs the baby from Rose and hands it back to Jackie.

The REAPER descends towards them.

THE DOCTOR I'm the oldest thing in here! Everyone get behind me!

The crowd run to obey him. The Reaper fixes on the Doctor. And leaps at him.

ROSE Doctor!

The Reaper envelops him and he's gone.

ROSE Doctor!

The Reaper leaps at the crowd, which parts, screaming.

The Reaper collides with the TARDIS key. And vanishes, destroyed in a blast of energy. The ship vanishes too. The key falls to the floor, clink clink clink . . . and lies there.

Silence. Everyone stares. That was their last chance.

ROSE Doctor . . . ?

She grabs the key, hoping that it'll be hot. But –

ROSE It's cold. The key is cold.

It takes her a moment to take it in.

ROSE Oh my God, he's dead.

PETE goes to comfort her, but she steps away. She can't accept it, can't deal with it. He hugs her anyway, and she gives in, holding on to him.

ROSE It's all my fault. Both of you. All of you! The whole world!

The power supply stutters and dies. The lights go out. From outside the building, we can even more clearly hear the noise of the Reapers, moving in. The crowd gathers together instinctively, looking around, waiting for the attack. Hushed, still:

SARAH What's happening ...?

STUART They're getting stronger.

BEV This is it. There's nothing we can do. No one to help. It's the end.

49 THRU 51 OMITTED

52 INT. CHURCH ANTEROOM DAY

PETE is pouring himself communion wine, his hands shaking. We can hear the sounds of the REAPERS outside, and the quiet, scared chatter of the crowd inside the church. And then, over that, the sound of a car.

Pete looks up. He goes to the window. Outside, MATT in his boy-racer car is still repeating his actions. Pete realises what he has to do.

53 INT. CHURCH DAY

PETE comes back into the church, with a strange smile. To STUART and SARAH:

PETE Stu, Sarah, the wedding's still on, okay?

And he keeps on walking, to ROSE:

PETE The Doctor really cared about you. He didn't want you to go through it again, not when there might be another way. But now there isn't.

ROSE What are you talking about?

PETE The car that should have killed me, love. It's here. It's come for me.
(weak smile)
See, I'm not so daft after all. The Doctor worked it out way back, soon as he saw the car, but he tried to protect me. Still. He's not in charge any more. I am.

Rose understands what he means, and is horrified.

ROSE No.

JACKIE comes over (she hands the BABY to BEV).

PETE It's another way to heal the wound. It has to be.

ROSE You can't . . .

He puts his hand to her face.

PETE Who am I, love?

ROSE My Daddy.

JACKIE What d'you mean . . . ?

PETE Jackie, *look* at her. She's ours.

Rose makes eye contact with Jackie. And Jackie knows it's true.

JACKIE Oh God. Oh God.

Rose reaches out. And Jackie takes her in her arms.

JACKIE Pete, I . . .

PETE I'm meant to be dead, Jackie. You're gonna get rid of me. Peace at last.

JACKIE Don't say that.

PETE For once in your life, trust me. It's gotta be done. You've got to survive, cos you've got to bring up our daughter. You old nag.

And he gives her a kiss. Then turns to Rose.

PETE I never read you those bedtime stories, or took you on those picnics. I was never there for you.

ROSE You would have been.

PETE But I can do this for you. I can be a proper Dad to you now.

ROSE It's not fair.

PETE I had all these extra hours, no one else in the world has ever had that. On top of that, I get to see you. And you're beautiful. How lucky am I? So come on. Do as your Dad says.

Rose hesitates. Then, her eyes blinded by tears, she grabs the vase, before she can think about it.

Pete gently takes the vase from Rose, vastly proud of her and sure of this.

PETE So. You gonna be there for me, love?

54 EXT. CHURCH DAY

Saint Etienne's 'Hobart Paving' murmurs onto the soundtrack. In slow motion, PETE, carrying the vase, starts to run towards the road, where the car's still materialising.

REAPERS run at him as JACKIE and ROSE walk out of the church, stand in the doorway. Jackie gives BABY ROSE to Rose. The Reapers turn to them instead.

55 INT. CHURCH DAY

The music continues. Flashback to ROSE and JACKIE saying goodbye to PETE. Heads together, intimate, a family.

PETE Thanks for saving me, love.

ROSE Thank you for saving all of us.

56 EXT. CHURCH DAY

The music continues, onto its chorus, 'Don't forget to catch me'. Close on PETE as he sprints towards Matt's car, holding the vase.

PETE Oh God. Oh God.

The REAPERS have begun to close in on ROSE and JACKIE and the BABY. ROSE stands there, brave: she won't move.

57 INT. JACKIE'S BEDROOM (1992)

The music continues. As before, JACKIE telling the story to LITTLE ROSE.

JACKIE He died, and I was so close. But not close enough.

58 EXT. CHURCH DAY

The music continues. PETE runs straight at the car. MATT throws his arm up for the last time.

PETE Goodbye, love.

Close on ROSE, as a REAPER rears up right in front of her. She closes her eyes.

ROSE Goodbye, Dad.

59 EXT. CHURCH DAY

Darkness. The music has stopped.

The sound of the car hitting PETE, exactly as before. The vase hits the road and smashes. The only differences from the first time are that we're in a different location and Pete, lying in the road, is in his wedding suit.

The REAPERS flash out of existence.

60 OMITTED

61 EXT. CHURCH DAY

ROSE still has her eyes closed. She can't bear to open them, until a hand grasps her shoulder. She looks up.

No Jackie; just THE DOCTOR, looking down at her. Sad, proud, aware of what's happened.

THE DOCTOR Go to him. Quick.

Rose runs to her Dad. The Doctor follows more slowly. All around is normal.

Matt gets out of his car, looking shattered. PETE looks up at Rose, just for a second, with what looks like recognition in his eyes. She takes his hand. A hint of a smile from him. Then he's gone.

62 INT. JACKIE'S BEDROOM DAY (1992)

As before, JACKIE is telling Pete's story to LITTLE ROSE, but with changes –

JACKIE The driver was just a kid. He stopped, he waited for the police. It wasn't his fault. For some reason, Pete just ran out.

She strokes Little Rose's hair.

JACKIE People say, there was this girl. She sat with Pete while he was dying. She held his hand. Then she was gone. We never found out who she was.

63 EXT. CHURCH DAY

On ROSE, slowly putting a hand to her mouth, shaking. The absolute full moment of grief, as never felt before.

People are coming out of the church now, looking at the accident from a distance. They include SONNY and many of the others who we've seen taken by the Reapers.

SONNY gently stops SARAH from running out, a nice gesture: hold on, let me see what's going on.

Rose sees JACKIE coming out of the church, looking puzzled, just starting to question people about what's going on. Rose only has a moment. She bends down to her Dad's body and kisses his forehead.

ROSE V/O Peter Alan Tyler, my Dad. The most wonderful man in the world.

She looks up, and there's THE DOCTOR. A good distance behind him stands the TARDIS. She goes to him and takes his hand.

ROSE Died the 7th of November, 1987.

The Doctor leads her towards the TARDIS; she does not look back.

The Empty Child and The Doctor Dances
By Steven Moffat

Back in the old days, when Russell and Julie and Phil and Helen were young, before they were all creased and spindled by filming schedules and Barry Island, they talked to me about their budget. 'Lots of money!' they said. 'Spend our budget!' they demanded.

'He's never had a budget before,' scoffed Russell to Phil. 'Writes sitcoms, he does. Three wall sets!'

And even then, in my head … Rose rising, hanging from a barrage balloon, heading right up into the middle of a German air raid. I'd show the twuckers! (For decency's sake, I'm conflating my profanities.)

Well, I did show them, and they didn't blink. And then they showed me, and then they showed you, and wow, how good did that look?

But before that, all those drafts – all those endless drafts. What changed, that's what you want to know as you flick through this book in WHSmith's like the skinflint you are. Well, actually, looking back at the first draft right now, not that much. All the important stuff – corridor chasing, scary lurching – was all there at the start. But there was a time when the Doctor and Nancy didn't meet till the very last scene of 'The Doctor Dances'. Yes, I know, how stupid was that? Oh, and there was no Chula ambulance – the mysterious crashed vessel was once Captain Jack's own ship, time-looped and invisible, having arrived the previous month from the near future. Yes, well, clever in its stupidly complicated way,

I suppose. But Chris would've need three extra pages to explain it all, plus a flip chart and a pointer. And possibly an oxygen cylinder for when he'd finished.

Anyway, as Phil wept like a grown man about the budget, Russell H Gardner (for decency's sake, I'm conflating the Welsh) guided me towards a simpler story. Julie would keep asking me to change my set descriptions from 'stunningly vast' to 'stunningly compact', and Helen would tactfully suggest that explaining the plot at some point would be a positive, and Russell would enthuse away Welshly, demanding more death and destruction, like Neddy Seagoon in a fit of blood-lust. (The RTD philosophy: 'Become a writer. Create interesting characters. *And melt them!!!*')

And finally they were filming, and I was done. Or so I thought, poor Scottish fool that I was.

Out on Barry Island, there was the director James Hawes, clutching the short straw and my scripts, trying to film the impossible at night in the rain. And there was the Doctor about to save the world with some fairy dust and a good throw. And they weren't going to finish in time! So, as they suffered in the bitter cold of those January nights, longing for the warmth of their pubs and mistresses, I sat down at the computer again, with instructions to lose two minutes from the climax. Yes, you've got it – for decency's sake, I conflated the nanogenes.

You remember that bit where Jack has just reappeared astride the bomb – oh, the imagery! – and the Doctor shouts 'Change of plan, we don't need the bomb'? 'What plan?' you ask. Well, the plan I cut, in fact. We just forgot to take out that line. Oops!

But, I hear you object, if you lose two minutes from the script, isn't the show going to be two minutes too short? Well that shows all you know! It's a lot more complicated than that, telly! It's not for amateurs, you know! Now off to the cash desk with you, and pay! Tchh!

And that's about it really. Except for that two-minute scene about the scary typewriter we had to stick in later cos the show was too short.

Steven Moffat

1 EXT. SPACE

A pin-prick of light, among the stars. Zooming towards us, bigger and bigger. It's a cylinder, like a big, dirty oil drum, tumbling through the void. Nasty, industrial, all battered and charred – and a nasty shade of mauve.

And pursuing it, absurd and heroic, a police telephone box . . .

ROSE V/O What's the emergency?

THE DOCTOR V/O It's mauve.

2 INT. THE TARDIS NIGHT

THE DOCTOR and ROSE clutching at the console as the TARDIS heaves, spins, lurches. The Doctor is working frantically at the controls, on the high seas again – and this time it's an emergency. Rose is wearing a Union Jack tee-shirt.

ROSE . . . Mauve?

THE DOCTOR Universally recognised colour for danger.

ROSE What happened to red?

THE DOCTOR That's only humans. By everyone else, red is camp. Oh, the misunderstandings! All those red alerts, all that dancing . . . !
(working frantically at the controls)
It's got a very basic flight computer – I've hacked in, slaved the TARDIS. Wherever it goes . . .
(looks up at her, grins delightedly)
. . . we go!!

ROSE And that's safe, is it?

THE DOCTOR Totally.

Whump!! A bang and a flash from the console – flames! The TARDIS buffets, spins.

The Doctor has leapt back, is now sucking his burnt fingers. He and Rose grab the console again.

THE DOCTOR Okay, reasonably! Shoulda said 'reasonably' there.

The cylinder is flickering out of existence on the scanner.

THE DOCTOR (racing round the console)
No, no, no! Jumping time tracks, getting away from us!!

He's off round the console, yanking at the controls.

ROSE So what *is* this thing?

THE DOCTOR No idea.

ROSE Then why are we chasing it?

THE DOCTOR It's mauve and dangerous . . .
(fixes her with a look – this is the headline)
. . . and about thirty seconds from the centre of London!

Shock zoom on Rose. She looks to the scanner again. Earth! The cylinder is tumbling towards it!

CUT TO OPENING TITLES.

3 EXT. LONDON ALLEYWAY NIGHT

A seedy back alley, blackened brickwork, overflowing bins, slinking cats – and then the grinding of ancient engines. The TARDIS materialises.

THE DOCTOR (emerging, mid-conversation)
Know how long you can knock around space without happening to bump into Earth?

ROSE Five days. Or is that just when we're out of milk?

THE DOCTOR All the species, in all the universe – and it's gotta come out of a cow.
(setting off down the alley)
Must've come down somewhere quite close – within a mile anyway. And it can't have been more than a few weeks ago. Probably a month.

ROSE A *month*?? We were right behind it.

THE DOCTOR It was jumping time tracks all over the place – you want to drive?? We're bound to be a little out.

We switch POV: we're above them now, hand-held – someone is watching from a rooftop.

ROSE How much is a little?

THE DOCTOR A bit.

ROSE Is that exactly a bit?

THE DOCTOR Ish.

The Doctor has come to a doorway – clearly a back entrance, dark and creepy. The kind of door you shouldn't go through in this kind of movie.

ROSE What's the plan? You gonna do a scan for alien tech, or something?

THE DOCTOR Rose, it hit the middle of London with a very loud bang. I'm gonna *ask*.

He proffers the little wallet with the psychic ID he used in 'The End of the World'.

ROSE 'Doctor John Smith, Ministry of Asteroids'.

THE DOCTOR Psychic paper, it tells you –

ROSE What you want it to tell me, I remember.

THE DOCTOR Come on then!

ROSE Not very Spock, is it, just *asking*.

The Doctor has put his head to the door, listening.

THE DOCTOR Door, music, people. What do you think?

ROSE I think you should do a scan for alien tech – gimme some Spock, just once! Would it kill you?

THE DOCTOR You sure about that tee-shirt?

He is frowning at the large Union Jack blazing from her chest.

ROSE Too early to say. Taking it out for a spin.

THE CHILD V/O (distantly)
Mummy?

ROSE, hears this, is instantly chilled. She looks around, unable to locate the source of the voice. The Doctor, whirring his sonic screwdriver at the door, hears nothing.

THE DOCTOR (door open now)
Come on if you're coming! This won't take a minute.

The Doctor heads through the door. Rose takes another troubled look round, then starts to head after him – but as she does so she glances up. And freezes. Rose's POV: standing at the edge of the rooftop above, dimly visible, a silhouette against the stars . . . a motionless child.

THE CHILD Mummy?

4 INT. DARKENED CORRIDOR NIGHT

The DOCTOR makes his way along a darkened, seedy corridor – at the far end, an arch, a bead curtain hanging across it. Beyond it lights, chatter, applause. He moves towards it.

5 INT. DRINKING DEN NIGHT

It's straight out of *The Singing Detective*. A GIRL singing at a big, chunky microphone. Lounging SPIVS with pencil moustaches. GIRLS with scarlet mouths. A lean, leathery BARMAN polishing a glass. We pan round this, coming to THE DOCTOR, taking it all in. He grins – a perfect specimen of its kind!

6 EXT. LONDON ALLEYWAY NIGHT

ROSE, staring at the CHILD above.

ROSE Are you all right up there?
(no reply)
Are you stuck?

She looks. A fire escapes zig-zags up the wall – she can climb to the child!

ROSE Do you need help?

Again, distantly:

THE CHILD . . . Mummy?

7 INT. DRINKING DEN NIGHT

The girl is finishing her song. THE DOCTOR is at the singer's mike stand.

THE DOCTOR Excuse me! Excuse me, could I have everyone's attention – just for a mo, very quick. Hello?

Reluctantly the room falls silent, turns to him. The Doctor fires off his best and widest grin.

THE DOCTOR Might seem like a stupid question. Has anything fallen from the sky recently?

Staring. Total silence. The Doctor, a little taken back. What's he got wrong? And then – someone laughs. Then someone else. The Doctor: wha-? The laughter slowly builds . . .

8 EXT. LONDON ALLEYWAY NIGHT

ROSE is racing up the last flight of the fire escape – to see that it doesn't go all the way to the top of the building. A few feet above Rose, the CHILD stands, silhouetted, motionless.

ROSE Okay, hang on, don't move . . .

Close on the Child, silhouetted. As he moves his head to look at Rose, light briefly catches his eyes. Two perfectly round disks flash in the moonlight . . .

Rose is looking around frantically for another way to climb up – and a length of metal cable clatters down from the roof, like it's been thrown down for her.

9 INT. DRINKING DEN NIGHT

The DOCTOR still at the mike. Everyone is laughing now.

THE DOCTOR Sorry, am I saying something funny? There's just this thing I need to find. Would've fallen from the sky, few days ago . . .

Dreadful mournful whine starts up.

THE DOCTOR . . . Would've landed quite near here . . .

The Doctor falters. That whine sounds familiar. And everyone's getting up, heading for the door . . .

THE DOCTOR . . . With a very loud . . .

The Doctor's eye falls on a poster on the wall. An air-raid warning poster.

THE DOCTOR (ending, a little lamely, the dumbest question he's ever asked) . . . bang?

He closes his eyes in despair.

10 EXT. LONDON ALLEYWAY NIGHT

ROSE is climbing up the cable, nearly at the top. She too has heard the sirens, is looking around in confusion. Doesn't recognise that sound – but it doesn't sound good!

THE CHILD Balloon.

She looks back up at the CHILD. The Child moves his head again. The disks flash. This time ROSE sees it, frowns, halts in her climb. There's something wrong with shape of the Child's head, something –

THE CHILD Balloon.

ROSE ... What?

The Child looks up – again, moonlight glimmers briefly on his disk eyes – and Rose follows his look. Hanging in the air 50 ft above them, like an elephant tethered in the sky, listing eerily, is a barrage balloon ...

THE CHILD Balloon.

A gust of wind – the barrage balloon shifts, silent and huge – and Rose shifts with it, away from the wall. The cable is trailing from the barrage balloon! Now she's hanging over the centre of the alley, spinning, clinging on frantically ... because the balloon is pulling her up, up, past the rooftops, and then – spinning around her the skyline of wartime London – searchlights, barrage balloons, the drone of the coming bombers ... the whole dreadful, epic panorama ...

The wind gusts again, turning the ponderous balloon, lifting it higher ... Rose is dragged up, yelling:

ROSE Doctor!!

Up, up ... searchlights sweeping round the sky, the pounding of the anti-aircraft guns just beginning, tracer fire ... and there, in the distance, here they come ... the German bombers. It's like there's hundreds of them, droning through the moonlight – like there's a great black cloud of them, swarming towards London – and straight towards Rose.

She hangs there, staring, terrified, a Union Jack spread across her chest.

ROSE Okay. Maybe *not* this tee-shirt.

11 EXT. LONDON ALLEYWAY NIGHT

THE DOCTOR comes out the door again, looking round.

THE DOCTOR Rose?

Not there.

THE DOCTOR (louder)
Rose?

A movement. He whirls. A cat is looking at him from the top of one of the bins. He sighs.

THE DOCTOR (to the cat)
You know, one day – one day just maybe – I'm gonna meet someone who gets the whole 'Don't wander off!' thing. Nine hundred years of phone-box travel, it's the only thing left would surprise me!

And right on cue – a telephone rings! The DOCTOR freezes – cos he knows exactly where it's coming from. He turns. He is staring, thunderstruck, at the TARDIS! We close in on the sign on the door, behind which the phone is ringing . . .

The Doctor strides over to the TARDIS, flips opens the little panel to reveal the ringing phone. He stares at it, almost indignantly. He prods at it with his sonic screwdriver.

THE DOCTOR How can you be ringing? What's that about, ringing? What am I supposed to do with a ringing phone??

The obvious answer pops into his head. He steels himself – and, feeling a little ridiculous, he reaches for the phone. Before he can lift it, a voice from behind him:

NANCY (from off)
Don't answer it.

He looks round, almost startled. A girl is standing in the shadows. A classic street urchin – dirt-streaked face, ragged clothes. She looks to be about 16 and, underneath the grime, pretty as a porcelain doll. Standing there, there is something eerie about her stillness, her calm, solemn stare. This is NANCY.

NANCY It's not for you.

The Doctor looks shrewdly at her.

THE DOCTOR And how do you know that?

NANCY Cos I do. And I'm telling you. Don't answer it.

THE DOCTOR If you know so much, tell me this. How can it be ringing?
(turns back to phone, prods it with his sonic screwdriver)
This isn't a real phone. Not wired to anything. So how come –

He breaks off, cos he's glanced back at Nancy – and she's gone. Like she's vanished . . .

Now thoroughly discomfited, the Doctor looks back to the phone. It's still ringing. Despite himself, he's unnerved. He resolves himself, picks up the phone – and for a comical moment doesn't quite know what to say into it.

THE DOCTOR . . . Hello?
(silence; self-conscious now, not used to this – he doesn't answer *phones*!)
This is the Doctor speaking.
(and then – well, what else could he say?)
How may I help you?

The DOCTOR frowns. What? And then, in his ear . . .

THE CHILD'S VOICE V/O (an eerie whisper)
. . . Mummy?

He stiffens. Wha–??

THE CHILD'S VOICE V/O (exactly the same tone as before – eerily identical)
. . . Mummy?

The Doctor hesitates, doesn't quite know what to say, trying to get his head round this.

THE DOCTOR Who is this? Who's speaking?

THE CHILD'S VOICE V/O . . . Are you my mummy?

The DOCTOR flounders, bewildered.

THE DOCTOR *Who is this??*

THE CHILD'S VOICE V/O *Mummy??*

THE DOCTOR How did you phone here? This isn't a real phone, this isn't connected. How did you –

The phone clicks in his ear, goes dead. He stands there, numbly holding the phone for a moment.

Slowly he hangs up. His face: what the hell was that?? He looks back to where Nancy was standing – there's a row of bins just behind where she stood, and then a low wall (cutting across the alleyway, ending it). Clearly this must have been her escape route.

He hesitates, unsure what to do for a moment. He looks back to the TARDIS. He pops open the door, calls inside.

THE DOCTOR Rose? Rose, are you in there?

No reply. He hops up on to the bins, looks over the wall . . . into a narrow passageway. Like the kind that you get at the back of terraced houses . . .

11A EXT. NARROW PASSAGEWAY NIGHT

THE DOCTOR drops down into the passageway, looks around. Which way did she go? There are some bins in this passageway, too, but one of them has been pulled away from the others, and now stands at a particular section of wall. The Doctor hops up on this bin, looks over.

12 EXT. GARDEN NIGHT

The back of a house, a nasty stretch of lawn and at the end of it, an Anderson shelter (submerged corrugated-iron shed, usually with turf over the top). An irate WOMAN is sticking her head out of the shelter, yelling at the back of the house.

WOMAN Arthur! Arthur, will you hurry up? Didn't you hear the sirens??

13 EXT. THE SKY NIGHT

Close on ROSE's hands gripping desperately to the steel cable. She slips a few inches – blood on the cable now, slippery.

Wider: she's hundreds of feet above London now – no hope of getting down. Just gotta hang on, just gotta not fall somehow! The drone of the bombers getting louder. The wind whipping at her. She looks desperately round – no hope, no help anywhere!

14 EXT. GARDEN NIGHT

The WOMAN is still yelling from the shelter.

WOMAN Arthur, *please*!

Finally ARTHUR comes out of the house – not in a good mood.

ARTHUR Middle of dinner, every time. Bloomin' Germans, don't they eat?

WOMAN I can hear the *planes*.

ARTHUR (yelling at the sky)
Don't you eat??

WOMAN (pulling him in)
Keep your voice down, it's an air raid!

The door slams behind them, and a head pops out from behind the shelter. Closer: it's NANCY again. She listens at the bunker door, checking they're all well ensconced – and darts towards the back door of the house!

As she does so we CUT TO THE DOCTOR, watching over the wall ...

15 INT. KITCHEN NIGHT

NANCY comes through the back door, straight into the kitchen. She looks around, heads straight for the cupboards ... She tosses a little canvas sack on the kitchen table, ready for her booty. It looks like what it is – a sandbag, slit open and redeployed.

16 EXT. THE SKY NIGHT

ROSE still frantically clinging on. Her POV: below her the bombs are falling; great blooms of flame, the sky turning red ...

She slips further. More blood on the cable! Her face: eyes screwed shut, teeth gritted – can't hold on much longer. Her feet kicking, the ground hundreds of feet below. She's getting higher and higher, nothing she can do.

A German plane zooms past, barely fifty feet away! A storm of turbulence! The balloon spins, buffets, rocks – Rose screams, slips further, no way she can keep doing this, can't last much longer ...!

17 EXT. BALCONY NIGHT

We're somewhere in Westminster, a fine old stone balcony. A lone figure stands at the stone balustrade, his back to us, framed against the infernal skyline of Blitz London. A silhouette in a peaked cap and greatcoat, collar turned up against the wind. Over his shoulder we can see in the middle distance the barrage balloon, its tiny, kicking passenger.

Close on a pair of binoculars standing on the balustrade next to the figure. He reaches for them.

ALGY (from off)
Jack?

Another uniformed man has popped out through the French windows leading onto the balcony, a drink in his hand. Beyond him we can see what looks like a gentleman's club – stuffed armchairs, stuffed shirts. Everyone seems to be heaving themselves to their feet, heading to the exit.

ALGY You going down the shelter? Apparently I've got to go off on some damn silly guard duty.

JACK doesn't reply. He has the binoculars trained on the sky. ALGY looks up where Jack is focusing his binoculars

ALGY Ah! Barrage balloon, eh? Must've come loose.

Through the binoculars, focusing. We're reasonably close on ROSE, twisting and struggling.

ALGY Happens now and then. Don't you RAF boys use 'em for target practice?

Algy turns, starts to head back in, clearly expecting Jack to follow. As he does so, Jack touches a panel on his binoculars. A soft whine of advanced technology. Through the binoculars: we now zoom in improbably close on Rose.

JACK (under his breath; appreciatively)
Excellent bottom!

ALGY (turning, flustered)
I say, old man, there's a time and a place ...

He sees that Jack is still examining the balloon, making no move to follow.

ALGY Look, um, should really be off!

JACK Sorry, old man –

Jack turns. We see him for the first time – an iconic first-look-at-a-hero shot, the reddening sky of Blitz London behind him, the searchlights, the flaming buildings. He's impossibly handsome, dashing – the jawline of Dan Dare, the smile of a bastard.

JACK I've got to meet a girl.

He winks at Algy, heads past him in the doorway, and away.

For a moment Algy seems slightly crestfallen.

Jack pops back into view for a second.

JACK But you've got an excellent bottom too!

He claps a friendly hand on Algy's shoulder and off he goes.

18 INT. KITCHEN NIGHT

NANCY has finished her looting of the kitchen. All the cupboard doors stand open, stuff is scattered all over the floor – and Nancy's little sack is bulging.

19 INT. HALLWAY NIGHT

She starts heading down the hallway for the front door. A shot of her through an open doorway as she passes it.

She's gone for a beat, then pokes her head back round the door, stares at the (unseen by us) contents of room. Eyes like saucers!

She disappears again. We hear the front door, we hear her step outside. Through the window we can see her on the doorstep. She gives a loud whistle – three sharp blasts, clearly a signal.

Then she comes scurrying back in, back through the open doorway – and this time we widen the shot as she comes back to –

20 INT. DINING ROOM NIGHT

– a table fully set for dinner, for a whole family of five, clearly abandoned with barely a mouthful taken! NANCY goes quickly to the end of the table, where a joint is in the middle of being carved. She picks up the carving knife, sets to work, expertly.

A patter of feet in the hall! JIM – another urchin – comes tearing in; comes to a shuddering halt in the doorway, staring at all this wonderful food! Another urchin – ERNIE – slams into the back of him; also stares. Wow!

NANCY (still expertly carving)
Many kids out there?

JIM Yes, miss. Seen a few.

Ernie is already heading for the food, reaching to grab some potatoes from a bowl – Nancy's voice is a whip-crack:

NANCY (pointing her carving knife at the empty chairs)
Still carving. Sit and wait!

Cowed, Ernie and Jim do as they're told.

NANCY We've got the whole air raid!

She calmly resumes her carving.

21 OMITTED

22 EXT. SKY NIGHT

ROSE still clinging on for dear life! She slips again, while the sky roars and thunders around her. Her face: this is it! Can't keep doing this!

She slips again, further – too far, too fast. The cable slips from her grasp. Screaming, she falls! Shot from above – hundreds of feet over the streets of London, Rose is plunging down into them.

No hope of rescue, no hope of survival – and then something impossible happens. A searchlight is sweeping up from below, up and up, right at her – and it *catches* her. Suddenly she's just hanging there, bouncing slightly, like a mote of dust in a shaft of sunlight.

She looks around, bewildered, astonished. Nothing's holding her – except the light. Wha–?

A calm voice echoes round her.

JACK V/O Okay – I've got you.

ROSE (totally freaked)
Who's got me??
(looks around)
Who's got me and, you know, *how*??

JACK V/O I'm just programming your descent pattern. Stay as still as you can and keep your hands and feet inside the light field.

ROSE . . . Descent pattern?

JACK V/O Oh, and could you switch off your mobile phone?

She boggles at this.

JACK V/O No, seriously. It interferes with our instruments.

Rose fumbles for her mobile, switches it off.

ROSE (as she does so)
You know that no one ever *believes* that, right?

JACK V/O Thank you, that's much better.

ROSE (flaring)
Oh, yeah, that's a real load off, that is!! I'm hanging in the sky, in the middle of a German air raid, with a Union Jack on my chest, but hey, my mobile phone's off!

JACK V/O With you in a moment.

A click, like a line going dead. The light beam darkens to about half its former brightness.

ROSE Hey! Come back here!!
(yelling now)
You could have left the light on!!

23 INT. JACK'S COCKPIT NIGHT

A different shot of ROSE hanging there. We are now looking at her on a scanner – lots of readouts and numbers and stuff, flowing across it. This is hi-tech – way past anything in 1940. JACK is sitting at the instruments of what appears to be some kind of space vehicle – it isn't too dissimilar to the cockpit of a fighter plane; a mix of fighter pilot imagery and *Star Wars* . . . and a camper van. Does he *live* here??

COMPUTER VOICE V/O (deep, macho voice)
The mobile communication device indicates non-contemporaneous life form.

JACK She's not from round here, no.

24 EXT. SKY NIGHT

ROSE bobbing there, somewhere between terrified and self-conscious. There is a click and the beam brightens again.

JACK V/O Ready for you. Hold tight!

ROSE To what??

JACK V/O Fair point.

And then, with a terrifying whoosh Rose is spun round and then sucked feet-first down the light beam. Close on Rose as the world screams past her. She's screaming right along with it. She twists herself round, takes a quick look at where she's going – Rose's POV: London zooming up sickeningly to meet her – the Houses of Parliament – THUMP! CUT TO black . . .

Then –

24A INT. JACK'S COCKPIT NIGHT

JACK Okay, I've got you. You're fine, you're just fine. . . . That tractor beam, it can scramble your head a little.

The picture resolves into JACK holding ROSE. She clings to him, coughing, choking. They are standing in the cockpit of Jack's ship. The only illumination comes from the instruments and the cabin windows – the orange flare of a burning city.

ROSE I just . . . I can't . . . *I can't see!!*

JACK You've got your eyes shut.

ROSE Oh, right, yeah.

Rose opens her eyes. She is looking straight at impossibly handsome Jack, smiling at her.

ROSE (visibly disconcerted)
Oh. Hello.

JACK Hello.

ROSE . . . Hello.
(realises)
Sorry. That was 'hello' twice there. Dull but . . . you know, thorough.

JACK You all right?

ROSE (defiantly)
Fine, I'm fine. You expecting me to faint or something?

She is looking around frantically, taking in the ship. How did she get in here? She looks up. Above her, a hatchway open to the stars . . .

JACK You look a little . . . dizzy.

ROSE Well what about *you*?? You're not even in focus!
(considers that)
Oh boll–

And she collapses, face first, into Jack's chest.

25 EXT. STREET NIGHT

The front door of the house we saw earlier (where the kids are) is standing open. A couple more street URCHINS are racing across the road towards the door. As they go through it we CUT TO another POV, a higher one. From a low rooftop, the tiny figure ROSE saw, is watching. The light glimmers on the strange round eyes . . .

26 INT. DINING ROOM NIGHT

The table is now surrounded by URCHINS – seven or eight of them, sitting on the chairs, meekly waiting as NANCY carves and serves. The dining room is twee and refined – all plates framed on the wall, ornaments, and Best China. The kids, sitting round the table, are – incongruously – straight out of *Oliver*.

The two new arrivals stand meekly in the doorway – clearly there's a procedure to this. Nancy glances up at them.

NANCY You, come in! You, back out and wipe your feet.

One kid darts under the table, the other races back out to the front door. An explosion sounds from not far away. Nancy glances at the window.

NANCY (finishing up on the carving)
Sounds like it's gonna be a long one. Which is good cos there's pudding.

ERNIE Got to be black market, all this, look at it. Couldn't get all this on coupons.

NANCY Ernie, how many times?? We are guests in this house! We are not going to make comments of that kind.
(points a finger at him)
Washing up!

ERNIE (aggrieved)
Oh, Nancy!

NANCY (looking hard at one of the new arrivals – ALF)
Haven't seen you at one of these before.

ALF Please miss, he told me.

He nods at one of the other kids, who gives a nervous confirming nod to Nancy.

NANCY Sleeping rough?

ALF Yes, miss.

NANCY (a nod – he qualifies)
All right then.

She hands the plate of meat to the nearest urchin – JIM.

NANCY One slice each. And I want to see everyone chewing *properly*!

We pan with the plate as it is rapidly passed along the urchins.

JIM Yes, miss. Thanks, miss.

ERNIE (grabbing plate)
Thanks, miss.

THE DOCTOR (taking the plate)
Thanks, miss!

ALF (grabbing the plate off THE DOCTOR)
Thanks, miss!

ALF freezes. They all freeze and stare. The Doctor is just sitting there, as if he'd been there along – he's just magically appeared among them. He happily

takes his slice of meat, tucks in. He becomes aware of all the astonished staring. He gives a big, cheery grin.

THE DOCTOR Good here, innit? Who's got the salt?

As one, the kids throw themselves to their feet, launch themselves at the door, scarpering!

NANCY It's all right, everybody stay where they are!

They all freeze. They're more scared of Nancy.

NANCY Back in your seats. This isn't his house. He shouldn't be here either.

A little nervously, the kids are resuming their chairs.

THE DOCTOR (big smile)
So, you lot, what's the story?

The kids exchange glances nervously. Who is this guy, what does he want?

ERNIE What do you mean?

THE DOCTOR You're homeless, right? Living rough?

JIM What you wanna know for?
(new, alarming thought)
You a copper?

Another blast of tension round the kids. The Doctor instantly quells it.

THE DOCTOR I'm not a copper. What's a copper going to do to you lot anyway? Arrest you for starving?

ERNIE (through a crammed mouthful of food)
Put you in a home, coppers would. Soon as look at you.

An exchange of glances. This means something to all of them. The Doctor is consulting his watch.

THE DOCTOR I make it 1941. You lot shouldn't even be in London. Should've been evacuated to the country by now.

ALF I *was* vacuated. Sent me to a farm.

THE DOCTOR So why'd you come back?

ALF (hesitates, doesn't really want to get into this)
There was a man . . .

There are sombre nods from the other kids. They've all got stories like this.

JIM Yeah. Same with Ernie. Two homes ago.

ERNIE (embarrassed by this revelation)
Shut up! Better off on the streets anyway. Nicer food.

JIM Yeah. Nancy always finds the best meals.

The Doctor looks admiringly at Nancy, who is glowering suspiciously at him.

THE DOCTOR So that's what you do, is it, Nancy?

NANCY What is?

THE DOCTOR Soon as the sirens go, you find a big, fat family meal, still warm on the table with the whole family down the air-raid shelter – and bingo! Feeding frenzy for the homeless kids of London town. Puddings for all, as long as the bombs don't get you.

NANCY Something wrong with that?

THE DOCTOR *Wrong* with it?? It's *brilliant*. Not sure if it's Marxism in action or a West End musical.

NANCY Why did you follow me? What do you want?

THE DOCTOR I want to know how a phone that isn't a phone, gets a phone call. You seem to be the one to ask.

NANCY I did you a favour. I told you not to answer it. All I'm gonna tell you.

THE DOCTOR (grins at her, unabashed)
Thanks, great!
(to the other kids)
Also I need to find a blonde in a Union Jack. I mean a specific one, I didn't just wake up with a craving. Anyone seen a girl like that?

Nervous shakes of the head – and Nancy takes his plate away, bangs it down on the other side of the table.

THE DOCTOR (a little indignant, he was enjoying that)
What did *I* do wrong?

NANCY You don't close your mouth when you eat. No blondes, no flags. Anything else before you leave?

THE DOCTOR Yeah, actually, one more thing, thanks for asking . . .

The Doctor has pulled a little stubby pencil from his pocket. He grabs a napkin, starts to draw on it.

THE DOCTOR Something else I'm looking for. Would've fallen from the sky about a month ago – but not a bomb.

(The Doctor keeps talking, but we take the tiniest beat on Nancy. She registers this.)

THE DOCTOR Not the usual kind anyway. Wouldn't have exploded – probably just buried itself in the ground. And it would've looked something like this.

He holds up the napkin – a rough sketch of the cylinder we saw at the top of the show. The Doctor frowns, puzzled, cos no one is looking at him, and the room is suddenly cold and silent. Everyone is staring over his shoulder, at the window behind him. Fear in all their eyes.

THE DOCTOR (looking round them, puzzled)
Hello? Something wrong?

The Doctor looks to Nancy. She is also staring, wide-eyed, at a point just past his shoulder. He turns, following their look to the window (the one at the front, looking out onto the street). Silhouetted, the head and shoulders of a small child. The palm of one hand pressed against the glass. A tiny hand.

The Doctor frowns. What's frightening about that? Just a child's hand.

NANCY (whispering now)
Who was the last one in?

ERNIE (also whispering, nods at the Doctor)
Him.

NANCY (whispering)
He came in the back. Who was the last one in the front?

ALF (whispering also)
Me.

NANCY (whispering)
Did you close the door?

ALF (whispering)
I ... I don't ...

NANCY *Did you close the door??*

A gasp from one of the kids. Nancy looks back to the window. Just a moist palm print – the child is gone, has moved. And Nancy erupts into action, races into the hallway –

27 INT. HALLWAY NIGHT

Nightmare shot, the half-lit, shadow-barred hallway, zooming and tilting on the front door – it is ajar, a tiny, silhouetted figure is just appearing beyond it –

NANCY throws herself at the door, slams it shut, slams the bolt over. When she turns, THE DOCTOR is at the dining-room door, looking at her curiously.

THE DOCTOR What's this then?

NANCY Shh!

A knock at the door. The Doctor glances at the door, troubled. Why is she behaving like this?

THE DOCTOR Never easy. Being the only child left out in the cold.

NANCY Suppose you'd know

THE DOCTOR Yeah.

She looks hard at him – big, solemn eyes.

NANCY Mister ... it's not exactly a child.

The Doctor frowns. What does she mean? And then it comes ... from beyond the door ...

THE CHILD'S VOICE Mummy?

On the Doctor: he registers the same voice as he heard on the phone. A child's voice. But odd. Soft like a whisper but it carries all through the house. The Doctor stares at the door – riveted now.

THE CHILD'S VOICE Mummy?

Nancy pushes past the Doctor, into the dining room.

28 INT. DINING ROOM NIGHT

NANCY Right. Everybody out. Across the back garden, under the fence.

THE CHILD'S VOICE Mummy?

NANCY Now! Go! *Move!*

The kids are crowding into the hall, scurrying in the direction of the back door. A little girl remains locked where she is, fists clamped to the table, shaking . . .

THE CHILD'S VOICE *Mummy!*

NANCY Come on, baby, got to go . . . it's just like a game, just like chasing —

She grabs the little girl's hand, pulls her from her chair.

29 INT. HALLWAY NIGHT

And they're off down the hallway, out through the kitchen. THE DOCTOR watches them go, turns back to the door. The letter flap is opening. A tiny arm reaches through, a very pale, tiny hand gropes blindly. It's a perfectly ordinary human hand.

THE CHILD'S VOICE Let me in. Please, mummy.

The Doctor steps closer, staring at the hand . . .

THE DOCTOR Are you all right?

THE CHILD'S VOICE Please let me in?

THE DOCTOR (stepping closer; cautious but intrigued)
Are you looking for your mummy?

The hand is stretching towards the sound of the Doctor's voice.

THE CHILD'S VOICE I'm scared. Don't leave me alone. Please, mummy.

NANCY (from off)
Mister? . . .

The Doctor turns. NANCY is back. She has a vase in her hand, ready to throw. She hurls it at the flailing arm. The vase smashes against the door, the arm yanks back through the flap.

NANCY You mustn't let him touch you.

THE DOCTOR What happens if he touches me?

NANCY He'll make you like him.

THE DOCTOR And what's he like?

NANCY I've gotta go.

She turns to run. The Doctor grabs her, gently swings her back round.

THE DOCTOR Nancy! What's he like.

She looks at him for a moment. And then she leans in to him to whisper something, like it's the biggest, deadliest secret ever.

NANCY He's empty.

The Doctor frowns, not understanding. The phone rings, shattering the silence. Nancy stares at the phone, terrified.

NANCY It's him.

The Doctor looks curiously at the phone.

NANCY He can make phones ring. He *can*. Just like with that police box, you *saw*!

Impulsively, the Doctor steps forward lifts the phone. In his ear:

THE CHILD'S VOICE (phone distort)
Are you my mummy?

Nancy snatches the phone from the Doctor's hand, hangs it up. Almost instantly, a radio on a table flares into life. Music, and then, over it:

THE CHILD'S VOICE (radio distort)
Mummy? Mummy?

Something rattles behind them. They turn. A child's toy, a music box, lies discarded on the floor. The figurine on top starts to turn, but instead of music, we hear, crudely rendered through the mechanism:

THE CHILD'S VOICE (distort)
Mummy? Mummy? Mummy?

Nancy is completely freaked now. She breaks free of the Doctor.

NANCY You stay here if you want to!

She races away through the kitchen, out the back door. The Doctor looks back to the door. 'Mummy' is still sounding from the music box, the radio.

THE DOCTOR Your mummy isn't here.

Abruptly the radio and music box stop. A beat.

THE CHILD'S VOICE (from behind the door now)
Are you my mummy?

THE DOCTOR No mummies here. Nobody here but us kids.
(looks around)
Well. This kid.

THE CHILD'S VOICE I'm scared. Let me in. Please.

The Doctor takes a step closer to the door. His eyes go to the bolt, restraining it. He considers . . .

THE DOCTOR Why are those children frightened of you?

THE CHILD'S VOICE Please let me in, mummy. I'm scared of the bombs.

The Doctor takes another step closer. Reaches for the bolt. Hesitates.

THE CHILD'S VOICE Please, mummy. Please let me in. I'm scared of the bombs, mummy.

The Doctor is looking at the hand with which he is reaching for the lock. His hand is shaking. He blinks in surprise. Nerves aren't usually his problem. He steels himself.

THE DOCTOR Okay. I'm opening the door. I'm opening it now.

Almost having to force himself, he reaches for the bolt, slams it back, and then – it takes an effort – he pulls open the door ... to see ...

Nothing! The empty street. The child has gone!! The Doctor stands for a moment, stares. What now? He looks around – then, deciding, he closes the door, heads back along the hallway, after the others.

30 INT. JACK'S COCKPIT NIGHT

On ROSE, asleep but stirring. Her eyes flicker open. Rose's POV: her vision blurrily resolves into a shot of JACK, sitting at his controls, his back to us. The cabin is largely in darkness – the only lights from windows (the orange flare of a burning city) and from the instruments. She leans over, cranes to look out one of the cabin windows. The ship is hanging suspended above the streets of London – not very high, about fifty feet.

JACK (without turning)
All better now?

Rose startles. Jack turns in his chair. A shadow against the wartime skies.

ROSE You got lights in here?

Jack reaches over, clicks a switch. Rose's first impression was dead right. He's shockingly handsome.

A silence. They're looking at each other. And they're liking what they see. For Rose, this is a little disconcerting. Jack just smiles, wolfishly.

JACK Hello.

ROSE ... Hello.

Another silence.

JACK Hello.

ROSE Let's not start that again.

JACK (smiles)
Okay.

A little silence. Rose shifts, a little self-consciously – making all those awkward little flicks and tweaks of someone who's aware they might not be looking their best but suddenly would like to. She's a little thrown but she gives her best shot at defiance.

ROSE So. Who are you supposed be then??

JACK Currently? Captain Jack Harkness, 133 Squadron, Royal Air Force, American volunteer.

As he says this he passes her his wallet, displaying his credentials in a little window. Rose looks at this, grins.

ROSE Liar.

JACK You think?

ROSE This is psychic paper, isn't it? Tells me whatever you want it to tell me.

JACK (impressed)
How'd you know?

ROSE (smug now, getting in control of the conversation)
Two things. One, I've got a friend who uses it all the time, and two . . . you just handed me a piece of paper telling me you're single and you work out.

JACK (a little taken aback)
. . . Ah! Tricky thing, psychic paper.

ROSE (handing it back to him)
Yeah. Got to not let your mind wander when you're handing it over.

Jack is smirking at the paper she's handed back to him.

JACK Quite! So, you have a 'sort of' boyfriend called Mickey Smith but really you consider yourself footloose and fancy free.

ROSE (flushing)
What??

JACK Actually the word you use is 'available'.

ROSE No way!

JACK Also the word 'very'.

ROSE successfully snatches the paper from Jack, tosses it aside.

ROSE Okay, shall we try and get along without the paper?

JACK That might be better, don't you think?

Another awkward silence. Rose looks around.

ROSE (looking around)
Nice spaceship.

JACK Gets me around.

ROSE Very . . . Spock.

JACK Very what?

ROSE Guessing you're not a local boy then?

Jack has levelled a little hand-held computer at her. It beeps and chirps.

JACK A cell phone, a liquid crystal watch and fabrics that won't be around for at least another two decades. Guessing you're not a local girl.

Rose is at a window, peering out.

ROSE Guessing right.
(going to the window)
We're parked in mid-air. Can't anyone down there see us?

JACK No. Could I see your hands a moment?

ROSE Why?

JACK Please?

A little reluctantly – but he is terribly handsome – Rose gives him her hands. Gently, Jack takes hold of them, starts to examine the cuts and bruises with what looks like a pencil torch. As he does so:

JACK You can stop acting now. I know exactly who you are. I can spot a Time Agent a mile off.

ROSE A Time Agent?

JACK Been expecting one of you guys to show up. Though not, I have to say, by barrage balloon. Do you always travel that way?

He smiles at her, still holding her hands. And she's terribly aware of this very handsome man, very close.

ROSE Sometimes I get swept off my feet.
(colours; adds too hastily)
By balloons!

Jack is pulling his scarf off. He winds it gently round Rose's wrists, loosely binding her hands together –

ROSE What are you doing?

JACK Try to keep still.

He leans over, clicks a switch on the wall. Rose stares at her hands. A storm of what look like tiny golden fireflies are buzzing round them – and her hands are healing. The cuts and bruises disappearing!

ROSE How'd you do that?

The fireflies fade out of existence. Her hands are perfect again.

JACK Nanogenes. Subatomic robots, the air in here's full of them. They just rebuilt three layers of your skin.

ROSE Oh. Well tell 'em, thanks.

JACK Right then! Shall we get down to business?

ROSE Business?

He clicks another control. An ice bucket with a bottle of champagne in it pops out of the wall, James Bond style (along with two glasses).

JACK You're a Time Agent – and I've got a price on my head in two and a half solar systems. Shall we have a drink on the balcony?

He flicks another switch. The roof hatch slides open. He grabs the champagne and heads up the stairs. He disappears out onto the roof of the craft.

ROSE hesitates, a little uncertain.

JACK (calling, from off)
Bring the glasses.

A little hesitant, Rose takes the glasses, starts up the steps . . .

30A EXT. OUTSIDE BIG BEN NIGHT

... and finds herself ascending out of invisibility, a step at a time. She stares around, boggles – and sees that she's right next to Big Ben, the giant clock-face right in front of her (being the black-out, the clock-face is in darkness). A few feet away, JACK stands nonchalantly in mid-air, opening the champagne. ROSE nervously takes a step towards him. Her foot clangs down on the invisible hull. She looks down.

ROSE Well, I know I'm standing on *something* ...

Jack raises a little zapper (a little gadget like you open car doors with – he's currently using it to remove the foil from the champagne bottle) – and clicks it. For a moment a small space ship shimmers into visibility beneath their feet. Jack presses the zapper again. The ship disappears.

ROSE Okay. So you have an invisible spaceship.

JACK Yeah.

ROSE Tethered up to Big Ben for some reason.

Jack grins, passes her a glass of champagne.

JACK First rule of active camouflage. Park somewhere you'll remember.

He pops the cork from the bottle.

31 EXT. WASTELAND NIGHT

A patch of wasteland – bombed-out shells of houses. By a shattered wall, NANCY is crouched, sorting through the contents of her sack – the stuff she stole from the kitchen. She is then placing it in what is clearly a hollowed-out place in the wall – where she hides her stuff. The scrape of a foot – she whirls, looks round – and when she looks back, THE DOCTOR is there, leaning casually against the wall, smiling at her.

NANCY (looks at him sourly for a moment)
How'd you follow me here?

THE DOCTOR Good at following, me. I've got a nose for it.

NANCY People can't usually follow me if I don't want them to.

THE DOCTOR My nose has special powers.

NANCY Yeah? Is that why it's so –

She thinks better of it.

THE DOCTOR What?

NANCY Nuffing.

THE DOCTOR *What?*

NANCY *Nuffing.*
(a beat)
Do your ears have special powers too?

THE DOCTOR What are you trying to say?

NANCY (turning to go)
Good night, mister.

THE DOCTOR Nancy . . .

Despite herself, she hesitates.

THE DOCTOR There's something chasing you and the other kids. It looks like a boy but it isn't. And this all started about a month ago. Right?

This last piece of information impacts on her. She turns to look at him, curious now.

THE DOCTOR The thing I'm looking for. The thing that fell from the sky. That's when it landed. And you know what I'm talking about, don't you?

Nancy hesitates. Takes the decision to confide. It isn't easy.

NANCY There was a . . . a bomb. A bomb that wasn't a bomb. Fell on Limehouse Green Station . . .

THE DOCTOR Take me there.

NANCY (shakes her head)
Soldiers all round it. Barbed wire. You'd never get through.

THE DOCTOR Try me!

Nancy looks at him a moment, considering.

NANCY You really want to know what's going on in there?

THE DOCTOR I really want to know.

NANCY Then there's someone you need to talk to first.

THE DOCTOR And who would that be?

NANCY The Doctor.

On the Doctor: Wha–??

32 EXT. OUTSIDE BIG BEN NIGHT

The giant clock-face of Big Ben – and ROSE and JACK standing impossibly in mid-air a few feet in front of it. They both have glasses of champagne. Rose's is drunk – not unlike herself. She is giggling as Jack refills her glass.

ROSE You know, it's getting late, I really should be getting back.

JACK We're discussing business.

ROSE This isn't business, it's champagne.

JACK I try never to discuss business on a clear head. Are you travelling alone? Are you authorised to negotiate with me?

ROSE What would we be negotiating?

JACK I have something for the Time Agency. Something they'd like to buy. Are you empowered to make payment?

ROSE Well. I'd have to talk to my . . . companion.

JACK Your 'companion'.

His meaning is clear. And he's getting closer.

ROSE (smiles a little nervously)
Like I said, it's getting late – I should be getting back to him. What time is it?

JACK Him?

ROSE Do you have the time?

Without taking his eyes off her, Jack raises his zapper again, points it at the giant clock-face. The clock-face illumines, bathing them both in its light. This is now impossibly romantic. And half past nine.

ROSE Okay. That was flash. That was on the flash side.

JACK When you say 'companion' just how disappointed should I be?

ROSE eyes him for a moment. He's getting so close. His intent is clear.

ROSE Okay. We're standing in mid-air, on top of an invisible space ship, during a German air raid. Do you really think this is a good moment to come on to me?

JACK Perhaps not.

ROSE Well. It was only a suggestion.

Jack's face: he's in! This is not a drill!

JACK Do you like Glenn Miller? Become quite partial during my stay.

He raises his key zapper, clicks it. Glenn Miller starts playing; 'Moonlight Serenade'. He pulls her gently to him. They start to dance. In mid-air. In front of Big Ben. As the Blitz drones and booms around them. It's impossibly romantic.

JACK It's 1941. Height of the London Blitz. Height of the German bombing campaign. And something else has fallen on London. A fully equipped Chula warship. The last one in existence. The last of the Chula Death Squad, armed to the teeth. And I know where it is – cos I parked it. If the agency can name the right price, I can get it for you. In two hours' time a German bomb is going to land on it, and destroy it forever. That's your deadline. That's the deal. Shall we start talking payment?

ROSE You know what I think?

JACK What?

ROSE I think you were talking just there.

JACK Two hours. The bomb falls. There'll be nothing left but dust and a crater.

ROSE Promises, promises.

JACK You listening to any of this?

ROSE You used to be a Time Agent, now you're some kind of freelancer.

JACK That's a little harsh – I prefer to think of myself as a criminal.

ROSE I'll bet you do.

JACK Okay, this companion of yours. Does he handle the business?

ROSE I delegate a lot of that, yeah.

JACK Well! Maybe we should go find him!

ROSE (exactly what she wants!)
And how you gonna do that?

JACK Easy! I'll do a scan for alien tech!

He starts tapping away at his hand-held computer. On Rose: a tiny smile.

ROSE Finally! A professional!

33 EXT. WASTELAND NIGHT

Behind the houses, a patch of wasteland. A mess, bombed shells of houses . . .
THE DOCTOR and NANCY are picking their way across it.

THE DOCTOR So this guy, he's just called 'the doctor' . . . he doesn't have a name?

NANCY Dunno.

THE DOCTOR Ever think of asking him?

NANCY What's the point?

THE DOCTOR You don't think there's any point asking people their names?

NANCY What's your name?

THE DOCTOR I'm the –
(realises; ending a little lamely)
… other Doctor.

Nancy just gives him a look. They are rounding a shattered wall. The Doctor stops and stares at something. The Doctor's POV: ahead, in the centre of the waste-ground is what is clearly a new structure. A chain-link fence (or whatever they had then) enclosing a space about the size of a couple of tennis courts. Barbed wired round the top of the fence. A gate, padlocked. Keep Out signs everywhere. Clearly this place was once a railway station – there are tracks, old abandoned carriages.

The Doctor pulls something from his jacket. Looks like a cigarette case, but when he flips it open it becomes binoculars. He looks through them.

Through the binoculars: in the centre of the enclosure we can just see churned-up, scorched earth – a large mass sticking out of a hole in the ground. It is covered in tarpaulin.

NANCY (she points)
See that building? The hospital?

The Doctor glances briefly at a building looming beyond the crash site.

NANCY That's where the doctor is. You should talk to him.

THE DOCTOR (still examining the crash site)
For now, I'm more interested in getting inside there.

NANCY Talk to the doctor first.

THE DOCTOR Why?

NANCY Cos then maybe you won't want to get inside.

His curiosity now piqued, the Doctor raises his binoculars again. Through the binoculars: we pan up from the crash site to a large building some little distance beyond it. (Astute viewers may recognise it as Albion Hospital from 'Aliens of London'.) The Doctor presses a control. We zoom in on the gates to the hospital. They are chained up, padlocked. Keep Out signs everywhere.

With the Doctor's attention focused on the hospital, Nancy is using this moment to slip away.

THE DOCTOR (without even turning)
Where you going?

NANCY startles. Has he got eyes in the back of his head? He still hasn't even turned.

NANCY There was a lot of food in that house – I've got mouths to feed. Should be safe enough now.

THE DOCTOR Can I ask you a question?

NANCY Mister, it's all you ever do.

THE DOCTOR Who did you lose?

This question, out of nowhere, startles her.

NANCY … What??

THE DOCTOR The way you look after those kids. It's cos you lost someone, isn't it? And you're doing all this to make up for it.

Nancy's face: defiance, silence. But you know he's right. Almost in spite of herself:

NANCY (hesitates)
My little brother. Jamie.

She's breathing a little harder now. The way you do when you're Not Crying.

NANCY We had a place near here. Hovel more like. Might as well have been sleeping rough for all the roof there was. One night I had to go out looking for food. Same night that thing fell. Told Jamie not to follow me. Told him it was dangerous. But he . . .
(really steeling herself)
He didn't like to be alone.

THE DOCTOR What happened?

NANCY In the middle of an air raid? What do you think happened?

A moment's silence between them. The Doctor isn't going to do anything crass like comfort her. But he's respecting the moment.

THE DOCTOR (that sudden dazzling smile)
Amazing.

NANCY What is?

THE DOCTOR 1941. Right now, not very far from here, the German war machine is rolling up the map of Europe. Country after country, falling like dominoes. Nothing can stop it, nothing. Till one tiny, damp, little island says 'no'. Says 'no, not here'. A mouse in front of a lion, drawing a line in the sand. You're amazing. The lot of you. Dunno what you do to Hitler, but you scare the hell out of me.

She stares at him, struck by this. How does he know these things?

THE DOCTOR Now off you go. Do what you got to. Save the world.

He turns, heads off into the darkness. She stares after him, wondering. Then pulls herself together. She turns, heads away. As she clears frame, something stirs in the shadows. A tiny figure. Closer: as it turns its head, light glimmers on strange round eyes – and it starts after Nancy . . .

DISSOLVE TO:

34 EXT. ABANDONED HOSPITAL NIGHT

Looming over us, an abandoned hospital. Huge, rambling, all blacked stone and darkened windows. We crane down, coming to massive iron gates – they are chained and padlocked, Keep Out signs everywhere – and then to THE DOCTOR approaching.

The Doctor's POV: panning from one window to another. There are cracks of light showing through the black-out curtains. He has pulled his sonic screwdriver from his jacket, is whirring at the padlock. It springs apart in his hands. The gates – now released from their chains – are creaking slightly open. The abandoned hospital stands there in the moonlight, waiting . . .

35 INT. HOSPITAL CORRIDOR NIGHT

The empty hospital. A brightly lit, cavernous hallway of a corridor. Footfalls.

THE DOCTOR steps into shot at the far end. He looks around, heads to one of the wards.

36 INT. HOSPITAL WARD NIGHT

He's standing in a long hospital ward, rows of beds. And the beds are occupied. Motionless FIGURES lie on each. Ordinary men and women, clearly dead. Every single one of them wears a gasmask. Rows of round, hollow, staring eyes . . .

THE DOCTOR turns on his heel, stalks out –

37 INT. HOSPITAL WARD 2 NIGHT

– to another ward. The same rows of bodies, the same staring GASMASKS. He moves to one of the bodies, bends to inspect it – and there are footfalls behind him.

He turns. DOCTOR CONSTANTINE is standing in the doorway. He wears the traditional white coat. He's in his 60s, tired beyond reason, walks with a stick. There is both profound sadness and absolute determination. He looks at THE DOCTOR, seemingly without surprise. Like he's too tired to do surprise any more.

CONSTANTINE You'll find them everywhere. Every bed, every ward. Hundreds of them.

THE DOCTOR Yeah, I saw. Why are they still wearing gasmasks?

CONSTANTINE They're not. Who are you?

THE DOCTOR I'm –
(hesitates)
Are you the doctor?

CONSTANTINE Doctor Constantine. And you are?

THE DOCTOR Nancy sent me.

CONSTANTINE Nancy? Then you must have been asking about the bomb.

THE DOCTOR Yeah.

CONSTANTINE What do you know about it?

THE DOCTOR Nothing. Why I was asking. What do *you* know?

Constantine is coming into the room now, shakes his head. He waves his hand at the gasmask people.

CONSTANTINE Only what it did.

THE DOCTOR All these people, they were caught in the blast?

CONSTANTINE No. No, as a matter of fact, none of them were.

The Doctor looks bewildered at this answer. Constantine chuckles at his confusion. The chuckle becomes a cough, becomes a retch. The Doctor steps forwards to help, Constantine waves him back, irritably.

THE DOCTOR You're very sick.

CONSTANTINE Oh, dying I should think. Just haven't been able to find the time.

He settles gratefully onto a chair. Looks sharply up at the Doctor.

CONSTANTINE Are you a doctor?

THE DOCTOR I have my moments.

CONSTANTINE Examined any of them yet?

THE DOCTOR No.

CONSTANTINE Don't touch the flesh.

The Doctor looks around, unsure what to do.

THE DOCTOR Which one?

CONSTANTINE Any one.

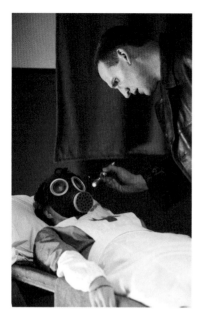

The Doctor crosses to the nearest cadaver, bends to look. He uses his sonic screwdriver to poke and prod at the body. He does so quickly, expertly.

CONSTANTINE (settling into a chair)
Conclusions?

THE DOCTOR Massive head trauma, mostly to the left side. Partial collapse of the chest cavity, mostly on the right. There's some scarring on the back of the hand and the gasmask seems to be fused to the flesh – but I can't see any burns.

CONSTANTINE Examine another one.

The Doctor glances at him, impatiently – but crosses to the next bed, repeats the procedure. Almost immediately he is frowning. Then he's frowning deeply. He looks up at Constantine.

THE DOCTOR This isn't possible.

CONSTANTINE Examine another.

The Doctor is already crossing to another body. He looks up after the briefest examination.

THE DOCTOR This *isn't possible*.

CONSTANTINE No.

THE DOCTOR They've got the same injuries.

CONSTANTINE Yes.

THE DOCTOR *Exactly* the same.

CONSTANTINE Yes.

He crosses to another body.

THE DOCTOR All of them, identical, right down to the scar on the back of the hand.

Constantine looks down at his hands clasped on the handle of his walking stick. He has the beginnings of exactly the same scar. The Doctor doesn't register this, examining another of the bodies. He looks up from it.

THE DOCTOR How did this happen? How did it *start*?

CONSTANTINE When that bomb fell, there was just one victim.

THE DOCTOR Dead?

CONSTANTINE (a beat; looks at him)
At first.

On the Doctor. This thought impacts.

CONSTANTINE His injuries were … truly dreadful. By the following morning every doctor and nurse who had treated him – who *touched* him – had those exact same injuries. By the morning after that every patient on the same floor – the exact same injuries. Within a week, the whole hospital.
(he looks around the bodies)
Physical injury … as *plague*. Can you explain that??

THE DOCTOR Why'd you put gasmasks on them?

CONSTANTINE I didn't. What would you say was the cause of death?

THE DOCTOR The head trauma.

CONSTANTINE No.

THE DOCTOR Asphyxiation?

CONSTANTINE No.

THE DOCTOR The collapse of the chest cavity – it could've –

CONSTANTINE No.

THE DOCTOR Okay. What was the cause of death?

CONSTANTINE There wasn't one.
(a beat; looks hauntedly at the Doctor)
They're not dead.

He raises his stick, whacks it against the radiator. A loud, dinning clang.
The Doctor turns to look down the ward, and all gasmasked heads turn
slowly to look at him. Unnerved, the Doctor takes a pace back.

CONSTANTINE Oh, don't worry. Quite harmless. They just sort of sit there.
No heartbeat. No life signs of any kind. They just ... don't ... *die*.

THE DOCTOR And they've just been left here. No one's doing anything??

CONSTANTINE I try to make them comfortable. What else is there?

THE DOCTOR Just you? You're the only one here?

CONSTANTINE Before this war began I was a father and a grandfather.
Now I am neither. But I am still a doctor.

THE DOCTOR Yeah. Know the feeling.

CONSTANTINE I suspect the plan is to blow up the building – blame it
on a German bomb.

THE DOCTOR What, to halt the spread? Probably too late.

CONSTANTINE I know. There have been isolated cases all over –
(coughs, recovers)
– isolated cases all over London, I –

He coughs again, can't control it. The Doctor steps forward, to help.

CONSTANTINE Stay back, *stay back*!!
(looks at the Doctor, now with the urgency of a man with seconds to live)
Listen to me! Top floor ... Room 802. That's where they took the
first victim. The one from the crash site!
(chokes again)
And you've got to find Nancy again.

THE DOCTOR Nancy?

CONSTANTINE (chokes)
It was her brother. Jamie, her brother.

Close on the Doctor. This impacts, he's thinking it through ...

THE DOCTOR But that means ... that means ...

CONSTANTINE There's something else. She knows more than she's saying. Wouldn't tell me, but she might –
(chokes, seems to stammer)
– she m– m– muh– muh–

His hand flies to his neck.

CONSTANTINE *Mummeeeee ...*

The Doctor stares at him in horror. Constantine is now staring at him, weirdly, all sense gone from his eyes.

CONSTANTINE (the words forcing, almost vomiting out of him)
... Are ... you ... my ... mummy?

And then his mouth is being forced open, by something inside. A flash of metal. And the nozzle of a gasmask starts to force its way out of his mouth ... On the Doctor, horrified, fascinated. The skin of Constantine's face is pulling back, stretching – slowly, horribly morphing into a gasmask.

It's over in a few seconds. The man on the chair is now identical to every other body in the room. He slumps, lolls ... On the Doctor, staring: what the hell happened there?? He steps away from him, looks round at the identical others. He clutches his head, despairing at himself.

THE DOCTOR Her brother! Should've *realised*!

JACK (calling from off)
Hello?

The Doctor turns, heads out into the corridor.

38 INT. HOSPITAL CORRIDOR NIGHT

JACK and ROSE are heading along to meet him.

JACK Good evening. Hope we're not interrupting?
(extending his hand to shake THE DOCTOR's)
Jack Harkness! Been hearing all about you on the way over.

ROSE He knows, I had to tell him.
(willing the Doctor to play along)
About us being Time Agents.

JACK And it's a real pleasure to meet you, Mr Spock.

The Doctor boggles at this – but Jack has noticed the bodies.

JACK So! What's this, then?

He heads through to the ward. We stay with the Doctor and Rose in the corridor – in the background, we see Jack in the ward, looking at the bodies.

39 OMITTED [38 CONTINUES]

THE DOCTOR looks at ROSE.

THE DOCTOR Mr Spock??

ROSE What was I supposed to say? You don't have a name. Don't you ever get tired of 'Doctor? Doctor Who?'.

THE DOCTOR Nine centuries in, I'm coping. Where have you *been*?? We're in the middle of the London Blitz, it's not a good moment for a stroll!

ROSE Who strolls? I went by barrage balloon. Only way to see an air raid.

THE DOCTOR *What??*

ROSE Never mind about that. Listen, what's a Chula warship? You ever heard of one of those?

On the Doctor's face: yes he has. And it's not good news!

THE DOCTOR *Chula??*

40 INT. DINING ROOM NIGHT

The dining room, much as we left it. A mess of food on the table, overturned chairs. NANCY appears at the door. She pulls a little sack from under her coat, heads to the table. As she clears frame, we go to a radio (wherever this is on set). Music starts to play (OR a hiss and crackle of static). Nancy startles, looks at it. And over the music/hiss, somehow filtering through the primitive mechanism . . .

THE CHILD'S VOICE Mummy? Where's my mummy?

NANCY stares in horror! Looks to the radio. And then a door bangs! Nancy whirls, looks to the dining-room doorway – in the hallway glimpsed outside, in the orange glow from the fires of the city, a shadow moves. A floorboard creaks – Nancy spins! Where to go?? No time, no time! She throws open a cupboard door. Shelves, crockery, no room for her!!

THE CHILD'S VOICE (from off; closer)
Mummy?

Nancy throws herself to the floor, rolls under the table. Nancy's POV: from under the table. We can only see the bottom section of the door. It stands ajar. A shadow passes the door – a pair of tiny feet ...

Nancy stares – and the pair of feet pass on down the hallway outside ...

On Nancy: where's he going? Is he leaving?

41 AND 42 OMITTED

43 INT. HOSPITAL WARD 2 NIGHT

Like THE DOCTOR before him, JACK is going from body to body in a state of mounting disbelief.

JACK This just isn't possible. How did this happen??

THE DOCTOR What kind of Chula ship landed here??

JACK ... What?

ROSE He said it was a warship. He stole it, parked it somewhere out there – somewhere a bomb's going to fall on it. Unless we make him an offer.

The Doctor staring at him, at his most menacing – a study in contained anger.

THE DOCTOR What kind of warship?

JACK (dismissively)
Does it matter? It's got nothing to do with *this*.

THE DOCTOR *This* started at the crash site. It's got *everything* to do with it. *What kind of warship??*

Jack looks mildly at him, not at all concerned at his anger.

JACK An ambulance.

The Doctor and ROSE exchange a glance. Not what they expected. Jack has pulled out his little hand-held computer. He projects a holographic image of the tumbling cylinder we saw at the top of the show.

JACK That's what nearly hit you in the time vortex, right? I threw it at you. Saw your time-travel vehicle – love the retro look, by the way, nice panels – threw you the bait.

ROSE *Bait??*

JACK A med-ship. Empty – I made sure. Nothing but a shell.

ROSE You said it was a warship.

JACK They have ambulances in wars.
(smiles)
It's a con! I was conning you. That's what I am, I'm a con man. Thought you were Time Agents. You're not are you?

ROSE (exchanges a glance with the Doctor)
Just a couple more freelancers.

JACK Should've known, the way you guys are blending with the local colour! Flag Girl was bad enough, but U-Boat Captain ...!

JACK turns back to the prone bodies, continues his examination.

JACK Anyway. Whatever's happening here – it's got nothing to do with that ship.

Rose moves to the Doctor's side.

ROSE What *is* happening, Doctor?

THE DOCTOR Human DNA is being rewritten.
(looks around the grotesque, lifeless creatures)
By an idiot.

ROSE What do you mean?

THE DOCTOR Some kind of ... virus, I don't know. Converting human beings, into these. But why? What could possibly be the point??

44 INT. DINING ROOM NIGHT

NANCY huddled, trembling, beneath the table. She is listening hard, peering out from underneath. Maybe he's gone? She makes a tiny, cautious move, starts to ease herself out from under the table – and then –

THE CHILD (from off)
Are you my mummy?

She freezes, scrambles back under!! Nancy's POV: the lower part of the door. In the doorway, a pair of tiny feet –

On Nancy: so scared she can hardly breathe. The feet advance towards the table ... Nancy shuffles back on her knees – instinctively moving away – and something dislodges from her little food bag.

On Nancy staring in horror – as an apple rolls slowly out from under the table! Nancy looks back to the CHILD's feet. The feet move; the Child walks round the side of the table, to where the apple now lies in full view on the carpet. A tiny hand reaches out to pick it up – Nancy looks from this to where the door still stands open. The Child has moved round the side of the table; the path is now clear! A chance! Maybe her only chance!

And she lunges out from under the table, scattering the chairs, throwing herself at the doorway – and a tiny hand raises, points, and *slam*!! The door is sucked shut as if by a wind.

Nancy freezes, trapped. Slowly turns. The Child is standing there, his hand still raised. Our first view of him. Just a small child, wearing a gasmask – like the bodies in the hospital. The disk-like glimmer of his eyes we saw earlier, the eyeholes of his mask.

A terrible silence.

THE CHILD Are you my mummy?

45 INT. HOSPITAL WARD 2 NIGHT

THE DOCTOR, ROSE and JACK as we left them. Every body in the ward sits bolt upright. And as one, they shout:

GASMASK PEOPLE Mummy?

The Doctor looks round, fascinated.

ROSE What's happening?

THE DOCTOR I don't know.

46 INT. DINING ROOM NIGHT

The CHILD starts advancing.

THE CHILD Are you my mummy?

NANCY moves now, keeping the table between herself and the Child. She is edging towards the window.

NANCY Jamie. It's me. Nancy. Can't you see it's me?

THE CHILD Where is my mummy?

Nancy, her back now to the window, whirls – frantically tries to open it. No good!

THE CHILD (advancing)
Where is my mummy?

47 INT. HOSPITAL WARD 2 NIGHT

The bodies, as one, swing their legs from the bed, onto the floor.

GASMASK PEOPLE Mummy?

THE DOCTOR, ROSE and JACK are at the wrong end of the ward for the door. They start drawing back as the GASMASKS lurch towards them . . .

THE DOCTOR Don't let them touch you!!

48 INT. DINING ROOM NIGHT

The CHILD is still advancing.

THE CHILD Mummy? Are you my mummy?

NANCY Jamie. It's me. Nancy.

49 INT. HOSPITAL WARD 2 NIGHT

THE DOCTOR, ROSE and JACK, shrinking back against the wall . . .

ROSE What happens if they touch us?

THE DOCTOR You're looking at it!

50 INT. DINING ROOM NIGHT

The CHILD, advancing.

THE CHILD Mummy?

NANCY It's Nancy. Your sister.

THE CHILD I'm scared. I'm scared of the bombs.

NANCY I know you're scared. I know you are.
(she swallows hard)
But you're dead, Jamie. You're *dead*.

The Child advancing right at us, filling the frame. As the light falls across the mask, we see for the first time . . . there is nothing inside. No eyes, no head. We can see right to the back of the mask.

THE CHILD Mummy?

51 INT. HOSPITAL WARD 2 NIGHT

On the GASMASK CREATURES, closer, closer.

GASMASK CREATURES *Mummmmeeeeeeee!*

Episode 10

The Doctor Dances
By Steven Moffat

1 INT. HOSPITAL WARD 2 NIGHT

(RECAP OF EPISODE 9.)

The GASMASK CREATURES closing in on THE DOCTOR, ROSE and JACK.

SMALL CHILD/GASMASK (closer)
Mummy?

LITTLE OLD LADY/GASMASK (closer)
Mummy?

ROSE (trying hard not to freak out)
Why do they keep saying that?

Close on the Doctor: why indeed? This gives him an idea! He takes a pace forward towards the creatures – that wild look on his face. He's going to take a gamble!! A poised moment, a confrontation –

THE DOCTOR (thundering)
Go to your room!

Jack and Rose: wha–? The creatures: frozen . . . heads tilt.

2 INT. DINING ROOM NIGHT

The EMPTY CHILD feels it too. Falters. What? NANCY staring – what's happening here?

3 INT. HOSPITAL WARD 2 NIGHT

THE DOCTOR (blazing, stern)
I mean it. I'm very very cross with you. I'm very very angry with you! Time out! Go to your room!

On the DOCTOR: eyes blazing, staring right at us –

4 INT. DINING ROOM NIGHT

On the EMPTY CHILD: the empty sockets glaring mutinously up at us – it's like THE DOCTOR and the Child are looking at each other. The Empty Child tilts his head, like he's trying to understand what this Doctor could be –

The Empty Child's POV: rapid cutting – the Doctor in the hospital ward from a whole succession of slightly different POVs – through the eyes of the GASMASK CREATURES surrounding him. It's like the Child can cut round all the viewpoints like a vision mixer. The image is drained of colour, like sepia, and weirdly pulled and distorted by the small glass panes of the gasmasks.

THE DOCTOR (giving it everything)
Go . . . to . . . your . . . ROOM!!!

A hanging moment, could go either way . . . and slowly the Child starts to turn, starts to walk from the room . . .

NANCY staring: what's happening, what saved her?

5 INT. THE HOSPITAL WARD 2 NIGHT

The GASMASK CREATURES are lurching back to their beds, climbing back in. ROSE and JACK exchange a bewildered look. THE DOCTOR slowly relaxes, takes a breath.

THE DOCTOR I'm really glad that worked. Those would've been rubbish last words.

CUT TO OPENING TITLES.

6 EXT. STREET NIGHT

The CHILD walking away from us, along the exact middle of the road.
We pull back.

7 INT. DINING ROOM NIGHT

We are seeing him through the window, the black-out curtain drawn back. NANCY is watching the CHILD from the dining-room window. There is terrible sadness on her face.

NANCY Jamie . . .

She flops back against the wall. There are tears in her eyes. She slowly slides down the wall, buries her face in her knees.

8 INT. HOSPITAL WARD 2 NIGHT

THE DOCTOR paces, thinking. JACK is lying on one of the free beds, relaxed, hands clasped behind his head. ROSE is looking in horror and pity at the GASMASK CREATURES.

ROSE Why are they all wearing gasmasks?

JACK They're not. Those masks are flesh and bone.

She cranes a little closer to look at one, slumped on its bed – an old man. The tufts of grey hair are growing directly from the leather of the mask.

THE DOCTOR How was your con supposed to work?

JACK Oh, you know, simple enough. Find some harmless piece of space junk, let the nearest Time Agent track it to Earth, convince him it's valuable, name a price. When he's paid fifty per cent up front, oops, a German bomb falls on it, destroys it forever. He never gets to see what he paid for, never knows he's been had, I buy him a drink with his own money and we talk about dumb luck. The perfect, self-cleaning con.

THE DOCTOR (looks at him, disgusted)
Yeah. Perfect.

JACK The London Blitz is great for self-cleaners, but Pompeii's nice if you want to make a holiday of it. Got to set your alarm for Volcano Day though.
(grins at the wintry look on the Doctor's face)
Getting a hint of disapproval.

THE DOCTOR Take a look around the room. This is what your harmless piece of space junk did.

JACK (shakes head, absolutely confident)
No way. It was a burnt-out medical transporter, it was empty.

The Doctor just looks at him – then he's marching for the door.

THE DOCTOR Rose!

ROSE We getting out of here?

THE DOCTOR We're going upstairs.

JACK I even programmed the flight computer so it wouldn't land on anything living. I harmed no one! I don't know what's happening here but believe me, I had nothing to do with it.

The Doctor turns in the doorway, glowers at him.

THE DOCTOR I'll tell you what's happening. You forgot to set your alarm. It's Volcano Day!

From outside the sirens are wailing again.

ROSE What's that?

JACK The all-clear.

THE DOCTOR I wish.

He turns and heads away along the corridor.

9 INT. THE CHILD'S BEDROOM NIGHT

NANCY slumped where we left her. She has raised her head at the sound of the all-clear (which is still wailing away). She scrambles to her feet, heads for the door.

10 INT. DOWNSTAIRS HALLWAY/KITCHEN NIGHT

NANCY comes haring down the stairs, through to the kitchen – she yanks open the door – and the EMPTY CHILD is standing right there!! Nancy reels back from the door, screaming! And so does the Empty Child. Because it's the not the Empty Child at all, just an ordinary boy in a gasmask – which he now pulls off, to get a better look at Nancy.

BOY (calling over his shoulder)
Mum, dad!

11 EXT. GARDEN NIGHT

The family we saw going to the Anderson shelter earlier are now re-emerging. NANCY races out into the garden, heading for the back fence.

DAD (seeing them)
Those ruddy kids ...!

Nancy is racing for the back fence – but the DAD lunges at her, grabs her.

NANCY Let me go! Get your hands off me!! Let me go!!

12 INT. HOSPITAL CORRIDOR/TOP FLOOR NIGHT

JACK and ROSE come pounding up the stairs.

JACK (calling)
Mr ... Spock?

ROSE (correcting him)
Doctor.

THE DOCTOR's head pops from round a corner.

THE DOCTOR You got a blaster?

JACK Sure.

They follow the Doctor round – he's standing at a locked door. The door is marked 802. This door has clearly been smashed open at some time, some great force having come through it. The door is now closed again and chained and padlocked.

THE DOCTOR The night your space junk landed, someone was hurt. This is where they took them.

ROSE (looking at the state of the door)
What happened?

THE DOCTOR Let's find out.
(to Jack)
Get it open.

Jack produces his blaster – as sleek, futuristic and exotic as you'd suppose – levels it at the padlock . . .

ROSE (out of Jack's hearing)
What's wrong with your sonic screwdriver?

THE DOCTOR (out of Jack's hearing)
Nothing.

The Doctor is examining Jack's blaster – clearly the real reason he asked him to use it. Jack blasts the padlock; the lock glows, disappears – as does an exactly square section of the door behind it. The door creaks open.

THE DOCTOR (eyes still on the blaster)
Sonic blaster, fifty-first century. Weapon factories of Villengard.

Jack looks at him, taken aback at his knowledge – allowing the Doctor to take the blaster from his hand, casually examine it.

JACK (impressed)
You've been to the factories?

THE DOCTOR Once.

JACK They're gone now, destroyed. Main reactor went critical – vaporized the lot.

THE DOCTOR (that sudden, scary grin)
Like I said. Once.

He holds Jack's look, shoves the blaster back at him (NOTE: we see the movement, but we don't actually see the gun itself returned); pushes past Jack and heads into the room.

THE DOCTOR There's a banana grove there now. I like bananas. Bananas are good.

Jack and Rose make to follow. Rose is looking at the perfectly square section missing from the door.

ROSE Nice blast pattern.

JACK (explaining)
Digital.

ROSE A squareness gun. I like it.

13 INT. THE ROOM NIGHT

THE DOCTOR clicks on the light switch. The room they're standing in has been torn apart. It looks a little like a recording studio. They're in what would be the producer's booth, packed with instruments – all clunky gasometer dials and bakelite – with a big glass screen looking out onto a larger, adjoining room. The glass of this dividing screen – clearly heavy duty, strengthened (whatever they had then) – has been smashed, the shards hanging into the booth. It's like something of enormous power has erupted through it from the other room.

The Doctor steps closer to the hole in the screen, looks through it. Jack and Rose stay where they are, unable to see what he can.

THE DOCTOR (to Jack)
Well? What do you think?

JACK (looking around)
Something got out of here.

THE DOCTOR Yes. And . . . ?

JACK (looking at the wreckage; shrugs)
Something powerful. Angry.

THE DOCTOR Powerful, angry, yeah. And here's the headline.

The Doctor steps to the metal door, opens it. He steps aside for Jack to go through. A little nervously Jack complies. Close on his face as he stares around the room he finds himself in. Incomprehension.

We are pulling back from Jack. Toys all over the floor, childish drawings all over the wall, a tiny bed . . .

JACK A child . . .

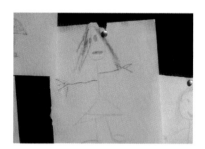

Rose joins him. Through the shattered glass, we can see the Doctor in the control room, examining the instruments.

JACK Suppose this explains 'mummy'?

ROSE (looking at the shattered glass)
How could a child do this?

Jack frowns at this, a little haunted. The Doctor is examining a big, clunky reel-to-reel tape recorder. He clicks the switch . . . the hiss of the tape, then:

CONSTANTINE V/O *Do you know where you are?*

THE CHILD'S VOICE V/O *Are you my mummy?*

Jack and Rose are chilled by the voice, exchange a glance.

CONSTANTINE V/O *Are you aware of what's around you. Can you . . . see?*

THE CHILD'S VOICE V/O *Are you my mummy?*

The Doctor comes through to the room, joins them.

CONSTANTINE V/O *What do you want? Do you know what –*

THE CHILD'S VOICE V/O *I want my mummy! Are you my mummy?*

Close on the Doctor listening to this. He turns his head to look at one of the walls. The Doctor's POV: close shot, a small child's drawing of a woman – barely a stick figure. A triangular skirt, scraggy hair . . .

THE CHILD'S VOICE V/O *Are you my mummy?*

Pulling out – other drawings, surrounding the first. The same stick woman, drawn by the same child . . .

THE CHILD'S VOICE V/O *Mummy? Are you there, mummy?*

Still pulling out. More and more near-identical drawings. The wall is covered in them.

THE CHILD'S VOICE V/O (imploring now)
Mummy? Mummy?

Jack has joined the Doctor and Rose. They all stare at the wall, all the pictures, all the stick women . . .

ROSE Doctor, I've heard that voice before. When we first arrived.

THE DOCTOR Me too.

ROSE Always 'are you my mummy?'. Like he doesn't know. Why doesn't he know?

THE CHILD'S VOICE *Mummee?*

13A, 13B AND 14 OMITTED

14A INT. DINING ROOM NIGHT

The table has been cleared. NANCY sits, solemnly, at the end of the table. The DAD we saw before comes into the room, looking fat and self-important. He sits at the other end of the table.

DAD The police are on their way.

Nancy just looks back at him, calm, unmoved – like she's biding her time.

DAD I pay for the food on this table. The sweat on my brow, that food is. The sweat on my brow!

Nancy says nothing, gives nothing away.

DAD Anything else you'd like? Got a whole house here – anything else you'd like to help yourself to?

Nancy looks at him for a moment. Then:

NANCY Yes.

The Dad is momentarily startled.

DAD . . . What?

NANCY I'd like some wirecutters, please. Something that would cut through barbed wire. Oh, and a torch.

He just stares at her.

NANCY Don't look like that, Mr Lloyd – I know you've got plenty of tools here, been watching this house for ages. Also, I'd like another look round your kitchen cupboards. I was in a hurry the first time, I want to see if there's anything I missed.

The Dad is staring, hardly able to believe his ears. He finally summons the ability to speak.

DAD The food on this table –

NANCY – is an awful lot of food, isn't it, Mr Lloyd? Lot more food than on anyone else's table. Half this street thinks your missus must be messing about with Mr Haverstock, the butcher. But she's not, is she?

DAD Of course she's not.

NANCY You are.

Terrible silence. The Dad is staring, aghast.

NANCY Wirecutters. Torch. Food. And I'd like to use the bathroom before I leave, please.

The Dad is staring at her, now pale and slack-jawed. Nancy gives a small, cruel smile.

NANCY Oh look! There's the sweat on your brow!

15 INT. THE ROOM NIGHT

THE DOCTOR is staring at the drawings again – seems almost to shudder.

ROSE Doctor?

THE DOCTOR Can't you sense it?

THE CHILD'S VOICE V/O *Mummy? Please mummy?*

JACK Sense what?

THE DOCTOR Coming out the walls at you. Can't you *feel* it?

ROSE and JACK exchange a glance. Clearly they can't.

THE CHILD'S VOICE V/O *Mummy? Are you my mummy?*

THE DOCTOR (brusque – hiding his recovery from his emotional outburst)
Funny little human brains! How do you get around in those things?

ROSE (to Jack; apologising for the Doctor)
When he's stressed, he likes to insult species.

THE CHILD'S VOICE V/O *Mummy?*

THE DOCTOR Rose, I'm thinking!

ROSE Cuts himself shaving, he does half an hour on life-forms he's cleverer than.

THE DOCTOR There are children. Living rough, round the bomb sites, the waste-ground. They come out during the air raids, looking for food.

THE CHILD'S VOICE V/O *Mummy? Please?*

THE DOCTOR Suppose they were there when this thing – whatever it was – landed.

JACK It was a med-ship – harmless!

THE DOCTOR Yeah, you keep saying harmless.
(to Rose again)
Suppose one of them was ... affected. Altered ...

(Now in the background, though we don't especially notice it, a new sound – a continual, rhythmic swishing.)

ROSE Altered how?

THE CHILD'S VOICE V/O *I'm here!!*

Swish, swish, swish – keeps on going, under scene.

THE DOCTOR It's afraid. Terribly afraid. And powerful – but doesn't know it yet. But it will.
(almost laughs)
It's got the power of a god ... and I just sent it to its room!

A new thought flickers across his face. A trace of alarm. In the silence, very clear now – swish, swish, swish –

THE CHILD'S VOICE V/O I'm here!

ROSE (picking up on the noise; a terrible sense of foreboding)
Doctor ...

THE CHILD'S VOICE V/O I'm here! Can't you see me? Can't you see me?

ROSE ... What's that noise?

Swish, swish, swish –

THE CHILD'S VOICE V/O I'm here!!

THE DOCTOR (frozen, tensed, that terrible forced calm)
The end of the tape. Ran out about thirty seconds ago.

Quick shot of the tape machine. The tape is finished, the end of it spinning free – swish, swish.

THE CHILD'S VOICE V/O I'm here now!!

Another moment of neck-prickling realisation. The child's voice is no longer a recording!! Hasn't been for a little time.

THE DOCTOR I sent it to its room. *This is its room!*

Through the shattered glass of the screen we can see the silhouette of the chair sitting on the other side. Two stubby little arms rise up from it – the CHILD is sitting right there, watching them. In the depths of the chair, light glimmers on the glass eye-pieces.

THE CHILD Can't you see me??

For a moment, deathly quiet – no one even dares to breathe. Finally:

JACK Full marks for child psychology, Doctor Spock.

THE DOCTOR Just Doctor.

THE CHILD Mummy? Are you my mummy?

We can just see the Child tilting its head inquisitively at Rose. Rose swallows hard, says nothing. A movement catches the Doctor's eye. He glances at Jack. Jack is slowly, carefully, reaching under his jacket for his weapon.

JACK (whispering)
On my signal, to the door ...

THE CHILD Mummy?

The Child is getting to its feet. The Doctor and Rose exchange a glance. The Doctor nods.

JACK Now!!

Jack, whirls, rolls, comes up on one knee, weapon levelled at the glass screen – it's classic James Bond – *except* – the weapon in his hand is a banana!

Wha–? He stares at it in astonishment – and hears the sound of his own blaster! It's in the Doctor's hand. And he is calmly blasting a hole in the rear wall of the room! A square section of the wall, about the size of a window, disappears –

THE DOCTOR (yelling at Jack and Rose – practically throwing them at the hole in the wall)
Move it, now, go, don't drop the banana!

JACK Why not?

THE DOCTOR Good source of potassium!

He bundles them both through the hole, first Rose then Jack –

16 INT. HOSPITAL CORRIDOR NIGHT

ROSE, JACK, THE DOCTOR come tearing out –

JACK Gimme that!!

Jack grabs the blaster from the Doctor, spins, aims at the square hole – the EMPTY CHILD is on their heels, just about to climb through –

Jack fires – and wham! The missing square of wall is back – only faintest fault-lines show it was ever gone.

Rose boggles.

JACK Digital rewind.

He looks at the Doctor, holds up the banana.

JACK Nice switch.

THE DOCTOR It's from the groves of Villengard – thought it was appropriate.

JACK (looks at him, smiles)
There's really a banana grove at the heart in Villengard? And you did that??

THE DOCTOR (shrugs)
Bananas are good.

Jack laughs. He's deciding he likes this guy.

A tremendous whump! The restored square of wall judders with a huge impact, heaves out a few centimetres.

ROSE (stepping back in alarm)
Doctor! . . .

THE DOCTOR Come on!!

They turn to run down the corridor and freeze! A few feet away, limping and lurching towards them, GASMASK PEOPLE (a nurse, a huge fat man, a pregnant woman) raising their arms – this is the signature move of these creatures – like a small child reaching up for a hug.

GASMASK/NURSE Mummy?

GASMASK/FAT MAN Mummy?

They turn to run the other way, and freeze again – Gasmask People!
An elderly man in striped pyjamas. Twin children, holding hands.

GASMASK/TWINS Mummy?

They're trapped – whump! the wall heaves, grinds – in a tiny section of
corridor, right where the Child is about to emerge!

Whump! The square section of wall judders out a few more centimetres,
a chunk of masonry smashes to the floor.

THE DOCTOR It's keeping us here till it can get at us!

Whump! The wall heaves.

JACK It's controlling them?

THE DOCTOR It is them. It's every living thing in this hospital.

Whump! The square section is bulging out now, listing, about to fall – our
three heroes, backs against the opposite wall; nothing they can do but wait.
Cool under fire, JACK is readying his weapon.

JACK Okay. This can function as a sonic blaster, a sonic cannon
and triple-enfolded sonic disruptor. Doctor, what you got?

THE DOCTOR (brandishing his screwdriver)
I've got a sonic – never mind.

JACK What?

Whump! The section bulges, starts to topple . . .

THE DOCTOR It's sonic, let's leave it at that.

JACK Disruptor, cannon, what??

THE DOCTOR It's sonic, okay, totally sonic, I am sonic-ed up!

JACK (flaring at him)
A sonic what??

THE DOCTOR (flaring back at him)
Screwdriver!!

Jack stares at him. Whump!! Chunks of masonry everywhere – it's almost out!!

As if this was a signal, the Gasmask Creatures start lurching and limping
towards them – the Empty Child is climbing through the rubble!

ROSE Fascinating chat, boys!

She grabs JACK's gun arm, pulls it so that it's aimed at the floor directly
beneath them and –

ROSE Going down!

– fires! The square section they're standing on disappears and they fall right
through to:

17 INT. LARGE ROOM NIGHT

THE DOCTOR, ROSE and JACK come plummeting through the ceiling, crashing to the floor. The large room they're in now is in darkness – they are in a square of light coming through the hole above.

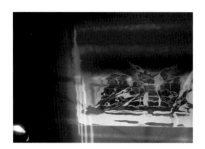

Jack rolls as he hits the floor, levels his gun at the ceiling, fires. The square of light snaps out. A shot of the ceiling, now perfectly restored – just a faint line indicating where the missing section was. There is now only moonlight filtering through the windows.

ROSE (scrambling up; straight to the Doctor)
Doctor, you okay?

THE DOCTOR (getting stiffly up)
Could've used a warning.

ROSE Oh, the gratitude!

JACK (still boggling; as is if there's been no interruption in the conversation)
Who has a sonic screwdriver??

THE DOCTOR I do!

ROSE (looking around)
Lights?

JACK (as he does so)
Who looks at a screwdriver and thinks, hmm, nice, but could be a bit more sonic?

THE DOCTOR What, you've never been bored??

ROSE There's gotta be a light switch.

THE DOCTOR (still going at Jack)
Never had a long night? Never had a lot of cabinets to put up??

Rose has scrambled to the wall, flicked on the lights – we're in another ward, rows of GASMASK CREATURES in their beds – raising their heads!

GASMASK CREATURES Mummy? Mummy?

The Gasmask Creatures are starting to climb from their beds – already the route out of the ward is blocked.

JACK Door!

Jack is racing to a door at the back of the ward. Locked! He tries his blaster on it, nothing!

JACK Damn it!

He bangs the weapon against the door jamb! The Doctor whirrs his screwdriver at the lock.

Gasmask Creatures, climbing out of bed –

JACK It's the special features, they really drain the battery.

ROSE The battery??

The Doctor has the door open, bundles them both into –

18 INT. STOREROOM NIGHT

– a middle-sized storeroom, full of various medical paraphernalia. One barred window. THE DOCTOR whirrs his screwdriver at the door, locking it.

ROSE (still going at JACK)
That is so lame!

JACK I was going to send off for a new one. But somebody's got to blow up the factory.

ROSE (sympathetic)
Oh, I know. First day I met him, he blew up my job. It's practically how he communicates.

THE DOCTOR Okay, that door's gonna hold for a bit –

JACK The door? The wall didn't stop it.

THE DOCTOR Well it's got to find us first! Come on, come on, we're not done yet. Assets, assets!

JACK Well, I've got a banana and at a pinch you could put up some shelves.

THE DOCTOR Window?

JACK (not looking; it's the first thing he checked)
Barred. Sheer drop outside – seven storeys.

ROSE And no other exits.

A slightly lame moment.

JACK (grins)
Well! The assets conversation went in a flash, didn't it?

The Doctor looks at him sourly – not in the mood for flippancy, certainly not from Jack.

THE DOCTOR (looks sourly at Jack; to Rose)
So! Where'd you pick this one up?

ROSE ('give him a break')
Doctor . . . !

JACK She was hanging from a barrage balloon, I had an invisible space ship . . .
(shoots her a flirtatious smile)
I never stood a chance.

The Doctor resumes his frantic pacing.

THE DOCTOR Okay! One – we've gotta get out of here. Two – we *can't* get out of here. Have I missed anything?

Rose is staring off-screen in astonishment at something.

ROSE Yeah. Jack just disappeared.

A wider shot, as the Doctor follows her look. Impossible, they are alone in the storeroom. Jack is gone!

19 OMITTED

19A1 INT. OUTHOUSE/DEN NIGHT

A small dark place, full of old junk. ERNIE, ALF, two of the other kids. Huddled, waiting. Alf is crouched on the floor at an old, broken typewriter. He has shoved an old scrap of paper into it, is laboriously hitting the keys. Clack! Clack!

The door opens – they all tense, terrified that it's the CHILD. But NANCY walks in. A beat; they all stare at her.

ALF Thought you were dead.

ERNIE (loyally)
I didn't. Knew you'd come back. You always do. With food, I bet.

Nancy looks at him for a beat, doesn't smile. Like she's worried. Clack! Clack! She looks curiously at Alf, typing away.

ERNIE Found that old thing in all the junk. Thinks he can write now.

ALF Writing a letter to me dad.

ERNIE You don't even know where your dad is. How you gonna send it?

ALF I think you just put it in an envelope.

ERNIE You can't even read or write.

ALF Don't have to now! I've got a *machine!*

Clack! Clack!

NANCY (flaring at Alf)
Will you stop making that noise!

ALF, terrified, snatches his hands from the keyboard. They all stare at her. This is unprecedented. Nancy does not shout. She looks around them, a little grumpy, a little guilty.

NANCY Sorry, Alf. On you go, you write to your dad if you want to.

She starts unpacking her little bag onto the floor. The food from the house.

NANCY Ernie . . .

ERNIE Yeah?

NANCY What if . . . one night . . . I *didn't* come back?

In the background, the others are listening now. Alf is typing.

ERNIE . . . What do you mean?

NANCY There's a war on. People don't always come back, do they? What would you do then?

From the bottom of her sack, Nancy has produced the wirecutters. She examines them with a professional eye. Very worried now. Ernie's eye goes to the cutters.

ERNIE Those are wirecutters.

NANCY You've gotta think about that. Cos you'd be in charge then. Someone's gotta look after this lot. And I need to know I can count on you.

ERNIE (still eyeing the wirecutters suspiciously)
Why? You going somewhere?

NANCY ... The bomb site. The one at the railway station.

ERNIE (Staring at her, wide-eyed, horrified at the mere idea)
... *Why??*

NANCY Whatever's going on ... that's where it all started.

ERNIE How'd you mean?

NANCY The Child. That's where he was killed. And that's where he rose from the dead. And I'm gonna find out how.

ERNIE He'll get you. He'll make you empty like him. Then he'll come for us. He *always* comes after us!

NANCY No, Ernie, he doesn't.
(a beat; a painful revelation)
He always comes after *me*.

Ernie frowns, not understanding. A little silence. Just the occasional clack! of Alf's typewriter. Nancy looks round them all. Tearful but fighting it. This is a confession.

NANCY Listen to me. All of you. You think I keep you safe. But you're wrong. I'm the one who keeps you in danger. The Child isn't after you. He never has been. He's after me.

ERNIE Why?

NANCY There are things I haven't told you. Things I *can't* tell you. Just understand this: every second you're with me, you're in danger. Even right now. Sitting here. You're in danger because of *me*.

ERNIE No. We're *safe* with you. The Child can't get us here.

NANCY looks sadly at him. Such faith in her. So wrong.

NANCY You think so, Ernie? You think you're safe here? Then answer me this. Alf's sitting right next to you now ...

Clack! Clack!

NANCY ... So who's typing?

Clack! Clack!

Slowly, fearfully, they look round. The typewriter sits unattended in the corner. With one final clack! it falls silent. The children stare. Nancy steps to the typewriter, pulls the sheet from it. (For the moment we don't see what it says.)

ERNIE Is he coming?

NANCY Only if I stay.

She drops the paper, picks up the wirecutters, goes to the door. Turns in the doorway.

NANCY He'll never come for you again, I promise.

She goes.

Ernie goes to the piece of paper, picks it up. CLOSE on the sheet: a few lines of gibberish (what Alf was typing) then: 'are you my mummy are you my mummy are you my mummy are you my mummy . . .'.

DISSOLVE TO:

19A EXT. THE CRASH SITE ENCLOSURE (OUTSIDE THE WIRE) NIGHT

NANCY, picking her way through the wasteland. She is keeping low, careful not be seen. As she scrambles up to a suitable vantage point (the bridge?) we go with her – we see the crash site enclosure, sinister in the moonlight, the tarpaulined bulk looming in the middle. Close on Nancy's face: she swallows hard, resolving herself. She fumbles inside her sack, produces wirecutters – and starts towards the fence!

20 INT. THE STOREROOM NIGHT

THE DOCTOR and ROSE. Rose is checking the other walk-in cupboards.

ROSE Okay, so he vanished into thin air. It's always the great-looking ones who do that!

THE DOCTOR (gives her a look)
I'm making an effort not to be insulted.

ROSE I mean *men*.

THE DOCTOR Okay, thanks, that really helped.

A hiss of static. An old radio – clearly abandoned, not plugged in anywhere – has come to life. Then, a voice from it!

JACK V/O (through radio)
Rose? Doctor?

The Doctor exchanges a puzzled look. They step closer. The Doctor picks up the radio, sees that it isn't even plugged in.

JACK V/O (through radio)
Can you hear me?

21 INT. JACK'S SHIP NIGHT

JACK is in his pilot's chair, talking into a mike. We now INTERCUT between the ship and storeroom as required.

JACK V/O (through radio)
Back on my ship – used the emergency teleport. Sorry I couldn't take you, it's security-keyed to my molecular structure. Hang in there, working on it.

THE DOCTOR (still examining the radio)
How are you talking to us?

JACK V/O (through radio)
Om-Com – I can call anything with a speaker grille.

THE DOCTOR Now there's a coincidence!

JACK V/O (through radio)
What is?

THE DOCTOR (puzzled thinking)
The child can Om-Com too.

ROSE It can?

THE DOCTOR Anything with a speaker grille. Even the TARDIS phone.

ROSE What, you mean the child can phone us?

THE CHILD V/O (from the radio)
And I can hear you.

THE DOCTOR and ROSE turn, look to the radio, chilled.

THE CHILD V/O (sing-song, mocking, a game)
Coming to find you. Coming to find you.

22 INT. JACK'S SHIP NIGHT

JACK is hearing the CHILD's voice too.

JACK Doctor, can you hear that?

THE DOCTOR V/O (through radio)
Loud and clear.

ROSE V/O (through radio)
And just a shade creepy.

JACK (pressing switches)
I'll try and block the signal. Least I can do.
(smiles)
Remember this one, Rose?

He clicks a final switch –

23 INT. STOREROOM NIGHT

– and from the radio comes 'Moonlight Serenade'. ROSE smiles, THE DOCTOR looks at her curiously.

ROSE (shrugs, a little embarrassed)
Our song.

The Doctor's face. The tiniest blink, the tiniest flicker; you'd have to be fast to spot it. If you did, you'd think maybe the Doctor doesn't like this . . .

24 EXT. THE CRASH SITE ENCLOSURE (OUTSIDE THE WIRE) NIGHT

Sentries guard the entrance as before.

Closer shot of a detail of the enclosure. We are looking through the barbed-wire fence to the compound with the large, central hole within.

We are pulling back – bringing NANCY into shot. Her face: set, determined. She steps forward, kneels by the wire. Clumsily but carefully – she hasn't done this before – she raises the wirecutters to the wire. Chunk!

We track on past her, through the fence, towards the tarpaulined bulk thrusting up through the crater … Chunk!

25 INT. STOREROOM NIGHT

THE DOCTOR is still at work on the bars, probing the concrete round them with his sonic screwdriver. ROSE sits on the shelf next to him, knees drawn up to her chin. 'Moonlight Serenade' continues to play.

ROSE What you doing?

THE DOCTOR Trying to set up a resonation pattern in the concrete, loosen the bars …

ROSE You don't think he's coming back, do you?

THE DOCTOR Wouldn't bet my life.

ROSE (looks curiously at him for a moment)
Why don't you trust him?

THE DOCTOR Why do you?

ROSE Saved my life. Bloke-wise, that's up there with flossing.
(a beat; looks at him)
I trust him cos he's like you. Only with dating and dancing.

The Doctor shoots her a slightly odd look – maybe slightly vulnerable, even slightly hurt – resumes his work on the bars.

ROSE (picking up on the look)
What?

THE DOCTOR You just assume I'm …

ROSE What?

THE DOCTOR You just assume I don't … dance?

ROSE (stares at him; slow smile)
What? Are you telling me you do … dance?

THE DOCTOR Nine hundred years old, me. Been around. I think you can assume at some point I've … danced.

ROSE You??

THE DOCTOR Problem?

ROSE (staring at him, intrigued, fascinated – is he a bloke after all?)
Doesn't the universe implode or something if *you* … dance?

THE DOCTOR Well I've got moves but I wouldn't want to boast.

She laughs, then looks at him for a moment as he works away at the bars. She skips off the shelf, heads off out of frame – she has a plan.

We hold on the Doctor, working. He stiffens. Cos the music just got louder. Rose has turned it up. He turns to look at her. Barely able to suppress her giggles, she is waiting for him in the middle of the floor. Demurely she puts out a hand to him, for him to take, for him to dance with her. Totally innocent, of course – and terribly sexy.

ROSE You've got moves? Show me your moves!

The Doctor's face: hesitation, vulnerability. Never expected this turn in the conversation. We haven't quite seen him like this before – floundering slightly . . .

THE DOCTOR Rose, I'm trying to resonate concrete . . .

ROSE Jack's coming back. He'll get us out. So come on. The world doesn't end cos the Doctor dances.

The Doctor is looking at her oddly. We can't quite read his face. He steps down from the window, approaches her, takes her hands, and we don't quite know what's going to happen here –

She moves her hands as if to dance with him, but no – he turns her hands over, looks at the palms.

THE DOCTOR A barrage balloon?

ROSE (taken aback)
What?

THE DOCTOR You were hanging from a barrage balloon.

ROSE (laughs)
Oh that, yeah. About two minutes after you left me. Thousands of feet above London. Middle of a German air raid, Union Jack all over my chest!

THE DOCTOR I've travelled with a lot of people, but you're setting new records for jeopardy-friendly.

He's still studying her hands.

ROSE Is this you dancing? Cos I've got notes.

THE DOCTOR Hanging from a steel cable. Thousands of feet above London.
(shows her her own hands)
Not a cut, not a bruise . . .

ROSE Yeah, I know. Captain Jack fixed me up.

THE DOCTOR We're calling him Captain Jack now?

ROSE Well. His name's Jack, he's a captain.

THE DOCTOR He's not really a captain, Rose!

ROSE You know what? I think you're experiencing captain envy.

ROSE (pulls him closer, positions his hands correctly for dancing)
You will find your feet at the end of your legs. You may care to move them.

THE DOCTOR If he ever was a captain he's been defrocked.

ROSE (grins)
Yeah? Shame I missed that.

JACK Actually I quit.

Close on the Doctor, and Rose turning in shock. JACK is smiling at them from the command chair of the cockpit.

JACK Nobody takes my frock.

And the Doctor and Rose are no longer in the storeroom, they are in . . .

26 INT. JACK'S SHIP NIGHT

THE DOCTOR and ROSE – still ready to dance – stare at JACK, who is sitting in the pilot's chair. Behind him it looks like he's taken half the dashboard apart and he's holding a screwdriver.

JACK Most people notice when they're teleported. You guys are so sweet.

The Doctor and Rose look at each other, spring apart. Jack grins, reaches over, clicks off the music.

JACK Sorry about the delay. Had to take the nav-com off line to override the teleport security.

THE DOCTOR You can spend *ten minutes* overriding your own protocols?? Maybe you should remember whose ship it is!

JACK Oh, I do. She was gorgeous.
(heading to the back of the ship)
Like I told her – back in five minutes.

He ducks down under his console, starts working away with his screwdriver.

THE DOCTOR (looking around)
This is a Chula ship.

JACK (calling from off)
Yeah, just like that medical transporter. Only this one *is* dangerous.

The Doctor is thinking, rapidly. He's getting it, he's putting it together. Very deliberately, he raises one hand, snaps his fingers. Instantly there's a little swarm of what seem like fireflies dancing round his hand.

ROSE They're what fixed up my hands. Jack called them . . .

THE DOCTOR Nanobots? Nanogenes?

ROSE Nanogenes, yeah.

THE DOCTOR Subatomic robots. Millions of them in here. In every square foot probably.
(shows his hand)

See? Burned my fingers on the console when we landed. All better now. They activate when the bulkhead's sealed, check you out for damage, fix any physical flaws.

ROSE Still the same dress size.

THE DOCTOR They have their limits.

ROSE What are you trying to say??

The Doctor waves his hand – the nanogenes scatter.

ROSE How'd you make them do that?

THE DOCTOR Bullying subatomic life-forms. Easy. Learned when I was a kid.

ROSE There are so many different ways to say: 'I had a lonely childhood'.

The Doctor goes to the console, hunkers down next to Jack.

THE DOCTOR Take us to the crash site. I need to look at your space junk.

JACK Soon as I get the nav-com back on line. Make yourselves comfortable. Carry on with ... whatever you were doing.

THE DOCTOR We were just ...
(slightly embarrassed look at Rose)
... talking about dancing.

JACK Didn't look like talking.

ROSE Didn't sound like dancing.

27 EXT. THE CRASH SITE ENCLOSURE (INSIDE THE WIRE) NIGHT

NANCY is crawling to the hole, clutching the torch. She stops, looks around, cautiously – guards visible on the other side of the fence, none looking at her, and it's dark anyway. She should be okay! She carries on crawling, she's right at the structure – reaching for the tarpaulin . . .

And wham! The lights go on. Big arc lights – or whatever they'd have – positioned around the hole.

Nancy whirls. The gates have been flung open, the guards are in the enclosure. And their rifles are levelled at her!

28 INT. JACK'S SHIP NIGHT

JACK is still working away at the nav-com; ROSE is with him, chatting. In the background, a little away from them, THE DOCTOR is slumped, brooding.

ROSE So. You used to *be* a Time Agent, now you're trying to con them?

JACK If it makes me sound any better, it's not for money.

ROSE For what?

JACK (glances at her; she's not the type to stop asking)
Woke up one morning – when I was still working for them – found they'd stolen two years of my memories. They've got 'em on file somewhere – I'd like them back.

ROSE They stole your *memories?*

In the background, we see the Doctor – listening now.

JACK Long story. Wish I knew what it was about.

Rose looks at him, visibly shocked. This is unsettling information.

JACK Two years of my life. No idea what I did.
(glances over at the Doctor)
Your friend doesn't trust me. And you know what? For all I know, he's right not to.
(sits up, finished)
Okay! We're good to go! Crash site?

29 OMITTED

30 INT. SHED NIGHT

A lone soldier is sitting inside the shed – crudely, simply furnished, a place for a coffee and a fag. He is sitting shivering on a chair, looks feverish. This is JENKINS.

The door opens, ALGY drags NANCY inside. Jenkins is immediately on his feet – though he looks barely capable of it.

ALGY As you were. Feeling any better?

JENKINS (blinking, a little fuzzily)
Just a turn, sir.

Nancy looks at the man. Close on the man's hand – the first thing Nancy looks at. A scar is there. The identical scar we saw on the hands of the Gasmask People! She looks at Jenkins in alarm, and, before she knows it, ALGY is handcuffing her to the table.

NANCY No! Not in here! Not with him.

ALGY Shouldn't have broken in here if you didn't want to stay.

NANCY You don't understand!! Not with him!!

Jenkins has slumped back in his chair. He is running a shaking hand through his hair – the hand with the scar on the back. Nancy can't take her eyes off that scar!

ALGY (oblivious)
This is a restricted area, miss. You can just sit here for a bit, we're going to have a few questions.

A SOLDIER appears at the door, holding Nancy's wirecutters.

SOLDIER Found these, sir. How she got in.

Algy takes them, interested now.

ALGY Very professional.
(looks at Nancy shrewdly)
A little bit too professional. Didn't just drop in by accident then, did you?

She looks coldly at him.

NANCY My little brother died here. I wanted to see what killed him.

This clearly impacts on Algy. But there isn't time for that now!

ALGY (to soldier)
Take the men, check the fence for any other breaches. And search the area, she may not have come here alone.

SOLDIER Yessir!

The soldier goes.

NANCY Please. Listen to me. You can't leave me here.

Algy just looks at her, coldly.

ALGY (to Jenkins)
Keep an eye on her, Jenkins!

JENKINS Yes, mummy.

ALGY (double-takes)
Jenkins?

JENKINS Sorry. Sir.
(rubs his sweating forehead)
Don't know what's the matter with me.

Nancy is staring at Jenkins – mounting alarm. She knows what's coming, has seen it before.

NANCY (to Algy)
Look, lock me up, fine, but not here. Please, anywhere but here!

Algy just shoots her a cold look – and walks out, closing the door. Nancy looks in open terror at Jenkins – who is shaking his head in confusion.

JENKINS You'll be all right, miss, I'm just a little ... just a little ...

Nancy is now yanking at her handcuffed hand – she can barely move the table! Now she's clawing at her hand, trying to pull it from the cuff, anything to get away –

JENKINS What's the matter with you?

NANCY You got a key for these handcuffs?

JENKINS Yeah, why?

NANCY Give it to me. Please. Let me go.

JENKINS Why would I do that?

NANCY Cos you've got a scar on the back of your hand.

JENKINS Well, yeah, but I don't –

NANCY And you can't remember how you got it, can you? And there's another across your shoulders and you don't know how you got that either. And another one up the side of your chest.

JENKINS (staring at her)
How did you ... how could you know that??

NANCY And they're getting worse, aren't they? And you feel like you're gonna be sick. Like there's something forcing its way up your throat.
(almost gently now)
I know because I've seen it before.

JENKINS (haunted now, almost believing her)
What's ... what's happening to me?

NANCY In about a minute you won't be you anymore. You won't even *remember* you. And if you don't let me go, it'll happen to me, too. Please!

JENKINS What are you talking about?

NANCY What's your mother's name?

JENKINS Matilda.

NANCY You married?

JENKINS Yes.

NANCY Wife's name?

Jenkins opens his mouth to speak – and his mind is a blank.

NANCY You got kids?

JENKINS I ...
(eyes widen in horror)
I don't know?

NANCY What's *your* name?

He stares at her. Lost now.

NANCY Please. It's too late for you. I'm sorry. But *please*. Let me go.

JENKINS What do you m– ... What do you m– ... m– m– m– m–

Nancy stares at him knowing exactly where this is going!

JENKINS Mummeeeee ...

His mouth is starting to bulge out – like something is about to emerge.

31 OMITTED

32 EXT. WASTE-GROUND/OUTSIDE THE CRASH SITE NIGHT

THE DOCTOR, ROSE and JACK are scrambling up a small hill on the approach to the crash site. They keep low, out of sight. As the crash site becomes visible over the brow of the hill, we see ALGY standing outside the gates (smoking, if he's allowed to).

JACK Well, there it is!
(looks closer)
They've got *Algy* on duty here?? Must be important.

THE DOCTOR Well we've got to get past him.

ROSE Are the words 'Distract the guard' heading in my general direction?

JACK I don't think that's such a good idea.

ROSE Don't worry – I can handle it.

JACK Got to know Algy quite well, while I've been in town. Trust me, you're not his type.
(he winks at her)
I'll distract him!

On Rose: wha–?? Unabashed, Jack grins at her.

JACK Don't wait up!

And off he goes, straightening his tie, smoothing back his hair. Rose stares after him, a little flummoxed by this turn of events. Something in her face is screaming 'No, no, not on that team!'

THE DOCTOR Relax! He's a fifty-first century guy. He's just a bit more flexible when it comes to ... dancing.

ROSE ... How flexible?

THE DOCTOR Well, by his time, you lot are spread out across half the galaxy.

ROSE Meaning?

THE DOCTOR So many species, so little time.

ROSE (appalled)
What, that's what we do when we get out there? That's our mission?? We seek out new life and ... and ...

THE DOCTOR (nods happily)
Dance!

Close on Algy, and Jack as he joins him. Jack is unscrewing the lid on his hipflask.

JACK Hello, tiger. How's it hanging?

Algy looks at him, a little blankly. Unfocused, almost as if drunk.

ALGY Mummy?

JACK (frowns)
Algy, old sport, it's me.

ALGY Mummy?

JACK It's *me*. Jack!

ALGY Jack? Are you ... my ... mummy?

And he coughs, chokes – and like Constantine before him, the nozzle of a gasmask is suddenly forcing its way out of his mouth.

He drops to his knees, his hands clawing at his neck – and his head morphs into a gasmask! He slumps sideways to the ground. Not unconscious – just unmoving.

Rose and the Doctor come racing to his side. The Doctor looks grimly at the fallen officer.

THE DOCTOR The effect is becoming airborne. Accelerating.

ROSE What's keeping us safe?

THE DOCTOR Nothing.

Air-raid sirens are sounding again. JACK glances up.

JACK Here they come again.

ROSE All we need!
(to Jack, worried now)
You said a bomb's gonna land *here.*

JACK According to the history books. We've got about ten minutes.

THE DOCTOR Never mind about that.
(eyes still on Algy)
If the contaminant is airborne now, there's only hours left.

JACK Till what?

THE DOCTOR Till nothing! Forever! For the whole Human Race.
And can anyone else hear singing?

They all turn – looking to the shed where NANCY was locked up. Faintly: Nancy's voice – singing 'Rock-a-bye baby'.

32A THE SHED NIGHT

JENKINS – now a GASMASK CREATURE – is curled on the floor. A terrified – but keeping-it-together – NANCY is singing a lullaby. Only the slightest crack in her voice gives away the terrible strain she's under.

NANCY (sings)
'– on the treetops. When the bough breaks the cradle will drop –'

Behind her the door is slowly easing open. THE DOCTOR pokes his head round, cautiously. Focused on what she's doing, Nancy doesn't notice.

The Doctor takes in what's happening; Nancy glances round, sees him – he puts a finger to his lips, moves silently to her side, whirrs the sonic screwdriver at the handcuffs. He looks at the sleeping Gasmask Creature, back to Nancy. He grins, loving the simplicity of her solution.

THE DOCTOR Nice one!

The handcuffs spring apart – Nancy stares at this in wonder. He takes her hand, leads her from the shed. As they go, we close in on the slumping, sleeping JENKINS . . .

32B THRU 34 OMITTED

35 EXT. CRASH SITE ENCLOSURE (INSIDE THE WIRE) NIGHT

Wham! The arc lights go on and illumine the tarpaulined bulk in the centre of the enclosure, just as THE DOCTOR yanks at it, ripping it down – to reveal the big, charred, mauve cylinder we saw at the top of the show, half buried in the ground. NANCY stares at this, amazed. ROSE – standing by her, a comforting arm around her shoulders – also stares.

JACK (smugly, to the Doctor)
You see? Just an ambulance!

NANCY (staring in confusion)
That's an ambulance?

Rose glances at her, sympathetically.

ROSE It's hard to explain, it's . . . it's from another world.

JACK has moved closer to the cylinder. He's confident now, certain that he's proved his innocence. He examines a control panel on the side. Clearly some work has been done on this.

JACK They've been trying to get in.

THE DOCTOR Of course they have. They think they've got Hitler's latest secret weapon –
(he breaks off)
What are you doing?

Jack is tapping away at his wristwatch while aiming it at the access hatch.

JACK Sooner you see this thing is empty, sooner you'll know I had nothing to do with –

A crack, a fizzle. Jack jumps back from the cylinder. (At the same moment the hatchway clangs, like it's been released.)

JACK Didn't happen the last time.

THE DOCTOR It hadn't crashed the last time. There'll be emergency protocols.

The Doctor has stepped forward, is now looking at the cylinder in mounting alarm. Closer on a detail: on the control panel on the side. A light is flickering on, glowing red.

ROSE (following his look)
Doctor? What is that?

36 EXT. OUTSIDE THE CRASH SITE ENCLOSURE (OUTSIDE THE WIRE) NIGHT

ALGY, where he lies slumped – he twitches, starts to clamber to his feet . . .

37 INT. HOSPITAL WARD 2 NIGHT

The GASMASK CREATURES, all in their beds: they raise their heads.
Shot of CONSTANTINE, slumped where he sat: raises his head.

38 OMITTED

39 INT. HOSPITAL CORRIDOR NIGHT

A shot zooming insanely fast along the corridor to the CHILD standing at the far end, his back to us. He turns, fast.

His empty eye-sockets fill the screen!

40 EXT. THE CRASH SITE ENCLOSURE (INSIDE THE WIRE) NIGHT

Thump! Thump! The door to the shed is battered from within.

ROSE (nervously observing this)
Doctor!

THE DOCTOR is deep in troubled thought. Now he comes to life!
He glances round to where the gates are still hanging open.

THE DOCTOR Captain, secure those gates.

JACK Why?

THE DOCTOR Just do it!

JACK heads off.

THE DOCTOR Nancy, how did you get in here?

NANCY Cut the wire.

THE DOCTOR Show Rose where.
(tosses his sonic screwdriver to ROSE)
Setting two-thousand-four-hundred-and-twenty-eight-D.

ROSE What?

THE DOCTOR Reattaches barbed wire. Go!

Close on the Doctor's face, studying the control panel. Very, very worried.
He goes to the panel, starts jabbing buttons like he's trying to turn it off.

40A EXT. HOSPITAL NIGHT

The Hospital, looming above us. We pan down – to see the GASMASK CREATURES streaming out of the double doors of the building, down the steps. (The doors have been smashed aside and are hanging drunkenly from their hinges.)

40AA EXT. CRASH SITE ENCLOSURE (INSIDE THE WIRE) NIGHT

We are close on the cut section of barbed wire. ROSE is working at the wire, reattaching it using the sonic screwdriver, while NANCY holds it in place. Nancy is watching the operation of the sonic screwdriver in astonishment. She looks at Rose, solemn, intense.

NANCY Who are you? Who are any of you?

ROSE Never believe me if I told you.

NANCY (almost laughs)
You just told me that's an ambulance from another world. There's people all over with gasmask heads calling for their mummies. And the sky's full of Germans dropping bombs on me. Tell me. Do you think there's anything left I couldn't believe?

Rose looks at her a few seconds, considering. This is a girl at the end of her tether. She owes her the truth.

ROSE We're time travellers. From the future.

Nancy stares at her for a moment – then laughs.

ROSE Told you.

NANCY Mad, you are!

ROSE We have a time-travel machine. Seriously.

NANCY It's not that, love. All right, you got a time-travel machine, I'll believe you. Believe anything, me.

She looks to the skies, stormy and red.

NANCY But what future?

It takes a moment for Rose to comprehend. She follows her look to the terrible London sky.

ROSE Nancy, this isn't the end. I know how it looks, but it's not like the end of the world or anything.

NANCY How can you say that? Look at it.

ROSE Listen to me. I was born in this city. I'm from here. In fifty years' time.

NANCY From here?

ROSE I'm a Londoner. I'm from your future.

NANCY But ... but you're not ...

ROSE What?

NANCY German.

Again it takes a moment for the penny to drop.

ROSE Nancy. The Germans never come here. They don't win.
(a beat; she smiles)
Don't tell anyone I said so. But you know what? You win.

Nancy stares at her, like this is the most impossible thing ever.

Rose has finished her work.

NANCY (boggling)
We win??

ROSE Only down side? All the movies!

The girls jump up and head back towards the cylinder.

40B EXT. CRASH SITE ENCLOSURE (INSIDE THE WIRE) NIGHT

JACK has climbed on top of the cylinder, THE DOCTOR watching him.
The girls arrive just as Jack wrenches the hatch open.

JACK (to the Doctor)
It's empty. Look at it.

THE DOCTOR What would you expect in a Chula Medical Transporter?
Bandages? Cough drops?
(looks to ROSE)
Rose?

ROSE Dunno.

THE DOCTOR Yes, you do.

He takes her hands, shows them to her. And wham! She gets it.

ROSE Nanogenes!

The Doctor rounds on Jack. By Jack's ashen face, he knows where this is going.

THE DOCTOR It wasn't empty, Captain. There were enough nanogenes
in there to rebuild a species.

JACK (shaken to the core – he's understanding now, he's getting it)
Oh God. Oh God!

THE DOCTOR Getting it now, are we? When the ship crashes, the
nanogenes escape. Billions upon billions of them. Ready to fix all
the cuts and bruises in the whole world. But what they find first
is a dead child. Probably killed earlier that night. And wearing
a gasmask.

ROSE And they brought him back to life?? They can do that??

THE DOCTOR What's life? Life's easy. A quirk of matter. Nature's
way of keeping meat fresh. Nothing to a nanogene. One problem
though. These nanogenes, they're not like the ones on your ship.
This lot have never seen a human being before. Don't know what a
human being's supposed to look like. All they've got to go on is one
little body – and there's not a lot left. But they carry right on, they
do what they're programmed to, they patch it up. Can't tell what's
gasmask and what's skull but they do their best. And then off they
fly, off they go, work to do! Cos you see, they think they know what
people should look like now. And it's time to fix all the rest. And
they won't ever stop. They won't ever, ever stop. The whole Human
Race is gonna be torn down and rebuilt in the form of one terrified
child, looking for its mother. And nothing in the world can stop it!

JACK (crushed, shaking, understanding)
I ... I didn't know ...

THE DOCTOR Yeah. Whatever.

The Doctor strides away from him, disgusted. He goes to the flashing light
on the cylinder, makes another attempt on it with his sonic screwdriver.
(NOTE: Jack is still in earshot.)

ROSE (frowning, watching him work)
Doctor, what is that? What's it doing?

NANCY (clutching Rose's arm)
Rose?

She points. Rose follows her look. Rose's POV: the fence and wasteland beyond it – explosions are booming out there, flames flickering – and glimpsed in that flickering glow, the GASMASK CREATURES from the hospital, advancing towards the enclosure . . .

Faintly, on the wind:

GASMASK CREATURES Mummy? . . . Mummy? . . .

Rose looks back to the Doctor, getting it now!

ROSE It's bringing the gasmask people here, isn't it?

THE DOCTOR (as he works at the revealed circuits)
The ship thinks it's under attack. It's calling up the troops. Standard protocol.

ROSE But the gasmask people aren't troops!

THE DOCTOR They are now. This is a *battlefield* ambulance. The nanogenes don't just fix you up, they get you ready for the front line. Equip you, programme you . . .

ROSE That's why the child is so strong? Why it could do that phoning thing?

THE DOCTOR It's a fully equipped Chula warrior, yes. All that weapons tech in the hands of an hysterical four-year-old. And now there's an army of them – all looking for mummy!

ROSE And all headed here.

Then, from off . . .

GASMASK CREATURES (from off; overlapping, eerie, whispering, rising in volume as they come closer)
Are you my mummy? Are you my mummy? Are you my mummy?

They look around. The Gasmasks are approaching the fence.

JACK Why don't they attack?

THE DOCTOR Good little soldiers. Waiting for their leader.

JACK (getting it)
The child!

NANCY is glaring at Jack.

NANCY Jamie.

JACK What?

NANCY Not 'the child'. Jamie.

ROSE So how long before that bomb falls?

JACK Any second now!

THE DOCTOR (shoots him a look)
What's the matter, Captain? Little too close to the volcano for you?

Nancy is staring tearfully out into the wasteland, lost in her own misery.

NANCY He's just a little boy.

THE DOCTOR I know.

NANCY Just a little boy who wants his mummy.

THE DOCTOR I *know*. There isn't a little boy born who wouldn't tear the world apart to find his mother. And this little boy can.

ROSE So what are we gonna *do*?

The Doctor looks at her – and his look is simple and terrifying. Because this time he really doesn't have anything.

THE DOCTOR I don't know. I'm sorry.

Nancy is sobbing uncontrollably now.

NANCY It's my fault.

THE DOCTOR No.

NANCY It is. It's all my fault.

THE DOCTOR How can it –

The Doctor breaks off. His mind is racing now. From all around: 'Are you my mummy? Are you my mummy?'

THE DOCTOR Nancy, what age are you?

No answer, sobbing.

THE DOCTOR Twenty, twenty-one? Older than you look, right?

Nancy shakes her head, won't answer.

JACK Doctor, that bomb – we've got seconds!

ROSE (to Jack)
You can teleport us out.

JACK Not *you*. The nav-com's back on line, gonna take too long to override the protocols –

THE DOCTOR (doesn't even spare him a glance – still focused on Nancy)
So it's Volcano Day. Do what you've got to!

ROSE (stares at him, ashen)
Jack?

Agony on Jack's face – then decision. He raises his zapper, clicks it. And disappears in a green flash. On Rose; horrified! He's saved himself!

The Doctor – he's paid no attention at all to the above – steps towards Nancy, tenderly takes her face in his hands.

THE DOCTOR Five years ago, you'd have been, what? Fifteen? Sixteen? Old enough to give birth anyway.
(a beat)
He wasn't your brother, was he?

Tearful, Nancy shakes her head. Her cheeks are burning. She can't even look at the Doctor now. This is the most unimaginable shame!

THE DOCTOR A teenage single mother. In 1941. So you hid. You lied. You even lied to him.

Suddenly, eerily, all the Gasmask chanting stops. There is a crash! The gates of the enclosure slowly creak open – and a lone tiny figure is standing there.

THE CHILD Are you my mummy?

The Doctor hasn't turned, hasn't even looked at the CHILD. His eyes are fixed on Nancy.

THE DOCTOR He's gonna keep on asking. He's never gonna stop. Never.
(looks hard at her – really fixes her with his eyes)
Nancy ... tell him.

Nancy raises her head, stares at him in astonishment.

THE DOCTOR Nancy, the future of the Human Race is in your hands. Trust me and *tell him.*

He gently takes her shoulders, turns her to face the CHILD, now only a few feet away.

THE CHILD Are you my mummy?

A beat; on Nancy: terrified, sobbing – can she do this?

NANCY (finally, torn from her, a terrible sob)
Yes.

The Child starts to advance towards Nancy.

NANCY Yes, I'm your mummy.

Rose plucks at the Doctor's sleeve.

ROSE Doctor, the bomb . . .

The Doctor is watching raptly as Nancy and the Child now approach each other, a few feet apart.

THE CHILD Mummy?

Nancy steps forward, swallows hard. They stand facing one another, a few feet apart.

NANCY I'm here.

THE DOCTOR He doesn't understand, there's not . . .
(gentler)
There's not enough of him left.

NANCY (kneeling now, reaching out her arms to the Child)
They threw me out. Both of us. Had to hide you, had to lie. And then . . . and then you died. And you came back. I thought God was punishing me. They said God would punish me. I am your mummy. I will always be your mummy.

Nancy is on her knees now, opening her arms to the Child. Doesn't care what's gonna happen.

NANCY I'm so sorry. I'm so, so sorry.

The Child approaches, Nancy wraps her arms around him. The golden fireflies start storming around them.

ROSE Doctor, it's changing her, we've gotta –

THE DOCTOR Shh!
(staring raptly, under his breath)
Come on. Please!

What he's staring at: the mother and child. The golden fireflies are flashing red . . .

THE DOCTOR Come on, you clever little nanogenes. Figure it out!
The mother – she's the mother. Gotta be enough information.
Figure it out!

ROSE What's happening?!

THE DOCTOR (pointing at the fireflies – like Rose could possibly understand)
See? Recognising the same DNA!

ROSE Which means?

A terrible silence. The Doctor doesn't even dare voice his hopes.

And suddenly it's over. Nancy reels back, flops to the ground. She looks imploringly up at the Doctor. What happened there? The Doctor is looking at the Child, who stands motionless a few feet away. He hesitates – then starts slowly towards the tiny figure. Rose and Nancy: watching, exchanging a glance. There is wild hope on the Doctor's face as he hunkers down in front of the Child. He so wants this. Almost can't bear to see if it's worked – if he's right.

THE DOCTOR Come on! Gimme a day like this! Gimme this one!

Hardly daring to hope any more, he reaches behind the Child's head, undoes the straps of the gasmask – and the gasmask falls, revealing the face of a perfectly ordinary, perfectly restored child. The Doctor lets out a wild laugh of joy, grabs the Child, kisses him on the forehead.

THE DOCTOR Welcome back! Twenty years to pop music, you're gonna love it.

Nancy: staring in wonder and disbelief.

NANCY What ... what happened?

THE DOCTOR The nanogenes recognised superior information. The parent DNA. They didn't change you, cos you changed them. (looks at her, realises he's talking gibberish as far as she's concerned) Mother knows best.

Nancy barely understands but doesn't care. She extends her arms to JAMIE.

NANCY Jamie ...

As she hugs the child, explosions sound from nearby. Rose glances nervously at the sky.

ROSE Doctor, that bomb ...

THE DOCTOR Taken care of it.

ROSE How?

THE DOCTOR Psychology.

And then, from above, a terrible descending whistle. Rose looks up, sensing it! From way above: the POV of the bomb streaking down at the crash site enclosure, zooming right down on them – a searchlight sweeping up from nowhere – and then Rose just staring.

The bomb is hanging just above their heads, bobbing gently, caught – it seems – in a searchlight. (Just like Rose in ep.9.) We pan. At the other end of the searchlight, hovering, is Jack's ship, projecting it. In a green flash, Jack materialises on top of the bomb – greatcoat flying, he never looked finer. He pulls a pair of metal clamps from his pockets, slams them on either side of the bomb. The Doctor is watching. He smiles.

THE DOCTOR Good lad.

JACK (calling out)
Doctor – the bomb's already commenced detonation. I've put it in stasis, but it won't last!

THE DOCTOR Change of plan! Don't need the bomb – can you get rid of it, safely as you can?

JACK Rose?

ROSE Yeah?

JACK Goodbye!

And in a green flash, Jack and the bomb have disappeared. A second later, in another green flash, Jack and the bomb reappear exactly where they were, like he's had an afterthought.

JACK Oh!
(giving Rose his cheesiest grin)
Loved the tee-shirt!

And he disappears again. A moment later, his ship (still hanging, suspended) roars into life, rears back till it points straight up – and zooms off into the sky.

Nancy with her child: she is touching his face, unable to believe what's happened.

The Doctor is extending his arms. The fireflies are streaming towards him, flocking round his hands.

ROSE What are you doing?

THE DOCTOR Software patch. Gonna email the upgrade.
(his sudden wild grin)
You want moves, Rose. I'll show you moves!

And he throws his arms. And the nanogenes stream from him, a golden storm of them – straight to the Gasmask Creatures. The creatures stagger, some of them fall – the Doctor, at the centre of the storm, arms flung wide, loving this, roaring the laughter, absolutely joyous –

THE DOCTOR Everybody lives, Rose. Just this once! Everybody lives!!

Close on one of the gasmask creatures: it is the one who used to be CONSTANTINE. He drops to his knees as he changes from a Gasmask Creature, back into Constantine – perfectly restored, exactly the man we first met – and the Doctor is helping him to his feet.

THE DOCTOR Doctor Constantine – who never left his patients. Back on your feet, constant doctor. World doesn't want to get by without you yet – and I don't blame it one bit.

Constantine is looking around in bewilderment.

THE DOCTOR These are your patients. All better now.

CONSTANTINE (looking around in confusion)
Yes. Yes, so it would seem.
(can't get his head round where he is)
They would also seem to be standing around in a disused railway station. Is there a particular reason for that?

THE DOCTOR Yeah, well, you know … cutbacks.
(conspiratorial)
Listen, whatever was wrong with them before, you're probably gonna find they're cured. Just tell 'em what a great doctor you are, don't make a big thing of it. Okay?

And off he goes. We stay with Constantine.

MRS HARCOURT (calling from off)
Doctor Constantine.

Constantine turns to see an indignant, elderly lady struggling to her feet.

CONSTANTINE Ah, Mrs. Harcourt! How much better you're looking!

MRS HARCOURT My leg's grown back!

Constantine looks to her fully restored leg.

MRS HARCOURT When I came to the hospital, I had one leg!

CONSTANTINE (floundering a little)
Well there is a war on, Mrs Harcourt – is it possible you miscounted?

On the Doctor, racing back to the cylinder.

THE DOCTOR (bellowing)
Right you lot, lots to do. Off you go, beat the Germans, save the world, don't forget the Welfare State!

Closer on him as he goes to one of the thrusters on the cylinder, whipping out his sonic screwdriver. Rose joins him.

THE DOCTOR (to Rose)
Setting this to self-destruct when everyone's clear. History says there was an explosion here. Who am I to argue with history?

Rose smiles at him, as he works away, enjoying his victory as much as he is.

ROSE Usually, the first in line.

40C INT. THE TARDIS NIGHT

THE DOCTOR and ROSE, coming through the doors: the Doctor is still buzzing from his victory – he probably hasn't stopped talking all the way back.

THE DOCTOR The nanogenes will clear up their mess and switch themselves off. Cos I just told them to. Nancy and Jamie will go to Doctor Constantine for help – ditto. All in all, all things considered – sorted!

ROSE Look at you, beaming away like you're Father Christmas!

THE DOCTOR Who says I'm not? Red bicycle when you were twelve.

ROSE (startled, he's bang on)
What??

THE DOCTOR (starting up the engines)
And everybody lives, Rose. Everybody lives. I need more days like this!

ROSE (a new thought, a troubling one)
Doctor . . .

THE DOCTOR Go on, ask me anything. I'm on a roll.

ROSE What about Jack?

The Doctor hesitates, carries on with his work. Like he doesn't want to get into this.

ROSE Why did he say goodbye?

41 EXT. SPACE

JACK's spaceship zooms through the void.

42 INT. JACK'S SHIP

The bomb hangs suspended in a green glow in the middle of the cabin. JACK is at the controls. He doesn't look so happy.

JACK Okay, computer – how long can we keep the bomb in stasis?

COMPUTER Stasis decaying at ninety percent per cycle. Detonation in three minutes.

JACK Can we jettison it?

COMPUTER Any attempt to jettison the device will precipitate detonation. One hundred percent probability.

JACK We could stick it in an escape pod?

COMPUTER There is no escape pod on board.

JACK Okay, see the flaw in that. I'll get in the escape pod.

COMPUTER There is no escape pod on board.

JACK Did you check everywhere?

COMPUTER Affirmative.

JACK Under the sink?

COMPUTER Affirmative.

JACK Okay. Out of a hundred, exactly how dead am I?

COMPUTER Termination of Captain Jack Harkness in under two minutes, one hundred percent probability.

JACK Lovely, thanks, good to know the numbers. Okay then! Think we'd better initiate emergency protocol 417.

COMPUTER Affirmative.

A drink materialises on Jack's dashboard. He takes a sip.

JACK A little too much vermouth. See if I come here again.

He stands, ready to face his doom like a man. Or at any rate, like a man with a drink. We start pulling back from him, as he looks out over the stars one final time. It's a pull-out that feels like the end of the show, like this is the last we'll see of him.

JACK You know, funny thing. Last time I was sentenced to death, I asked for four hyper-vodkas for my last breakfast. All a bit of a blur after that. Woke up in bed with both my executioners. Lovely couple. They kept in touch. Can't say that for many executioners. Anyway. Thanks for everything, computer – it's been great.

We are pulling back and back ... and now, magically, we are pulling back through the police-box doors of the TARDIS!

And suddenly there's music – 'Moonlight Serenade'. Jack – slowly, disbelieving – turns. Jack's POV: absurdly, there's a police box standing at the back of his ship, the doors open, light spilling magically from within.

ROSE (from inside)
Well! Hurry up then!

For a moment, Jack doesn't know what to do – then he races for the TARDIS doors, throws himself through them –

43 INT. TARDIS

– into the huge, magical room. 'Moonlight Serenade' playing, and THE DOCTOR and ROSE dancing. She's teaching him; he moves awkwardly.

ROSE Okay, try and spin me again. But this time don't get my arm up my back. No extra points for a half-nelson.

THE DOCTOR I'm sure I used to know this stuff.
(calling to JACK)
Close the door, would you. Your ship's about to blow up, there's gonna be a draft.

Hurriedly – and a little dazedly – Jack closes the doors. The Doctor flicks a switch. The TARDIS engines grind into life.

THE DOCTOR Welcome to the TARDIS.

JACK (looking numbly round the room)
Bigger on the inside . . .

THE DOCTOR You'd better be.

ROSE I think what the Doctor is trying to say is . . . you may cut in.

She puts her hand out to him. The music's still playing. They're going to dance.

THE DOCTOR Rose! I've just remembered!

ROSE What?

The Doctor hits a switch on the console. The music changes – up tempo: Glenn Miller's 'In the Mood'.

THE DOCTOR I can dance!

He grabs Rose, spins her perfectly, and they're off round the console. And if you thought Jack could dance, this guy's got nine hundred years on him.

ROSE Actually, Doctor, I thought that Jack might like a dance.

THE DOCTOR I'm sure he would, Rose, I'm absolutely certain . . .

He spins her, twirls her . . .

Jack stands there, starting to smile, taking in this strange new world he's suddenly a part of.

THE DOCTOR . . . But who with?

Episode 11

Boom Town
By Russell T Davies

'The Gang Show', Helen Raynor called this. More like 'The Bottle Show'. In the US, a bottle show is an episode of a long-running series which saves money. A bottle episode of *Enterprise* would be set entirely on board the ship, cos those sets are already standing.

The great advantage of *Doctor Who* is that its bottle is as big as the Earth. Well, it *is* the Earth. We can film anywhere in the present-day world, without needing a time warp to explain how we got there. Thank God for the TARDIS.

We had tuppence for this show. We'd just done World War Two, and had the final battle of the Time War to come, so the money had to be saved, somewhere. (This is nothing new, every show spreads its costs like this.) I looked at the stock material – yes, there's Cardiff Bay outside my window, a location waiting and deserving to be used. Yes, there's a Slitheen costume, and a CGI Slitheen already fully rendered. Yes, there's a wonderful TARDIS crew, all under contract, including the brilliant Noel Clarke. And yes, in the so-classy-you-couldn't-buy-it-with-a-gold-mine bracket, there's Annette Badland. Complete and utter quality. Who needs laser-beams, when she and Chris can act together? During rehearsals for Episodes 4 and 5, Chris had gone for a costume fitting and I'd stood in for him. I had faced Margaret Slitheen.

And my God, she was terrifying. More than scary; she was *real*.
Right there and then, I'd resolved to bring Annette back.

Of course, having promised a cheap show, I then fiddled
a bit. When I handed 'Boom Town' in, Phil Collinson phoned me up:
'I thought you said this was cheap.' 'It is.' 'There's an earthquake!
In Cardiff!!'

This script is also paving the way for the big showdown in the
next two episodes. There are structural tasks which 'Boom Town'
must fulfil. The Writer's Checklist, again. Jack's now established
as a fine member of the crew, a technician, a strategist and a
fighter, ready for the Daleks to come. I wanted them all to be
more of a team, and good friends, because in a week's time, they'll
be split up and never able to relax again. I knew also that the
TARDIS would need a forcefield in Episode 13, so I laid down the
extrapolator (and I really must do something about its mysterious
origins, one day). And I wanted a Doctor who, for a brief time,
was happy.

Out of all that comes a show which is pure atmosphere and
dialogue. It exists on a charm; 'When the wind's in the right
direction', says the Doctor, as though summoning a spell.
And while I love spaceships and monsters and intergalactic
wars, the simplicity of this episode makes it, just sometimes,
when the wind's in the right direction, my favourite.

Russell T Davies

1 INT. LORD MAYOR'S OFFICE DAY

Modern day. An elegant, spacious, wood-panelled room. MR CLEAVER – 50, Welsh, glasses, worried – is pacing up and down, addressing an OOV person seated behind the desk.

MR CLEAVER I've checked the figures, I've checked them again and again. Always the same result. The design is not safe. It could result in the death of millions. I beg of you, stop the Project, right now, before it's too late.

Reveal, behind the desk: MARGARET BLAINE – concerned, kind.

MARGARET Well. Goodness me. Obviously, Mr Cleaver, you're the expert.

MR CLEAVER Then you'll stop it?

MARGARET Seems I have no choice.

She shifts; her stomach rumbles.

MARGARET Ooh. Do excuse me. Civic duties leave little time for a sandwich.

MR CLEAVER But you promise, you'll stop it today, immediately?

MARGARET Well of course! Nothing's more important than human life. What do you take me for, some sort of maniac?

MR CLEAVER Well no! Clearly not!

MARGARET Am I right in thinking, you've shown your results only to me?

MR CLEAVER Just you, no one else.

MARGARET Wise move.

MR CLEAVER I can't tell you, Mrs Blaine, this is such a weight off my mind. Good Lord. I've barely slept.

He's relieved, crosses to the window, looks out. He takes off his glasses, wipes them – very short-sighted, squinting.

MR CLEAVER I couldn't believe my own readings. The scale of it. Destruction, like the British Isles has never seen before.

On Cleaver; behind him, a flickering blue light.

MR CLEAVER We'll have to do a full analysis – if I didn't know better, I'd almost think someone *wanted* this Project to go wrong. As though they intended this city to be wiped off the map. Madness, I know!

The blue light fades, as he puts his glasses back on.

MR CLEAVER Thank goodness we've got you. Our esteemed leader –

He turns round, and a SLITHEEN is standing right behind him!

Mr Cleaver screams – the huge claw grabs his neck.

CU MARGARET/SLITHEEN: laughing, as she murders him.

CUT TO OPENING TITLES.

2 EXT. CARDIFF TRAIN STATION DAY

The train pulls up.

Doors open, PASSENGERS get out. And here's MICKEY SMITH, walking along. Looking a bit grim.

3 EXT. CARDIFF BAY DAY

LONG LENS SHOT: background, people, reduced to a blur; on MICKEY, ignoring it all, walking along, still grim.

4 EXT. MILLENNIUM CENTRE SQUARE DAY

MICKEY walks down the steps. Reveal: the square, the looming bronze of the Millennium Centre, the silver water sculpture, and in the centre of the wooden-floored square: the TARDIS.

Mickey walks up. Deep breath. Knocks on the door.

CAPTAIN JACK pops his head out.

CAPTAIN JACK Who the hell are you?

MICKEY What d'you mean, who the hell am I? Who the hell are you?

CAPTAIN JACK Captain Jack Harkness – whatever you're selling, we're not buying.

MICKEY Out of the way!

And Mickey pushes his way in –

5 INT. TARDIS DAY

MICKEY stomps in, CAPTAIN JACK following –

CAPTAIN JACK Don't tell me, this must be Mickey –

ROSE is by the console. THE DOCTOR is way up in the gantries, above them all, calling down. He's strapped up with toolkits full of equipment, using an industrial drill on the central column.

THE DOCTOR Here comes trouble. How've you been, Ricky boy?

MICKEY It's Mickey!

Rose heads for Mickey (as Jack goes to the console – he's helping the Doctor). Awkward meeting – do they kiss?

ROSE Oh don't listen, he's winding you up, is that a new jacket?

MICKEY Yeah, got it down the market.

ROSE It's smart, I like it. Nice to see you.

MICKEY And you, yeah.

Then they decide on a kiss on the cheek. But then, a smile:

MICKEY You look fantastic.

ROSE Thanks.

And they give each other a proper hug.

CUT TO Captain Jack, calling over to the Doctor.

CAPTAIN JACK Hey look at these two, sweet. How come I never get any of that?

THE DOCTOR Buy me a drink, first.

CAPTAIN JACK You're such hard work.

THE DOCTOR But worth it!

CUT TO Rose and Mickey.

ROSE Did you manage to find it?

MICKEY Yeah, took me half an hour to get past your mother, I was lying through my teeth. There you go –

Hands over her passport. Rose calls up to the Doctor:

ROSE I can travel anywhere now!

THE DOCTOR I've said, you don't need a passport.

The Doctor now starts heading down . . .

ROSE No, it's all very well, going to Platform One and Justicia and the Glass Pyramid of San Kaloon, but what if we end up in Brazil? I might need my passport. Y'see, I'm prepared for anything.

MICKEY Sounds like you're staying, then.

ROSE How d'you mean?

MICKEY On board this thing.

Awkward pause, no reply.

MICKEY So what are you doing in Cardiff? And who the hell's Jumping Jack Flash? I mean, I don't care if you're travelling about with old big-ears up there –

THE DOCTOR Oy!

MICKEY Look in the mirror! But him. He's all sort of, I dunno . . .

CAPTAIN JACK Handsome?

MICKEY More like, cheesy.

CAPTAIN JACK Early twenty-first century slang, is cheesy good or bad?

MICKEY It's bad.

CAPTAIN JACK But bad means good, is that right?

THE DOCTOR You saying I'm not handsome?

ROSE We've just stopped for a while, we need to refuel. Thing is, Cardiff's got this rift, running through the middle of the city, it's invisible, but it's like an earthquake fault, between different dimensions –

The Doctor now arrives back at the centre, stands alongside Rose and Jack, all three facing Mickey. Fast, snappy, a team:

THE DOCTOR The rift was healed, back in 1869 –

ROSE Thanks to a girl called Gwyneth, cos these creatures called the Gelth were using the rift as a gateway, but she saved the world and closed it –

CAPTAIN JACK But closing a rift always leaves a scar, and that scar generates energy, harmless to the Human Race –

THE DOCTOR But perfect for the TARDIS; I just park it here for a couple of days, right on top of the scar –

CAPTAIN JACK Open up the engines and soak up the radiation –

ROSE Like filling her up with petrol, and off we go –

CAPTAIN JACK (high-fives Doctor)
... Into time –

THE DOCTOR (high-fives Rose)
... And space!

Mickey's just staring at them.

MICKEY God, have you seen yourselves? You think you're so clever.

THE DOCTOR/ROSE/CAPTAIN JACK Yeah/Yes/Yup!

6 EXT. MILLENNIUM CENTRE SQUARE DAY

THE DOCTOR, ROSE, MICKEY and CAPTAIN JACK walk out (it'll be cold, but they're dressed for it, big coats, gloves).

THE DOCTOR Should take another twenty-four hours. Which leaves us with time to kill.

MICKEY That old woman's staring.

CAPTAIN JACK Probably wondering what four people can do inside a small wooden box.

MICKEY What are you captain of, the Innuendo Squad?

The Doctor and Rose are heading off.

MICKEY But – hold on – the TARDIS, how can you just leave it, doesn't it get noticed?

CAPTAIN JACK What is it with the whole police-box thing anyway, why's it look like that?

ROSE It's a cloaking device.

THE DOCTOR It's called a chameleon circuit.

He walks round the TARDIS, smiling, so proud of it:

THE DOCTOR The TARDIS is meant to disguise itself, wherever it lands. Like, if this was ancient Rome, it'd be a statue on a plinth or something. But I landed in the 1960s, it disguised itself as a police box, and the circuit got stuck.

MICKEY What, so it copied a real thing – there used to be real police boxes?

THE DOCTOR Yeah, on street corners. Phone for help, before they had radios and mobiles. If they arrested someone, they could shove 'em inside, till they could get help. Like a little prison cell.

CAPTAIN JACK Why don't you fix the circuit?

THE DOCTOR I dunno. I like it! Don't you?

ROSE I love it.

MICKEY But that's what I meant – there's no police boxes any more, doesn't it get noticed?

THE DOCTOR Ricky, let me tell you about the Human Race. Put a mysterious box slap bang in the middle of town, and what do they do? Walk past it. Now stop your nagging, let's go and explore –

The Doctor strides off, taking Rose's arm, others follow.

ROSE So what's the plan?

THE DOCTOR Anything! It's Cardiff, early twenty-first century, and the wind's coming from the east. Trust me. Safest place in the universe . . .

7 INT. TOWN HALL EXHIBITION ROOM DAY

MARGARET This nuclear power station, right in the heart of Cardiff City, will bring jobs for all!

Applause!

It's a big, classy, marbled room, filled with CIVIC DIGNITARIES, JOURNALISTS, and WAITERS and WAITRESSES carrying wine and canapés. MARGARET's in full regalia, wearing her chain of office – she's the Lord Mayor. Behind her, a huge sign, 'BLAIDD DRWG', and displays of architect's diagrams and artists' impressions.

Now, Margaret walks down the room, following the length of a long, central table, on which is built a model of the city (buildings of white card, like a set model) with a great big NUCLEAR POWER STATION in place of Cardiff Castle.

MARGARET As you can see, as Lord Mayor, I've had to sanction some radical redevelopments –

A camera flash goes off. Margaret suddenly snarls –

MARGARET No photographs! What did I say? Take pictures of the Project, by all means, but not me, thank you.
(smiling again)
So! Cardiff Castle will be demolished, allowing the Blaidd Drwg Project to rise up, tall and proud, a monument to Welsh industry! And, yes, some of you might shiver. The words 'nuclear power station' and 'major population centre' aren't exactly the happiest of bedfellows. But I give you my personal guarantee that as long as I walk upon this Earth, no harm will come to any of my citizens – now drink up! A toast –
(raises a glass)
To the future!

ALL The future!

MARGARET And believe me. It will glow. Thank you!

Behind her, a quiet, thin, young Welsh journalist, CATHY SALT. She summons the nerve –

CATHY Um, excuse me, Mrs Blaine, my name's Cathy Salt, I represent the *Cardiff Gazette* –

MARGARET I'm sorry, I'm not doing interviews, I can't bear self-publicity –

CATHY But, are you aware of the curse?

Margaret stops. Still smiling, turns back to Cathy.

MARGARET Whatever do you mean? Cathy, wasn't it?

CATHY Cathy Salt. That's what some of your engineers are saying – that the Blaidd Drwg Project is cursed.

MARGARET Sounds rather silly to me.

CATHY Well, that's what I thought, I was just chasing a bit of local colour. But the funny thing is, you start piecing it all together, and it does begin to look a bit odd.

MARGARET In what way?

CATHY The deaths. The number of deaths associated with this Project. First of all, there was the entire team of European Safety Inspectors –

MARGARET But they were French! It's not my fault if 'Danger, Explosives!' was only written in Welsh.

CATHY Then, there was that accident with the Cardiff Heritage Committee –

MARGARET The electrocution of that swimming pool was put down to natural wear and tear.

CATHY And then, the architect –

MARGARET It was raining, visibility was low, my car simply couldn't stop.

CATHY And then just recently, Mr Cleaver, the government's nuclear adviser –

MARGARET Slipped on an icy patch.

CATHY He was decapitated.

MARGARET It was a very icy patch. I'm afraid these stories are nothing more than typical small-town thinking – I really haven't got time, if you'll excuse me –

She makes to go, but Cathy's more steely than she appears –

CATHY Except, before he died, Mr Cleaver posted some of his findings online.

MARGARET . . . Did he now?

CATHY If you know where to look. He was worried about the reactor –

MARGARET Oh, all that technical stuff –

CATHY Specifically, that the design of the suppression pool would cause the hydrogen recombiners to fail, precipitating the collapse of the containment isolation system and resulting in a meltdown.

MARGARET (cold smile)
Who's been doing her homework?

CATHY That's my job.

MARGARET I think . . . Cathy Salt, I think you and I should have a word in private. Off we go.

She links arms with Cathy, and they walk off. Margaret smiling with a deadly sweetness.

8 INT. TOWN HALL CORRIDOR DAY

Long, marbled, echoing. MARGARET and CATHY SALT walk along, and Margaret clutches her stomach, as it rumbles.

MARGARET Ooh, my little tum is complaining, I think we might have to make a detour to the Ladies.

CATHY I'll wait here.

MARGARET Oh come on. All girls together.

Margaret heads into the Ladies, Cathy follows.

9 INT. TOWN HALL LADIES TOILETS DAY

Small and functional. MARGARET heads in, CATHY following. Margaret heads for the cubicle, Cathy waits by the sinks.

MARGARET So, you were saying? These outlandish theories of yours.
(locks the door)
Keep talking, I can listen – ooh –

Margaret clenches, farts.

CATHY Sounds like we got here just in time.

MARGARET Continue!

CATHY Well, I don't know much about nuclear physics. But from what I could make out, Cleaver was saying the whole Project could go up, worse than Chernobyl.

INT CUBICLE: Margaret reaches up, unzips her forehead. Blue light flickers (not as strong as ep.4, more contained).

INT TOILET: Cathy looks up.

CATHY Is there something wrong with the lights?

MARGARET Oh, they're always on the blink, I can't tell you how many memos I've sent. So, Chernobyl?

CATHY Apparently, but a thousand times worse. It sounds absurd, there must be so many safety regulations, but Cleaver seemed to be talking about a nuclear holocaust.

INT CUBICLE, FX SHOT: the SLITHEEN shucking out of its Margaret-skin.

CATHY He almost made it sound deliberate. And I mean, we're hardly the *Sunday Times*, it's only the *Cardiff Gazette*, but we still have a duty to report the facts.

INT CUBICLE: the Margaret-suit gets hung on the door-hook. Reveal the full Slitheen, now crammed into the space. Her voice is now modulated (in post-production; though less than in eps 4 and 5, Margaret has refined the process.)

MARGARET/SLITHEEN Then you're going to print this information?

CATHY Are you alright? You sound a bit . . .

MARGARET/SLITHEEN Sore throat. Ahem. Just a little tickle. But tell me, do you intend to make this information public?

CATHY I have to.

MARGARET/SLITHEEN So be it.

And the Slitheen rears its claws, about to burst out –

CATHY Mind you, my boyfriend says I'm mad. We're getting married next month, and he says, if I make a fuss, I could lose my job, just when we need the money.

The Slitheen stops dead.

MARGARET/SLITHEEN . . . Boyfriend?

CATHY Jeffrey. Civil servant, he's nothing exciting. But he's mine!

MARGARET When's the wedding . . . ?

CATHY The nineteenth, it's really just to stop my mother nagging. But the baby sort of clinched it, I suppose.

And the Slitheen is sad, eyes drooping. Sits on the toilet.

MARGARET/SLITHEEN You're with child?

CATHY Three months, it's not showing yet. Wasn't planned, bit of an accident. Nice accident, though.

MARGARET/SLITHEEN Congratulations.

CATHY Thank you. What about you, have you got kids?

MARGARET/SLITHEEN No.

CATHY Is there a *Mister* Blaine . . . ?

MARGARET/SLITHEEN Not any more. I'm all on my own. Had quite a sizeable family, once upon a time. Wonderful brothers, oh they were bold! But all of them gone, now. Maybe you're right. Maybe I'm cursed.

CATHY Oh, I don't think so, not really.

MARGARET/SLITHEEN You're very kind. Um. If you don't mind, I might be a while. You run along. Perhaps we could do this another day.

CATHY Are you all right?

MARGARET/SLITHEEN Fine.

CATHY Um. Okay, tell you what, I'll leave my details with your office, and, uh . . . thanks for talking.

MARGARET/SLITHEEN Thank you.

Cathy goes.

On Margaret/Slitheen, slumped on the toilet. A sad sigh.

10 EXT. CARDIFF BAY DAY

Laughter. THE DOCTOR, ROSE, CAPTAIN JACK and MICKEY sitting outside one of the bars – again, cold, but loving it, all wrapped up, enjoying the sheer outdoorsness. And enjoying each other's company. Even Mickey; he's looking round, nervous, but excited, smiling, like he's allowed to be part of this lot, and likes it. (Dialogue overlapping, lively, relaxed.)

ROSE Oh my God, I wish I'd seen it!

CAPTAIN JACK I swear, sixty foot tall, and with tusks, it turns out, the white things were tusks, and I mean, *tusks*. And it's woken up! And it's not happy! And we're standing there, all fifteen of us, naked, and I'm like going, nothing to do with me!

THE DOCTOR You're lying through your teeth!

ROSE I'd've gone bonkers! That's the word, bonkers!

THE DOCTOR How could you not know it was there?

ROSE Naked!

CAPTAIN JACK And then it roars! And we're running! Oh my God, we are running, and Brakovitch falls over, and I turn back and I say to him –

MICKEY I knew we should've turned left!

Big laugh, claps, he's guessed the punchline.

CAPTAIN JACK That's my line!

ROSE I don't believe it, I don't believe a word you say, ever. That is so brilliant! Did you ever get your clothes back?

On the Doctor, as his smile stops dead. Dialogue cont., b/g, but stay on the Doctor –

CAPTAIN JACK No, I just picked him up and ran, back to the ship, full throttle, kept going till I hit the spacelanes and then I was shaking! Didn't hit me till I was fifteen light years away. I was like this!

... as the Doctor stands. Walks forward. Towards another table. A newspaper has been left behind, pinned under an ashtray, to stay put. The corner is flapping in the wind. The Doctor picks up the paper. Sighs. Now, the others have stopped, watching, as he looks round.

THE DOCTOR And I was having such a nice time.

He holds up the paper, to show them. HEADLINE: NEW MAYOR, NEW CARDIFF. Below: a photo of Margaret – as sc.7 – caught, hand out, annoyed, objecting to the photographer.

11 INT. TOWN HALL CORRIDOR DAY

Wham! Doors slam open. Filled with sunlight, silhouetting: THE DOCTOR, ROSE, CAPTAIN JACK and MICKEY. The team! Walking, determined, maybe even slo-mo. *The Right Stuff.* Big, epic, hero shot, striding into action.

12 INT. TOWN HALL STAIRCASE DAY

A junction, with corridors leading off in all directions, at the base of a sweeping marble staircase. THE DOCTOR, ROSE, MICKEY stop, CAPTAIN JACK takes charge, rattles off:

CAPTAIN JACK According to intelligence, the target is the last surviving member of the Slitheen family, a criminal sect from the planet Raxacoricofallapatorious, masquerading as a human being, zipped inside a skin-suit. Okay! Plan of attack, we assume a basic fifty-seven/fifty-six strategy, covering all available exits on the ground floor, Doctor, you go face-to-face, so let's designate that as Exit One, I'll cover Exit Two, Rose, you're Exit Three, Mickey Smith, you take Exit Four, have you got that?

THE DOCTOR (stern)
Excuse me. Who's in charge?

CAPTAIN JACK Sorry. Waiting for orders, sir.

THE DOCTOR Right. Here's the plan.
(pause; big smile)
Like he said. Nice plan! Got anything else?

CAPTAIN JACK Present arms.

All four get out mobile phones.

THE DOCTOR/ROSE/MICKEY Ready/Ready/Ready.

CAPTAIN JACK Speed dial?

All four press a button, beep.

THE DOCTOR/ROSE/MICKEY Yup/Ready/Check.

CAPTAIN JACK Then let's go. See you in hell.

The Doctor strides up the stairs, Rose, Captain Jack, Mickey scatter in all directions.

13 INT. LORD MAYOR'S OUTER OFFICE DAY

THE DOCTOR walks in, all smiles. The Lord Mayor's SECRETARY is a young man, IDRIS HOPPER, sitting at his desk.

THE DOCTOR Hello! I've come to see the Lord Mayor.

IDRIS Have you got an appointment?

THE DOCTOR No, I'm just an old friend, passing by, bit of a surprise. I can't wait to see her face.

IDRIS Well, she's just having her cup of tea, she loves her cup of tea, she wouldn't want to be disturbed.

THE DOCTOR Just go in there, and tell her, the Doctor would like to see her.

IDRIS Doctor who?

THE DOCTOR Just the Doctor. Tell her exactly that. The Doctor.

IDRIS Hold on a tick ...

Idris heads off. Inner office stays OOV, just on the door, as Idris goes inside, closes it behind him. Pause on the Doctor.

A smash; a teacup, dropping, off. Pause on the Doctor.

Idris comes out – inner office OOV – closes the door behind him, flustered, nervous.

IDRIS Um. The Lord Mayor says, thank you for popping by. She'd love to have a chat. But she's up to her eyes in paperwork, perhaps if you could make an appointment for next week ...?

THE DOCTOR She's climbing out of the window, isn't she?

IDRIS Yes she is.

Sudden action, the Doctor pushes past him –

14 INT. LORD MAYOR'S OFFICE DAY

THE DOCTOR slams through the door. The window's open, the Doctor strides over, leans out –

15 EXT. LORD MAYOR'S OFFICE DAY

THE DOCTOR leans out. Vicious grin. Bellows:

THE DOCTOR *MARGARET!*

His POV: MARGARET is halfway down the fire escape. She looks back, utter terror – runs. The Doctor clicks on his mobile phone.

THE DOCTOR Slitheen heading north!

16 INT. TOWN HALL CORRIDOR #1 DAY

ROSE on her mobile –

ROSE On my way –

And she starts running . . .

17 INT. TOWN HALL CORRIDOR #2 DAY

CAPTAIN JACK on his mobile –

CAPTAIN JACK Over and out –

And he starts running . . .

18 INT. TOWN HALL CORRIDOR #3 DAY

MICKEY on his mobile –

MICKEY Oh my God!

And he starts running . . .

19 EXT. LORD MAYOR'S OFFICE DAY

THE DOCTOR goes to get out of the window, but IDRIS is there, faithful to his boss, throwing himself halfway out of the window, grabbing the Doctor – a tussle. CUT TO MARGARET, further down, running. At the same time, she's intent on her brooch, taking it off, fumbling –

20 INT. TOWN HALL CORRIDOR #1 DAY

ROSE runs down the corridor. Ahead of her, SECRETARIES in the corridor, chatting. Rose doesn't stop, barges through – a woman goes flying, papers in the air – Rose keeps running . . .

21 INT. TOWN HALL CORRIDOR #2 DAY

CAPTAIN JACK runs down the corridor. Ahead of him, a TEA LADY pushes a TEA TROLLEY out of a doorway, right across the corridor. Captain Jack doesn't stop, leaps – great big hidden-trampoline-style stunt; Captain Jack bounding UP and OVER the trolley, and down, and running . . .

22 INT. TOWN HALL CORRIDOR #3 DAY

MICKEY runs down the corridor. Ahead of him, a CLEANER pushes a CLEANING TROLLEY out of a doorway, right across the corridor. Mickey smacks right into it, toilet rolls and detergent and mops and legs go flying ...

23 INT. TOWN HALL CORRIDOR #1 DAY

ROSE slams out of a fire door, into sunlight –

24 INT. TOWN HALL CORRIDOR #2 DAY

CAPTAIN JACK slams out of a doorway, into sunlight –

25 INT. TOWN HALL CORRIDOR #3 DAY

MICKEY clomps along, wet, trailing toilet roll, his foot stuck in a metal mop-bucket –

26 EXT. LORD MAYOR'S OFFICE DAY

THE DOCTOR shoves IDRIS inside, belts down the fire escape –

27 EXT. BACK OF TOWN HALL DAY

A general area, all bins and tarmac and cars. MARGARET reaches the base of the fire escape – as she runs, she clutches her brooch, taking off an earring. But then Margaret stops, horrified, seeing ... HER POV: ROSE running from one direction –

Margaret hisses like a lizard, turns to run another way. Her POV: CAPTAIN JACK running towards her –

Margaret turns, back the way she came – but there's THE DOCTOR, belting towards her –

(NB, a wide area, so the Doctor, Rose and Captain Jack are still a good distance away.) Margaret looks round – there's a fourth direction! An alleyway, leading off. Margaret runs down it, pulling off her second earring.

A distance back, the Doctor, Rose, Captain Jack converging –

CAPTAIN JACK Who was on Exit Four?

ROSE That was Mickey!

A huge distance behind, MICKEY appears, running, wet.

MICKEY Here I am!

THE DOCTOR Mickey the idiot.

ROSE Oh be fair, she's not exactly gonna outrun us, is she?

CUT TO Margaret, still running, but as she does so, she's clipping her brooch and the two earrings together, so they become a gizmo. And grinning, she presses them, *ka-chick* – Margaret vanishes. No FX, just an instant blink, gone.

CUT TO Captain Jack, outraged, the Doctor and Rose calm.

CAPTAIN JACK Teleport! She's got a teleport! That's cheating, now we're never gonna get her –

ROSE Ohh, the Doctor's very good with teleports.

The Doctor smiles, holds up the sonic screwdriver, whirrs. Margaret blinks into existence, much closer to the Doctor and the others, now – but in the blink, she's been switched round, so that she's now running *towards* them!

She stops, realises this, horrified – about turns, runs away – on the hoof, she presses her device, *ka-chick* – Margaret vanishes.

The Doctor whirrs. Margaret reappears running towards them. Stops, turns. Runs. *Ka-chick* –

The Doctor whirrs. Margaret reappears, running towards them. And now she's knackered, gasping for breath, stops. (As Mickey, running, finally reaches them.)

THE DOCTOR I could do this all day.

MARGARET I couldn't.
(puts hands up)
This is persecution, why can't you leave me alone? What did I ever do to you?

THE DOCTOR You tried to kill me and destroy this entire planet.

MARGARET Apart from that?

28 INT. TOWN HALL EXHIBITION ROOM DAY

THE DOCTOR, ROSE, CAPTAIN JACK, MICKEY and MARGARET walk in, the Doctor fascinated by the model city; studying it.

THE DOCTOR ... So you're a Slitheen, you're on Earth, your family gets killed, but you teleport out, just in the nick of time. You're alone, you're trapped, no means of escape, what do you do? You build a nuclear power station! But what for ...?

MARGARET A philanthropic gesture. I've learnt the error of my ways.

THE DOCTOR And it just so happens to be right on top of the rift.

MARGARET What rift would that be?

CAPTAIN JACK A rift in space and time. Now closed, but the scar is right underneath the reactor. If that power station went into meltdown ...

ROSE Would it open the rift?

CAPTAIN JACK Oh yeah. Catastrophe! Whole planet would just ... schwwwup!

THE DOCTOR (studying the model)
This station is designed to explode, the moment it reaches capacity.

ROSE ... But didn't anyone notice? Isn't there someone in London, checking this sort of stuff?

MARGARET We're in Cardiff, London doesn't care! The South Wales coast could fall into the sea, and they wouldn't notice –
(stops)
Oh, I sound like a Welshman. God help me, I've gone native.

MICKEY But why would she do all that? Great big explosion, she'd just end up killing herself.

MARGARET She's got a name, you know.

MICKEY She's not even a she, she's a thing.

THE DOCTOR Oh but she's clever!

He's prised his fingers under the model, hauls up a panel – the model buildings go flying, as the panel lifts up in a neat, solid, flat 2 ft x 4 ft. Underneath, it's a giant circuit board – intricate metal patterns, a motherboard.

THE DOCTOR Fantastic!

CAPTAIN JACK (awestruck)
... Is that a tribophysical waveform macro-kinetic extrapolator?

THE DOCTOR Couldn't put it better myself. Look at it! The workmanship!

He rips it free, hands it to Jack. (Then lose the Doctor b/g; he wanders off, seeing something more interesting ...)

CAPTAIN JACK Genius! You didn't build that?

MARGARET I have my hobbies. A little tinkering.

CAPTAIN JACK No, I mean you *really* didn't build that. Way beyond you.

MICKEY I bet she stole it.

MARGARET It fell into my hands.

ROSE Is it a weapon?

CAPTAIN JACK It's transport! Y'see, the reactor blows up, the rift opens, phenomenal cosmic disaster, but this thing shrouds you in a forcefield, you've got this energy bubble, zzhum, all around you, so you're safe – then you just feed it coordinates, stand on top, and ride the concussion, way out of the solar system –

MICKEY It's a surfboard!

CAPTAIN JACK A pan-dimensional surfboard, yup.

MARGARET And it would've worked. I'd have surfed away from this dead-end dump and back to civilisation.

MICKEY You'd blow up a planet? Just to get a lift?

MARGARET Like stepping on an anthill.

Suddenly, from the far end of the room:

THE DOCTOR How did you think of the name . . . ?

The Doctor's standing by the BLAIDD DRWG display: quiet, fascinated, dark; mind ticking over.

MARGARET What, Blaidd Drwg? It's Welsh.

THE DOCTOR I know, but how did you think of it?

MARGARET Chose it at random, that's all, I don't know. Just sounded good. Does it matter?

THE DOCTOR (at Rose)
Blaidd Drwg.

ROSE What's it mean?

THE DOCTOR Bad Wolf.

Everyone else irrelevant, this is just between them:

ROSE But . . . that keeps cropping up. Bad Wolf. I've heard it before, I've heard it lots of times.

THE DOCTOR Everywhere we go. Two words. Following us. Bad Wolf.

ROSE How can they be following us?

Pause, the Doctor dark; then a big smile, shakes it off –

THE DOCTOR Naah, just coincidence. Like hearing a word on the radio, then hearing it all day. Never mind! Things to do . . .
(walks back to them)
Margaret, we're gonna take you home.

CAPTAIN JACK Hold on, that's an easy option, isn't that like letting her go?

THE DOCTOR It's a decent planet, nice people, they can decide what to do with her.

ROSE I don't believe it, we're actually gonna visit Raxaci – no, hold on, wait a minute – Raxa –

THE DOCTOR Raxacoricofallapatorius.

ROSE Raxacorico . . .

THE DOCTOR Fallapatorius.

ROSE Raxacoricofallapatorius!

THE DOCTOR That's it!

ROSE I got it!

MARGARET They have the death penalty.

Nasty silence.

MARGARET The family Slitheen was tried in its absence, many years ago, and found guilty. With no chance of appeal. According to the statutes of government, the moment I return, I am to be executed. What do you make of that, Doctor? Take me home, and you take me to my death.

She holds the Doctor's stare. He is quiet and cold:

THE DOCTOR Not my problem.

Silence. Then the Doctor turns, walks out – all the fun evaporated – as Rose follows the Doctor, then Mickey, then Captain Jack. He's carrying the panel – indicates that Margaret should walk ahead, so he can keep an eye on her.

Margaret walks out, head high, proud. Not finished yet.

29 INT. TARDIS NIGHT

THE DOCTOR at the console, checking the new floor-to-ceiling cables. ROSE, MICKEY and MARGARET stand around. Margaret's genuinely impressed.

MARGARET Oh but this ship is impossible! It's superb! How do you get the outside around the inside . . . ?

THE DOCTOR Like I'd give you the secret, yeah.

MARGARET I almost feel better about being defeated. We never stood a chance, this is the technology of the Gods.

THE DOCTOR Don't worship me, I'd make a very bad God. You wouldn't get a day off, for starters.
(calls down)
Jack, how we doing, big fella?

CAPTAIN JACK's under the flooring, attaching wires to the Slitheen 'surfboard', and joining the wires to the console.

CAPTAIN JACK This extrapolator's top of the range, where did you get it?

MARGARET I don't know, some airlock sale.

CAPTAIN JACK Must've been a great big heist, it's stacked with power.

THE DOCTOR But can we use it for fuel?

CAPTAIN JACK It's gonna take a bit of work, it's not compatible. But it should knock off about twelve hours, we'll be ready to go by the morning.

THE DOCTOR Then we're stuck here. Overnight.

MARGARET I'm in no hurry.

ROSE We've got a prisoner. That's weird. Like the police box really is a police box.

MARGARET You're not just police, though. Since you're taking me to my death, that makes *you* my executioners. Each and every one of you.

MICKEY You deserve it.

MARGARET You're very quick to say so. And yet, very quick to soak your hands in my blood. Which makes you better than me, how, exactly …?

Silence, all awkward. Smiling, elegant, Margaret sits in the TARDIS seat.

MARGARET Long night ahead. Let's see who can look me in the eye.

And calm, collected, she fixes her gaze on Mickey. He just stares back, folds arms, macho, bullish. But she keeps looking. And he's not so brave, weakens, looks away.

Margaret looks at Rose. And Rose is full of doubt. Feels guilty. She avoids Margaret, looks to the Doctor instead.

The Doctor – still working away – meets Rose's look, smiles, but weakly. And he avoids Margaret, too.

30 EXT. MILLENNIUM CENTRE SQUARE NIGHT

The glitter of lights in darkness. MICKEY sits alone on the steps, the TARDIS a distance away, windows bright.

ROSE is walking towards him.

ROSE S'freezing out here.

MICKEY Better than in there.

She sits next to him. Quiet:

MICKEY She does deserve it, she's a Slitheen, I don't care. It's just … weird, inside that box.

ROSE Yeah.

Silence.

ROSE I didn't really need my passport.

Meaning, she wanted to see him. Pause, as that sinks in. He smiles, she smiles, a gentle laugh, then both relax.

MICKEY I was thinking, y'know, we could … go for a drink, have a pizza or something. Just you and me.

ROSE That'd be nice.

MICKEY And, I mean, if the TARDIS can't leave till the morning. We could … go to a hotel. Spend the night. If you want to. I've got a bit of money.

ROSE Okay. Yeah.

MICKEY Is that all right?

ROSE Yeah.

MICKEY Cool. There's a couple of bars round here, let's give 'em a go. (indicates the TARDIS)
D'you need to go and tell him …?

ROSE None of his business.

And she takes his hand, both smiling, as they head off.

CUT TO TARDIS SCANNER POV: Rose and Mickey walking away –

31 INT. TARDIS NIGHT

SCANNER FOOTAGE: the end of sc.30, Rose and Mickey. THE DOCTOR watching; quiet smile, interrupted by –

CAPTAIN JACK What's on?

THE DOCTOR Nothing, just ...

He switches it off, fast, guilty of spying, walking away.

As he walks round – with CAPTAIN JACK now sitting on the metal walkway, working on the surfboard, running wires from it to the console – reveal MARGARET. She's now sitting towards the back, off the metal walkway, right down on floor level. Not chained, but prisoner-like in her position. Stay distant on her; a quiet, malevolent presence in the background. Night-time feel, *low-key*:

MARGARET I gather it's not always like this. Having to wait.

Silence, the Doctor busy. A good pause, then:

MARGARET I bet you're always first to leave, Doctor. Never mind the consequences, off you go. You butchered my family and then ran for the stars, am I right? But not this time. At last, you have consequences. How does it feel?

THE DOCTOR I didn't butcher them.

CAPTAIN JACK Don't answer back, that's what she wants.

THE DOCTOR But I didn't. You had an emergency teleport, you didn't zap them to safety, did you?

MARGARET It only carries one. I had to fly without coordinates. I ended up in a skip on the Isle of Dogs.

And the Doctor laughs, a little.

MARGARET It wasn't funny.

THE DOCTOR Sorry.
(pause)
It is a *bit* funny.

And she laughs, gently. Pause, more relaxed:

MARGARET Do I get a last request?

THE DOCTOR Depends what it is.

MARGARET I grew quite fond of my little human life. All those rituals. The brushing of the teeth. And the complicated way they cook things. There's a little restaurant, just round the Bay, it became quite a favourite of mine.

THE DOCTOR Is that what you want, a last meal?

MARGARET Don't I have rights?

CAPTAIN JACK Oh, like she's not gonna try to escape.

MARGARET Except I can never escape the Doctor, so where's the danger? I wonder if you could do it. To sit with a creature you're about to kill, and take supper. How strong is your stomach?

Staring at each other across the distance, a challenge.

THE DOCTOR Strong enough.

MARGARET I wonder. I've seen you fight your enemies. Now dine with them.

THE DOCTOR You won't change my mind.

MARGARET Prove it.

The Doctor's so tempted, fascinated; but he turns away.

THE DOCTOR There's people out there. If you slipped away for just one second, they'd be in danger.

CAPTAIN JACK Except, I've got these.

Holds up, from his satchel, two metal hoops, like bangles.

CAPTAIN JACK They can also be used as handcuffs. You wear one each, if she moves more than ten feet away, she gets zapped with ten thousand volts.

THE DOCTOR Margaret. Can I take you out to dinner? My treat.

MARGARET Dinner in bondage. Works for me.

32 EXT./INT. BAR night

Music linking sc.32–37. Seen from outside, through glass: ROSE and MICKEY, having a drink, having a laugh.

33 EXT. CARDIFF BAY night

Music continues. Long lens, beautiful lights. THE DOCTOR and MARGARET walk along, chatting, smiling. He holds her hand. Because of the handcuffs.

34 INT. TARDIS night

Music continues. Peaceful, calm, tracking round the console, CAPTAIN JACK standing there with the surfboard. He's still wiring it up. He's wearing his workman's utility belt, with sci-fi pliers, working away, happy.

35 EXT. CARDIFF BAY night

Music continues. ROSE and MICKEY wander in search of another bar. They huddle, in the cold, as they walk.

36 EXT./INT. RESTAURANT night

Music continues. Seen from outside, through the glass: A WAITER leads THE DOCTOR and MARGARET to their table.

37 INT. TARDIS NIGHT

Music continues. CAPTAIN JACK makes the final connection. Tiny, delicate white lights blink into life, all the way along the surfboard. It's beautiful. Jack smiling, admiring it.

38 INT. RESTAURANT NIGHT

Nice, intimate place. Big windows, the night outside. THE DOCTOR and MARGARET sitting, a glass of wine, with menus.

MARGARET Here we are, out on a date, and you haven't even asked my proper name.

THE DOCTOR It's not a date. So what's your name, then?

MARGARET Blon. I'm Blon Fel Fotch Passameer-Day Slitheen. That's what it'll say on my death certificate.

THE DOCTOR Nice to meet you, Blon.

MARGARET I'm sure. Look, that's where I was living, as Margaret, nice little flat, over there –

She points, the Doctor turns, looks right behind him. Margaret hinges open the stone on her ring, tips powdered poison into his wine, keeps talking to cover:

MARGARET On the top, next to the one with the light on, two bedrooms, bayside view, I was rather content –

She sits back, normal, as the Doctor turns back round.

MARGARET Don't suppose I'll see it again.

THE DOCTOR Suppose not.

And without a frown, without even needing to check, he picks up her glass, and his, and swaps them round.

MARGARET Thank you.

THE DOCTOR Pleasure.

MARGARET Tell me then, Doctor. What do you know of our species?

THE DOCTOR Only what I've seen.

MARGARET Did you know, for example, that in extreme cases, when her life is in danger, a female Raxacoricofallapatorian can manufacture a poison dart within her own finger –

And she points her finger at him – *ptssh*!

A dart flies out, and the Doctor calmly catches it in his fist, right in front of his face, without even blinking.

THE DOCTOR Yes I did.

MARGARET Just checking. And one more thing. Between you and me.

She looks secretive, beckons. Both lean in, a whisper:

MARGARET As a final resort, the excess poison can be exhaled through the lungs.

And she breathes on him, *haaaaaaaaah*!

He whips out a Gold Spot, gives her open mouth a squirt.

THE DOCTOR That's better.

And they both sit back, Margaret peeved.

THE DOCTOR Now then, what d'you think? Steak looks nice. Steak and chips!

39 EXT. CARDIFF BAY NIGHT

Long lens: ROSE and MICKEY walking along, drifting, close. Looking out, into the dark, musing:

ROSE The Doctor took me to this planet a while back. Much colder than this. They called it Woman Wept, the planet was actually called Woman Wept, cos if you look at it from above, there's this huge continent, all curved round, it looks a bit like a woman, sort of lamenting. And we went to this beach. No buildings, no people, just this beach, like a thousand miles across. And something had happened, something to do with the sun, I don't know, but the sea had frozen. In a split second. Like in the middle of a storm, waves and foam, just frozen, all the way to the horizon. Midnight, and we walked underneath these waves, a hundred feet tall, made of ice.

MICKEY I'm going out with Trisha Delaney.

And it all stays calm, civilised:

ROSE Oh, right. That's nice. Trisha from the shop?

MICKEY Yeah, Rob Delaney's sister.

ROSE She's nice, yeah.
(pause)
She's a bit big.

MICKEY She's lost weight. You've been away.

ROSE Well, good for you. She's nice.

MICKEY So tell us more about that planet.

ROSE Um. That was it, really.

They walk off. Pretending to be fine, but so far apart.

40 INT. RESTAURANT NIGHT

THE DOCTOR and MARGARET, having ordered, no food yet. Margaret genuinely trying to get through, now.

MARGARET Public execution is a slow death. They prepare a thin acetic acid. Lower me into the cauldron. And boil me. The acidity is perfectly gauged, to strip away the skin. Internal organs fall out, into the liquid. I become soup. And still alive. Still screaming.

THE DOCTOR I don't make the law.

MARGARET But you deliver it. Will you stay to watch?

Pause. It's getting through to him, now.

THE DOCTOR What else can I do?

MARGARET The Slitheen family's huge, there's a lot more of us, all scattered, off-world. Take me to them. Take me somewhere safe.

THE DOCTOR Then you'll just start again.

MARGARET I promise I won't.

THE DOCTOR You've been in that skin-suit for so long, you've forgotten. There was once a real Margaret Blaine. But you killed her and stripped her and used her skin. You're pleading for mercy out of a dead woman's lips.

MARGARET Perhaps I have got used to it. A human life, an ordinary life. That's all I'm asking. Give me a chance, Doctor. I can change.

THE DOCTOR I don't believe you.

Pause.

MARGARET There was this girl, just today. Young thing. And something of a danger, she was getting too close. I felt the blood-lust rising, just as the family taught me, I was going to kill her, without a thought. And then ... I stopped. She's alive somewhere, right now, she's walking round this city, because I can change, I did change. I know I can't prove it –

THE DOCTOR I believe you.

MARGARET Then you know I'm capable of better.

Pause. The Doctor sighs, so tired. Not hostile, but sad; completely understanding her.

THE DOCTOR It doesn't mean anything.

MARGARET I spared her life.

THE DOCTOR You let one of them go. But that's nothing new. Every now and then, one little victim is spared. Because she smiles. Cos he's got freckles. Cos they begged. And that's how you live with yourself, that's how you slaughter millions, because once in a while, just on a whim, if the wind's in the right direction ... you happen to be kind.

MARGARET Only a killer would know that.

And he's hurt by that, loses eye contact, thrown.

MARGARET Isn't that right? From what I've seen, your funny little happy-go-lucky life leaves devastation in its wake. Always moving on, cos you dare not look back. Playing with so many lives, you might as well be a God.
(more honest)
And you're right, Doctor, you're absolutely right, sometimes, you let one go.
(desperate)
Let me go.
(silence)
I don't want to die.

On the Doctor: what the hell does he do?

41 EXT. CARDIFF BAY NIGHT

ROSE and MICKEY now a good few feet apart, he's sitting, she's by a railing. Distant, calm, but flat:

MICKEY What d'you want to do now?

ROSE Don't mind.

MICKEY We could ask around. About hotels.

ROSE What would Trisha Delaney say?

MICKEY S'pose.

Good silence, five, six seconds. Still calm. Then:

MICKEY There was a bar down there, with a sort of Spanish name or something, we could try in there. It wasn't too full, we could find a table –

And then, with sudden heat, like teenagers:

ROSE You don't even like Trisha Delaney!

MICKEY Oh is that right? Well what the hell do you know?

ROSE I know you, and I know her, and I know that's never gonna happen, so who do you think you're kidding –

MICKEY At least I know where she is!

ROSE There we are then! This is nothing to do with Trisha Delaney, this is all about me, isn't it?

But suddenly, up a gear, furious –

MICKEY You *left* me! We were nice, we were happy, I did anything for you, and then you give me a kiss and run off with him and you make me feel like nothing, Rose! I was nothing! And now I can't even go out with some stupid girl from the shop, cos you pick up the phone and I get summoned! Is that what I am? On standby? Am I supposed to just sit there waiting for you for the rest of my life? Because I *will*!

He stops himself. Massive silence. Hold and hold.

Then, very quiet:

ROSE I'm sorry.

Silence.

ROSE I am, though.

Silence. She goes and sits by him. But not too close. Both feeling useless and lost.

42 INT. RESTAURANT NIGHT

MARGARET being honest, THE DOCTOR facing her.

MARGARET In the family Slitheen, we had no choice. I was made to carry out my first kill at thirteen. If I'd refused, my father would have fed me to the Venom Grubs. If I'm a killer, it's because I was born to kill, it's all I know.
(pause)
Doctor?
(pause)
Are you even listening to me?

THE DOCTOR ... Can you hear that?

MARGARET I'm begging for my life!

THE DOCTOR No, listen, shush ...

MARGARET I can't hear anything.

But there it is: a faint rumble.

Then a *ting-ting-ting*, the Doctor looks down. Their two wine glasses are close, almost touching; now *ting-ting-ting*ing against each other. The table beginning to shake –

43 EXT. CARDIFF BAY NIGHT

MICKEY facing ROSE, close, intimate.

MICKEY I'm not gonna ask you to leave him, cos I know that's not fair. But all I need is something, Rose. Some sort of promise, yeah? That when you do come back ... you're coming back for me.

ROSE ... Is that thunder?

MICKEY Does it matter?

ROSE That's not thunder.

As the mysterious rumble grows ...

44 INT. RESTAURANT NIGHT

Smash, glasses hitting the floor – CAMERA SHAKE, the restaurant shuddering, just a little. DINERS and STAFF looking round, alarmed. Bottles fall from behind the bar, a heavy crash – THE DOCTOR and MARGARET alarmed –

MARGARET What is it? What's happening?

FOREGROUND: SHEET OF GLASS shatters, as though the restaurant windows are caving in –

45 EXT. CARDIFF BAY NIGHT

CAMERA SHAKE, CU MICKEY looking around, astonished – the whole area beginning to shudder –

The neon sign outside a bar swings, falls – PRACTICAL FX, an explosion of sparks from the sign.

PEOPLE begin to run from the bars – screams –

46 EXT. CARDIFF BAY NIGHT

CAMERA SHAKE, screams and crashes all around, PEOPLE running foreground, background –

And through this, THE DOCTOR and MARGARET, running, though the Doctor's naturally faster, and she has to cry out –

MARGARET The handcuffs!

He has to hold her wrist, pulls off the bangle-handcuff. But then he grabs her wrist properly –

THE DOCTOR Don't think you're running off –

MARGARET I'm sticking with you!

As they run together –

MARGARET Some date this turned out to be!

47 OMITTED

48 EXT. CARDIFF BAY NIGHT

CAMERA SHAKE, screams, crashes, etc. THE DOCTOR and MARGARET run through panicking PEOPLE. An entire lamppost falls alongside them, glass shatters –

49 EXT. CARDIFF BAY NIGHT

ROSE is already running away, in the direction of the TARDIS. (ADR line over this? 'I've got to go!', maybe.) But MICKEY just stands there, calling after her:

MICKEY Go on, then, run! Cos it's him again, isn't it? It's the Doctor, it's always the Doctor, it's always gonna be the Doctor! And it's never *me*!

And with chaos all around, MICKEY just watches her go.

50 EXT. MILLENNIUM CENTRE SQUARE NIGHT

THE DOCTOR and MARGARET run round from the bayside, to see the square, and the cause of the trouble – the TARDIS. It is revolving! PRACTICAL FX: turning on the spot [if possible]. Windows blazing white. FX SHOT: a huge bolt of lightning rips out of the TARDIS roof-light, into the sky – magnificent, unearthly lightning. And the Doctor is horrified:

THE DOCTOR It's the rift. The rift is opening!

51 INT. TARDIS NIGHT

CAPTAIN JACK'S panicking. PRACTICAL LIGHTS throughout the ship rising, falling, flashing, the whole room shuddering – and the cause of the problem is the surfboard, its lights now blinking in a frantic pattern, Jack ripping out the wires connecting it to the console. PRACTICAL FX, explosions from the console –

52 EXT. MILLENNIUM CENTRE SQUARE NIGHT

WILD CAMERA SHAKE now, THE DOCTOR and MARGARET hand in hand, running across the square. The Doctor reaches the revolving TARDIS – hangs on tight, stopping it spinning, as he digs out his key –

53 INT. TARDIS NIGHT

CAPTAIN JACK thrown back, another PRACTICAL FX explosion. The door's thrown open, THE DOCTOR and MARGARET burst in, the Doctor runs to the console –

THE DOCTOR What the hell are you doing?

CAPTAIN JACK It just went crazy!

THE DOCTOR It's the rift! Time and space are ripping apart, the whole city's gonna disappear!

54 EXT. MILLENNIUM CENTRE SQUARE NIGHT

CAMERA SHAKE, ROSE running, round from the bayside, to see the TARDIS, still revolving. Another FX BOLT OF LIGHTNING, arcing up out of the TARDIS. She looks round – FX RIFT: a distortion in space, like an earthquake fault in the air itself, flexing along the entire square –

55 EXT. CARDIFF AT NIGHT

Aerial view of the city: FX SHOT, the convulsion of the RIFT, right across the landscape, with an awful, whip-crack, rupturing noise –

56 INT. TARDIS NIGHT

CAMERA SHAKE, lights still dipping and flaring: THE DOCTOR and CAPTAIN JACK at the console, slamming levers, frantic –

CAPTAIN JACK It's that extrapolator thing! I've disconnected it but it's still feeding off the engine, it's using the TARDIS, I can't stop it –

THE DOCTOR Never mind Cardiff, it's gonna rip open the planet –

MARGARET is at the top of the door-walkway as ROSE bursts in through the door, runs up, yells out to the Doctor –

ROSE What is it, what's happening?

MARGARET Oh, just little me.

And with her left hand, in one sharp *rrrrip!*, Margaret pulls off the right arm of her suit – both suits, fabric and skin – revealing her full SLITHEEN CLAW. And she grabs hold of Rose, round the neck!

MARGARET One wrong move and she snaps like a promise.

CAMERA SHAKE settles, now – though the danger, the pressure, maintains a constant rumble – as Margaret walks forward, with Rose, onto the walkway, facing the Doctor and Captain Jack, on the opposite side of the console.

THE DOCTOR I might have known.

MARGARET I've had you bleating all night, poor baby, now shut it. You! Fly boy! Put the extrapolator at my feet.
(tightens claw)
Do it!

Jack looks to the Doctor, who nods, grim.

Jack grabs the surfboard, darts forward, puts it at Margaret's feet, darts back to join the Doctor.

MARGARET Thank you. Just as I planned.

She stands on the surfboard, still holding Rose.

THE DOCTOR You knew this would happen.

ROSE But I thought you needed to blow up the nuclear power station ...?

MARGARET Failing that, if I were to be arrested, then anyone capable of tracking me down would have considerable technology of their own. Therefore, they would be captivated by the extrapolator. Especially a magpie mind like yours, Doctor. So the extraplolator was programmed to go to Plan B. To lock onto the nearest alien power source, and open the rift. And what a power source it found! I'm back on schedule. Thanks to you!

CAPTAIN JACK The rift is gonna convulse, you'll destroy the whole planet.

MARGARET And you with it!
(stands on the board)
While I ride this board over the crest of the inferno, all the way to freedom! Stand back, boys! Surf's up!

57 EXT. MILLENNIUM CENTRE SQUARE NIGHT

FX SHOT: a wild burst of lightning from the TARDIS light –

58 INT. TARDIS NIGHT

CHUNK! A whole panel of the TARDIS console, nearest to MARGARET and ROSE (roughly, facing the door), lifts up with a sudden thump. A hole in the console; underneath, massive energy, solid white PRACTICAL LIGHT, blazing out.

And THE DOCTOR is utterly calm.

THE DOCTOR Of course, opening the rift means you're gonna pull this ship apart.

MARGARET So sue me!

THE DOCTOR It's not just any old power source. It's the TARDIS. My TARDIS. The best ship in the universe.

MARGARET It'll make wonderful scrap.

ROSE What's that light?

The white light is burning bright, glowing, flaring. The shuddering and the dipping lights continue, but seem to be irrelevant now; the light spreads a powerful calm.

THE DOCTOR The heart of the TARDIS. This ship is alive. You've opened its soul.

MARGARET stares into the light.

MARGARET ... It's ... so bright ...

THE DOCTOR Look at it, Margaret.

MARGARET ... Beautiful ...

THE DOCTOR Look inside. Blon Fel Fotch! Look at the light!

Rose looks away. But Margaret is transfixed. Light reflects on her face, white, shining, glowing ... PRACTICAL LIGHT streams out of the console ... Margaret bathes in it. Smiles.

Her claw relaxes around Rose ... and CAPTAIN JACK leaps forward, shields his eyes, pulls Rose aside. But Margaret is just smiling. Heavenly light. Blissful. CU: she looks at the Doctor. Quiet:

MARGARET Thank you.

CU Margaret, glowing white, filling frame, white-out – and when it fades, she is gone. Her Margaret-suit flops to the ground, empty.

A second, as the Doctor, Rose, Captain Jack just stare. Then, it's as if the mayhem floods back in – the calm gone, the CAMERA SHAKE still rumbling, lights dipping, engines stressed and screaming –

THE DOCTOR Don't look – stay there, close your eyes, don't look at the light –

He runs, slams down levers. The gap in the console-panel closes, shutting off the white light – gone.

THE DOCTOR Now shut down! Jack, come on, shut it all down!

Captain Jack runs forward – slams down levers –

THE DOCTOR Rose! That panel, shut it down, all the switches, turn to the left –

And Rose runs forward, so the three of them are helping to close down the disaster. A great team, working well.

The shaking lessens. The lights begin to stabilise. The roar of the engines begins to fail and fall ...

59 EXT. MILLENNIUM CENTRE SQUARE NIGHT

And [if possible] the revolve of the TARDIS slows, stops. All back to normal.

60 INT. TARDIS NIGHT

... And peace is restored. Calm, still, lights normal. THE DOCTOR, ROSE and CAPTAIN JACK stand back from their respective sides of the console, against the handrails.

THE DOCTOR Nicely done. Thank you, all.

ROSE But what happened to Margaret?

CAPTAIN JACK Must've got burnt up. Carried out her own death sentence.

THE DOCTOR No, I don't think she's dead.

ROSE Then where's she gone?

THE DOCTOR She looked into the heart of the TARDIS. Even I don't know how strong that is. And the ship's telepathic – like I told you, Rose, it gets inside your head, translates alien languages for you. Maybe the raw energy can translate all sorts of thoughts.

And he's wandered round to the heap of the Margaret/Slitheen suit. He squats down, rummages in the rubber and clothing ... and pulls out an egg. A grey, leathery, big-enough-to-fit-in-an-open-palm egg.

THE DOCTOR Here she is.

ROSE She's an egg?

THE DOCTOR Regressed to her childhood.

CAPTAIN JACK She's an egg?

THE DOCTOR She can start again. Live her life from scratch. If we take her back home, give her to a different family, tell 'em to bring her up properly ... she might be all right.

CAPTAIN JACK Or she might be worse.

THE DOCTOR That's her choice.

ROSE She's an egg.

THE DOCTOR She's an egg.

ROSE Oh my God, Mickey –

And she runs, out of the door –

61 EXT. MILLENNIUM CENTRE SQUARE NIGHT

ROSE runs out, runs for the bayside –

62 EXT. STREET NEAR BAY NIGHT

A POLICE CAR and an AMBULANCE hurtle along, lights flashing, with more sirens in the air – the city repairing itself. They scorch past MICKEY, who's walking away. As the vehicles pass, he stops, looks round, in their direction; looking back towards the trouble, where Rose is, where the Doctor is.

Then Mickey turns his back on it. He walks away, off, alone, into the night.

63 EXT. CARDIFF BAY NIGHT

All around, PEOPLE recovering, sifting through broken glass, helping each other. Sirens, distant alarms. But ROSE is just walking to a halt. Stands there, looking round, but knowing he's gone.

Then she turns, and walks slowly back towards the TARDIS.

64 INT. TARDIS NIGHT

ROSE walks back into the TARDIS, quiet. Closes the door, but stays by it, keeping distant from the others. THE DOCTOR's at the console, CAPTAIN JACK on the other side. The Doctor looks at Rose, knows something's wrong.

THE DOCTOR We're all powered up, we can leave. Opening the rift filled us up with energy, we can go. If that's all right.

ROSE Yeah, fine.

THE DOCTOR How's Mickey?

ROSE He's okay. He's gone.

THE DOCTOR D'you want to go and find him? We can wait.

ROSE No need. He deserves better.

Pause.

THE DOCTOR Off we go then.
(as Margaret said)
Always moving on.

CAPTAIN JACK Next stop, Raxacoricofallapatorius. And you don't often get to say that.

THE DOCTOR We'll just stop off and pop her into the hatchery. Margaret the Slitheen can live her life all over again. A second chance.

CU Rose: a sad smile.

ROSE That'd be nice.

65 EXT. MILLENNIUM CENTRE SQUARE NIGHT

Mighty old engines engines rise and fall and roar, and the TARDIS fades away.

Episodes 12 & 13

Bad Wolf and The Parting of the Ways

By Russell T Davies

There are some things that have never been seen in *Doctor Who*. The show's history is so diverse and creative, involving comics and novels and audio adventures, as well as the million stories which viewers make up in their heads, that there are certain things you'd swear had been televised. But no, they didn't happen. Until I got the chance to write this.

A Dalek in the TARDIS. The TARDIS on board a Dalek ship. A Dalek Fleet. War between the Daleks and Earth. None of these had been shown properly before. And my God, I could've spent five billion quid showing the whole thing, but strangely, they didn't want to sell off the entire BBC in order to make this two-parter. I still find that odd.

But I love this show because its ambition should always exceed its reach. And the scale of events in this story is really a tribute to the beginnings of *Doctor Who*, way back in the black-and-white sixties. They were fearless, then. They'd create a Dalek invasion of Earth in the corner of a BBC cupboard, and make us believe it. Massive Dalek Empires existed, invisible on screen, but in surround-sound 3-D Technicolor inside my head. They let us imagine it; they made us imaginative. And for all the wonderful FX, I hope these scripts have something of the same. When Australasia is bombed out of existence, it's represented by a simple graphic and Lynda's horror. Creating an epic event and then placing it off-stage isn't a saving, it's a dare: imagine it!

But never mind the fanboy stuff. My real job was to give Christopher Eccleston's magnificent Doctor the best possible ending; to make him Rose's saviour. And he's encircled by the best kind of stories, those of ordinary people rising up to extraordinary deeds. In some ways, the Doctor, Rose and Captain Jack have no choice in their actions; free rein over time and space gives them a certain responsibility. But that's not true of the supporting characters, and that's what this adventure showcases. A handful of humans face half a million Daleks. Mickey Smith never gives up, even when unloved. Jackie Tyler is finally selfless, in memory of poor Pete. Lynda Moss, who's even been ignored by Big Brother, dies a brave, lonely death. And little, tiny people who don't even have names – the Controller, the Programmers, the Floor Manager – sacrifice themselves to buy the Doctor more time. Surrounded by us, inspired by us, the Doctor becomes like us. The Time Lord has never been more human than when he gives his life for the woman he loves.

There are some sniffy people in the TV industry who have asked, archly, why I'm now writing genre, instead of drama. Obviously, they've never watched a single episode of *Doctor Who*. It's the best drama in the world.

Russell T Davies

1 INT. CUPBOARD DAY

A small, plain, dark cupboard, barely big enough for one man.
Someone stirs, awakes, on the floor, groggy.

It's THE DOCTOR. He's got no idea where he is.

THE DOCTOR ... What's happening, what's ...?

He shakes off the dizziness. Then, sudden panic, realising he's trapped,
all elbows and knees against the walls. But there's a door. With a handle.
He opens it ...

2 INT. THE HOUSE DAY

THE DOCTOR stumbles out – but still woozy, he falls to the floor. TIGHT on
him, don't reveal surroundings. A woman, LYNDA, runs up – she's edge of
frame, stay on the Doctor.

LYNDA Oh my God! I don't believe it, why did they put you in there?
They never said you were coming!

THE DOCTOR But what happened ...? I was ...

He tries to get up, stumbles.

LYNDA Careful now, mind yourself, that's the transmat, it scrambles
your head, oh, I was sick for days! What's your name then,
sweetheart?

THE DOCTOR I'm the Doctor. I think. I was ... I don't know! What
happened ...?

LYNDA You got chosen.

THE DOCTOR Chosen for what ...?

LYNDA You're a housemate! You're in the house! Isn't that brilliant?
You're playing the game!

And the Doctor gives his head a good shake, blinks, looks. REVEAL: the
House. An open room with living area and kitchen. One exit door, sealed tight.
Big floor-to-ceiling windows along one wall, but with only black outside.
Dining table and chairs. A stylish, bright-block-of-colour sofa. Small cameras
mounted high up in the corners. And big mirror panels, all around. And one
entire wall is the LOGO, a huge, familiar eye.

During this, chat continues: STROOD – 28, male, sharp, gay – and another
woman, CROSBIE – 35, black, tough, shaved head – are on the sofa. LYNDA
is 30, northern, enthusiastic, gobby-but-nice. It's the late stages of the game,
their clothes reduced to tee-shirts, tracksuits, dressing gowns.

STROOD That's not fair, we've got an eviction in five minutes! I've
been here for all nine weeks, I've followed the rules, I haven't had
a single warning, then he comes swanning in!

CROSBIE If they keep changing the rules, I'm gonna protest, you
watch me, I'm gonna paint the walls!

LYNDA Oh stop your moaning, try to be nice. It's not his fault, is it?

And then the Doctor looks up, hearing from above, BIG BROTHER:
Would the Doctor come to the Diary Room? He looks round. Behind him,
the familiar door, with the old illuminated eye-shaped control on the side.

He runs over, shoves through the door –

3 INT. DIARY ROOM DAY

As always, CAMERA POV: small room, curvy chair. THE DOCTOR runs in,
to sit; looks to CAMERA.

BIG BROTHER You are live on Channel Forty-four Thousand.
Please do not swear.

THE DOCTOR ... You have *got* to be kidding.

CUT TO OPENING TITLES.

4 INT. STUDIO DAY

Darkness all around, a big, black, unlit space. ROSE is huddled on the floor,
waking, confused. A man, RODRICK – black, 25 – crouches beside her; stay
tight on Rose.

ROSE Owww ... What happened ...?

RODRICK It's all right, it's the transmat, it does your head in, you get
a bit of amnesia, what's your name?

ROSE Rose, but ... where's the Doctor ...?

RODRICK Just remember: do what the Android says. Don't provoke it.
The Android's word is law.

ROSE What d'you mean, android? Like a robot?

FLOOR MANAGER OOV Positions, everyone, thank you!

RODRICK Come on, hurry up ...

He helps Rose to her feet, and they walk across the space.

ROSE But I was travelling, with the Doctor, and a man called Captain
Jack, the Doctor wouldn't just leave me – what's all this ...?

Because they're entering a lit area. Six podiums, in a semi-circle; at the other,
four podiums, FOUR CONTESTANTS, all nervous (all, including Rodrick, wear
drab, grey clothes – society's in a recession). They face a central podium.

Centre, two TECHNICIANS work on a slumped FIGURE, attaching cables
to its body. The FLOOR MANAGER – 30, female, with clipboard and comms
headset – is with them.

FLOOR MANAGER That's enough chat, positions, final call. And good luck.

ROSE But I'm not supposed to be here –

RODRICK It says Rose on the podium, go on –

One of the podiums does say ROSE. Rose automatically goes there, Rodrick next to her. (Podiums left to right: AGORAX, FITCH, ROSE, RODRICK, COLLEEN, BROFF.) Rose's head clearing ...

ROSE Hold on, I must be going mad. It can't be. This looks like ...

FLOOR MANAGER Android activated!

A hiss, hum of power! The technicians stand back, disappear into darkness, as the FIGURE lifts its head, comes alive. It is a female robot quizmaster. Dressed in black, her black coat going all the way to the floor; like its body is a metal cone. The head is round, chrome, detailed, with thin wire glasses-frames welded over the optic circuits. The top of its head is a smooth, gleaming red.

ROSE Oh my God, the android. The Anne Droid.

ANNE DROID Welcome. To *The Weakest Link*!

5 INT. *WHAT NOT TO WEAR* STUDIO DAY

CAPTAIN JACK wakes. Blinks. Woozy. His POV: two blurry faces looking down at him.

TRIN-E Here we go again. We've got our work cut out with this one.

ZU-ZANA I don't know, he's sort of handsome. That's a good lantern jaw.

TRIN-E Lantern jaws are so last year.

And his focus resolves: two more DROIDS. One tall and thin, the other shorter. Chrome heads, gleaming. Again, elegant clothes widen out into a cone, so they have no legs; they glide on a base.

This is the MEDICAL ROOM from ep.7 – the same sterile space, Captain Jack in the chair (he's in Levis and tee-shirt). Around the room, mirrors, racks of clothes. No door.

CAPTAIN JACK Sorry, but ... nice to meet you, ladies ... Where am I exactly?

ZU-ZANA Oh, that's just the transmat, it always causes memory loss.

TRIN-E Never mind the past, you can shake it off like an old Afghan coat! We're giving you a brand-new image.

CAPTAIN JACK Yeah, but hold on, I was with the Doct – why, is there something wrong with what I'm wearing?

ZU-ZANA It's all very twentieth century, where did you get that denim?

CAPTAIN JACK Little place in Cardiff, it was called ... 'The Top Shop'.

ZU-ZANA Oh, design classic!

They glide to the far side of the room, to a free-standing laser device (bit like Van Statten's in ep.6), pointed at Jack.

TRIN-E But we're going to find you some new colours, maybe get rid of that Oklahoma farmboy thing.

ZU-ZANA Just stand still, and let the Defabricator work its magic.

CAPTAIN JACK What's the Defabricator?

The tip of the laser device glows [PRACTICAL, NO BEAM]. CUT TO Captain Jack, naked. And not remotely bothered.

CAPTAIN JACK Okay. Defabricator. Does exactly what it says on the tin. Am I naked in front of millions of viewers?

TRIN-E AND ZU-ZANA Absolutely!

CAPTAIN JACK Ladies. Your viewing figures just went up.

6 INT. THE HOUSE DAY

THE DOCTOR whirrs the sonic screwdriver around the closed door. LYNDA is with him. STROOD and CROSBIE stay on the settee.

THE DOCTOR Can't open it.

LYNDA It's got a deadlock seal, ever since *Big Brother* Five Hundred and Four when they all walked out, you must remember that.

He goes to one of the mirrors, whirrs at the edges.

THE DOCTOR What about this?

LYNDA That's exoglass, you'd need a nuclear bomb to get through.

THE DOCTOR Don't tempt me.

He moves on, checking the walls. Lynda gets close, nervous:

LYNDA I know you're not supposed to talk about the outside world, but you must've been watching. Do people like me? Lynda, Lynda with a Y, not Linda with an I – she got forcibly evicted cos she damaged one of the cameras. Am I popular?

THE DOCTOR Can't remember.

LYNDA Oh, but does that mean I'm nothing? Some people get this far just cos they're insignificant, doesn't anybody notice me?

He looks at her properly, now; feels sorry for her.

THE DOCTOR No, you're nice, you're … sweet. Everyone thinks you're sweet.

LYNDA Is that right, is that what I am? No one's ever told me that before, am I sweet? Really?

THE DOCTOR Yeah. Dead sweet.

LYNDA (genuinely moved)
Thank you.

The Doctor gets back to work, now at the black windows – it's not night outside, it's literally solid black.

THE DOCTOR It's just a wall. Isn't there supposed to be a garden out there?

LYNDA Don't be daft, no one's got a garden any more! Who's got gardens? Don't tell me you've got a garden!

THE DOCTOR No, I've just got the TARDIS –

The word's a trigger, like a punch in the stomach – he's winded, slides to the floor, staring ahead –

THE DOCTOR I remember!

LYNDA That's the amnesia! So what happened, where did they get you ...?

THE DOCTOR In the TARDIS. We were laughing ...

7 INT. TARDIS DAY

In flight, ROSE and CAPTAIN JACK laughing, having a good time. CAMERA is the Doctor's POV. No sound, only V/O:

THE DOCTOR V/O We left Raxacoricofallapatorius. Then we went to ... Kyoto, that's right, Japan, in 1336, and we only just escaped, we were together, we were laughing, and then ...

CU Rose. The picture starts to bleach [PRACTICAL LIGHT].

THE DOCTOR V/O ... There was a light, this white light, coming through the walls ...

Rose looks round, at the walls, alarmed, looks back. She reaches out, scared, to camera, to the Doctor – but it's as though she's stuck, can't reach him. Nightmare image, Rose reaching out, being pulled away. Picture flares to pure, full-frame white, and –

MIX TO:

8 INT. THE HOUSE DAY

THE DOCTOR staring into space, LYNDA beside him.

THE DOCTOR ... And then ... I woke up here.

LYNDA That was the transmat beam. That's how they pick housemates.

THE DOCTOR (grim smile)
Ohh, Lynda with a Y. Sweet little Lynda. It's worse than that.

Strong again, he stands. Looks at the mirror. REVERSE, from other side of the mirror, with that faint reflection of a camera lens. He stares at CAMERA.

THE DOCTOR I'm not just some passing traveller. No stupid little transmat can get inside my ship. That beam was fifteen million times more powerful. Which means, this isn't just a game. Something else is going on.
(even closer to CAM)
Well here's the latest update from the *Big Brother* House. I'm getting out. I'm gonna find my friends. And then! I'm gonna find *you*.

9 INT. FLOOR 500 DAY

SHOT TIGHT, not revealing location, just the hum of machinery; an air of concentration, quiet voices counting out codes and numbers. The Doctor's CU from sc.8, to CAMERA, is on a desktop screen. Watching the screen – a PROGRAMMER, a young man in short-sleeved shirt and tie and comms headset. The Doctor's worried him.

He stands – stay tight on him as he crosses, just the impression of OTHERS, at screens, hard at work – goes to the desk of a FEMALE PROGRAMMER, leans in, mutters –

MALE PROGRAMMER Need a word –

FEMALE PROGRAMMER Hold on, let me finish this –
(on headset mike)
Counting from 20, 19, 18 –

CUT TO her screen: W/S, *THE WEAKEST LINK* STUDIO.

10 INT. STUDIO DAY

ROSE at her podium, next to RODRICK. Other CONTESTANTS in position, the FLOOR MANAGER calling out:

FLOOR MANAGER – 17, 16, 15 – thank you, people, transmitting in . . . 12, 11, 10 –

Counting down 9, 8, 7 in b/g. On Rose, hushed, to Rodrick:

ROSE But I need to find the Doctor –

RODRICK Just shut up and play the game.

ROSE All right then. What the hell, I'm gonna play to win!

FLOOR MANAGER Aaaand, cue –

ANNE DROID Let's play, *The Weakest Link*!
(music sting)
Start the clock!
(music sting)

The game is seen as: TX FORMAT, with clock and bank graphics on-screen; INTERCUT with OFF-AIR FOOTAGE, on Rose – bemused but loving it. The other contestants are tense, scared.

ANNE DROID Agorax, the name of which basic foodstuff is an anagram of the word 'beard'?

AGORAX Bread.

ANNE DROID Correct – Fitch, in the Pan Taffic Calendar, which month comes after Hoob?

FITCH Is it . . . Clavadoe?

ANNE DROID No, Pandoff – Rose, in maths, what is 258 minus 158?

ROSE Um, one hundred!

ANNE DROID Correct – Rodrick –

RODRICK Bank!

ANNE DROID Which letter of the alphabet appears in the word dangle but not in the word gland?

RODRICK E.

ANNE DROID Correct – Colleen, in social security, what D is the name of the payment given to Martian Drones?

COLLEEN Default.

ANNE DROID Correct – Broff, the Great Cobalt Pyramid is built on the remains of which famous Old Earth Institute?

BROFF Touchdown.

ANNE DROID No, Torchwood – Agorax, in language, all five examples of which type of letter appear in the word facetious?

AGORAX Vowels.

ANNE DROID Correct – Fitch, in biology, which blood cells contain iron, red or white?

FITCH Um, white.

ANNE DROID No, red – Rose, in the holovid series 'Jupiter Rising', the Grexnik is married to whom?

ROSE (laughing)
How should I know?

ANNE DROID No, the correct answer is Lord Drayvole – / Rodrick, in maths, what is nine squared?

RODRICK Eighty-one.

ANNE DROID Correct – Colleen, who is the current God Emperor of Brazilia?

From / stay on Rose. Laughing at the absurdity of it.

11 INT. FLOOR 500 DAY

SHOT TIGHT, both PROGRAMMERS watching intently. Horrified.

FEMALE PROGRAMMER Why's she laughing . . . ? Oh my God, I don't think she knows.

MALE PROGRAMMER And I've got a housemate who appeared out of nowhere. I told you. It's like the game is running itself.

12 INT. *WHAT NOT TO WEAR* STUDIO DAY

CAPTAIN JACK admires himself in the full-length mirror, with the TRIN-E and ZU-ZANA DROIDS. He's in black leather trousers, big buckled belt, big buckled boots, white vest.

TRIN-E It's the buccaneer look. Little dash of pirate, and just a tweak of President Schwarzenegger – we're sort of embracing the hokum.

CAPTAIN JACK Not sure about the vest, think a bit of colour might lift it?

ZU-ZANA Absolutely not, never wear black with colour! It makes the colour look cheap and the black look boring. Now, let's talk jackets –

CAPTAIN JACK I kinda like the first one.

ZU-ZANA No, that's a bit too much Hell's Angel, I think I like the shorter one. Look! Waist length, nice and slimming, shows off the bum.

CAPTAIN JACK Works for me.

TRIN-E That's quite an asset you've got there, the viewers will love it.

CAPTAIN JACK If you don't mind me asking, who's watching this stuff? I mean the programme, not my assets. Who's the audience?

TRIN-E Everyone on Earth.

CAPTAIN JACK What, the whole planet?

TRIN-E Beaming direct into every household. The latest fashion is for vid-sockets, so we're transmitted right into the eyeball.

ZU-ZANA We're doing ever so well, we're number three in the ratings.

TRIN-E Just behind *Who Wants to Be a Trillionnaire*, and *Changing Moons*.

CAPTAIN JACK Thing is, I wasn't on my own, I was travelling with two other people, I should kind of hook up with them, where would they be?

ZU-ZANA They must be on board, in different games.

CAPTAIN JACK On board? Are we in orbit?

ZU-ZANA Of course we are, this is the Game Station.

CAPTAIN JACK And what exactly is the Game Station?

TRIN-E Men! All they want to do is talk hardware. Back to the clothes!

Trin-E glides away – go with her; Jack stays in b/g with Zu-Zana. She's holding up a number of belts.

ZU-ZANA Now, we need some sort of belt, something to punctuate the torso and draw attention to the waistline, what d'you think of this one?

CAPTAIN JACK Yeah, not bad. If it's gonna draw the eye to my waistline, let's do it. I was thinking maybe something in mookskin, would that work?

Trin-E foreground. She's unscrewing her right arm. (Jack busy with jackets, replies without looking around.)

TRIN-E Once we've got an outfit, we can look at the face. Ever thought about cosmetic surgery?

CAPTAIN JACK I've considered it, yeah. Bit of a lift around the eyes, maybe tighten the jaw, what do you think?

TRIN-E Oh let's have a bit more ambition!

Trin-E clicks on a new forearm, lifts it up, admires it. Her arm now ends in a gleaming chrome chainsaw.

TRIN-E Let's do something ... cutting edge.

13 INT. STUDIO DAY

Again, TX FOOTAGE INTERCUT with OFF-AIR FOOTAGE.

Now at the stage after voting, ROSE holding up her oval disc (it's the daytime version). She's handwritten 'Fitch' in black felt pen. (Other discs: 2 Fitch, 2 Broff, 1 Rose.) Rose is enjoying sparring with the ANNE DROID. RODRICK and OTHERS grim, looking at Rose like she's insane.

ANNE DROID So, tell me Rose, what do you do?

ROSE Um, well, I just travel about, bit of a tourist, I suppose.

ANNE DROID Is that another way of saying unemployed?

ROSE No!

ANNE DROID Have you got a job?

ROSE Well, not really, no –

ANNE DROID Then you're unemployed. And yet you've still got enough money to buy peroxide. Why Fitch?

ROSE Well, I think she just got a few questions wrong, that's all.

ANNE DROID And you'd know all about that.

ROSE Yeah, but I can't vote for myself, so ... it had to be Fitch.

Only now does Rose realise that FITCH – 40, female – is terrified. Crying. Rose disturbed, mutters to Fitch:

ROSE Sorry, that's the game, that's how it works, I had to nominate someone.

Fitch ignores her, begs the Anne Droid:

FITCH Let me try again, it was the lights and everything, I couldn't think –

ANNE DROID In fact, with three answers wrong, Broff was the weakest link in that round. But it's votes that count!

FITCH I'm sorry oh please oh God help me –

ANNE DROID Fitch, you are the weakest link. Goodbye!

The Anne Droid's jaw hinges down, like Marley's ghost ... the mouth is a gun. FX SHOT: it FIRES – a huge, thick, fast bolt of white light, fringed with burning red –

FX SHOT, the bolt *SLAMS* into Fitch, massive force – *FATOOM*!

The light clears. Fitch is gone. Nothing but a thin curl of dust, a wisp of smoke.

FLOOR MANAGER Aaaand, we've gone to adverts, coming back in three minutes.

CUT TO Rose. Staggered. To Rodrick:

ROSE But ... what was that, what happened?

RODRICK She was the weakest link, she gets disintegrated. Blasted into atoms.

ROSE But I voted for her! Oh my God, this is sick – all of you, you're just sick, I'm not playing this –

But as she goes to step forward –

BROFF I'm not playing, I can't do it, let me out, please, oh God, let me out of here –

BROFF – 18, male, terrified – runs across the studio, but the Anne Droid swivels round – *whoosh!* – vicious speed –

ANNE DROID You are the weakest link, goodbye!

Jaw hinges down – FX SHOT: bolt shoots from the Anne Droid to Broff – *FATOOM*!

And he's gone. Dust and smoke.

CUT TO Rose. Shaken, terrified. Rodrick mutters:

RODRICK Don't try to escape. It's play or die.

14 INT. THE HOUSE DAY

THE DOCTOR whirring away at the wall, while LYNDA, STROOD, CROSBIE all sit on the settee – nervous, looking up.

LYNDA Doctor, they said, all housemates gather on the sofa, you've got to!

THE DOCTOR I'm busy getting out, thanks.

LYNDA If you don't obey, then all the housemates get punished.

He accepts that, grudgingly joining them.

THE DOCTOR Maybe I'll get voted out, then.

STROOD How stupid are you? You've only just joined, you're not eligible.

LYNDA And don't try anything clever, or we all get it in the neck.

Then, from above:

BIG BROTHER Crosbie, Lynda and Strood, you have all been nominated for eviction. And the eighth person to leave the *Big Brother* House is – (long pause . . .) Crosbie!

Strood and Lynda go to her, hug her. The Doctor bemused.

LYNDA Oh I'm sorry I'm sorry I'm sorry –

STROOD Oh it should've been me, that's not fair, oh Crosbie love . . .

[Speeches run simultaneously.]

BIG BROTHER Crosbie, you have ten seconds to make your farewells and leave the *Big Brother* House, ten ... nine ... eight ... seven ... six ... five ... four ... three ... two ... one ... Crosbie, you have been evicted, please leave the *Big Brother* House. / Please leave the *Big Brother* House.

LYNDA I won't forget you!

CROSBIE Sorry I stole your soap.

LYNDA I don't mind, honestly!

STROOD And thanks for all the food, you were a smashing cook, bless you –

CROSBIE Bye then – bye Lynda –

At / the door has opened; a small, plain, pure white corridor beyond, reaching a dead end. Crosbie upset as she walks through; Lynda and Strood emotional as they go to the door with her – 'bye', kisses, etc. Then the door closes and she's gone. Lynda's bereft.

LYNDA I can't believe it. Poor old Crosbie.

THE DOCTOR It's only a gameshow! She'll make a fortune outside, sell her story, release a record, fitness video, all of that, she'll be laughing.

LYNDA What d'you mean, outside?

STROOD Here we go –

The plasma screen on the wall has come on, showing Crosbie in the white corridor. She's crying, just standing there.

THE DOCTOR Why don't they let her out, what are they waiting for?

LYNDA Stop it, it's not funny.

A hum of power, building, rising ... Crosbie looks up, in fear ... Strood and Lynda in anguish – staring – the Doctor realising ...

And FX SHOT: the bolt of white light, fringed with red, blasts down from the roof, slams into Crosbie – *FATOOM!*

Light clears, and she is gone. Dust and smoke.

THE DOCTOR ... What was that ...?

STROOD Disintegrator beam.

LYNDA She's been evicted. From life.

15 INT. FLOOR 500 DAY

The MALE and FEMALE PROGRAMMER in secret conference, hushed:

MALE PROGRAMMER No one programmed the transmat, no one selected the new contestants. It's exactly like those stories.

FEMALE PROGRAMMER Oh don't start that again. I think you need to take a session off.

MALE PROGRAMMER I would, if you'd take it with me.

FEMALE PROGRAMMER And don't start that again either.

Beat; a smile between them. Then serious again:

MALE PROGRAMMER But the rumours go back decades. Saying that something's been hidden up here. Underneath the transmissions.

FEMALE PROGRAMMER Like what, exactly?

MALE PROGRAMMER That's where the story ends. No one knows.

FEMALE PROGRAMMER But the Controller would know. She watches everything.

MALE PROGRAMMER Maybe she just can't see it, you've got to allow for human error.

FEMALE PROGRAMMER Well that's your problem, then.
(leans in, a secret)
I don't think she's been human for years.

2-SHOT, both cautiously look round, to the far end ... CUT TO sudden, shocking CU: THE CONTROLLER – a deathly white face, to CAMERA, staring, mad, muttering, like an insane albino – but just a glimpse and then CUT TO:

16 INT. THE HOUSE DAY

LYNDA and STROOD on the settee as THE DOCTOR rages –

THE DOCTOR Are you *insane?* You just step into the disintegrator? Is it that important? Getting your face on telly, is that worth dying for?

LYNDA You're talking like we've got a choice!

And the Doctor stops dead. Disarmed.

THE DOCTOR I thought you had to apply.

STROOD Don't be so stupid, that's how they played it centuries back.

LYNDA You get chosen whether you like it or not. Everyone on Earth is a potential contestant, the transmat beam picks you out at random. And it's non-stop, there are sixty *Big Brother* Houses all running at once.

THE DOCTOR How many? Sixty?!

STROOD Yeah, they've had to cut back, it's not what it was.

THE DOCTOR It's a charnel house. What about the winners, what do they get?

LYNDA They get to live.

THE DOCTOR Is that it?

LYNDA Isn't that enough?

THE DOCTOR Rose is out there. She was caught in the transmat, she's a contestant –

Sudden action, he strides across the room, grinning:

THE DOCTOR Time I got out. That other housemate, Linda with an I, she was forcibly evicted for what?

LYNDA Damage to property.

THE DOCTOR What, like this?

And he holds the sonic screwdriver up to a wall-camera. PRACTICAL – camera sparks!

17 INT. *WHAT NOT TO WEAR* STUDIO DAY

CAPTAIN JACK now in tennis whites and racket, with ZU-ZANA.

CAPTAIN JACK Naah, I'm not getting this, it's just too safe, y'know? Too decent. And you'd never keep it clean.

ZU-ZANA Well, the sporting theme is very popular these days. Maybe we should go for something else physical. Maybe . . . swimming?

CAPTAIN JACK (smiling)
And what does that mean?

ZU-ZANA Nice little pair of trunks.

CAPTAIN JACK And nothing else?

ZU-ZANA Absolutely nothing else.

CAPTAIN JACK You're a very cheeky robot, did you know that?

ZU-ZANA Now don't overheat my circuits. Anyway, you ponder that, we need to move on to Stage Two.

Zu-Zana glides across to join TRIN-E, at the far end, by the Defabricator.

TRIN-E Stage Two ready and waiting.

CAPTAIN JACK Bring it on, girls.

ZU-ZANA Okay, stand by to be defabricated –

The tip of the laser glows [PRAC LIGHT]. Captain Jack's covered with the whip-crack FX SHIMMER again. It clears, and his clothes have gone.

TRIN-E Excellent. And now it's time for the face-off!

CAPTAIN JACK What does that mean? Have I got to compete with another contestant?

TRIN-E No, like I said . . . face . . . off!

And both DROIDS lift their arms – with four vicious new limbs, whirring! Trin-E's right arm is the chainsaw. Her left arm is a huge pair of glinting scissors! Zu-Zana's right arm is a huge chopping axe! The fingers of her left hand are five hypodermics. All chrome, gleaming.

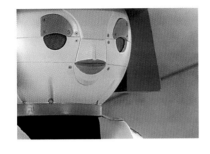

ZU-ZANA I think you'd look good with a dog's head!

TRIN-E Or maybe no head at all, that would be so outrageous!

ZU-ZANA And we could stitch your legs to the middle of your chest!

TRIN-E Nothing is too extreme! It's to die for!

And they glide towards him, glittering, whirring, slicing. But Captain Jack stays utterly calm.

CAPTAIN JACK Now hold it there, ladies. I don't want to shoot either one of you.

TRIN-E But you're unarmed!

ZU-ZANA You're naked!

On MID-SHOT Captain Jack – facing the Droids, he reaches behind.
And when he brings his hand front again, he's holding a small knuckle-duster-shaped gun.

ZU-ZANA But that's a Compact Laser Deluxe!

TRIN-E Where were you hiding that?

CAPTAIN JACK You really don't want to know.

The Droids move forward, fast –

TRIN-E Give me that accessory!

And he fires. The [PRAC] tip of the gun glows – PRAC EXPLOSION – Trin-E's head blows up!

Jack fires again, gun glows – PRAC EXPLOSION – Zu-Zana's head blows up!

18 INT. STUDIO DAY

CU the ANNE DROID:

ANNE DROID You are the weakest link, goodbye!

Jaw hinges down, FX BOLT – FX BOLT hits COLLEEN – *FATOOM*!
Colleen's gone, a scattering of dust, a trail of smoke.

CUT TO the FLOOR MANAGER:

FLOOR MANAGER Going to the break, two minutes on the clock,
just a reminder, we've got solar-flare activity coming up in ten,
thanks everyone –

CUT TO, l to r: AGORAX, ROSE, RODRICK, the only survivors. Rose shaken, furious, Rodrick with a 'Colleen' placard (Rose's says 'Agorax', Agorax's 'Colleen'). Hushed, upset:

ROSE Colleen was clever, she banked all the money, why d'you vote for her?

RODRICK Cos I want to keep you in! You're stupid, you didn't even know the Princess Vossaheen's surname. When it gets to the final, I want to be up against you. So you get disintegrated, and I get a stackload of credits. Courtesy of the Bad Wolf Corporation.

Rose suddenly chilled.

ROSE What d'you mean, who's Bad Wolf?

RODRICK They're in charge, they run the Game Station.

ROSE But why are they called Bad Wolf?

RODRICK I dunno, it's just a name, it's like an Old Earth nursery-rhyme sort of thing, what does it matter?

CU Rose, looking to the distance:

ROSE I keep hearing those words. Everywhere we go. Bad Wolf . . .

CUT TO rapid, snatched images – flashbacks, not new footage:

ep.3, Gwyneth scared, saying, 'The big, bad wolf' –

ep.4, the words BAD WOLF graffiti'd on to the TARDIS –

ep.6, Van Statten's helicopter: 'Bad Wolf One descending' –

ep.7, CU TV screen on Floor 139, Badwolf TV –

ep.10, Written on Captain Jack's bomb, Schlechter Wolf –

ep.11, the *BLAIDD DRWG* banner, the Doctor saying 'Bad Wolf' –

CUT BACK TO to Rose, lost in thought.

ROSE Different times, different places. Like it's written across the universe.

RODRICK What's that supposed to mean?

ROSE I don't know. But if the Bad Wolf is in charge of the quiz, then maybe I'm not here by mistake. Someone's been planning this . . .

19 INT. THE HOUSE DAY

THE DOCTOR, happy, with LYNDA and STROOD on the sofa.

BIG BROTHER The Doctor has broken the House Rules. Therefore, Big Brother has no choice but to evict you. The Doctor, you have ten seconds to make your farewells –

The Doctor runs to the door, eager.

BIG BROTHER Ten . . . nine . . . eight . . . seven . . . six . . . five . . . four . . . three . . . two . . . one . . . The Doctor, you have been evicted, please leave the *Big Brother* House. / Please leave the *Big Brother* House.

THE DOCTOR That's more like it! Come on, open up!

LYNDA You're mad, it's like you want to die!

STROOD I reckon he's a plant, he was only brought in to stir us up.

At / the door opens, and he happily goes through.

20 INT. *BIG BROTHER* CORRIDOR DAY

THE DOCTOR walks in, the doors close behind him.

THE DOCTOR Come on then! Disintegrate me!

(Keep this going, the Doctor gesturing up, 'What you waiting for? Blast me! Do it!', etc, to play in to sc.21 and 22.)

21 INT. THE HOUSE DAY

LYNDA and STROOD watch the Doctor on the screen, horrified.

LYNDA He is, he's mad. He's bonkers!

22 INT. FLOOR 500 DAY

The FEMALE and MALE PROGRAMMER, both hushed, intense –

FEMALE PROGRAMMER I said keep an eye on him, not kill him.

MALE PROGRAMMER He damaged the property, it's an automatic process, I can't stop it –

Above his screen, a countdown. EVICTION: 8, 7, 6, 5, 4, 3 –

23 INT. *BIG BROTHER* CORRIDOR DAY

THE DOCTOR grins, looking up. The sound of power rising . . . and then it stops. Fails. Noise spirals down. Victorious:

THE DOCTOR I knew it!

24 INT. FLOOR 500 DAY

The MALE PROGRAMMER stabbing buttons, confused.

FEMALE PROGRAMMER What happened, what did you do?

MALE PROGRAMMER Nothing, it's like there's some sort of override. It's not me!

25 INT. *BIG BROTHER* CORRIDOR DAY

THE DOCTOR plays all this to the high wall-mounted CAMERA.

THE DOCTOR Y'see? Someone brought me into this game. But if they wanted me dead, they could've transmatted me into a volcano – they want me alive!

Walks away, to the far wall, gets out the sonic screwdriver.

THE DOCTOR Now then! No one's ever got this far, maybe the security's not so tight, at this end. You following this? I'm getting out!

And as he sonics away at the join in the wall –

26 INT. FLOOR 500 DAY

MALE and FEMALE PROGRAMMER watching the Doctor on screen.

FEMALE PROGRAMMER This is going way too far. You've got to tell the Controller.

27 INT. *BIG BROTHER* CORRIDOR DAY

THE DOCTOR sonics away at the wall, and – *ping*! A second set of doors opens. The Doctor looks round – the doors to the other end have opened also, the end adjoining the House. LYNDA and STROOD look out, scared, like animals preferring their cage.

THE DOCTOR Come with me.

STROOD We're not allowed.

THE DOCTOR Stay in there and you stand a 50/50 chance of disintegration. Stay with me, and I promise to get you out alive. Come on!

LYNDA I can't!

THE DOCTOR Lynda, you're sweet. From what I've seen of your world, d'you think anyone votes for sweet?

On the Doctor, holding out his hand to her. Hero shot.

Deep breath, and then Lynda runs – joins the Doctor. He grabs her hand, big smile, energised – and they run out –

28 INT. FLOOR 56 DAY

THE DOCTOR and LYNDA run out – he stops dead.

WIDE MATTE SHOT, FLOOR 56 written above, in huge letters. It's Satellite Five, a hundred years later. The food stands have gone, it's all more industrial – less gloss, more pipes visible, girders, etc. The Doctor and Lynda have emerged through an old Spike Room door. The Doctor amazed:

THE DOCTOR Hold on. I've been here before. This is Satellite Five!

29 EXT. FX SHOT: SATELLITE FIVE

Satellite Five in all its glory – busier than it was, plastered with more adverts and icons. Suspended against a backdrop of space (keeping Earth OOV for now).

30 INT. FLOOR 500 DAY

MALE and FEMALE PROGRAMMER study the screen, hushed –

FEMALE PROGRAMMER What about security? He's outside, why hasn't the alarm gone off?

MALE PROGRAMMER Okay, you win, the Controller's got to handle this. But go and check the Archive, we need evidence – the Archive makes a record of all transmat activity, find out how he got on board. Archive Six, go on.

Male Programmer walks off. Female Programmer heads the other way, but follow Male Programmer. And REVEAL LOCATION: WIDE MATTE SHOT, with the FLOOR 500 sign looming above. The old Floor 500 and the old Control Room have become one, the dividing wall gone, steps leading up to the old Control Room. The Control desks have spread – long strips of desks, PROGRAMMERS at MONITORS, now running down from the Control Room, along the whole length of Floor 500. (If this means too many prac monitors, then some workers just work at perspex panels.) Staff with headsets, muttering, counting – a constant hum.

Male Programmer approaches the Control Room end, unnerved. Sitting centre, surrounded by monitors, is the CONTROLLER. Female, deathly white, like a human automaton; long ago, she surrendered herself to the process. Her eyes flit from screen to screen, and she never stops counting – specified lines surrounded by a muttered, '*10, 9, 8, 7, 6, 5, 4, 3, 2, 1,* transmit, *46, 45, 44,* close, *116, 117, 118 ...*' Italics muttered, non-italics clear:

MALE PROGRAMMER Controller, we have a problem.

CONTROLLER – *8, 9, 10* – continue working – *15, 16, 17, 18* –

MALE PROGRAMMER We have a security problem –

CONTROLLER – delta *90, 91, 92, 93* – continue working – *6, 5, 4, 3, 2, 1, transmit* –

MALE PROGRAMMER I'm sorry, but I can't, we have contestants outside the games, but the alarms haven't gone off –

CONTROLLER – *51, 52, 53, 54* – no security, the games continue – *48, 49* –

MALE PROGRAMMER But we can't just let them wander –

CONTROLLER – *93, 94, 95, 96* – they are no one – *55, 54, 53, 52* – they are no one –

Suddenly, the Controller jerks, gasps, in pain –

MALE PROGRAMMER What is it?

CONTROLLER Archive Six!

WHIP-PAN from Male Programmer to Female Programmer, right at the far end of the floor, at an old Spike Room door.

FEMALE PROGRAMMER I'm sorry, I was just, um – I need to consult the Archive –

CONTROLLER Archive Six is out of bounds – *27, 28, 29, 30*, stop, *5, 6, 7* –

FEMALE PROGRAMMER I need to check the transmat log –

CONTROLLER Archive Six is out of bounds, no one may enter Archive Six – *52, 53, 54, 55* – return to work –

Male and Female Programmer puzzled, but return to their desks. CU Controller, lost in her own mind.

CONTROLLER – *13, 14, 15, 16* – inform all staff, solar flares in delta point seven – *19, 20, 21, 22, 23, 24* . . .

31 INT. FLOOR 56 DAY

THE DOCTOR's walking the length of the wall, testing it with the screwdriver – loves investigating. LYNDA follows.

THE DOCTOR No guards. That makes a change. You'd think a big business like Satellite Five would be armed to the teeth.

LYNDA No one's called it Satellite Five in ages. It's the Game Station now, hasn't been Satellite Five for about a hundred years –

THE DOCTOR (looks at watch)
Hundred years exactly. It's the year two zero-zero/one zero-zero.

CU the Doctor, excited, remembering –

THE DOCTOR I was here before, on Floor 139 – the satellite was broadcasting news channels, back then –

CUT TO rapid, snatched images – flashback, not new footage – ep.7, WIDE SHOT: FLOOR 139, breaktime, full of workers; shot of the Mighty Jagrafess; shot of the Doctor and Rose running as Floor 500 collapses; shot of the Editor and the Jagrafess dying.

CUT BACK TO the Doctor, smiling, even cocky.

THE DOCTOR Had a bit of trouble upstairs. Nothing too difficult. Gave 'em a hand – easy, home in time for tea.

LYNDA Hundred years ago? You were here, a hundred years ago?

THE DOCTOR Yup.

LYNDA Well you're looking good on it.

THE DOCTOR I moisturise.

He checks the screwdriver, slaps it, like it's faulty.

THE DOCTOR Funny sorts of readings. Lots of energy. Place is humming. Weird. This goes way beyond normal transmissions, what do they need all this power for . . . ?

LYNDA I dunno, I think we're the first contestants ever to get outside.

He keeps going, panel to panel, whirring away, investigating, LYNDA following.

THE DOCTOR I had two friends, travelling with me, they must've got caught in the same transmat. Where would they be?

LYNDA Dunno, they could have been allocated anywhere, there's a hundred different games.

THE DOCTOR Like what?

LYNDA Well there's ten floors of *Big Brother*, there's a different house behind all of those doors. But beyond that, there's all sorts of shows, it's non-stop. There's *Call My Bluff*. With real guns. There's *Countdown*, where you've got thirty seconds to stop the bomb going off. *Ground Force*, that's a nasty one, you get turned into compost. *Wipeout*, speaks for itself. Oh, and *Stars In Their Eyes*. Literally, stars in their eyes, if you don't sing, you get blinded.

THE DOCTOR And you watch this stuff?

LYNDA Everyone does. How come you don't?

THE DOCTOR I never paid for my licence.

LYNDA Oh my God, you get executed for that!

THE DOCTOR Let them try.

LYNDA You keep on saying things that don't make sense. Who are you though, Doctor? Really?

THE DOCTOR Doesn't matter.

LYNDA It does to me. I've just put my life in your hands.

He looks at her properly. Maybe even fancying her a bit!

THE DOCTOR I'm just a traveller. Wandering past. Believe it or not, all I'm after is a quiet life.

LYNDA So if we get out of here, what are you gonna do? Just wander off again?

THE DOCTOR Fast as I can.

LYNDA I could come with you.

Beat. He studies her. Smiles.

THE DOCTOR Maybe you could.

LYNDA I wouldn't get in the way.

THE DOCTOR Wouldn't mind if you did. Good idea, yeah. Lynda with a Y. (brisk again)
First of all, let's concentrate on the getting out. And to do that, you've got to know your enemy – who's controlling it, who's in charge of the satellite now?

LYNDA Hold on. Your lords and masters –

She presses a wall switch: the *chunk!* of powerful lights – NEW WIDE MATTE SHOT: the opposite end to the usual Floor signs – spotlights on huge lettering: BAD WOLF CORPORATION.

CUT TO the Doctor. Disturbed, wondering what this means . . .

32 INT. *WHAT NOT TO WEAR* STUDIO DAY

TRIN-E and ZU-ZANA are broken, smoking, on the floor. CAPTAIN JACK's wearing a combination of outfits, and he's just attaching his Compact Laser to the Defabricator.

CAPTAIN JACK Compatible systems, just align the wave signature . . . Thattaboy! Got myself a gun!

He pulls – the top of the Defabricator lifts off, so it becomes like a big, space-age laser rifle. He looks at the Droids' bodies.

CAPTAIN JACK Ladies, the pleasure was all mine. Which is the only thing that matters, in the end.

He presses three buttons on a computer panel, click, door unlocked, he heads out of the door –

33 AND 34 OMITTED

35 INT. FLOOR 299 DAY

CAPTAIN JACK, carrying gun, steps out, REVEAL – WIDE MATTE SHOT, FLOOR 299. (Same as Floor 56, there's no difference between lower Floors now, only 500 is special.) Captain Jack hasn't been here before, doesn't recognise it. He consults his wrist device. It pings!

CAPTAIN JACK Two hearts, that's him, which floor?

It burbles, and Jack's already heading for the lift –

36 INT. OBSERVATION DECK (FLOOR 56) DAY

THE DOCTOR walks through, LYNDA follows. Up the steps . . . and the Doctor looks at the view. Dismayed.

FX SHOT: the Earth – as in ep.7, but more so. More towers and industrial arrays extending out of Earth's atmosphere. Tiny pin-points of light, spaceships, buzzing about. But the Earth itself is grey; the swirl of heavy, rotten clouds.

LYNDA Blimey, I've never seen it for real, not from orbit. Planet Earth!

THE DOCTOR . . . What's happened to it?

LYNDA It's always looked like that, ever since I was born. See there? The Great Atlantic Smog Storm, that's been going for twenty years. We get newsflashes, telling us when it's safe to breathe outside.

THE DOCTOR So the population just sits there. Half the world too fat, half the world too thin, and you lot just watch telly.

LYNDA Ten thousand channels. All beaming down from here.

THE DOCTOR The Human Race! Mindless sheep, being fed a diet of ...
(beat)
Mind you, have they still got that programme where three people have to live with a bear?

LYNDA Oh, *Bear with Me*, I love that one!

THE DOCTOR And me, that celebrity edition where the bear got in the bath –
(snaps out of it)
But it's all gone wrong! I mean *history*'s gone wrong. Again!
This should be the Fourth Great and Bountiful Human Empire.
I don't understand. When I was here last time, I put things right.

LYNDA No, but that's when it first went wrong. A hundred years ago. Like you said, the news channels, they all shut down overnight.

THE DOCTOR But that was me. I did that.

LYNDA There was nothing left in their place. No information. Whole planet just froze – the government, the economy, they collapsed, that was the start of it. One hundred years of hell.

THE DOCTOR Oh my God ...

Silence; devastated, he walks forward, to the glass. His POV: the wasted, sick, boiling, dark planet.

THE DOCTOR I made this world.

37 INT. STUDIO DAY

CU AGORAX screaming – FX SHOT: *FATOOM*! And he's gone. Smoke and dust.

CUT TO the ANNE DROID, which swivels to face ROSE and RODRICK.

ANNE DROID That leaves Rose and Rodrick, you're going head-to-head. Let's play, *The Weakest Link*!

Under the music sting, Rodrick mutters to Rose:

RODRICK That's the end of tactical voting. You're on your own now.

38 INT. OBSERVATION DECK (FLOOR 56) DAY

CAPTAIN JACK strides in, to find THE DOCTOR and LYNDA. The Doctor's frantic, dismantling the computer terminal.

CAPTAIN JACK Hey handsome. Good to see you, any sign of Rose?

THE DOCTOR Can't you track her down?

CAPTAIN JACK She must be still inside the games, all the rooms are shielded.

THE DOCTOR If I can get inside the computer – she's got to be here somewhere –

CAPTAIN JACK Better hurry up, these games don't have a happy ending.

THE DOCTOR (snaps)
D'you think I don't know that?

Jack takes off his wrist-device, gives it to the Doctor.

CAPTAIN JACK Here we go, patch that in, it's programmed to find her.

THE DOCTOR Thanks.

The Doctor keeps working, fast. Jack acknowledges Lynda.

CAPTAIN JACK Hey there.

LYNDA Hello.

CAPTAIN JACK Captain Jack Harkness.

LYNDA Lynda Moss.

CAPTAIN JACK Nice to meet you, Lynda Moss –

THE DOCTOR D'you mind flirting outside?

CAPTAIN JACK I'm just saying hello!

THE DOCTOR For you, that's flirting.

LYNDA I'm not complaining.

CAPTAIN JACK Muchas gracias.

THE DOCTOR (angry, wrist-device:)
It's not compatible! This stupid system doesn't make sense, hang on –

And the Doctor abandons subtlety, pulls away at the console –

THE DOCTOR Give's a hand –

Captain Jack helps, they pull at the metal. The entire unit rips free, exposing wires.

THE DOCTOR It's weird, this place should be a basic broadcaster. But the systems are twice as complicated. What for? It's more than just television, the station's transmitting something else.

CAPTAIN JACK Like what?

The Doctor grabs wires and the wrist-device, frantic now:

THE DOCTOR I don't know! This Bad Wolf thing, it's all tied up with me, someone's manipulating my whole life, it's some sort of trap. And Rose is stuck inside it!

39 INT. STUDIO DAY

ROSE and RODRICK face the ANNE DROID. INTERCUT TV footage – with graphics, Rose and Rodrick's score counting out in crosses and ticks – and OFF-AIR COVERAGE, on Rose's fear.

ANNE DROID Rodrick, in science, what is the boiling point of Draffalon?

RODRICK Is it two hundred degrees?

ANNE DROID That is the correct answer!

Rodrick gets a tick.

ANNE DROID Rose, in geography, the Grand Central Ravine is named after which Ancient Britain City?

ROSE Um. Is it … York?

ANNE DROID No, the correct answer is Sheffield.

Rose gets a X.

40 INT. OBSERVATION DECK (FLOOR 56) DAY

THE DOCTOR's got the wrist-device plugged into the gutted console.
The device chimes –

THE DOCTOR Found her! Floor Four Zero Seven.

LYNDA Oh my God, she's with the Android – you've got to get her out!

41 INT. STUDIO DAY

ROSE and RODRICK play on, one tick to Rodrick –

ANNE DROID Rodrick, in literature, the author of *Lucky* was Jackie who?

RODRICK Stewart.

ANNE DROID No, the correct answer is Collins.

Rodrick gets a X.

ANNE DROID Rose, the oldest inhabitant of the Isop Galaxy is the Face of what?

ROSE Boe! The Face of Boe!

ANNE DROID That is the correct answer!

Rose gets a tick.

42 INT. LIFT SHAFT

(FX SHOT?) Lift ascending –

43 INT. LIFT DAY

The counter racing up, 110, 111, 112, 113 – CAPTAIN JACK and LYNDA b/g,
THE DOCTOR raging at the dial –

THE DOCTOR Come on. *Come on!*

44 INT. STUDIO DAY

ROSE and RODRICK and ANNE DROID, equal score –

ANNE DROID Rodrick, in history, who was the President of the Red Velvets?

RODRICK Was that ... Hoshbin Frane?

ANNE DROID That is the correct answer!

Rodrick gets a tick.

ANNE DROID Rose, in food, the dish Gaffabeque originated on which planet?

ROSE ... Mars?

ANNE DROID No, the correct answer is Lucifer.

Rose gets a X; Rodrick's one tick ahead –

45 INT. LIFT DAY

Counter rising, 360, 361, 362, 363, 364 –

46 INT. STUDIO DAY

ROSE and RODRICK and ANNE DROID, he's ahead by one tick –

ANNE DROID Rodrick, which measurement of length is said to have been defined by the Emperor Jate as the distance from his nose to his fingertip?

RODRICK ... Would that be a goffle?

ANNE DROID No, the correct answer is a paab.

Rodrick gets a X.

ANNE DROID Rose, in fashion, Stella Pok Baint is famous for what?

ROSE Um ... shoes?

ANNE DROID No, the correct answer is hats.

Rose gets a X, Rodrick still one tick ahead –

47 EXT. FLOOR 407 DAY

THE DOCTOR, CAPTAIN JACK and LYNDA belt out of the lift – WIDE MATTE SHOT, the FLOOR 407 sign above, as the three scatter across the floor, fast, frantic, checking the doors –

THE DOCTOR Game Room Six, which one is it? –

LYNDA Over here!

48 INT. STUDIO DAY

ROSE and RODRICK and ANNE DROID, the final round –

ANNE DROID Rodrick, in physics, who discovered the Fifteen-Dash-Ten Barric Fields?

RODRICK Um. San Hazeldine?

ANNE DROID No, the correct answer is San Chen.

Rodrick gets a X, they're level –

49 INT. FLOOR 407 DAY

THE DOCTOR sonicking at the door control panel, CAPTAIN JACK stands back, lifts up the Defabricator –

CAPTAIN JACK Stand back, let me blast it open –

THE DOCTOR You can't, it's made of Hydra Combination – I can do it – (at the screwdriver)
Come *on*!

50 INT. STUDIO DAY

ROSE, RODRICK and ANNE DROID, the final question –

ANNE DROID Rose, in history, which Icelandic city hosted Murder Spree Twenty?

ROSE Was it … Reykjavik?

ANNE DROID No, the correct answer is Pola Ventura.

Rose gets a X. Music cue! Lights go up! It's over!

RODRICK Oh my God! I've done it! You've lost!

51 INT. FLOOR 407 DAY

THE DOCTOR sonicking away like mad, desperate, muttering –

THE DOCTOR Come on come on come on –

52 INT. STUDIO DAY

ROSE terrified, RODRICK happy, the ANNE DROID remorseless [speeches run simultaneously] –

ANNE DROID Rodrick, you are the strongest link, you will be transported home with one thousand six hundred credits.	**ROSE** (desperate) But I'm not meant to be here, I need to find the Doctor – he must be here somewhere, he's always here, he wouldn't just leave me –
RODRICK Oh thank you, thank you so much –	(scared, strong)
ANNE DROID Rose, you leave this life with nothing –	This game is illegal, I'm telling you to stop –

CUT TO THE FLOOR MANAGER, off-set, turns, hearing –

THE DOCTOR Rose!

DOCTOR, CAPTAIN JACK and LYNDA come running in (NB, a good distance away from the set, as far as possible) – all yelling across the room –

CAPTAIN JACK Stop the game!	**FLOOR MANAGER** We're live on air!
ROSE Look out for the Android, it's armed –	**THE DOCTOR** Stop the game! I order you to stop the game!

And Rose runs towards the Doctor –

ANNE DROID You are the weakest link. Goodbye!

The Anne Droid's jaw hinges down – FX SHOT: the bolt shoots out. FX SHOT: THE BOLT HITS ROSE – *FATOOM*! Light clears. Nothing left of her. Just a drift of ashes, a curl of smoke.

Silence. On the Doctor. Shattered. Hold on him. No tears; deeper than that. Hollow.

Then bring in voices. They're audible but remote, irrelevant to the Doctor. People moving b/g, high emotion –

CAPTAIN JACK: (raging) *What the hell did you do?*

FLOOR MANAGER: *I'm calling security, right now, you have no permission to be here – deactivate the Android –*

RODRICK: *But I've won, right? I still get the money, right?*

CAPTAIN JACK: *You just killed her and you're worried about money? You just back off, mister! Back off!*

FLOOR MANAGER: *Control, I'm overriding your commands, I need security, and I need it here, right now –*

And throughout, stay close on the Doctor.

He walks forward. He kneels down. He reaches forward. Carefully picks up the dust. Stares at it. Runs it through his fingers.

Then just stares ahead.

Footsteps in b/g, heavy –

FLOOR MANAGER: *It's that lot, they interrupted the game –*

CAPTAIN JACK: *Leave him alone, don't you touch him –*

SECURITY GUARD: *Sir, put down the gun or I'll have to shoot –*

CAPTAIN JACK: *It's too late for the gun – you killed her! Your stupid freaking gameshow killed her –*

Now, TWO SECURITY GUARDS appear at the Doctor's side – edge of frame – haul him to his feet. Stay on him; he just goes with them, dead. Just voices around him:

SECURITY GUARD: *Sir, I'm arresting you under Private Legislation Sixteen of the Game Station Syndicate, you do not have to respond, but anything you say, or fail to say, may be held against you in a court of law –*

They're frogmarching him out. He just walks. A dead man. JUMP CUT TO:

53 INT. FLOOR 407 DAY

THE DOCTOR'S slammed against a wall – STAY TIGHT on him, as the SECURITY GUARD frisks him, rough.

The Security Guard holds the sonic screwdriver in front of the Doctor's face. The Doctor doesn't respond.

SECURITY GUARD: *Sir, can you tell us the purpose of this device? Can you tell us what it's for? We will be holding this device as evidence against you, d'you understand that?*

JUMP CUT TO:

54 INT. FLOOR 407 DAY

A different end of 407 (still shot tight, location irrelevant, it's just being used as a holding area). Tight on THE DOCTOR. CAPTAIN JACK and LYNDA near him, the SECURITY GUARD in front, two GUARDS behind.

SECURITY GUARD: *Can you tell us how you got on board?*

LYNDA: *It's not my fault, he just arrived in the House –*

SECURITY GUARD: *I'm asking him – sir? Can you tell us who you are? Who do you represent?*

JUMP CUT TO:

55 INT. FLOOR 407 DAY

CU THE DOCTOR – another wall of 407, just a background. CAMERA FLASH, a convict's photo.

Still numb, the Doctor turns to profile, CAMERA FLASH – JUMP CUT TO:

56 INT. FLOOR 407 DAY

CU THE DOCTOR, sitting. CAPTAIN JACK next to him, edge of frame, LYNDA edging the other side, SECURITY GUARD f/g.

SECURITY GUARD: *You will be taken from this place to the Lunar Penal Colony, there to be held without trial. You may not appeal against this sentence, is that understood?*

Pause, the Doctor says nothing. Security Guard walks away. At last, the Doctor is left alone. His first sign of life, a weary sigh. Then he turns to Captain Jack – lose Lynda, allow Jack into the frame – the Doctor calm and straightforward.

THE DOCTOR Okay. Let's do it.

And Captain Jack leaps up. CAMERA stays on the Doctor, who stands, grim, storms forward –

B/g: an impression of Captain Jack, fighting two GUARDS; f/g: the Doctor grapples with the Security Guard – just two seconds, and the Doctor sends him flying, easy – then he keeps walking forward, the screwdriver back in his hand –

57 INT. FLOOR 500 DAY

MALE PROGRAMMER's watching this on screen –

MALE PROGRAMMER Ohhh my God, now we're in trouble –

58 INT. LIFT DAY

THE DOCTOR, CAPTAIN JACK and LYNDA step into the lift. Jack's now got two guards' guns – typical blasters – but the Doctor's got the heavy Defabricator. And he means business.

THE DOCTOR Floor 500.

59 INT. FLOOR 500 DAY

The MALE PROGRAMMER smashes a security wall-box. An alarm sounds, EVERYONE looks round –

MALE PROGRAMMER Clear the floor! He's on his way up here. With a gun!

60 INT. LIFT SHAFT DAY

Lift ascending.

61 INT. LIFT DAY

JACK and LYNDA b/g, CU THE DOCTOR, to CAMERA. Dark as hell. He hoists the Defabricator, gives a *ka-chik*! Safety catch off.

62 INT. FLOOR 500 DAY

Alarm sounds, B/G WORKERS running out (some doors lead to stairs). The MALE and FEMALE PROGRAMMER face the CONTROLLER. She keeps staring ahead, refuses to listen, muttering.

FEMALE PROGRAMMER This is an emergency, you've got to close down the lift –

CONTROLLER All staff are reminded that solar flares commence in delta point two – *97, 98, 99, 100* –

MALE PROGRAMMER Never mind solar flares, he's gonna kill you! –

63 INT. LIFT DAY

The counter reaches 497, 498, 499 – 500!

64 INT. FLOOR 500 DAY

Alarm still ringing, the lift door opens. THE DOCTOR walks out. LYNDA stays back, but CAPTAIN JACK wields his blaster-guns –

CAPTAIN JACK Step away from the desks. No one try anything clever, okay, just stand to the side and stay there –

There's about TEN STAFF left, including MALE and FEMALE PROGRAMMER – they scatter back. The Doctor strides forward, dark as hell, carrying the Defabricator.

He reaches THE CONTROLLER. Points the gun up. A fury.

THE DOCTOR Who's in control of this place? What does Bad Wolf mean, who's behind all of this? Who is it?

CONTROLLER – *15, 16, 17, 18, 19, 20, 21, 22* –

THE DOCTOR This satellite is more than a Game Station, what exactly is going on?

CONTROLLER – *77, 78, 79, 80* – all staff are reminded that solar flares occur in delta point one – *15, 14, 13* –

THE DOCTOR I want an answer! Who killed Rose Tyler?! TELL ME!

The Male Programmer steps forward, tentative –

MALE PROGRAMMER She can't reply . . .

The Doctor swings round, gun still pointing –

MALE PROGRAMMER Don't shoot!

THE DOCTOR Oh don't be so thick, like I was ever gonna shoot –

And he chucks the gun to the Male Programmer. The Doctor brisker now (still furious, but using it, being practical).

THE DOCTOR Captain, we'd better secure this floor, we've got more guards on the way up. Seal the exits.

CAPTAIN JACK Yes sir!

Jack goes to one of the undamaged consoles, at the back.

THE DOCTOR You! What were you saying?

MALE PROGRAMMER But ... I've got your gun.

THE DOCTOR Okay, so shoot me, but why can't she answer?

MALE PROGRAMMER She's, um ... Can I put this down?

THE DOCTOR If you want, just hurry up.

MALE PROGRAMMER Thanks. Sorry. Um.
(puts it down)
The Controller is linked to the transmissions, the entire output goes through her brain. You're not a member of staff, so she doesn't recognise your existence.

THE DOCTOR What's her name?

MALE PROGRAMMER I don't know. She was installed when she was five years old, that's the only life she's ever known.

A shout from the back of the room:

CAPTAIN JACK Doors sealed! We should be safe for about ten minutes.

THE DOCTOR Keep an eye on 'em.

MALE PROGRAMMER But that stuff you were saying – that something's going on with the Game Station, I think you're right. I've kept a log. Unauthorised transmats, encrypted signals ... it's been going on for years.

THE DOCTOR Show me.

CUT TO Captain Jack, at his desk. His wrist-device burbles. He reads it, then looks round. Puzzled, uncertain of his readings, he stands, crosses to an old Spike Room door.

FEMALE PROGRAMMER You're not allowed in there. Archive Six is out of bounds.

CAPTAIN JACK Do I look like an out-of-bounds sort of man?

And he goes inside –

65 INT. ARCHIVE SIX DAY

– the old Spike Room. CAPTAIN JACK walks in. And smiles . . .

Centre is the old, low circular desk – but no workers, no central chair. Instead, REVEAL, slap bang in the middle . . . the TARDIS.

66 INT. TARDIS DAY

CAPTAIN JACK walks in (he's got his own key). The old place humming and creaking inside, the same as ever. He walks up the ramp, notices an old, distinctive jacket of Rose's, slung over the handrails. Captain Jack picks it up. Thinks of her.

Then he puts it back where it was, goes to the console. Presses a button. A beep from the scanner. He's puzzled, leans in, peers at scanner properly. Mystified.

CAPTAIN JACK . . . What the hell . . .?

67 INT. FLOOR 500 DAY

CU THE CONTROLLER:

CONTROLLER Solar-flare activity in delta point zero fifteen – *44, 45, 46* –

CUT TO THE DOCTOR, with the MALE PROGRAMMER at his desk, studying the screen. The FEMALE PROGRAMMER approaching.

FEMALE PROGRAMMER If you're not holding us hostage then open the doors and let us out, the staff are terrified –

THE DOCTOR And that's the same staff who execute hundreds of contestants every single day, yeah?

FEMALE PROGRAMMER That's not our fault, we're just doing our jobs –

THE DOCTOR And with that sentence you just lost the right to even talk to me, now back off!

All the lights go down. Pools of light only. A noise of energy, dying away. The entire floor, hushed.

THE DOCTOR What's that for? –

MALE PROGRAMMER That's just the solar flares. They interfere with the broadcast signal, so this place automatically powers down. Planet Earth gets a few repeats. It's all quite normal, only lasts for about two minutes.

FEMALE PROGRAMMER Doctor.

THE DOCTOR Whatever it is, you can wait.

FEMALE PROGRAMMER I think she wants you.

The Doctor looks round: the Controller still stares front – she seems to be blind, when not looking into the computer – but she intones, more human:

CONTROLLER ... Doctor doctor where are you doctor where is the doctor doctor doctor doctor doctor ...?

The Doctor walks forward; in awe, respecting this creature.

THE DOCTOR I'm here.

CONTROLLER ... Can't see, blind, so blind, all my life blind, all I can see is numbers. but I saw you, travelling so far, so wild, so free –

THE DOCTOR What do you want?

CONTROLLER Fast talk fast, solar flares hiding me, they can't hear, my masters listen but they can't hear me now, the sun the sun is so bright –

THE DOCTOR Who are your masters?

CONTROLLER ... Can't say their name, they wired my head, the name is forbidden, they control my thoughts, my masters my masters, I had to be careful –

THE DOCTOR You did it. You brought me here. You saved my life in the Big Brother House, cos you want me alive ...

CONTROLLER ... They monitor transmission, but they don't watch the programmes, I could hide you inside the games, knew you would find me find me –

THE DOCTOR My friend died inside your games –

CONTROLLER ... She doesn't matter –

THE DOCTOR Don't you *dare* tell me that!

CONTROLLER ... They've been hiding, my masters, hiding in the dark space, watching and shaping the Earth, so many so many so many years, they have always been there, guiding humanity, hundreds and hundreds of years –

THE DOCTOR Who are they?

CONTROLLER ... They wait and plan and grow in numbers, they're strong now, so strong, my masters my masters –

THE DOCTOR Who are they?

CONTROLLER ... But they speak of you, my masters my masters, they fear the doctor –

THE DOCTOR But who are they? Tell me!

And the lights go back to normal. And the Controller goes back to her normal counting.

CONTROLLER – *22, 23, 24, 25, 26, 27, 28* –

The Doctor furious, to the Male Programmer –

THE DOCTOR When's the next solar flare?

MALE PROGRAMMER Two years' time.

THE DOCTOR Fat lot of good that is!

CAPTAIN JACK saunters out of Archive Six.

CAPTAIN JACK Found the TARDIS.

THE DOCTOR We're not leaving now.

CAPTAIN JACK No, but the TARDIS worked it out, you wanna watch this – Lynda, could you stand over there for me?

LYNDA I just want to go home.

CAPTAIN JACK Won't take a second. Stand in that bit. Quick as you can.

Lynda stands in an empty area of floor.

CAPTAIN JACK Okay, everybody watching? And three, two, one –

He leans over a desk, stabs a button – FX SHOT: the white bolt of light slams down from the roof and blasts Lynda – *FATOOM*!

Light clears, she's gone. Dust and smoke.

THE DOCTOR But – you killed her!

CAPTAIN JACK Oh d'ya think?

And he presses the button again – FX SHOT: the white bolt slams down from the roof, right next to the Doctor – *FATOOM*!

And Lynda reappears! Light clears, she's standing there, dazed, unharmed.

LYNDA ... What the hell was that ...?

CAPTAIN JACK It's a transmat beam! It's not a disintegrator, it's a second transmat system! People don't get killed in the games, they get transported across space – she's alive, Doctor! Rose is still alive!

On the Doctor, ecstatic.

68 INT. SPACESHIP DAY

ROSE on the floor, waking. Head aching. Confused. All around, very dark. Hints of metal and grime. And as Rose sits up, groans, clears her head –

CUT TO ALIEN POV: gliding forward. Looking down at her.

ROSE No ... it can't be ...

Terrified, still on the floor, she scrabbles backwards, till she reaches the wall. The POV follows, remorseless.

ROSE But you're dead. I saw you die!

69 INT. FLOOR 500 DAY

THE DOCTOR and CAPTAIN JACK frantically at work, running from one console to another, the MALE PROGRAMMER helping; LYNDA, the FEMALE PROGRAMMER and STAFF watching, fascinated.

THE DOCTOR She's out there somewhere!

The CONTROLLER looks down, determined, in pain –

CONTROLLER Doctor! Coordinates five point six point one seven slash nine –

THE DOCTOR Don't! The solar flare's gone, they'll hear you!

CONTROLLER Point four three four –
(pain)
– no, my masters, no – I defy you – sigma seven seven seven –

And then she screams – [NEW] FX SHOT: *FATOOM*! The bolt hits the Controller, and she's gone. The wires swing free, empty.

THE DOCTOR They took her.

69A INT. SPACESHIP DAY

CU CONTROLLER in the same dark space, though giving nothing away. And at last, she's human, defiant, proud:

CONTROLLER Oh my masters. You can kill me. For I have brought your destruction.

[NEW] FX SHOT: a familiar ray-gun noise, and the Controller screams, glows negative, then slumps. Dead.

69B INT. FLOOR 500 DAY

CAPTAIN JACK tracking coordinates at one of the desks, all gathered around him.

THE DOCTOR She gave us the coordinates, but she didn't finish the sequence – where did they take her?

MALE PROGRAMMER Look, use that –
(gives Jack a disk)
It might contain the final numbers, I kept a log of all the unscheduled transmissions –

CAPTAIN JACK Nice one, thanks. Captain Jack Harkness, by the way –

MALE PROGRAMMER Right, yeah, I'm Davitch Pavale.

CAPTAIN JACK Nice to meet you, Davitch Pavale –

THE DOCTOR There's a time and a place.

FEMALE PROGRAMMER Are you saying this whole set-up's been a disguise all along?

THE DOCTOR Going way back. Installing the Jagrafess a hundred years ago. Someone's been playing a long game. Controlling the Human Race from behind the scenes for generations.

CAPTAIN JACK Here we go, click on that –

He throws THE DOCTOR a small hand-held clicker device. The Doctor points it up, clicks. It's like a remote. A huge scanner picture [ONLINE EDIT] materialises in the air, at the Control Room end, above the CONTROLLER. Picture fizzes, resolves into an image of empty space.

A gleeful Doctor, Jack, PROGRAMMERS and LYNDA look up. All a bit in awe now, scared, out of their depth.

CAPTAIN JACK The transmat delivers to that point. Thirty trillion kilometres away, right on the edge of the solar system.

FEMALE PROGRAMMER But there's nothing there.

THE DOCTOR It *looks* like nothing, because ...
(realises)
That's what this satellite does! Underneath the transmissions, there's another signal.

MALE PROGRAMMER Doing what?

THE DOCTOR Hiding. Hiding whatever's out there. Hiding it from radar and sonar and scanners. Something's sitting right on top of Planet Earth, but completely invisible.

CAPTAIN JACK But what is it? Who's out there?

THE DOCTOR If I cancel the signal . . .

He enters a code into a desk panel. And all look up, in amazement and fear.

FX SHOT: SCANNER PICTURE shimmers, uncloaking, revealing . . .
A SPACESHIP. A mighty bronze and gold spinning saucer. (Exactly like the old 1960s' TV21 comic strip saucers.)

FEMALE PROGRAMMER A spaceship . . .

MALE PROGRAMMER Hundreds of spaceships.

70 FX SHOT: THE FLEET

PULL OUT from the central spaceship. More ships, turning, spinning, beautiful, silent in space . . .

Pull out further, ship after ship after ship, all identical. A magnificent, shining, immaculate fleet.

71 INT. FLOOR 500 DAY

THE DOCTOR, CAPTAIN JACK, LYNDA, MALE and FEMALE PROGRAMMER looking up at the image, dwarfed by the scale of it.

CAPTAIN JACK But that's impossible. I recognise those ships. They were destroyed!

THE DOCTOR Obviously, they survived.

LYNDA Who did? Who are they?

THE DOCTOR Two hundred ships. More than two thousand on board each one. That's just about half a million of them.

MALE PROGRAMMER Half a million what?

THE DOCTOR Daleks.

72 INT. SPACESHIP DAY

ROSE is huddled on the floor, against the wall, terrified.

CUT TO WIDE SHOT: FX/SPLIT SCREEN – TEN DALEKS around her. Only one wall of the ship visible – very dark, pools of light, metal glinting as Daleks turn and manoeuvre. The wall is ridged, floor to ceiling, with intricate control panels and small lights. Daleks – some with sucker arms, some with claws, some with new attachments – glide to and fro, interfacing with the wall. All around Rose.

SUDDEN CUT TO DALEK #1 – its eyestick swings round, fast.

DALEK #2 Alert! Alert! We are detected!

DALEK #1 It is the Doctor! He has located us! Open communications channel!

A Dalek glides up to Rose.

DALEK #2 The female will stand! STAND!

73 AND 74 OMITTED

75 INT. FLOOR 500/INTERCUT WITH SPACESHIP DAY

FX SHOT: the mid-air scanner fizzes, blinks, a new image – ROSE, terrified, flanked by THREE DALEKS.

(CAPTAIN JACK, LYNDA, MALE and FEMALE PROGRAMMER and STAFF all looking up at the scanner, but they're b/g – THE DOCTOR steps forward, foreground, to face the Daleks.)

DALEK #1 I will talk to the Doctor.

THE DOCTOR Oh will you? That's nice. Hello!

DALEK #1 The Dalek Stratagem nears completion. The Fleet is almost ready. You will not intervene.

THE DOCTOR Oh really? Why's that then?

DALEK #1 We have your associate. You will obey, or she will be exterminated.

THE DOCTOR No.

Beat.

DALEK #1 Explain yourself.

THE DOCTOR I said, no.

DALEK #1 What is the meaning of this negative?

THE DOCTOR It means, no.

DALEK #1 But she will be destroyed!

The Doctor stands forward, magnificent; portrait shot.

THE DOCTOR No, cos this is what *I'm* gonna do. I'm gonna rescue her. I'm gonna save Rose Tyler from the middle of the Dalek Fleet. And then I'm gonna save the Earth. And then, just to finish off, I'm gonna wipe every last stinking Dalek out of the sky!

DALEK #1 But you have no weapons! No defences! No plan!

THE DOCTOR Yep.
(big grin)
And doesn't that scare you to death?

He holds up the clicker. Still smiling away.

THE DOCTOR Rose?

ROSE Yes, Doctor?

76 INT. SPACESHIP/INTERCUT WITH FLOOR 55 DAY

Now, the REVERSE of sc.75 – FX SHOT, a big scanner projection of THE DOCTOR's face, on the dark wall; ROSE and the three DALEKS facing it.

The Doctor with a smile –

THE DOCTOR I'm coming to get you.

He clicks – the picture fizzes, blinks off, dead.

DALEK #1 The Doctor is initiating hostile action!

DALEK #2 The Stratagem must advance! Begin the invasion of Earth!

DALEK #3 The Doctor will be exterminated!

DALEKS Exterminate! Exterminate! Exterminate!

Rose turns round, horrified.

CUT TO WIDE FX SHOT: from above Rose, looking down, revealing DOZENS OF DALEKS around her.

CUT TO WIDER FX SHOT: Rose smaller, a HUNDRED DALEKS.

CUT TO WIDER FX SHOT: dark metal gantries criss-crossing above, in the darkness, every level, every platform lined with HUNDREDS AND HUNDREDS OF DALEKS, some levitating across the empty space, all with their dome-lights flashing in anger, the terrible cry of 'Exterminate'.

Rose in the middle of a huge, insane army.

Episode 13
The Parting of the Ways
By Russell T Davies

1 THRU 7 OMITTED

(RECAP OF EPISODE 12.)

8 INT. SPACESHIP DAY

FX SHOT/SPLIT SCREEN: establish NINE DALEKS at work, ROSE centre. The room's still dark, she's spotlit from above.

CUT TO Rose, as one Dalek advances on her.

DALEK #1 You know the Doctor. You understand him. You will predict his actions!

ROSE I don't know! And even if I did, I wouldn't tell you –

DALEK #1 Predict! Predict! Predict!

But its eyestick swivels round, hearing –

DALEK #2 TARDIS detected, in flight.

9 EXT. FX SHOT: SPACE

A gorgeous, rich panorama of deep space. Against it, the valiant TARDIS, spinning through the void.

10 INT. SPACESHIP DAY

DALEK #1 Launch missiles! Exterminate!

11 EXT. FX SHOT: DALEK FLEET

On the main saucer, OTHER SHIPS circling behind. *Foom! – Foom!* Two bright bolts of dazzling energy fire out of vents in the ship –

12 INT. TARDIS DAY

THE DOCTOR slamming controls like a madman, with his hammer, gleeful; CAPTAIN JACK clinging on, watching the scanner –

CAPTAIN JACK We've got incoming!

13 INT. SPACESHIP DAY

ROSE flanked by DALEK #1, desperate:

ROSE But you can't! The TARDIS hasn't got any defences, you're gonna kill him –

DALEK #1 You have predicted correctly.

14 EXT. FX SHOT: SPACE DAY

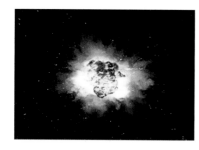

FX SHOT: the TARDIS spinning in space; FX SHOT: the two dazzling bolts scorch in; FX SHOT: the bolts hit the TARDIS – a huge explosion, a wipe-out of hot orange energy, obscuring the TARDIS –

15 INT. TARDIS DAY

Picture shaking: THE DOCTOR at the controls – CAPTAIN JACK holding up the SLITHEEN-EXTRAPOLATOR from ep.11. Its lights glittering; it's now wired up to the console.

CAPTAIN JACK The extrapolator's working, we've got a fully functional forcefield – try saying that when you're drunk.

THE DOCTOR And for my next trick ...

He slams every lever available, wild with energy.

16 INT. SPACESHIP DAY

ROSE with DALEK #1 – they both look up, around, as the familiar materialisation noise roars and bellows; CU Rose: astonished, realising, as the wind blows her hair.

CUT TO the control wall, THREE DALEKS swivel round, to see ...

FX SHOT: the outline of the TARDIS begins to fade in – squarely around Rose and the Dalek!

17 INT. TARDIS DAY

FX SHOT: ROSE and DALEK fade into vision, top of the ramp –

CUT TO THE DOCTOR –

THE DOCTOR Rose, get down!

Rose throws herself to the floor –

DALEK #1 Exterminate! –

FX SHOT: the Dalek fires; FX SHOT: the Doctor ducks, the bolt whizzes overhead. CAPTAIN JACK leaps out, fires the DEFABRICATOR – [PRAC] the Dalek explodes!

And at last . . . calm. Quiet. The top half of the Dalek is a smouldering mess, dead blue tentacles poking out. Rose looks up, scarcely able to believe it.

ROSE You did it . . .

She stands, he goes to her, and very simply, they embrace.

ROSE Feels like I haven't seen you for years.

THE DOCTOR I said I'd come and get you.

ROSE Never doubted it.

THE DOCTOR (laughs)
I did. You all right?

ROSE Yeah. And you?

THE DOCTOR Not so bad. Been better. Wouldn't mind a cup of tea.

CAPTAIN JACK Don't I get a hug?

ROSE You bet, come here.

CAPTAIN JACK I was talking to him.

Rose just laughs, hugs him.

CAPTAIN JACK Welcome home.

ROSE Thought I'd never see you again.

CAPTAIN JACK (of the Defabricator)
You were lucky, I was a one-shot wonder. Drained the gun's power supply, it's a piece of junk now.

ROSE (to the Doctor)
But it's the Daleks, you said they were extinct. How come they're still alive?

THE DOCTOR That's what I need to find out.

CAPTAIN JACK But they disappeared, way back in history. After the Tenth Dalek Occupation. One minute, they're the greatest threat in the universe, next minute they vanish out of time and space.

THE DOCTOR They just went to fight a bigger war. The Time War.

CAPTAIN JACK Thought that was just a legend.

THE DOCTOR (quiet, anguished)
I was there. The War between the Daleks and the Time Lords, with the whole of creation at stake. Think you've seen fighting, Jack? You've seen *nothing*. Two battle fleets. Millions of ships. Burning, and screaming. My people were destroyed, but they took the Daleks with them. I almost thought it was worth it. And now it turns out they died for nothing. The Daleks survived.

CAPTAIN JACK And so did you. How come?

THE DOCTOR I've spent a long time wondering if I was lucky, or cursed.

ROSE But Doctor, there's thousands of them now, we could hardly stop *one*. What are we gonna do?

Big smile, all chipper again:

THE DOCTOR No point standing here, chinwagging. Human race, you'd gossip all day. The Daleks have got all the answers. Let's go and meet the neighbours.

And he heads off down the ramp –

ROSE You can't go out there – !

18 INT. SPACESHIP DAY

FX SHOT/SPLIT SCREEN: TARDIS centre, spotlit from above. NINE DALEKS surround it. THE DOCTOR steps out of the door –

DALEKS Exterminate! *Exterminate!*

FX SHOT: all fire bolts of energy – and all the bolts bounce off, ricochet into the roof (as if the spotlight is delineating the circumference of the forcefield).

THE DOCTOR Is that it? Useless. Nul points.

ROSE and CAPTAIN JACK are edging out of the TARDIS, wary.

THE DOCTOR 'S all right, come on out, that forcefield can hold back anything.

CAPTAIN JACK Almost anything.

THE DOCTOR Yeah, but I wasn't going to tell them that, thanks.

CAPTAIN JACK Sorry.

The Doctor steps forward. Dark as hell. Taking his time. Daleks studying him, eyestalks twitching, as though nervous. (Shoot tight to play this off the three 'real' Daleks now.)

THE DOCTOR D'you know what they call me in the ancient legends of the Dalek Homeworld? The Oncoming Storm. You might have removed all your emotions, but I reckon, right down deep in your DNA, there's one little spark left. And that's *fear*. Doesn't it just burn, when you're facing me? So tell me. How did you survive the Time War?

EMPEROR DALEK They survived through me.

The Doctor, Rose, Captain Jack turn – till now, the only visible part of the ship has been the control wall; the reverse a black void. Now, the void lights up.

FX SHOTS: a layout much like ep.2's Fan Room. Far back (like where Platform One's reset switch was, through the fans) is the EMPEROR DALEK. A huge, hundred-foot metal thing of beauty; more complicated, but based on Dalek design. Pipes and tubes spreading out to the ship. At the centre – not the very top – a glass bowl, in which something blue twitches, suspended in swirling fluids. (For CUs in dialogue, CUT TO the ep.6 [PRAC] model Dalek creature, now 'upright', splayed out on wires and tubes in its bowl.)

The Emperor has a Dalek-like grate to its voice, but it's much more subtle. It's not Davros, but it's as eloquent. And all around the Emperor, gantries and walkways. Going way up high; and way down low, as wide and as deep as the Fan Room. FX DALEKS moving about on all levels.

The Doctor walks forward, Rose and Captain Jack behind, amazed

THE DOCTOR Rose. Captain. This ... is the Emperor of the Daleks.

EMPEROR DALEK You destroyed us, Doctor. The Dalek race died in your inferno. But my ship survived, falling through time, crippled, but alive.

THE DOCTOR Ohh, I get it –

DALEK #1 Do not interrupt!

DALEK #2 Do not interrupt!

DALEK #3 *Do not interrupt!*

FX SHOT: they fire, bolts scorching out, bouncing off – but it doesn't *feel* safe, Rose and Captain Jack flinching. Only the Doctor's unafraid, strong:

THE DOCTOR I think you've forgotten, I am the Doctor, and if there's one thing I can do, it's talk, I've got five billion languages and you haven't got *one* way of stopping me, so if anyone's gonna shut up, it's YOU!

He's so powerful that the THREE DALEKS retreat slightly. The Doctor turns back to the Emperor. Light again:

THE DOCTOR Okey doke. So! Where were we?

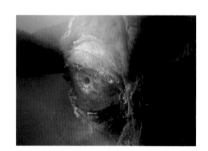

EMPEROR DALEK We waited here, in the dark space, damaged, but rebuilding. Centuries passed, and we quietly infiltrated the systems of Earth. Harvesting the waste of humanity.

THE DOCTOR (to Rose)
That's what happened to you. All the game contestants – they're not disintegrated, they're sent here.

EMPEROR DALEK More than that. The prisoners, the refugees, the dispossessed, they all came to us. The Human Race was happy to look away.

ROSE What does he mean, harvesting . . . ?

CAPTAIN JACK Raw stock. They used the people, to breed more Daleks.

EMPEROR DALEK The bodies were filleted. Pulped. Sifted. The seed of the Human Race is perverted, only one cell in a billion was fit to be nurtured.

THE DOCTOR You created an army of Daleks. Out of the dead.

ROSE But that makes them . . . half human.

EMPEROR DALEK Those words are blasphemy!

DALEK #1 Do not blaspheme!

DALEK #2 Do not blaspheme!

DALEK #3 Do not blaspheme!

EMPEROR DALEK Everything human has been purged. I cultivated pure and blessed Daleks.

THE DOCTOR (disturbed, now)
. . . Since when did the Daleks have a concept of blasphemy?

EMPEROR DALEK Since I led them from the wilderness. I am far more than Emperor. I reached into the dirt and made new life. I am the God of all Daleks!

DALEK #1 Worship him!

DALEK #2 Worship him!

THE DOCTOR (quiet, to the others)
… They're insane.

EMPEROR DALEK The beginning and end of all things!

And the Doctor's actually sad for them:

THE DOCTOR Hiding in silence for hundreds of years, that's enough to drive anyone mad. But it's worse than that … driven mad by your own flesh. The stink of humanity. Oh, you hate your own existence. (to Rose and Jack)
And that makes them more deadly than ever, come on, we're going.

EMPEROR DALEK You may not leave my presence!

[Speeches run simultaneously.]

DALEK #1 Stay where you are!   **EMPEROR DALEK** You will be exterminated!

DALEK #2 Stay where you are!   **DALEKS** Exterminate! Exterminate!

FX SHOT, WIDE SHOT: the Emperor and his Dalek army, all screaming, mad and wild, the whole ship echoing, as the Doctor, Rose and Jack step into the TARDIS. CU the Doctor, defiant, last to go though the doors –

19 INT. TARDIS DAY

CU THE DOCTOR, as he closes the door, leans against it. All his defiance gone. He's terrified.

20 OMITTED

21 INT. FLOOR 500 DAY

The wooden blue door swings open – CU THE DOCTOR, striding out of the TARDIS (already materialised), ROSE – looking round, bemused – and CAPTAIN JACK following. As the Doctor walks, reveal FLOOR 500 – LYNDA, MALE and FEMALE PROGRAMMERS (looking astonished at the TARDIS) are the only people left now.

THE DOCTOR Turn everything up! All transmitters, wide open, full power, now! Do it!

MALE and FEMALE PROGRAMMER run, slam switches.

MALE PROGRAMMER What does that do?

THE DOCTOR Stops the Daleks from transmatting on board – how did you get on, did you contact the Earth?

MALE PROGRAMMER We tried to warn them, but all they did was suspend our licence cos we've stopped the programmes.

THE DOCTOR So the planet's just sitting there. Defenceless. Lynda, what are you doing still on board?
(to the Programmers)
I told you to evacuate everyone!

MALE PROGRAMMER She wouldn't go.

LYNDA Didn't want to leave you.

FEMALE PROGRAMMER There weren't enough shuttles anyway, or I wouldn't be here. We've got about a hundred people stranded on Floor Zero –

22 INT. FLOOR ZERO DAY

FX SHOT, WIDE SHOT: a massive FLOOR ZERO sign. SPLIT SCREEN to create lots of PEOPLE: STAFF, including the FLOOR MANAGER; GUARDS; but mostly CONTESTANTS. Confusion, panic – some sit on the floor, despairing, some bang on the doors. CUT TO RODRICK yelling into an intercom.

RODRICK I won the game, where's my money? Anyone listening? Where's my money?

23 INT. FLOOR 500 DAY

MALE PROGRAMMER is at a desk, reading a signal.

MALE PROGRAMMER Oh my God. The Fleet is moving. They're on their way!

24 EXT. FX SHOT: DALEK FLEET DAY

The saucers begin to spin faster, the Fleet on the move, the sound of mighty engines whining up to maximum power.

25 INT. SPACESHIP DAY

FX SHOT: the DALEK EMPEROR, with FX DALEKS all around.

EMPEROR DALEK The Fleet will attack Planet Earth. My vessel will destroy the Game Station. This will be our Paradise!

26 EXT. FX SHOT: DALEK FLEET DAY

The Fleet spins away, in beautiful formation, led by the Emperor's ship. A terrifying armada.

27 INT. FLOOR 500 DAY

THE DOCTOR full of life, ripping wires out of desks; ROSE, LYNDA, MALE and FEMALE PROGRAMMER watching. CAPTAIN JACK's hard at work, wiring up the extrapolator to the station's systems.

THE DOCTOR Dalek plan, big mistake, cos what have they left me with? Anyone? Anyone? Oh come on, it's obvious! A great big transmitter – this entire station! Catch up! If I can change the signal, fold it back, sequence it? Anyone?

CAPTAIN JACK (quiet, horrified)
You've got to be kidding.

THE DOCTOR Give the man a medal!

CAPTAIN JACK A Delta Wave?

THE DOCTOR A Delta Wave!

ROSE What's a Delta Wave?

CAPTAIN JACK A wave of Van Cassadyne energy. Fries your brain. Stand in a Delta Wave and your head gets barbecued.

THE DOCTOR And this place can transmit one massive wave. Wipe out the Daleks!

LYNDA Well get started and do it then!

THE DOCTOR Trouble is, wave that size, building this big, brain as clever as mine, should take about, ooh, three days. How long till the Fleet gets here?

MALE PROGRAMMER Twenty-two minutes.

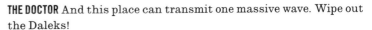

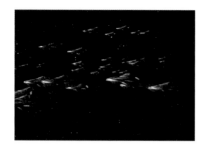

28 EXT. FX SHOT: DALEK FLEET DAY

Formations of Dalek saucers, spinning, gliding, fast.

29 INT. FLOOR 500 DAY

CAPTAIN JACK plugs the final wire into the extrapolator. Its lights start blinking.

CAPTAIN JACK Done it! Now let's have a look –

He runs to an intact desk, ROSE, LYNDA, MALE and FEMALE PROGRAMMER huddle round to study a monitor; intense, a team. THE DOCTOR in b/g, screwdriving masses of wiring. On the monitor: a schematic of the Game Station (the old Satellite Five diagram). Lines indicate extrapolator energy.

CAPTAIN JACK We've now got a forcefield, so they can't blast us out of the sky. But it doesn't stop the Daleks from physically invading.

MALE PROGRAMMER Do they know about the Delta Wave?

CAPTAIN JACK Yep, they'll have worked it out at the same time. So, if they want to stop the Doctor, they've got to get to this level, 500. Now I can concentrate the extrapolator around the top six floors, 500 down to 495. So they'll penetrate the station below that, at Floor 494, and fight their way up.

MALE PROGRAMMER Who are they fighting?

CAPTAIN JACK Us.

MALE PROGRAMMER And, uh, what are we fighting with?

CAPTAIN JACK The guards had guns, with bastic bullets, that's enough to blow a Dalek wide open.

FEMALE PROGRAMMER There's five of us.

THE DOCTOR Rose, you can help me, I need all these wires stripping bare.

FEMALE PROGRAMMER Right, and now there's four of us!

CAPTAIN JACK Then let's move it! Into the lift, come on, isolate the lift controls –

Male and Female Programmer head off, Lynda goes to the Doctor.

LYNDA Just wanna say … thanks, I suppose. I'll do my best.

THE DOCTOR Me too. See you later.

Both awkward, and decide on a handshake. And Lynda heads off to the lift. Lose the others in b/g, as Captain Jack lingers, with the Doctor and Rose. Serious, quiet:

CAPTAIN JACK Anyway. It's been fun. But I guess this is goodbye.

ROSE Don't talk like that. The Doctor's gonna do it, you just watch him.

He turns to Rose, puts one hand to her face, gentle.

CAPTAIN JACK Rose. You're worth fighting for.

Gives her a quick kiss on the lips. Turns to the Doctor, one hand to his face, gentle.

CAPTAIN JACK Wish I'd never met you, Doctor. I was much better off as a coward.

Gives him a quick kiss on the lips.

CAPTAIN JACK See you in hell.

And he turns, runs off.

ROSE He's gonna be all right, isn't he?

No reply, the Doctor just keeps working, grim.

30 INT. FLOOR ZERO DAY

The CROWD on their feet, shouting, angry, led by RODRICK.

CUT TO the reverse: CAPTAIN JACK standing on a box, flanked by LYNDA, the MALE and FEMALE PROGRAMMER. Also around them, SIX CONTESTANTS; they've crossed the room, to join Jack. Jack's got a guard's gun, fires in the air [PRAC bullets]. And the crowd quietens, muttering.

CAPTAIN JACK One last time. Any more volunteers? There is an army, about to invade this station, and I need every last citizen to mount a defence. Anyone else?

The FLOOR MANAGER sighs, crosses the floor, to Jack.

RODRICK Don't listen to him, there aren't any Daleks, they disappeared, thousands of years ago.

But the Floor Manager completes her walk. And Jack is completely in control, at his best:

CAPTAIN JACK Thanks. As for the rest of you. This is Floor Zero, the Daleks are going to enter at Floor 494, and as far as I can tell, they'll head up, not down. But that's not a promise, so here's a word of advice. Keep quiet. Don't let them know where you are.
(at Rodrick)
And if you hear fighting up above. If you hear us dying. Then tell me that the Daleks aren't real.
(very quiet)
Don't make a sound.

Then Jack walks out, his team following.

On Rodrick, unnerved . . .

31 INT. FLOOR 500 DAY

THE DOCTOR at work. He's got *huge* swathes of wires running out of all the desks, from the walls, from the Controller's position, lashing them together. ROSE is stripping down wires with a pen-knife. The intimacy of being all hushed and busy, alone in the huge space of floor 500. They keep working throughout:

ROSE S'pose . . .

Silence. Good long pause.

THE DOCTOR What?

ROSE Nothing.

THE DOCTOR You said 'suppose'.

ROSE No, I was just thinking ... and I mean, obviously, you can't, but ... you've got a time machine. Why can't you go back to last week and warn them?

THE DOCTOR Soon as the TARDIS lands, in that second, I become part of events. I'm stuck in the timeline.

ROSE Thought it was something like that.

She keeps working. But, hands still busy, he's looking at her, smiling. Like she means the world to him.

THE DOCTOR There's another thing the TARDIS could do. It could take us away. We could leave. Let history take its course, and we go to Marbella in 1989.

ROSE Yeah, but you'd never do that.

THE DOCTOR But you could *ask*. Never even occurred to you, did it?

ROSE Yeah, well. I'm just too good.

The Doctor just smiles. Then looks round, alert.

THE DOCTOR The Delta Wave's started building, how much time does it need ...?

The Doctor runs to a desk, stabs buttons. A monitor displays a long series of equations. CU the Doctor, lost in thought, Rose approaching.

ROSE Is that bad ...?
(no reply)
Doctor, is that bad?
(reply)
Okay, that's bad. How bad is it?

THE DOCTOR I'm not gonna do it. Unless ...
(realises)
... I could use the TARDIS.

He's suddenly gleeful, like a kid, kisses her forehead.

THE DOCTOR Rose Tyler, you're a genius! We can do it! If I use the TARDIS to cross my own timeline ... Yes!

And he runs into the TARDIS; Rose runs after him –

32 INT. TARDIS DAY

THE DOCTOR runs up the ramp, stabs buttons, ROSE following. He grabs hold of her hand, makes her hold down a lever.

THE DOCTOR Hold that down and keep position –

ROSE What does it do?

THE DOCTOR Cancels the buffers. If I'm very clever – and I'm more than clever, I'm brilliant – I might just save the world. Or rip it apart.

ROSE I'd go for the first one.

THE DOCTOR Me too. Now I need to power up the Game Station, hold on –

And he runs out, all puppy-dog energy –

33 INT. FLOOR 500 DAY

THE DOCTOR runs out of the TARDIS, all energy – but he pulls the door closed behind him, and immediately the energy dies. He just stands there, takes a breath. Desolate; he looks all of his 900 years. Then he gets out his sonic screwdriver. Looks at it, holds it up, whirrs it.

The TARDIS engines start up, the ancient grind and groan –

34 INT. TARDIS DAY

Engine noise – the rotor starts to rise and fall. ROSE panicked, still holding down the lever, yells:

ROSE Doctor, what are you doing? Can I take my hand off?
It's moving . . .

35 INT. FLOOR 500 DAY

THE DOCTOR watches, so sad. FX SHOT: the TARDIS simply fades away.

36 INT. TARDIS DAY

ROSE still holding the lever, but the TARDIS is rocking and swaying a little, clearly in flight – she begins to twig, takes her hand off, runs to the door. She heaves on it, but it won't open –

ROSE Doctor! Let me out – !

37 EXT. FX SHOT DAY

The time vortex. The TARDIS whirls on its final mission . . .

38 INT. FLOOR 500 DAY

CU THE DOCTOR. He rubs his face, so very, very tired. Deep breath, then he gets back to work. WIDE SHOT as he walks along the gutted desks. All alone.

39 INT. TARDIS DAY

The TARDIS in flight, ROSE hammering on the door –

ROSE What have you done? Doctor? What have you done?! –

Then she hears a noise, like a signal tuning in, and turns. At the console, FX SHOT: THE DOCTOR appears. A HOLOGRAM, projected from the console, with a slight flicker. He's formal, brave, talks facing dead ahead (i.e. he was alone, facing a camera, recording this, some time in the past).

THE DOCTOR This is Emergency Programme One. Rose, now listen, this is important. If this message has activated, then it can only mean one thing.

Rose amazed, walks up the ramp. The projection keeps talking as she goes up to it – FX: puts her hand through it. She stands back to listen – though he stares ahead, so she's never right on his eyeline. (The Doctor settles into a 'real' shot, FX only for the occasional flicker.)

THE DOCTOR We must be in danger. And I mean, fatal. Emergency Programme One means that this is the big one. I'm dead. Or I'm about to die, any second, with no chance of escape. And that's okay. Hope it's a good death. But I promised to look after you, and that's what I'm doing. The TARDIS is taking you home.

ROSE No . . .

THE DOCTOR And I bet you're moaning and fussing now. Typical! Just hold on a minute and listen a bit more –

ROSE I won't let you –

THE DOCTOR The TARDIS can't return for me. Emergency Programme One means that I'm facing an enemy who should never get their hands on this machine. So this is what you do: let the TARDIS die. When you get back to London, walk out of here, and lock the door, and throw away the key. Just let this old box gather dust. No one can open it; no one will even notice it. Let it become a strange little thing standing on a street corner. And over the years the world will move on and the box will be buried. And as for you . . .
(holding back emotion)
You were the best, Rose Tyler. And if you want to remember me, then you can do one thing. That's all. One thing.

And then, calmly, all compassion, the image turns its head, looks right at her. Like he *knows* she's there.

THE DOCTOR Have a good life. Do that for me, Rose. Have a fantastic life.

FX SHOT: he fizzes, blinks, and disappears. And Rose is horrified, stands there, as it sinks in. Hold for a few seconds. Then she rages, slams every button –

ROSE You can't do this to me, you can't –
(at the console)
take me back! *Take me back!*

But then the engine noise stops, the interior settles. Rose filled with dread, runs to the door, out –

40 EXT. ROSE'S ESTATE DAY

Rose opens the door and steps out. The worst thing of all: plain daylight; the real world. Home, London, Earth. The concrete, the flats, the sky.

She's horrified, runs back inside –

41 INT. TARDIS DAY

ROSE runs back to the console, pulls levers, raging –

ROSE You've got to take me back! Come on, *fly*! How do you fly? What do I do? Help me!

42 EXT. ROSE'S ESTATE DAY

MICKEY running, from a great distance. Exhilarated, seeing –

His POV: ROSE steps out of the TARDIS, slow, defeated.

MICKEY I knew it! I was all the way down by Clifton's Parade, I heard the engines, I thought, there's only one thing makes a noise like that . . .
(realises)
What is it?

And as he reaches her, she starts to cry. He hugs her. And she clings to him, crying her heart out.

43 INT. FLOOR 500 DAY

PROFILE CU THE DOCTOR, at work, frantic. Over the intercom:

CAPTAIN JACK OOV Rose, I've called up the internal laser codes, there should be a different number on every screen, can you read them out to me?

THE DOCTOR She's not here.

CAPTAIN JACK OOV Of all the times to take a leak! When she gets back, tell her to read me the codes.

THE DOCTOR She's not coming back

CAPTAIN JACK OOV What d'you mean, where's she gone?

44 INT. FLOOR 494 DAY

INTERCUT with sc.43: THE DOCTOR on FLOOR 500.

CAPTAIN JACK on his wrist-device. (At the same time, he's working on a wall panel, rewiring, and works throughout.)

THE DOCTOR OOV Just . . . get back to work.

Silence, and Jack realises:

CAPTAIN JACK You took her home, didn't you?

THE DOCTOR Yeah.

Silence. Jack grim, realising it's hopeless.

CAPTAIN JACK That Delta Wave. Is it ever gonna be ready?

But Captain Jack hears –

45 INT. FLOOR 500 DAY

EMPEROR DALEK Tell him the truth, Doctor.

THE DOCTOR looks up: on every surviving [PRAC] monitor, an image of the EMPEROR DALEK appears (CU, filling the screen, the [PRAC] creature). Its voice calm and subtle, across the empty floor. (INTERCUT with sc.44: CAPTAIN JACK on FLOOR 494; Jack still working, listening, but alone, no one nearby to hear this.)

EMPEROR DALEK There is every possibility the Delta Wave could be complete, but no possibility of refining it. The Delta Wave must kill every living thing in its path, with no distinction between Human and Dalek. All things will die. By your hand.

CAPTAIN JACK OOV . . . Doctor? The range of this transmitter covers the entire Earth.

EMPEROR DALEK You would destroy Daleks and Humans together. If I am God, the creator of all things, then what does that make you, Doctor?

THE DOCTOR There are colonies out there. The Human Race would survive, in some shape or form. But you're the only Daleks in existence, the whole universe is in danger if I let you live.
(raw, full of doubt)
D'you see, Jack? That's the choice. That's the decision I've got to make, for every living thing. Die as a Human. Or live as a Dalek.
(then, helpless:)
What would you do?

CAPTAIN JACK I think . . .
(pause)
You sent her home. She's safe. Keep working.

EMPEROR DALEK But he will exterminate you!

CAPTAIN JACK Never doubted him, never will. You get on with it, Doctor, I'm manning the defences –

Jack clicks off his comms (lose him from the scene). The Doctor's energised by Jack's trust, smiling, strides across the room, busy, trailing wires.

THE DOCTOR Now you tell me, God of all Daleks, cos there's one thing I haven't worked out. The words Bad Wolf. Spread across time and space, everywhere, drawing me in, how d'you manage that?

EMPEROR DALEK I did nothing.

THE DOCTOR Come on, there's no secrets now, your worship. How d'you connect me to those two words? Bad Wolf?

EMPEROR DALEK They are not part of my design.

THE DOCTOR Seriously?

EMPEROR DALEK This is the Truth of God.

THE DOCTOR Then what does it mean ...?

He looks up, completely mystified, but fascinated ... FX WIDE SHOT: the BAD WOLF CORPORATION sign.

46 INT. CHIP SHOP DAY

Plonk! A parcel of fish and chips is thumped down. It's the most ordinary chip shop in the world – formica, nothing fancy. A little table. JACKIE's bought fish and chips for all. MICKEY sits there, ROSE sitting, lost, silent with anger. All on eggshells, the most awkward ordinary conversation in the world. (No one else around – staff in b/g – but they still keep it a bit hushed.)

JACKIE Now that's on me, my treat. And it's gone upmarket, this place, they're doing little tubs of coleslaw now. It's not very nice, it tastes a bit sort of clinical, but it's there if you want it. Then we can go up town. Bit of shopping! Just like the old days.
(pause, carefully)
Welcome home.

Silence. Rose, head down.

MICKEY Have you tried that new pizza place? Down by Minto Road.

JACKIE Where's that, then?

MICKEY On the corner, at the far end, used to be the Christmas shop.

JACKIE Oh, I know, what's it selling?

MICKEY Well. Pizza.

JACKIE That's nice. Do they deliver?

MICKEY Yeah.

JACKIE That's handy.

Good, awkward pause. Then, kind:

JACKIE Rose. Have something to eat.

ROSE He is dying. Two hundred thousand years in the future, he's dying, and there's nothing I can do.

JACKIE Yeah, but like you said. Two hundred thousand years, that's way off.

ROSE But it's not, it's now. For me, it's happening now, that fight is happening *right now*. And he's fighting for us. For the whole planet. And I'm just sitting here, eating chips.

MICKEY But that's what he wanted.

ROSE Don't I get a say?

MICKEY No you don't. Not this time. You were never equals on board that TARDIS – you're kidding yourself, if you think you were. He was captain of the ship. And he makes the decisions.

ROSE Well then. For once in his life, he's wrong.

JACKIE Now listen to me. God knows, I've hated that man, and with good reason, but right now, I *love* him, and d'you know why? Cos he did the right thing.
(upset, tearful)
He sent you back to me.

ROSE But what do I do now? What do I do, every day? Get up, catch the bus, go to work and come back home and have chips and go to bed, is that it?

MICKEY (quiet, hurt)
That's what the rest of us do.

ROSE Well I can't.

MICKEY What, cos you're better than us?

ROSE No, I didn't mean . . .
(pause; then quiet and strong)
But it *was*. It was a better life. I don't mean all the travelling and seeing aliens and spaceships and things, that doesn't matter. The Doctor showed me a better way of *living* your life. You saw him, he showed you too. That you don't just give up. You don't just let things happen. You make a stand. You say no. You have the guts to do the right thing, when everyone else runs away.
(despairs)
Now I'm just sitting here. I can't –

Upset, she gets up, runs out.

Look between Jackie and Mickey; he'll follow. Heads out.

47 INT. ROSE'S ESTATE DAY

ROSE on a concrete bench, miserable. MICKEY walks up, cautious. Quiet, kind:

MICKEY I didn't mean . . .

ROSE I know.
(pause)
How's Trisha Delaney?

MICKEY Don't care. You came back.

Which makes her smile, a little.

MICKEY You can't spend the rest of your life thinking about the Doctor.

ROSE But how do I forget him?

MICKEY You've got to start living your own life, a proper life. Like he's never had. The sort of life you could have with . . . me.

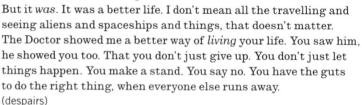

In saying that, he goes to sit next to her – REVEALING, behind him: graffiti, on the wall. *BAD WOLF.*

On Rose. Staring. Astonished. And beginning to realise . . .

48 EXT. ROSE'S ESTATE DAY

ROSE running across the estate – general area, bins and walls – inspired, thinking wild thoughts. MICKEY following. *Fast:*

ROSE Over here, it's over here as well –

On another wall – different, faded graffiti, *BAD WOLF.*

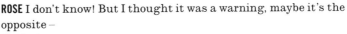

MICKEY That's been there for years, it's just a phrase, it's just words –

ROSE But we kept seeing those words, me and the Doctor, everywhere we went – it's like they just crop up, spontaneously, sort of bleeding through . . .

MICKEY But what's making it happen?

ROSE I don't know! But I thought it was a warning, maybe it's the opposite –
(excited)
Maybe it's a message! The same words written down now, and two hundred thousand years in the future – it proves the two different times are connected! It's a link, between me and the Doctor, Bad Wolf here, Bad Wolf there.

MICKEY If it's a message, what's it saying?

ROSE It's telling me I can get back!

MICKEY A message from who – ?

But she's off, running, so fast –

49 INT. TARDIS DAY

ROSE walking round the console, excited (a bit like the Doctor!); MICKEY listening.

ROSE All the TARDIS needs to do is make a return trip. Just . . . reverse!

MICKEY Yeah, but we still can't do it!

ROSE The Doctor always said the TARDIS is telepathic! Like, the way it gets inside your head and translates alien languages. This thing's alive, it can listen.

MICKEY Not listening now, is it?

ROSE We need to get inside it. Last time I saw you, with the Slitheen. This middle bit *opened*. And there was this light, the Doctor said it was the heart of the TARDIS –

CUT TO: rapid, snatched images – flashbacks, ep.11/58: the TARDIS console opening; the Doctor saying 'You've opened its soul'; beautiful white light streaming out –

ROSE If we can open it, I can make contact, I can tell it what to do.

MICKEY Rose, if you go back, then you're going to your death.

ROSE Well then. That's a risk I've got to take. Cos there's nothing left for me here.

MICKEY Nothing?

ROSE No.

And that hurts him so much; he's nothing. And she knows it, but has to say it. On Mickey, with dignity:

MICKEY Okay. If that's what you think. Let's get this thing open.

50 INT. OBSERVATION DECK (FLOOR 56) DAY

CAPTAIN JACK with LYNDA. Crouching over the deck's gutted terminal, wires exposed, the monitor showing the station schematic.

CAPTAIN JACK Right then Lynda, you're my eyes and ears. Soon as the Daleks get in, you can follow them on screen, and report that to me.

LYNDA Understood, yeah.

CAPTAIN JACK Trouble is, they'll detect you. But the door's made of Hydra Combination, should keep them out.

LYNDA Should?

CAPTAIN JACK Should. That's the best I can do.
(on his wrist device)
How long till the Fleet arrives?

MALE PROGRAMMER OOV About six minutes.

VRAAAAAAAAAAAM!

FX SHOT: the view from the deck – the DALEK SAUCER scorches in overhead, vast, making the station shudder (with the Earth in b/g, behind the saucer).

CAPTAIN JACK You said six minutes!

MALE PROGRAMMER OOV They accelerated!

FX SHOT: the view from the deck. The saucer stops in front of the station, other saucers fly past, head for the Earth.

CAPTAIN JACK This is it! Ladies and gentlemen, we are at war!

51 EXT. FX SHOT DAY

FX SHOT: the Emperor's DALEK SAUCER, other saucers in b/g flying in formation down to Earth. On the side of saucer, a huge ramp lifts upwards ...

FX SHOT: DALEKS fly out. Hundreds of them. Lifting in formation, flying through space; FX SHOT: CU DALEK, others around it, turning in space; FX SHOT: GAME STATION b/g, DALEK ARMY flying towards it ...

52 INT. OBSERVATION DECK (FLOOR 56) DAY

LYNDA, watching out of the window, on a hand-communicator.

LYNDA You were right. They're forcing the airlock on 494.

53 INT. FLOOR 499 DAY

FX SHOT: the sign looming, FLOOR 499. CUT TO ground level, a huge barricade – desks, girders, anything – laid out across the floor. CAPTAIN JACK – with a guard's gun and the Defabricator – is behind the barricade, at a gutted terminal: wires, monitors – an improvised command post. MALE and FEMALE PROGRAMMER and FOUR CONTESTANTS beside him, scared, armed with guards' guns.

Jack addressing the troops on his wrist-device:

CAPTAIN JACK Stand your ground, everyone. Follow my commands. And good luck.

They hear the grind of metal, from below ...

54 INT. FLOOR 500 DAY

THE DOCTOR working like a madman, lashing wires together.
He hears a far-off explosion – the whole chamber shudders –

55 INT. FLOOR ZERO DAY

All the CONTESTANTS are now sitting on the floor, huddled like refugees, some clinging to each other. In silence. All, including RODRICK, look up. Above them, the sound of huge swathes of metal, groaning, creaking, ripping open –

56 INT. FLOOR 494 DAY

FX SHOT: WIDE, FLOOR 494 sign above. Out of all the Spike Room doors, on every side: DALEKS. As many as possible –

57 INT. FLOOR 494 CORRIDOR DAY

(The CORRIDORS are long, one Dalek in width.) The FLOOR MANAGER is crouched down, holding a hand device, a monitor in front of her. Whispering into a communicator:

FLOOR MANAGER They're inside.

CAPTAIN JACK OOV Okay, activate internal lasers. Slice 'em up!

Floor Manager presses a button on the device. Nothing.

FLOOR MANAGER It's not working!

57A INT. OBSERVATION DECK (FLOOR 56) DAY

LYNDA on her communicator, studying the screen.

LYNDA Defences have gone off line! The Daleks have overidden the lot!

58 OMITTED

59 INT. FLOOR 494 CORRIDOR DAY

DALEKS enter the corridor, single file. The FLOOR MANAGER and two CONTESTANTS open fire.

FX SHOTS, as ep.6: SLOW-MOTION BULLETS stopping before they hit the Dalek casing, dissolving.

Floor Manager keeps firing, yells down her communicator:

FLOOR MANAGER They don't work! You lied to me! The bullets don't work!

FX SHOT IF POSSIBLE?: the Dalek ray hits the three of them, the image goes negative, they scream and die.

59A THRU 64 OMITTED

65 EXT. ROSE'S ESTATE DAY

A hand turns ignition – engine starts up. Handbrake off, foot on the accelerator, CU MICKEY, at the wheel of his Beetle –

MICKEY Come on!

CUT TO wheels, spinning, fast, dust, smoke – but not moving, revolving on the spot, the car held back. CUT TO REVEAL the Beetle with a huge, thick, rusty, industrial chain hooked to its bumper (can a Beetle have a tow-bracket?). The chain leads away, taut ... through the TARDIS doors ...

66 INT. TARDIS DAY

The chain in mid-air, taut, coming through the doors and, at the other end – with a huge hook, it's attached to a big, hefty bolt – a catch, on the console. Pulling at it. (NB, given the height of the console, the angle of the chain inside-to-out will have to be carefully determined, and dictates the distance between the Beetle and the TARDIS; but as far apart as possible.)

ROSE at the console, yells out:

ROSE Faster!

67 EXT. ROSE'S ESTATE DAY

WIDE SHOT (FX?): see the whole set-up – the car – straining at the leash – the chain – leading into the flimsy, wooden, but unmovable box.

CUT TO JACKIE standing there, horrified. CUT TO MICKEY at the wheel, grinding his teeth, more speed. CUT TO the wheels, spinning on the spot –

68 INT. TARDIS DAY

ROSE standing over the hook in the console, despairing.

ROSE It's not moving!

69 INT. FLOOR 495 DAY

CU Spike Room door: the THREE DALEKS glide through –

70 INT. OBSERVATION DECK (FLOOR 56) DAY

LYNDA watching the monitor, on her communicator:

LYNDA Advance guard has made it to 495 –

71 INT. FLOOR 500 DAY

THE DOCTOR at work – no comms, he calls out to the air –

THE DOCTOR Jack, how are we doing?

72 INT. FLOOR 499 DAY

CAPTAIN JACK 495 should be good, I like 495 –

And he presses a button on his command-post, activating –

73 INT. FLOOR 495 DAY

The THREE DALEKS turn, suddenly alerted –

DALEK #1 Identify yourself!

And at the far end stands the ANNE DROID.

ANNE DROID You are the weakest link, goodbye!

FX SHOT, WIDE SHOT: *FATOOM – FATOOM – FATOOM*! Like a whip-crack, the Anne Droid fires, all three Daleks disappear –

CUT TO THREE MORE DALEKS, gliding in –

ANNE DROID You are the weakest link, goodbye!

FX SHOT: CU ANNE DROID, firing, *FATOOM*!

74 INT. FLOOR 499 DAY

CAPTAIN JACK hears this, punches the air, 'Yes!'.

75 INT. FLOOR 495 DAY

FX SHOT: THREE DALEKS, all firing; FX SHOT? PRAC?: the ANNE DROID explodes, head falls off.

DALEK #1 Proceed to next level!

76 INT. OBSERVATION DECK (FLOOR 56) DAY

LYNDA watching her monitor, on comms:

LYNDA They're flying up the ventilation shafts, they've made it to 496 – (sees, horrified:)
No, wait a minute. Oh my God. Why are they doing that ...?

77 INT. FLOOR ZERO DAY

CONTESTANTS huddled, holding their breath, so scared. A Spike Room door opens. THREE DALEKS.

Another Spike Room door opens. THREE DALEKS. The lift opens. THREE DALEKS.

Panic, people running, screaming, all directions (with just sound) – 'Exterminate!' – guns, screams. Stay CU on RODRICK (no FX), desperate, on the floor, backing away like an animal; people a blur, foreground and background.

RODRICK You don't exist! You can't, you don't exist, it's not fair! I won the game! I should be rich! I'm a winner, you can't do this to me –

And he shields his face, screams –

78 INT. OBSERVATION DECK (FLOOR 56) DAY

LYNDA, the screams of the dying. Clicks it off in disgust.

LYNDA Floor Zero. They killed them all.

79 INT. TARDIS DAY

The chain still taut, the sound of revving from outside. But ROSE is despairing. The console hasn't budged.

The engine stops. The chain goes slack, clunks to the ground. Rose slams the console, wretched, beaten.

80 EXT. ROSE'S ESTATE DAY

MICKEY stepping out of the car, helpless. JACKIE nearby.

81 INT. TARDIS DAY

ROSE on the floor at the centre, desolate. Looks up: JACKIE's standing over her. Quiet, kind:

JACKIE It was never gonna work, sweetheart. And the Doctor knew that. He just wanted you to be safe.

Rose stands, anguished.

ROSE I can't give up.

JACKIE Do what the Doctor said. Lock the door. Walk away.

Rose quiet, hard, right at Jackie:

ROSE Dad wouldn't give up.

JACKIE Well he's not here, is he? And even if he was, he'd say the same.

ROSE No he wouldn't, he'd tell me to try anything. If I could save the Doctor's life, try anything.

JACKIE Well, we're never gonna know.

ROSE I know. Cos I met him. I met Dad.

JACKIE (hushed)
... Don't be ridiculous.

ROSE The Doctor took me back in time. I met Dad. I was with him.

JACKIE Don't say that.

ROSE You remember, when Dad died, there was someone with him? A girl. A blonde girl. She held his hand. You saw her from a distance, you saw her, Mum. Think about it. That was me. You saw me.

JACKIE Stop it –

ROSE That's how good the Doctor is.

JACKIE Stop it just stop it, just –

And Jackie's crying, runs out of the TARDIS –

82 EXT. ROSE'S ESTATE DAY

JACKIE runs out of the TARDIS, upset – keeps running.

83 INT. TARDIS DAY

CU ROSE, upset, giving way to tears, now.

84 INT. FLOOR 500 DAY

CU THE DOCTOR, at work.

THE DOCTOR Lynda? What's happening on Earth?

85 INT. OBSERVATION DECK (FLOOR 56) DAY

LYNDA studies her monitor. Quiet, horrified.

LYNDA The fleet's descending. They're bombing whole continents. Europa, Pacifica, the New American Alliance. Australasia's just … gone.

86 OMITTED

87 INT. FLOOR 499 DAY

CAPTAIN JACK walks the barricade, grim. The MALE and FEMALE PROGRAMMER and FOUR CONTESTANTS armed, scared.

CAPTAIN JACK Floor 499, we're the last defence. The bullets might work if you concentrate them on the Daleks' gunstick. Stand by.

On the Male and Female Programmer, quiet:

MALE PROGRAMMER I'm only here cos of you. Joined the Programme cos you were on it.

FEMALE PROGRAMMER Am I supposed to say, when this is all over, and if we're still alive, maybe we could go for a drink?

MALE PROGRAMMER That'd be nice.

FEMALE PROGRAMMER Yeah, well, tough.

And both smile. Pull back safety catches, ready to fire.

87A AND 88 OMITTED

89 EXT. ROSE'S ESTATE NIGHT

MICKEY'S outside the car, despairing of his Beetle, ROSE miserable beside him.

MICKEY There's gotta be something else we can do!

ROSE Mum was right. Maybe we should just lock the door and walk away.

MICKEY I'm not having that! I'm not having you, giving up, no way! We just need something bigger than my car, something stronger, something …

The roar of an engine, Mickey looks round, gobsmacked.

MICKEY … Something like that.

Driving towards them, a big, dirty old garage pick-up truck, a hefty beast of a vehicle. Driven by JACKIE!

It comes to a halt, she climbs down.

JACKIE Right, you've only got this till six o'clock, so get a move on.

ROSE (astounded)
Mum ...? Where the hell did you get that from ...?

JACKIE Rodrigo, he owes me a favour, and never mind why. But you were right, sweetheart. Your Dad was full of mad ideas, and this is exactly what he would have done. Now get on with it before I change my mind.

And she chucks the keys to Mickey.

90 INT. OBSERVATION DECK (FLOOR 56) DAY

LYNDA watching her monitor.

LYNDA They're climbing the western duct, should be with you in two minutes. And ... I've got a problem.
(looks across)
They've found me.

On the door: [PRAC?] a point of light appears ...

91 INT. FLOOR 56 CORRIDOR DAY

THREE DALEKS surround the door (the deck now has a thick, metal door, not the iron gate from ep.7). The lead Dalek has a special gun, glowing at the tip with a [PRAC] light. It's cutting open the door [PRAC?], melting a line ...

92 INT. FLOOR 500 DAY

THE DOCTOR frantic, wiring away. To the air:

THE DOCTOR You'll be all right, Lynda, that side of the station's reinforced against meteors, it should hold.

93 INT. OBSERVATION DECK (FLOOR 56) DAY

LYNDA manages a smile.

LYNDA Hope so. You know what they say about Earth workmanship.

And saying that, she stands. FX SHOT: behind Lynda, the observation window. Rising into shot, DALEKS. Hovering in space, just outside the deck. Close. Facing her. Taking aim.

Instinct. CU Lynda, turning round, slowly, fearful. FX SHOTS, Lynda's POV: the DALEKS' dome-lights flash, a silent 'Exterminate!' and they fire – CU Lynda, [PRAC] glass shattering foreground, she screams –

94 INT. FLOOR 500 DAY

THE DOCTOR hears Lynda's last scream. It cuts off.

95 INT. FLOOR 499 DAY

Behind the barricade: CAPTAIN JACK, MALE and FEMALE PROGRAMMER and FOUR CONTESTANTS, taking aim. CUT TO a Spike Room door – THREE DALEKS; CUT TO another Spike Room door – THREE DALEKS; CUT TO the lift – THREE DALEKS; CUT TO Captain Jack and the others. All open fire!

96 INT. FLOOR 500 DAY

THE DOCTOR working, desperate now – he can hear the bullets –

97 INT. FLOOR 499 DAY

FX SHOT: bolt hits FEMALE PROGRAMMER – she falls dead. MALE PROGRAMMER screams with rage, stands, fires like a madman, not caring, facing them –

FX SHOT: DALEK fires; FX SHOT: bolt hits the MALE PROGRAMMER – he falls, dead; CU CAPTAIN JACK, firing away with the Defabricator, enraged –

98 INT. SPACESHIP DAY

FX SHOT: the EMPEROR, DALEKS gliding all around.

EMPEROR DALEK This is perfection. I have created Heaven on Earth.

99 INT. FLOOR 499 CORRIDOR DAY

CAPTAIN JACK running – fires back down the corridor –

CAPTAIN JACK Last man standing! For God's sake, Doctor, finish that thing and kill them!

100 INT. FLOOR 500 DAY

THE DOCTOR sees the [PRAC] EMPEROR on the monitor.

EMPEROR DALEK Finish that thing and kill mankind.

On the Doctor. His torment.

101 EXT. ROSE'S ESTATE DAY

MUSIC! 'Can You Feel It' – cover version by V.

ENGINE REVS! The great big pick-up truck, driven by MICKEY, is now attached to the chain – truck radio blaring away. The chain, stretched taut, extends through the door of the TARDIS – CU Mickey, pounding the wheel, willing the truck on.

CUT TO a couple of KIDS and an OLD WOMAN, watching. CUT TO JACKIE, watching, in charge, yelling:

JACKIE Give it some more!

CU the tow-bar, the chain s-t-r-e-t-c-h-i-n-g –

102 INT. TARDIS DAY

The chain's reaching through the door, to the console, hooked into the same bolt. Pulling taut. And at last, the metal is beginning to creak ...

ROSE Keep going! *Keep going!*

103 EXT. ROSE'S ESTATE DAY

CU CHAIN, creaking, at its limit ... CU MICKEY, bouncing in his seat, giving it everything –

104 INT. TARDIS DAY

Wham! The catch rips off – the panel flies open – !

105 EXT. ROSE'S ESTATE DAY

The truck shoots forward a few feet. The chain drops, goes slack – the truck brakes, sharp – MICKEY leaps out, exultant –

MICKEY Did we do it? Rose – ?!

106 INT. TARDIS DAY

ROSE looks down at the panel. Like this moment is holy. PURE WHITE LIGHT [PRAC?] is streaming out, shining up.

CU ROSE: bathed in light. She looks down deep ...

107 EXT. ROSE'S ESTATE DAY

Whap! The TARDIS door slams shut. MICKEY runs up, hammers on the door –

MICKEY Rose? Rose – !

108 INT. TARDIS DAY

ROSE looks into the light. FX LIGHT, now: streaming around her, beautiful . . .

FX LIGHT. And curling slipstreams of ethereal white light pour into her eyes . . .

109 EXT. ROSE'S ESTATE DAY

JACKIE with MICKEY, standing back. Both fearful, now, as a wind blows up around them . . . FX SHOT: the TARDIS dematerialises, more mighty than ever before, wind, dust, the engines roaring, and it's gone.

110 INT. FLOOR 500 CORRIDOR DAY

CAPTAIN JACK runs along the corridor, to the door at the far end; this leads to FLOOR 500. Yells through the door:

CAPTAIN JACK Doctor! You've got twenty seconds maximum –

Far end of the corridor: DALEKS appear. On Captain Jack, firing, wild, demented –

111 INT. FLOOR 500 DAY

THE DOCTOR runs, grabs things, jamming equipment together –

112 INT. FLOOR 500 CORRIDOR DAY

CU CAPTAIN JACK, firing the Defabricator; scream of Daleks –

113 EXT. FX SHOT

The time vortex. The TARDIS, spinning, wilder than ever, its light and windows blazing with unnatural light –

114 INT. TARDIS DAY

FX SHOT: CU ROSE's eyes, wide open. The kaleidoscope whirl of the time vortex inside them.

115 INT. FLOOR 500 CORRIDOR DAY

CAPTAIN JACK's Defabricator clicks. Empty. A grim smile. His POV: the corridor filled with bits of burnt, shattered Dalek, but with THREE NEW DALEKS pushing through.

DALEK #1 Exterminate!

CAPTAIN JACK Yeah. I kinda guessed that.

FX SHOT: three Dalek bolts slam into him! Captain Jack falls down dead.

116 INT. FLOOR 500 DAY

THE DOCTOR jams in the final wire, he's holding a big, central circuit with a big lever attached, amazed –

THE DOCTOR It's ready!

The door opens. THREE DALEKS glide in. The Doctor looks round – another door, THREE DALEKS. Looks round – another door, THREE DALEKS. FX WIDE SHOT, SPLIT SCREEN: the Doctor centre, all the Daleks gliding forward. (When out of the FX shot, then the same three in the b/g of every shot.)

THE DOCTOR You really wanna think about this. Cos if I activate the signal. Every single creature dies.

The [PRAC] DALEK EMPEROR on the monitors:

EMPEROR DALEK I am immortal.

THE DOCTOR D'you wanna put that to the test?

EMPEROR DALEK I want to see you, become like me. Hail the Doctor, the Great Exterminator.

THE DOCTOR *I'll do it –!*

EMPEROR DALEK Then prove yourself, Doctor! What are you? Coward or killer?

And he's shaking, trembling, gripping the lever.

Hold the silence. Then he just lets go. Drops the whole device.

THE DOCTOR Coward. Any day.

EMPEROR DALEK Mankind will be harvested, because of your weakness.

THE DOCTOR Yeah. And what about me? Am I becoming one of your angels?

EMPEROR DALEK You are the Heathen. You will be exterminated.

THE DOCTOR Maybe it's time, yeah.

He closes his eyes, head up. Prepared. But then it starts ... the faint, familiar, wheezing, groaning sound ...

The Doctor looks round, horrified ... FX SHOT: the TARDIS starts to appear. Its lamp and windows blazing. A vicious wind. Dust rises, it becomes solid ...

On the Doctor, knowing something is very wrong.

CUT TO the DALEKS, agitated.

DALEK #1 Alert! TARDIS materialising!

EMPEROR DALEK You will not escape!

The TARDIS is solid now. And *both* doors shoot inwards. From inside, a [PRAC] blazing white light – the Doctor shields his eyes, but has to look, awestruck –

THE DOCTOR Rose . . . ?

But he flinches back, drops to the floor, as – FX SHOT: with an inrush of air, a figure rushes out of the TARDIS, in the air, a blur, then rapidly reassembling, snapping into shape, some distance in front of the TARDIS.

This is ROSE. And something more. Shining white; backlit, hair blowing, ethereal, the face of an angel. The room filled with the hum of enormous power. (FX on certain shots only; otherwise, a genuine glow using PRAC light, and the grade, only; the whole room bleached, now.)

The Doctor crouching, some feet away, looking up. Scared:

THE DOCTOR What did you do . . . ?

And she looks round, calm, slowly, like a Goddess; London accent gone, voice with reverb, infinite wisdom.

ROSE I looked into the TARDIS. And the TARDIS looked into me.

FX SHOT: CU Rose's eyes. With the vortex whirling within.

THE DOCTOR You went deeper than that. You looked into the Time Vortex. Rose, no one's meant to see that –

EMPEROR DALEK This is the Abomination!

DALEK #1 Exterminate!

FX SHOT: DALEK #1 fires, a bolt shoots out. Rose holds up her hand. FX SHOT: bolt freezes, reverses, slides back into the gun.

THE DOCTOR Rose, you've got to stop this, you've got to stop this now!

ROSE I am the Bad Wolf. I create myself. I take the words . . .

She gestures. FX SHOT: the BAD WOLF lettering on the wall lifts off, the separate letters gently dancing in the air.

ROSE I scatter them, in time and space, a message to lead myself here.

The letters rise, spin, shoot into the ether, gone.

THE DOCTOR You've got the entire vortex running through your head, you're gonna burn! Is that what you want?

ROSE I want you safe. My Doctor. Protected from the false God.

EMPEROR DALEK You cannot hurt me! I am immortal!

ROSE You are tiny. I can see the whole of time and space. Every single atom of your existence.

She turns, elegantly, to Dalek #1. Holds out her hand.

ROSE And I divide them.

FX SHOT: the DALEK – elegantly, gently, it divides into separate particles, which hang in the air –

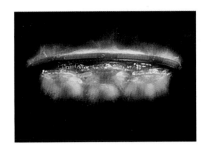

ROSE Every thing must come to dust.

FX SHOT: the particles become dust, spiralling in the air.

ROSE All things.

She gestures. FX SHOT: three more DALEKS, the same effect: all separate into particles, then float into dust.

ROSE Everything dies.

She opens her arms.

117 INT. SPACESHIP DAY

FX SHOT: all the DALEKS throughout the ship, going through the same effect, becoming particles, dust.

EMPEROR DALEK I will not die! I cannot die!

FX SHOT: the EMPEROR's casing divides into particles. PRAC SHOT?: CU the creature in the central bowl. Glass cracks. Screaming its rage, it shrivels and turns to dust.

118 EXT. FX SHOT: SPACE DAY

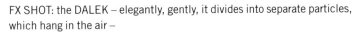

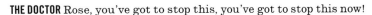

FX SHOT: the DALEK SAUCER begins to disassemble, calmly separating into drifts of particles . . .

119 INT. FLOOR 500 DAY

CU ROSE, shining white.

ROSE The Time War ends.

120 EXT. FX SHOT: SPACE DAY

FX SHOT: the last particles of saucer dissolve into trails of dust, dispersing, gone . . .

121 INT. FLOOR 500 DAY

Just ROSE and THE DOCTOR now, all Daleks turned to dust. He's still crouching, scared. She's smiling, blissful.

THE DOCTOR That's it, Rose, you've done it, now let go, just stop –

ROSE How could I ever let this go? . . . I bring life.

She gestures –

122 INT. FLOOR 500 CORRIDOR DAY

CU CAPTAIN JACK, dead on the floor. Sudden intake of breath – his eyes snap open!

123 INT. FLOOR 500 DAY

THE DOCTOR stands, raging at ROSE.

THE DOCTOR But this is wrong! You can't control life and death – !

ROSE But I can. The sun and the moon and the light and the dark . . .
(child-like)
But why do they hurt . . . ?

The hum of power dips, becomes discordant. The Doctor gentler now, compassionate.

THE DOCTOR It's eating you alive. The power's gonna kill you.
And it's my fault.

ROSE But . . . I can see everything. All that is. All that was.
All that ever could be.

THE DOCTOR That's what I see. All the time. And doesn't it drive you mad . . . ?

ROSE (more human, scared)
My head . . .

THE DOCTOR Come here.

He holds out his hand. She's shaking a little, scared, takes his hand.

ROSE . . . It's killing me . . .

THE DOCTOR I think you need a Doctor.

FX SHOT: Rose blazing with light, the Doctor holding her hand. And gently, carefully, he leans in. Presses his lips against hers. FX SHOT: the light streams from Rose, to the Doctor. Fills him; makes him shine.

They separate. Rose falls to the floor, unconscious. FX SHOT: the Doctor stands there, the unearthly light playing round his body, glowing with power. FX SHOT: the Doctor's eyes, containing the time vortex. And then he takes a huge, deep breath, tenses himself – FX SHOT: and the Doctor, alive with light, becomes utterly calm. Holds his breath. And Zen-like, simply breathes out. And the light streams away.

FX SHOT, WIDE: the Doctor as still as a statue, expelling the light, as it streams away and curls out, fading, gone . . .

And it's over. Silence. The aftermath of war.

The Doctor just walks around a bit, almost on the spot. Exhausted, stunned. And maybe feeling just a bit lucky. A trail of dust on the floor; the Doctor stirs it with his foot, then leaves it.

Then he kneels by Rose. She's still unconscious. He touches her face. Then leans down to lift her up.

124 INT. FLOOR 500 CORRIDOR DAY

CAPTAIN JACK stands. Shakes his head. Biggest hangover ever. Lost, dazed … but then, a smile. Looks at his hands. Feels his head. Alive! Then he hears the groan of old engines – runs through –

125 INT. FLOOR 500 DAY

CAPTAIN JACK runs in –

CAPTAIN JACK Doctor, what the hell . . ?

FX SHOT, his POV: the TARDIS fades away . . .

126 INT. TARDIS DAY

ROSE, on the floor, blinks, awakes, confused. She looks round: THE DOCTOR's at the console, slamming levers, the rotor rising and falling, the room swaying a little, in flight. He's smiling, happy; and underneath that, so sad.

ROSE . . . What happened?

THE DOCTOR Don't you remember – ?

ROSE It's like . . . there was this singing.

THE DOCTOR That's right, I sang a song and the Daleks ran away!

Rose stands, recovering.

ROSE . . . I was at home . . . No, I was in the TARDIS, then there was this light, and . . . I can't remember anything else.

But during that speech, on the Doctor. (Rose not seeing this.) He lifts up his hand, looks at it. FX SHOT: his hand shimmers with strange, hot, boiling orange energy, then gone.

He winces, shakes his hand. Manages to stay smiling.

THE DOCTOR Rose Tyler. I was gonna take you to so many places. Barcelona! Not the city Barcelona, the planet Barcelona, you'd love it. Fantastic place, they've got dogs with no noses, imagine how many times a day you end up saying that joke. And it's still funny!

ROSE Then . . . why can't we go there?

THE DOCTOR Maybe you will. And maybe I will. But not like this.

ROSE (smiling, bemused)
You're not making sense.

THE DOCTOR I might never make sense again. I might have two heads. Or no head. Imagine me, with no head! And don't say that's an improvement. But it's a bit dodgy, this process, you never know what you're gonna get – *aah!*

He convulses, a little, a shot of pain – FX SHOT: again, the orange energy ripples all over him – just his skin, not his clothes, then gone.

Rose alarmed, makes to go towards him –

ROSE What was that – ?

THE DOCTOR Stand back! Ohh, it's gonna be a big one!

ROSE Doctor. Tell me what's going on.

THE DOCTOR I absorbed all the energy of the Time Vortex.
And no one's meant to do that.
(serious, now)
Every cell in my body is dying.

ROSE But ... can't you do something?

THE DOCTOR Yeah. I'm doing it now.
(grimaces)
Ouch. Time Lords have got this little trick. Sort of a way of
cheating death. Except ...

And the pain doesn't matter now, as he looks at her.

THE DOCTOR It means I'm gonna change. And I won't see you again.
Not like this. Not with this daft old face. And before I go ...

ROSE (upset)
Don't say that.

THE DOCTOR Rose, before I go, I just want to tell you. You were
fantastic. Absolutely fantastic. And d'you know what?
(big smile)
So was I.

Beat. And then his head arches back – he convulses, as though every muscle
is tense – still standing, arms splayed out. FX WIDE SHOT: orange energy
EXPLODES out of his skin! Strong, like a blast of steam, of lava, though the
clothes stay untouched, energy funnelling out of the neck of his jumper, out
of the sleeves of his jacket –

Rose staggers back, feeling the heat, though she can't look away –

FX SHOT: CU his head, though now there's no head, just a fountain of energy,
pouring up –

CU Rose, staring, scared, but fascinated –

FX MID SHOT: the energy streaming out of the Doctor's neckline and sleeves,
the orange now turning pure white –

FX SHOT: CU the Doctor. As the energy streams away, fades, revealing a
brand new man, still wearing the same old clothes. He blinks, shakes his
head, then is completely normal.

THE DOCTOR Right then. There we are. Hello! Oh, new teeth, that's
weird. Okay, so where was I? Oh that's right –
(BIG SMILE)
Barcelona!

127 EXT. FX SHOT

The TARDIS tumbles away, into the vortex, smaller and smaller. Gone ...

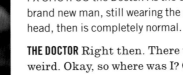

Published by BBC Books, BBC Worldwide Ltd, Woodlands, 80 Wood Lane, London W12 0TT

First published 2005
Reprinted 2005

Doctor Who is a BBC Wales production for BBC1
Format © BBC 2005
Executive producers: Russell T Davies, Julie Gardner and Mal Young
Producer: Phil Collinson
Script editors: Helen Raynor and Elwen Rowlands

ISBN 0 563 48641 4

Commissioning editor: Stuart Cooper
Project editor: Charlotte Lochhead
Consultant editor: Helen Raynor
Design: Smith & Gilmour, London
Screengrab editor: Justin Richards
Production controller: Peter Hunt

Set in New Clarendon, Trade Gothic and Deviant
Colour separations by Dot Gradations, Wickford, England
Printed and bound in Great Britain by CPI, Bath

For more information about this and other BBC books, please visit our website at www.bbcshop.com